T5-CQB-374

Also in the Variorum Collected Studies Series:

C.R. BOXER
Portuguese Merchants and Missionaries in Feudal Japan, 1543–1640

C.R. BOXER
Portuguese Conquest and Commerce in Southern Asia, 1500–1750

C.R. BOXER
From Lisbon to Goa, 1500–1750
Studies in Portuguese Maritime Enterprise

C.F. BECKINGHAM
Between Islam and Christendom
Travellers, Facts and Legends in the Middle Ages and Renaissance

ROBERT MANTRAN
L'Empire ottoman du XVIe au XVIIIe siècle

HALİL İNALCIK
The Ottoman Empire: Conquest, Organization and Economy

JEAN DAUVILLIER
Histoire et institutions des Eglises orientales au Moyen Age

PETER LINEHAN
Spanish Church and Society, 1150–1300

C.J. BISHKO
Spanish and Portuguese Monastic History, 600–1300

C.J. BISHKO
Studies in Medieval Spanish Frontier History

JEAN GAUTIER DALCHÉ
Economie et société dans les pays de la Couronne de Castille

JOSEPH F. O'CALLAGHAN
The Spanish Military Order of Calatrava and its Affiliates

JACQUES HEERS
Société et économie à Gênes (XIVe-XVe siècles)

JOHN W. O'MALLEY
Rome and the Renaissance: Studies in Culture and Religion

ROBERT M. KINGDON
Church and Society in Reformation Europe

Jesuit and Friar in the Spanish Expansion to the East

J. S. Cummins

Jesuit and Friar in the Spanish Expansion to the East

VARIORUM REPRINTS
London 1986

British Library CIP data

Cummins, J.S.
Jesuit and Friar in the Spanish expansion to the East. — (Collected studies series; CS237)
1. Catholic Church — Missions — China — History
2. Missionaries — Spain — History
I. Title
266'.023'46051 BV3417

ISBN 0-86078-185-2

Published in Great Britain by Variorum Reprints
20 Pembridge Mews London W11 3EQ

Printed in Great Britain by Galliard (Printers) Ltd
Great Yarmouth Norfolk

VARIORUM REPRINT CS237

CONTENTS

This volume contains a total of 334 pages.

INTRODUCTION

Our contemporary China-watchers have a long ancestry. China, the 'Middle Flowery Kingdom', exerted a peculiar fascination over Europeans from the Middle Ages to the Enlightenment. The travels of Marco Polo, the efforts of Franciscan and Dominican friars to establish their Faith in thirteenth-century China, the appearance of such exotic figures as the convert Rabban Sauma from Peking (who gave Communion to Edward I of England), all kept this fascination alive.

The selection of articles in this volume deals with this phenomenon, concentrating on one particular aspect of it: the lure of China for those Jesuits and mendicant friars who sought to convert the Middle Kingdom throughout the sixteenth and seventeenth centuries. Our modern efforts to enter China merely reflect this earlier, two-pronged, assault upon the Middle Kingdom by Jesuits based in India and by friars based in the Indies. Just as China today is courted for its commercial possibilities, so in the sixteenth century it was seen as a desirable spiritual prize; and not only for itself but also for its 'domino effect' upon the surrounding kingdoms of East Asia. Japan, for instance, was a cultural colony of China and, it was conjectured, might well follow her if she took the path to Rome. But in the end these optimistic evangelists' only success lay in the Philippines. (Vietnam, is so far as it is Catholic today, is another, a largely French, story.)

The Catholic Religious Orders — 'the flying squads of the Church Militant' (IV, 130) — who managed to enter China (friars first, Jesuits later) ought, ideally, to have settled down amiably to a partition of the rich harvest before them: the would-be Jesuit mandarins concentrating on the conversion of the Chinese elite by subtle infiltration; the friars, those ecclesiastical coolies, on the conversion of artisans and peasants by plain-spoken confrontation. The ideal did not happen.

Unfortunately the two groups of missionaries had already clashed at home in Spain, where the Jesuits and Dominicans, in particular, had differed on almost everything from choir practice to Freewill. These differences ripened into hostility, and in some cases hardened into something akin to hatred. When the missionaries left for fresh fields overseas they inevitably took their opinions with them. So just as some Spaniards hoped to keep their new-found world of America free of such undesirables as lawyers, Jews and bishops, the Jesuits wanted to keep China to themselves, as being best suited to its challenges, and thus friar-free. But this was not a viewpoint that the mendicants could be expected to share, and so the old rivalries were given fresh nourishment in Asia, especially in Japan where, said the early twentieth-century historian James Murdoch, 'between Jesuits and Franciscans it was all but war to the knife.'

In discussing the Jesuits' work in China I am putting forward the less popular side of that story and attempting to explain the motives of the Jesuits' friar opponents. The reader should therefore be aware that mine is 'a dissenting viewpoint'; see David E. Mungello, *Curious Land: Jesuit Accommodation and the Origins of Sinology* (Stuttgart, 1985), p. 49. The articles reprinted are in roughly chronological order. The first, introductory, article discusses the spiritual motivations and fantasies behind Columbus's search for China. Many Spaniards declared that they sought 'to serve God and get rich'; aims which are both laudable and nowadays fashionable. Columbus, however, sought rather to get rich in order to serve God the better; his economic motives had a spiritual basis: China was to be the means of liberating Jerusalem. Two other essays (II, V) deal with aspects of Catholic missionary activities in Japan and China, and above all with the friction between the rival Religious. But wherever their privileges, interests or ambitions were concerned, the Jesuits were always ready to adopt a positive stance. This is nowhere more vividly shown than in their notorious controversy with Bishop Palafox in Mexico (III). This turned out to be no merely parochial affair; it echoed — it was made to echo — in cloister, curia and carrel for over two centuries, and, with the Chinese Rites controversy itself, played a significant part in Clement XIV's disbanding of the Jesuits in 1773. I have discussed the significance of that event in 'The Suppression of the Jesuits, 1773', *History Today* (1973), 839–48 (not included here). The fourth article has this rivalry as a low-key note in the background but deals mainly with the Spanish 'Struggle for Justice' in the Philippines: it shows the reverse side of the anti-Spanish 'Black Legend' and reveals the spirit of Las Casas in Spain's East Asian colonies. The sixth article shows how, following classical and later precedent, some Spaniards could find lessons abroad for their own people at home: friar Domingo Navarrete, in the Spain of the 1670s, then emerging from decades of depression, points to China as a possible model for imitation, incidentally making the most forceful Spanish contribution to the *rêve chinois* of the eighteenth century. The selection concludes with an indication of the whereabouts (in 1965) in Peking of the old Jesuit library of European scientific and other books. A catalogue of the Rare Book section of the Peking Library is apparently being prepared; meantime, however, since travel to Chjina is now easier, it is hoped that the 'Brief Note' may still be found to be of some assistance.

It is a pleasure to thank C. R. Boxer and Nicholas Cushner, and the publishers who have given permission for these articles to be reproduced; in particular I should also like to thank C. R. Boxer for first revealing to me the endlessly fascinating — I had almost said entertaining — history of the Iberians in their wider world. In 1964 I was granted a Rockefeller Fellowship which enabled me to travel to East Asia and to work in India, Japan and the Philippines. I remain profoundly grateful for that opportunity. I should perhaps make clear that, presumably for political reasons, the Foundation was in no way connected with my visit to Peking in 1965.

The spelling of names in this volume is not always consistent, as different journals prefer different systems; the spelling of Chinese names is in the Wade-Giles style. It should not be necessary — but experience has proved it is — to explain that throughout these essays the word 'mendicant' refers to friars of the three Orders of Dominicans, Augustinians and Franciscans. Jesuits enjoy the spiritual and other privileges of the mendicant Orders but in Catholic sociology are never referred to as mendicants. The opportunity has been taken in this reprint to correct numerous misprints in the texts, and to add to each article except the last some additional notes and references.

J. S. CUMMINS

London
October 1985

PUBLISHER'S NOTE

The articles in this volume, as in all others in the Collected Studies Series, have not been given a new, continuous pagination. In order to avoid confusion, and to facilitate their use where these same studies have been referred to elsewhere, the original pagination has been maintained wherever possible.

Each article has been given a Roman number in order of appearance, as listed in the Contents. This number is repeated on each page and quoted in the index entries.

It has not been possible to reproduce all the illustrations originally included in these articles; in some cases new illustrations have been substituted.

I

Christopher Columbus: crusader, visionary, and Servus Dei

«Messer Marco Polo discovered China in the thirteenth century, when he was alive, and in the fifteenth, when he was dead, he discovered America.» [1] Yet many others could share the claim to have co-operated with Columbus: Aristotle, Albertus Magnus, Roger Bacon, Vincent de Beauvais, Pierre d'Ailly, Toscanelli, and «Sir John Mandeville». [2] But the scientific learning derived from these was later supplanted in Columbus's mind by the spiritual, visionary influence of Ramon Lull, Joachim de Fiore, and St. Francis, among others. It was this later source of inspiration that Columbus himself eventually claimed as the greater force. Of course, he was «modern», too, in that he was outstripping the deeds of the Ancients: Peter Martyr was impressed by his town-building, his sowing of European crops and breeding of European cattle in the New World: «¿Cómo hemos de admirar ya que los Saturnos, las Ceres y los Triptolemos enseñaran nuevos inventos a los hombres...?» [3] Yet though Columbus could be shown to be competing with the Ancients, this was only incidental to his aim, for if we are to believe him, the only city he wanted to build was Jerusalem. In his mind, the whole *empresa de Indias* was only a means to that pre-destined end: the New World was to redeem the old City. Columbus, who was re-drawing the map of the world (even if he was putting the wrong names on it), and shifting the intellectual and geographical centre of gravity, failed in his chief object: to fulfil the medieval ideal of freeing the Holy Sepulchre, and, further, to make straight the way for the

[1] Eileen Power, *Medieval People* (Harmondsworth, 1951), p. 70.

[2] Some enthusiasts, however, may seem to go too far: e. g. José María Salaverría, «El Cid como precursor de los conquistadores de América», *Hermes* (Bilbao), I (1917), 3 unnumbered pages. A concise survey is to be found in Egmont Zechlin, «Columbus als Ausdruck der mittelalterlich - neuzeitlichen Epochenscheide», in *Studi Colombiani*, II (Genova, 1952), pp. 101-111.

[3] Peter Martyr de Angleria, *Epistolario*, ed. and tr. J. López de Toro *(Documentos inéditos para la historia de España*, IX, Madrid, 1953), p. 281.

conversion of the world. In so far as his mind increasingly turned for inspiration to the spiritual rather than the humanistic trends about him, he may be seen as a man of the Middle Ages. His passion was aroused by Old Testament and Christian influences rather than by the classics: the Prophets came to replace Aristotle and Ptolemy, and in the manner of the medieval mystics, Columbus began to reject that learning of which he had once boasted, and claimed «en la ynpresa de las Yndias no me aprovechó rasón, ny matemática, ny mapamundos».[4] Yet he must not be taken too literally. To the very end he remained so interested in natural phenomena that Humboldt can enthuse over «that wonderful man whom nothing escaped ... unremittingly alive to all natural objects»,[5] and who was capable of such details as bottling samples of the milk-white sea-water off the southern Cuban coast in order to have it analysed in Spain. He himself saw nothing new in this search for knowledge: «los romanos ... pusieron mucha diligençia en saber los secretos del mundo y darlos a entender a los pueblos.»[6] Even at his most «mystic» he remained practical, and when he stopped to observe the flight of birds to the left or right, it was not to read the omens, but to seek a landfall.[7]

As Humboldt first pointed out, Columbus was deeply influenced by the religious atmosphere of the Spain of the Catholic Monarchs. In particular, he was affected by the prevalent crusading spirit which seems absent from the mental world of his pre-Hispanic years.[8]

Phelan can claim that the «discovery and conquest of America, among many other things, was the last Crusade. If Columbus had had his way, this would have been literally so», and Aziz S. Atiya states «it would not be imprudent to argue that the discovery of America was an indirect byproduct of the Crusading movement».[9] The Holy See appreciated

[4] Lollis, Part I, vol. II, p. 82. (Unless otherwise stated all quotations from Columbus's writings come from *Raccolta di documenti e studi pubblicati dalla r. commissione colombiana pel quarto centenario dalla scoperta dell' America*, ed. Cesare de Lollis, 6 parts, 12 volumes, Roma, 1892-94.)

[5] A. von Humboldt, *Cosmos*, I (London, 1848), 272 and note 329. S. E. Morison, *Christopher Columbus: Admiral of the Ocean Sea* (Boston, 1942), p. 6, discusses Columbus's «modern» characteristics.

[6] Lollis, Pt. I, v. II, p. 39. His royal masters also showed a keen interest in the phenomena of the New World with which he had presented them.

[7] Bartolomé de las Casas, *Historia de las Indias*, Book I, chap. 131; Ramón Iglesia, *El hombre Colón y otros ensayos* (México, 1944), p. 23.

[8] This is fully discussed by John Leddy Phelan in his illuminating and absorbing study, *The Millennial Kingdom of the Franciscans in the New World* (Berkeley, 1970), esp. chapter 2, upon which I have drawn. P. E. Russell, *Prince Henry the Navigator*, also brings out «the importance of medieval crusading and chivalric ideas in Prince Henry's life» and draws a parallel between Columbus and the Prince (Diamante XI, London, 1960, pp. 29-30). See also Pedro de Leturia, S. J., «Ideales político-religiosos de Colón en su carta institucional del 'Mayorazgo': 1498», in *Studi Colombiani*, II (Genova, 1952), pp. 249-275.

[9] Phelan, p. 22, and Atiya, *Crusade, Commerce and Culture* (Oxford, 1962), p. 128.

the importance of the crusading ideal in Spain: Sixtus IV, for instance, presented the Catholic Monarchs with a silver Crucifix as a standard for the final campaign against Spanish Islam. Columbus himself apparently took part in the siege of Baza in which the «flower of Spanish chivalry» engaged in 1489. Further to inflame his zealous indignation, he was a witness to the arrival there of ambassadors from the Sultan of Egypt who was threatening reprisals, including the destruction of the Holy Sepulchre, if the Catholic Monarchs did not cease their campaign against Granada. Doubtless it was this military experience that led Columbus to think of himself as a «capitán que fue d'España ... Yo devo de ser judgado como capitán que de tanto tiempo fasta oy trae las armas a cuestas, sin las dexar una ora, y de cavalleros de conquistas». [10] Nor did the fall of Granada, which Columbus witnessed, see the disappearance of the crusading spirit, for the cry was now «Tras Granada, Jerusalén». [11] Columbus links the *reconquista* and the discovery of America in the address to the Catholic Monarchs which prefaces the Journal of his first voyage. The plan to use new-found gold to free the *Casa Santa* is noted in a journal entry for 26 December, 1492: «protesté que toda la ganançia d'esta mi empresa se gastase en la conquista de Hierusalem.» [12] And for this purpose he later provided a trust fund in six per cent stocks in the Genoese bank of St. George. The subject recurs like a refrain in other writings by him: e.g. in the preface to his *Libro de profecías*, or in the draft letter to Pope Alexander VI written in 1502 to inform his Holiness of his plan to finance an army of 100,000 infantrymen and 10,000 cavalry to free the Holy Sepulchre.

Columbus's concern for gold became a kind of mystical cult: gold, he pointed out, could be used for supernatural ends: «llega a que echa las ánimas al Paraíso», [13] and it could ultimately be used to usher in the

For the general background see Fernand Braudel, *La Méditerranée et le monde méditerranéen à l'époque de Philippe II* (Paris, 1949), pp. 516-18; Marcel Bataillon, *Erasmo y España* (México, 1966), pp. 51-61; José Goñi Gaztambide, «The Holy See and the Reconquest of Granada (1479-1492)», in *Spain in the Fifteenth Century*, ed. Roger Highfield (London, 1972), pp. 354-379.

[10] Lollis, Pt. I, v. II, p. 73.

[11] Leturia (255-56) emphasises the closeness of Columbus to the Prince don Juan, whose teacher and whose favourite poet both urged upon him the «empresa jerosolimitana». This hope survived at least until 1530 (see the *Convocatoria a la guerra contra los Turcos* [BAE, XVI, 150-51]); and for official cognisance of Charles V's providential mission in Jerusalem, see Bataillon, 226.

[12] Lollis, Pt. I, v. I, p. 83; he also noted (Journal, 6 November, 1492; Lollis, Pt. I, v. I, p. 38) that Spain was now purged of those who «would not confess the Trinity»: her next task, then, was to convert the «Indies». He may well have seen significance in a ship carrying Spanish Jews into exile and leaving on the same tide as he did on the first voyage (Morison, p. 149).

[13] Lollis, Pt. I, v. II, p. 201. This expression reflects an unquestioning (and ill-informed) age of faith; soon another voice was to be heard: «parece estar el paraíso cerrado a los que no tienen dineros» (Alfonso de Valdés, *Diálogo de las cosas ocurridas*

Apocalypse. Consequent upon this imaginative line of thought, Columbus came to equate himself with David, who had bequeathed to Solomon the riches with which to build the Temple on Mount Zion: «Hierusalem i el monte Sion ha de ser reedificado por mano de cristiano: quien a de ser, Dios por boca del Propheta en el déçimo quarto Psalmo lo diçe. el abbad Joachín dixo que este avía de salir de España.....el emperador del Cataio ha días que mandó sabios que le ensẽnen en la fe de Cristo; ¿quién será que se ofrezca a esto? Si Nuestro Señor me lleva a España, io me obligo de llevar[les] con el nombre de Dios en salvo.» [14]

Thus another medieval ambition which Columbus hoped to fulfil is here touched upon: to spread the Gospel to China. This had always been a Franciscan ideal, and no doubt it helped to draw Columbus to that Order. His devotion to the friars was often noted; he sometimes wore their habit in public, and he died a member of the Franciscan Third Order. During the last eight years of his life, to quote Phelan, the Admiral's «religious sentiments were increasingly phrased in observant Franciscan terms». [15] Apart from his gratitude to the Franciscans of La Rábida, there were other reasons to draw Columbus to the Order. A great part of the geographical writings and accounts of travel in the last three centuries of the Middle Ages was the work of Franciscans [16]. They were also the traditional Custodians of the Holy Places in Jerusalem, which they never abandoned, despite persecution and even martyrdom. (Later there was a legendary connection between the Order and America, for, during the vision that accompanied the stigmata, Christ is said to have told St. Francis «the secret of America».) Because of such traditions, and because of their missionary work among Jews and Moors, the Franciscans were judged especially fitted for the task of converting America in the 16th century. [17] Columbus even shared the Franciscan love of Nature, which, *pace* Ramón Iglesia, sincerely marks his writings. [18]

en Roma, Part II). Almost a century later the Jesuit José de Acosta also sought a teleological explanation for the riches of the New World: see his *Historia natural y moral de las Indias*, Book IV, ch. 2.

[14] Lollis, Pt. I, v. II, p. 202. For the problems raised by the prediction of salvation from Spain, allegedly made by Joachim de Fiore, repeated in Columbus's *Libro de profecías* (Lollis, Pt. I, v. II, p. 148), see Phelan, p. 135.

[15] Phelan (pp. 18-22) sees the fourteenth-century Franciscan, Johannis de Rupescissa, as a precursor of Columbus. On Franciscan illuminism in the early sixteenth century, see Bataillon, 61.

[16] E. g. John de Pian de Carpine, William Rubruk, Odoric de Pordenone, Ramon Lull; and the *Libro del conoscimiento de todos los reynos* was allegedly by an anonymous Spanish Franciscan of the fourteenth century. See Jaime Cortesão, «O franciscanismo e a mística dos descobrimentos», *Revista de las Españas*, Nos. 65-66 (Madrid, Jan-Feb. 1932), 37-42.

[17] Richard Konetzke, «History of Missions in Hispanic America», *The Americas*, XIV (1958), 528.

[18] «Jamás hay en Colón una descripción desinteresada. Colón era un hombre de

Columbus's view of himself as a divinely-chosen instrument developed until he came to see himself as one called to fulfil both the prophecies of the Old Testament and the injunctions of the New, such as «Go ye and teach all nations». Perhaps to protect himself from the disappointments suffered in his later years he began to seek refuge in mystical dreams and visions. Phelan writes that he «consciously sought to surround himself with the magic aura that over the centuries had enveloped the name of Joachim of Fiore, by proclaiming himself the Joachimite Messiah» (p. 22). This led him into a further stage of apocalypticism. The «ships of Tarshish» had reached the distant islands, now that Columbus had «unlocked the enchained Ocean», and it seemed to him that the climax of Christian history was at hand. Claiming to follow Alfonso el Sabio, he worked out that the end of the world was only 155 years away. The «Man out of Spain», called to free Jerusalem with the riches of «Asia», had progressed into being the man destined to bring about the Second Coming. Christ gave the keys of the Kingdom to Peter; to Columbus he gave «las llaves de los atamientos de la mar Occéana ... del nuevo çielo e tierra que hasía Nuestro Señor, escriviendo sant Juan el Apocalis, después de dicho por boca de Ysaỳa, me hiso d'ello mensagero». [19] He believed that from his first voyage onwards his work had been aided by miracles; he concludes his Journal for that voyage («peregrinación», says Las Casas) with the words: «muchos milagros señalados [Dios] a mostrado en el viaje». [20] Besides being a new Moses, he is also a latter-day Tiphys, fulfilling not only scriptural prophecies, but also that discerned in Act II of Seneca's *Medea:* «There shall come a time when the ocean shall break its bounds, and a vast world shall appear.» [21]

This apocalyptic mysticism is revealed most clearly in a letter written in the autumn of 1501 to the Catholic Monarchs, stating «la rasón, que tengo, de la restituçión de la Casa santa a la santa Yglesia militante». [22] This letter was also intended as a prologue to his *Libro de profecías*, an anthology of all the biblical references to the discoveries and to the liberation of Mount Zion. [23] He claimed to be inspired by the Lord, «y con este

negocios y es inútil pedirle delicadezas líricas que no sentía» (R. Iglesia, p. 34). But Morison (pp. 265, 459) praises his «love of natural beauty, a trait unusual in that era and still uncommon among navigators...»; and of a description from the second voyage: «it reads like an idyl of Theocritus; only the nymphs and shepherd's pipe are wanting». See also von Humboldt, *Cosmos*, II, pp. 52-56.

[19] Lollis, Pt. I, v. II, pp. 66, 192.

[20] Lollis, Pt. I, v. I, p. 119.

[21] Columbus's son annotated his father's copy of the text with the words: «Haec prophetia expleta ẽ per patrẽ meum Christoforũ Columbũ Almirãtẽ Anno 1492» (quoted in J. B. Thacher, *Columbus, his Life, his Work and his Remains*, I [New York, 1903], p. 170). See also Lollis, Pt. I, v. II, 192 n.

[22] Lollis, Pt. I, v. II, p. 79.

[23] The *Libro* has baffled, distressed, or irritated the commentators: «He must

fuego vine a Vuestras Altezas ... ¿quién dubda que esta lunbre no fuese del Espíritu Santo?», and again comes the insistence that worldly learning has been of no use: «dexo las tantas artes y escrituras, de que yo dyxe ariba; solamente me tengo a la santa y sacra Escritura, y a algunas abtoridades proféticas de algunas personas santas [Joachim de Fiore?], que por revelaçión divina han dicho algo d'esto». This accords with the theme of inspired ignorance: «de la boca de los niños e ynoçentes se pronunçia la verdad.» There follows a eulogy of the Prophet Isaiah: «de Ysaýa disen que no solamente proheta, mas hevangelista, éste puso toda su diligençia a escrevir lo venidero, y llamar toda la gente a nuestra santa fee católica». [24] Since Isaiah's prophecy about America had now been fulfilled, so too Columbus expected to see the freeing of Jerusalem. [25] And it is against this ecstatic background that the accounts of the third and fourth voyages must be read.

Columbus's special devotion to the Blessed Trinity is most marked on the third voyage, which was made «en nombre de la Santísima Trinidad», and with a resolution to dedicate to the Trinity the first land he came upon. [26] His exalted mood is shown in a letter written to the Monarchs during the voyage: «todo pasará, y no la palabra de Dios, y se complirá todo lo que dixo, el qual tan claro habló d'estas tierras por la boca de Isaýas en tantos lugares de su escriptura, afirmando que de España les sería divulgado su sancto nombre». [27] The third voyage continued, with constant references to the Trinity: «Iba en nombre de la Sancta Trinidad ... despidió los otros tres navíos en nombre de la Sancta Trinidad ... quiere ir al Austro, porque entiende con ayuda de la Sancta Trinidad, hallar islas ... Aquel que es

have been a little crazed from his sufferings at this period, yet he never ceased to be magnificent» (W. T. Walsh, *Isabella of Spain: The Last Crusader* [New York, 1930], p. 453); «This deplorable lucubration, which we sincerely hope will never be published in full... forcibly reminds everyone of Newton's *Observations upon the Prophecies* [of Daniel] and *Apocalypse*» (H. Harrisse, *Notes on Columbus* [New York, 1866], pp. 84, 156); «Una compilación farragosa e inútil, pero que ilustra perfectamente la tendencia del Renacimiento al epítome erudito, enciclopédico y especializado a la vez» (A. Cioranescu, *Colón, humanista* [Madrid, 1967], p. 56); «su credulidad en ocasiones bordea y hasta invade el campo del ridículo» (A. Ballesteros y Beretta, *Cristóbal Colón y el descubrimiento de América*, II [Barcelona, 1945], p. 692).

[24] Lollis, Pt. I, v. II, pp. 79-82.

[25] Others, too, have found the linking of America and the Old Testament to be quite credible, for it seemed that what Humboldt has described as a «doubling of the act of Creation» (*Cosmos*, II, pp. 230-1) could not go unmentioned in the Scriptures. See Fr. M. F. Miguélez, OSA., «Fr. Luis de León y el descubrimiento de América», *La Ciudad de Dios*, XXX (1893), 167-184; José de Acosta, S. J., *Historia natural y moral de las Indias*, Book I, ch. XV; Gaspar de San Agustín, OSA., *Conquistas de las islas Philipinas: la temporal ... y la espiritual*, I (Madrid, 1698), p. 3.

[26] «A los españoles se les solía considerar en Italia como rebeldes al dogma de la Trinidad ... *peccadiglio di Spagna* la falta de fe en la Trinidad, dogma que tanto repugnaba a árabes y judíos» (Bataillon, pp. 60, 121n); Lollis, Part I, v. II, p. 1.

[27] Lollis, Pt. I, v. II, pp. 8, 27.

trino y uno me guíe ... la Sancta e Individua Trinidad». [28] On 31st July, 1498, land was sighted and Columbus was struck by what seemed to him to be marvellous: the first land they saw revealed three mountains joined at the base in a symbol of the Trinity: «es cierto que la fallada d'esta tierra, fue gran milagro, atanto como la fallada del primer viaje». [29] Inevitably, therefore, he christened the newly discovered land «Trinidad».

Still out at sea, lying off the Orinoco delta, he noted a new phenomenon: the sea water was sweet and fresh. He rightly concluded that this was due to the entry into the sea of a river, or rivers, of such size and strength that they came not from an island, but from a mainland. He decided that this was the edge of the Asian continent. The two sides of his mind were reflected in this conclusion: the rational, and the visionary («la razón me ayuda grandemente por esto ... y después me ayuda el dezir de Esdras»). [30] The apocryphal Book of Esdras, which asserted that six parts of the globe were dry land, and only one was covered by water, was his authority for the nearness of Asia to Europe. Consequently he must also be near the Earthly Paradise which was known to be «en fin de Oriente, y es éste». The waters of the Orinoco, dividing into rivers, were for Columbus those «that went out of Eden to water the Garden»: Pison, Gihon, Hiddekel and Euphrates.

Las Casas, when writing the *Historia de las Indias*, thought that, though Columbus was of course wrong in his second deduction, he was not being absurd: «no irracionablemente, sino con probables y razonables motivos podía opinar o sospechar al menos estar por aquella tierra ... donde esta situado el Paraiso terrenal.» [31] The delightful climate, the fresh cool air, the exotic vegetation, the delicious fruits, the beauty of the trees, and the gentle character of the natives combined to make one feel that that this might indeed be Paradise. [32] Nor does Morison scorn Columbus's «paradisiacal conceits», and he finds here striking evidence of the dualism in his nature: «in the very same week of August 1498, when he was working up a fantastic cosmographical hypothesis, [he was also] successfully concluding one of the finest bits of dead-reckoning in his maritime career...» This latest discovery was reported to the Queen, but, says Morison, «there is no indication that even the pious Isabella was impressed by the notion that the Garden of Eden had been annexed to her empire.» One would

[28] Las Casas, *Historia*, Bk. I, chs. CXXX-CXXXI; and cf Lollis, Pt. I, v. II, pp. 5, 28-9.

[29] Las Casas, *Historia*, Bk. I, ch. CXXXI; Lollis, Pt. I, v. II, pp. 8.

[30] Lollis, Pt. I, v. II, p. 22.

[31] Las Casas, *Historia*, Bk. I, chs. CXLI and CXLIV.

[32] The mighty waters of the Orinoco fitted in conveniently with popular legend: it was known that those born near the four rivers of Paradise were deafened by their roar, and Pero Tafur, for one, knew that they sweetened and rendered drinkable the sea itself.

like to have Alexander VI's reactions to Columbus's letter on the subject. [33]

The account of the third voyage, a piece of mystical geography, is outstripped by that of the fourth, in the *Lettera rarissima*, which gives a vivid insight into Columbus's mind at this time. One of the aims of this voyage (the so-called *alto viaje)*, was to find a way through Panama to Jerusalem. Fittingly, the journey started with a detour to relieve Arzila, on the Moroccan coast, then under siege by Muslims. Afterwards the journey continued «en nombre de la Santa Trinidad, y espéro d'él la vitoria». [34] On his arrival in Española he found a fleet of thirty ships about to leave for Spain. He warned the captains of an approaching storm and urged them to delay for a week, but was jeered at: «unos burlaron dello y quizá dél; otros lo tuvieron por adevino; otros mofando, por profecta». [35] Las Casas, relating the episode, adds with relish that they suffered for their disrespect, for almost the entire fleet was lost; Thacher, too, enthusiastically comments that «no Greek drama ever more completely filled the demands of vengeance». [36]

Columbus's subsequent voyage along the Panama coast was troubled. He sought the strait leading into the Indian Ocean (no one suspected the existence of the Pacific) and believed he was within ten days' sail of the Ganges, and was near to the Golden Chersonese whence, said Josephus, Solomon's gold came to build the Temple. But there were also hostile natives and fearful storms; hurricanes lashed the ships; such rains fell that it seemed a Second Deluge; the sky «ardió como forno», while the sea («fecha sangre, herviendo como caldera por gran fuego») was like the legendary *Mare tenebrosum*. [37] Not even Job himself, thought Columbus, could bear such martyrdom. At one moment, alone on board, delirious with fever, he climbed to the main top and, Lear-like, cried out: «subí assi, trabaxando, lo más alto, llamando a voz temerosa, llorando, i mui a prisa, los maestros de la guerra de Vuestras Altezas, a todos quatro los vientos, por socorro; mas nunca me respondieron. Cansado, me dormeçí, gimiendo: una voz muy piadosa oí ...» Then, a vision comforted him, reminding him that God had as much care for him as for Moses and David, and urging, finally, «no temas, confía: todas estas tribulaciones están escritas en piedra mármol, i no sin causa» (pp. 191-2). But even then his trials had not ended, and he was marooned on Jamaica for a year before being rescued dramatically from Española.

The account of the fourth voyage has aroused great admiration: Morison sees there «a story of adventure which imagination could hardly

[33] Morison, 557-8; Phelan, 134.
[34] Lollis, Pt. I, v. II, p. 173.
[35] Las Casas, *Historia*, Bk. II, ch. V.
[36] Thacher, II, 579.
[37] Lollis, Pt. I, v. II, p. 186.

invent», and though he calls the *Lettera rarissima* an «incoherent, exaggerated screed», yet he finds that it «concludes with a noble and eloquent peroration».[38] Humboldt goes further and enthuses over the beauty, nobility and poetry of Columbus's descriptions: «Voilà un tableau de tempête comme les donnent nos *romans maritimes*»;[39] for him at least, Columbus can be «if not more eloquent, yet far more moving than the allegorical pastoral romance of Boccaccio ... Sannazaro ... Sydney ... Garcilasso ... Jorge de Montemayor».[40]

The *alto viaje*, then, was very different, both in reality and symbolically, from the first encounter with that tropical paradise which was to be his means of freeing *la casa santa*, but to the end, wildly consistent as ever, Columbus died thinking of Jerusalem.

* * *

Columbus had his detractors who jeered at his dreams, or thought him entirely motivated by greed. But equally he had his defenders, of whom some accepted him on his own terms. Already, in 1495, Jaime Ferrer saw him as within the tradition of «el Caballero Hercules» and «el gran Alejandre, y el principe de caballeria, Julio Cesar»,[41] and regarded him as a divinely-chosen legate, a latter-day counterpart to the Apostle Thomas who had been despatched to preach in India. For Ferrer, Columbus was an «Apostolo y Ambajador de Dios». Then, in 1516, Agostino Giustiniani, seizing upon the same Psalm-verse as Ferrer («*in omnem terram exivit sonus eorum*»), depicted Columbus as fulfilling the prophecy of David. Later, Las Casas, in both his *Historia* and *Apologética*, described the Admiral warmly, linking him with a figure in Tacitus, and seeing divine providence in his very names, which defined his life's tasks: to be the «Christ-bearer» and the «poblador de nuevo». Las Casas, too, saw him as divinely elected from out of the sons of Adam, and as a near-prophet, who, if he had faults, paid dearly for them.[42] Columbus's son, Hernando, also saw a mysterious significance in his father's life and name Colombo, «o Palomo, en cuanto trajo la gracia del Espíritu Santo a aquel nuevo mundo».[43] Later elaborations might have surprised even the Admiral himself. Peter Sebastian Kreuzer counted thirty-six parallels between *Christus und Columbus* (Graz, 1856). The character of this

[38] Morison, pp. 584, 644.
[39] Von Humboldt, *Examen critique*, III (Paris, 1837), p. 231 n.
[40] *Cosmos*, II (London, 1848), p. 56.
[41] Thacher, II, 365-6.
[42] Las Casas, *Historia*, Bk. I, chs. II, CXXI.
[43] *Historia del Almirante Cristóbal Colón por su hijo don Hernando*, I (Madrid, 1932), pp. 13-15.

study may be gauged from its comparison of Columbus's return from the first voyage with the Resurrection, or between the second out-going voyage and the Ascension «into the happy kingdom to which He had shown the way». Columbus is shown to be the man by whom the first two petitions of The Lord's Prayer are given wider fulfilment. The Admiral's achievement is put to apologetical use: those who deny the existence of an after-life are like the «learned» ones who doubted the existence of America. In short, this is a work of ingenuity and imagination.

For Alfonso de Ulloa, Columbus had outstripped the achievements of ancients and moderns alike, but other early writers (Benzoni, Giustiniani, Modelo) thought him unfortunate not to have lived in classical times, for in a just world he would have been deified and had temples and statues raised in his name. However, in the nineteenth century there was an attempt to make amends. A proposal for his canonisation was launched by a life-long, and long-lived, champion of the «Servant of God, Christopher Columbus». This was Count Antoine Roselly de Lorgues, who, under the somewhat tactless banner of «la vérité a besoin de la France», published a number of works during his campaign which lasted from 1856 to 1892.

Roselly compared Columbus to Moses and St. Peter, hailed him as the «messenger of the Gospel and amplifier of the Universe», and indulged in mystical equations. He noted that 1,500 years before Christ, Moses had brought the true faith to the people of God, just as 1,500 years after Christ, Columbus had brought a new people into the church of God. Pius IX, as the first Pope ever to have crossed the Atlantic, was petitioned on behalf of the «predestined herald of the Faith to half the World». Papal approval was encouraging, if cautious: «Tentare non nocet.» Roselly was allowed to make an address to the Fathers of Vatican I, upon whom he made a favourable impression, and he gathered a large number of signatures for the Postulatum of 1870. Delayed, however, by the occupation of Rome and the resultant upheaval, the case was reopened in 1877, when the Minister-General of the Franciscan Order appointed Roselly as Postulator of the Cause. (Roselly, like Columbus, was a Franciscan Tertiary.) By 1881 the movement had attracted the support of almost a thousand prelates, including 6 patriarchs, 35 cardinals (among them was Manning of Westminster), and 146 archbishops.

But there was also opposition. Some objections were technical, and based on the elaborate rules for canonisation procedure laid down by Benedict XIV. The main obstacle, however, was the belief held by some, hotly denied by others, that Columbus's second son, Hernando, was illegitimate. Roselly saw this as a calumny, based upon a mere inference drawn from a copy of the Admiral's will which, by ill-luck, had come into possession of a mere compiler, annotator and cataloguer, Nicolás Antonio: it was a calumny, said Roselly, that «Nicolao l'a tirée de sa lourde cervelle». [44] Since Roselly was confident that the great mission of the Discovery could never have been entrusted to a sinner, he was therefore quite undeterred, and throwing himself into the acrimonious controversy with zest and zeal, the Postulator continued his vigorous campaign, firing his last shot at the age of 92, aided by Léon Bloy's satire *Colomb devant les taureaux* (1890). But in the event, although Leo XIII marked the anniversary year of 1892 by proclaiming «Columbus noster est», the attempt to canonise a second St Christopher failed. [45]

University College,

London.

[44] A. Roselly de Lorgues, *L'Ambassadeur de Dieu et le Pape Pie IX* (Paris, 1874), pp. 381-3.

[45] However, perhaps some sort of amends had already been made, for in 1882 an Order bearing his name, the Knights of Columbus, was founded in America. I am grateful to Professor Alan Deyermond, Dr Roger Walker and Professor A. I. Watson for reading and making useful comments on the manuscript of this article.

ADDITIONAL NOTES

P. 50: The emphasis on devotion to the Trinity shown by Columbus and Las Casas has led some to detect attempts to distract attention from their Jewish origins. But the suggestion is not proven; see E. Asencio, La España imaginada de Américo Castro (Barcelona, 1976), p. 95. On the widespread popularity of the Trinitarian cult in fifteenth- and sixteenth-century Spain (e.g. Ignatius Loyola) see Pedro Leturia, SJ., 'Libros de horas', Archivum Historicum Societatis Jesu, XVII (1948), esp. 26-29. For a recent discussion of themes touched on in the present article, see P.M. Watts, 'On the Spiritual Origins of Columbus's "Enterprise of the Indies"', American Historical Review, 90 (1985), pp. 73-102.

II

THE DOMINICAN MISSION IN JAPAN (1602-1622) AND LOPE DE VEGA

In collaboration with C. R. Boxer

Rev. P. F. Bennoni Biermann Ord. Praed., rerum a praeconibus christianae fidei inter gentes praeclare gestarum scriptori praeclaro, octogesimum recurrente natali die D.D.D.

In comparison with the well-publicised Jesuit and Franciscan missions in feudal Japan, the Dominicans and the Augustinians have remained very much in the background. To a large extent, this is perfectly understandable. The Jesuits were the first and for a long time the only missionaries in Japan, and the regular publication of their Annual Letters assured them of a wide and interested audience in all save the most bigotedly Protestant countries of Western Europe. The Franciscans, though their mission was established forty four years after St. Francis Xavier had landed at Kagoshima, quickly achieved renown throughout Christendom with the spectacular martyrdom at Nagasaki on the 5 February 1597 in which they provided the great majority of the victims. Moreover, the success of the Christian *daimyos*' embassy to Rome, Madrid and Lisbon which had been organised and publicised by the Jesuits in 1583-90, was emulated within three decades by the dispatch of Daté Masamune's embassy accompanied by Friar Luis Sotelo, O.F.M., and which attracted almost as much notice in Western Europe. Finally, the Jesuit and Franciscan records of their respective missions in Japan, both published and unpublished, are evidently much more voluminous than those of either the Dominicans or the Augustinians. For these and other reasons which need not be mentioned here, historians both clerical and lay, European and Japanese alike, have tended to concentrate on the activities of the two former Orders in the Japanese mission-field, and have left the others to their contemporary chroniclers and hagiographers [1]. While not disputing the primacy of the Jesuits and the Franciscans in the Land of the Rising Sun, it is the object of this essay to show that the Dominicans' missionary efforts were far from negligible and that they secured the sympathy and support of Spain's most famous playwright. The Augustinians do not fall within the scope of this article, save incidentally, but it is to be hoped that the remarkable life and labours of Fray Bartolomé de Gutiérrez, O.E.S.A., (to mention only one of their martyrs) will attract a modern biographer before long. Nor are we concerned in this article with the last fourteen years (1623-1637) of the Dominican mission in feudal Japan.

The first recorded Dominican friar to set foot in Japan was Fr. Juan Cobo, who landed at Satsuma in 1592 as envoy from the Governor of the Philippines to Toyotomi Hideyoshi. Nothing came of his visit, since he was shipwrecked on the return voyage and perished at the hands of the head-hunters of Formosa. Ten years elapsed after Cobo's death before the Dominicans tried to get another footing in Japan, but then they were more successful. The exact origins of the mission which they founded in Satsuma in 1602 are still not altogether clear, but Dr Antonio de Morga's version is probably not far from the truth. The martyrdom of 5 February 1597, though primarily a Franciscan triumph, had quickened the interest in Japan of all the four Religious Orders represented at Manila. Fr. Jerónimo de Jesús, O.F.M., who had returned to that country in 1598, and been well received by Tokugawa Ieyasu, the military dictator who became the effective ruler of the island empire after the battle of Sekigahara (20 October 1600), claimed that there was a rich harvest of souls awaiting Jesuits and friars alike. In 1601, the Dominican Prior at Manila, Fr. Francisco Morales, became very friendly with some Japanese Christians from Satsuma

---

[1] The principal sources for the Dominican mission in feudal Japan are the original letters preserved in the archives of the Philippine Province of the Rosary at Manila, many of which have been published serially in an obscure periodical entitled " Misiones Dominicanas " (vols. II-VIII, Madrid-Alcalá, 1919-1925) and hereinafter referred to as MD.; Jacinto Orfanel, O.P., and Diego Collado, O.P., Historia eclesiástica de los sucessos de la christiandad de Iapón, 1602-1622 (Madrid, 1633); Diego Aduarte, O.P., Historia de la provincia del Santo Rosario de la Orden de Predicadores en Philippinas, Iapon, y China (Manila, 1640). A second edition of Aduarte's *Historia* was published at Saragossa in 1693, but our quotations are from the first edition. For a short, factual modern survey cf. Pablo Fernández, O.P., Dominicos donde nace el sol (Barcelona, 1958), pp. 81-97.

and he asked them about the possibility of opening a Dominican mission in that fief. The Japanese were most optimistic, and the Father Provincial accordingly gave them a letter addressed to the ruling *daimyo*, Shimazu Yoshihiro, asking if missionaries of that Order would be allowed to work there. An affirmative reply was received in the following year, and despite some misgivings on the part of the newly-arrived Governor of the Philippines, Don Pedro de Acuña, and a few of the lay authorities at Manila, a party of five friars headed by Fr. Francisco Morales left for Satsuma in June, 1602 [2].

Having fought on the losing side against Ieyasu at the battle of Sekigahara, Yoshihiro had been forced to resign the fief (in 1602) to his son, Tadatsune, who took the name of Iehisa in the following year. It was, however, apparently the former who received Morales and his companions at Kagoshima, kindly enough at first, but later with more reserve when he realised that they had not come with the intention of attracting Spanish traders and merchant shipping from Manila, as he had hoped, but solely with the object of making converts to Christianity. As late as February 1606, however, Friar Juan Rueda de los Angeles O.P., who had joined the mission two years previously, wrote that " El Rey nos tiene mucha aficion, hacenos limosna, y no le hemos pedido cosa que nos la haya negado ". The Dominicans were allowed to remain in Satsuma until the year 1609, but there were never more than six of them there at any given time, and they never had more than one small church — at first on the off-shore island of Koshiki, and from June 1606 at the little port of Kyodomari on the opposite coast.

Unfortunately, we have very little information about this Dominican mission in Satsuma, neither Orfanel nor Aduarte devoting much space to it in their respective chronicles [3]. It is obvious that the friars made relatively few converts, despite the exemplary lives they led and the

---

[2] Dr. Antonio de Morga, Sucesos de las islas Filipinas (Mexico, 1609), reprinted with copious notes and an introduction by W. E. Retana (Madrid, 1909), from which edition our references are taken, pp. 101-103, 128-30; Diego Aduarte, O.P., Historia, Libro I, cap. 55. Fr. Lorenzo Pérez, O.F.M., in his lavishly documented monograph on " Fr. Jerónimo de Jesús, restaurador de las misiones del Japón, sus cartas y relaciones, 1595-1604 " (Firenze, 1929), pp. 18-40, points out that Morga was mistaken on some points of detail; but he accurately reflected the mixed feelings in Manila about the pros and cons of reopening missionary and commercial contacts with Japan in 1598-1603.

[3] Orfanel, Historia (1633), ff. 1-8; Aduarte, Historia, Libro I, caps. 55, 64, 67 and 68. Only a few original letters from this period are published in the MD.

rigour with which they followed the Constitutions of their Order. Nor is this surprising, as the difficulties in the way of evangelisation which St. Francis Xavier experienced during his stay at Kagoshima were still more formidable half a century later. Buddhism was very strongly established here, and the Bonzes were more respected than they were in many other regions. The inhabitants prided themselves on their fanatical loyalty to their *daimyo*, and these *daimyo* let it be clearly understood that they did not favour converts to Christianity. As elsewhere in Japan at this time, the conversion of nobles and *samurai* was forbidden on pain of death, but the prohibition was enforced more rigorously in Satsuma than in most other fiefs. It was a breach of this prohibition which provided the Dominicans with their first Japanese martyr, a *samurai* named Leon Shichiyemon who was baptized in July 1608, and executed when he refused to renounce his faith four months later.

Even though they did not make many converts during their seven-year stay in Satsuma, the friars were not entirely wasting their time. They earnestly studied the Japanese language, manners and customs; and if two of the missionaries could not last the course and had to return to Manila, the others became remarkably proficient linguists. Fr. Juan Rueda de los Angeles wrote, in his above-quoted letter of 24 February 1606, that the friars took daily lessons in Japanese and often spoke it among themselves. By this time, he averred, " Todos los Padres han salido con la lengua, confiesan, y predican y catequizan en ella " [4]. He himself became so expert that by the time of the general persecution in 1614 he could pass himself off as a Japanese. The friars naturally had to contend with much opposition and counter-propaganda from the local Bonzes. Orfanel also mentions one who was certainly no bigot, but whose polite evasions were more difficult to overcome than argumentative hostility:

" Era este de buen natural, y hombre a mi parecer que se le dava poco de passar dos, o tres dias sin rezar. Solia ir algunas vezes a casa de los Padres, pareceme que mas porque le conbidassen a bever, que por otra cosa. Quando le dezian algo de nuestra ley, oialo, y luego respondia: Que lo mismo tenian ellos puntualmente en la suya sin discrepar en nada. A todo dava esta respuesta, con que no se le hallava pies ni cabeça, y si le queria hablar mas en ello, luego dezia que estava de priessa, y se despedia ".

---

[4] Fr. Juan Rueda de los Angeles, O.P., to the Provincial, Kiyodomari, 24 February, 1606 in MD. IV (1921), pp. 370-71, 399-400.

This attitude reminds one of St. Francis Xavier's friend at Kagoshima, the abbot of the Zen monastery of Fukushoji, who likewise tried to avoid becoming enmeshed in abstruse theological arguments, without giving offence to his interlocutor [5].

Although the Dominicans had never made any secret of the fact that they had come to Satsuma solely for the purpose of preaching the Gospel, the Shimazu family evidently hoped that the presence of the friars would act as a bait to Spanish traders in much the same way as the presence of the Jesuits at Nagasaki facilitated the trade with the Portuguese merchants of Macao. If the Shimazu did not actively encourage the friars to remain when the ships from Manila failed to come, at least they tolerated them for some years, giving them land for the construction of their two churches and sending them occasional gifts in money and kind in lieu of the fixed income they had originally offered and which the friars had politely declined. With the gradual, if modest, expansion of their missionary work, and the continued absence of shipping from Manila, the *daimyo* began to lose patience. The conversion and martyrdom of Leon Shichiyemon evidently proved the last straw. The blow did not actually fall till May 1609, but the friars had some warning that their expulsion was contemplated, although the *daimyo* politely dissimulated with them personally up to the last moment. When he dropped the mask, he was frank enough, as Fr. José de San Jacinto Salvanés reported in a letter dated 27 January 1610:

" El recado nos dieron a dos de mayo, diciendo que el Rey aborrecia nuestra Ley y que después que estábamos allí, habíamos hecho muchos cristianos y que se iba perdiendo la adoración de sus dioses, que en su Reino mas que en otros del Japon se estimaba en mucho, y que por otra parte, no le eran [*sic*; eramos ?] de ningun provecho, porque no venia nunca nao — ésto se quede en casa — y que asi nos fuésemos presto a otra parte ". For these reasons, as Fr. José wrote in the same letter: " De Satsuma nos desterraron después de haber renegado muchos cristianos y salido desterrados otros muchos por no querer renegar " [6].

Fortunately for the friars, they had already managed to establish a foothold elsewhere in Kyushu, as well as in Kyoto, by the time of

---

[5] Orfanel, Historia, fl. 2. For Xavier's relations with the Zen abbot of the Kagoshima Fukushoji, see Michael Cooper, S.J., The early Jesuits and Zen (The Month, May, 1962, pp. 261-74), especially, pp. 263-5.

[6] José de Salvanés, O.P., to the Padre Provincial, Kyoto, 27 January 1610 in MD. V (1922), p. 61.

their expulsion from Satsuma in May 1609. Henceforth the province of Hizen became their principal mission-field, for they had been given an unexpectedly cordial welcome there by Nabeshima Naoshige, *daimyo* of Saga, three years earlier. When Friar Alonso de Mena was granted a preliminary audience by Nabeshima, the friar, mindful of the trouble brewing with the Shimazu of Satsuma, pointed out that if the Dominicans were allowed to settle in Hizen, they could not guarantee that Spanish ships would visit his ports. Nabeshima gave a reassuring reply, saying that " ni el tampoco les admitia en su Reino por essos respetos, que no tuviessen pena ". He added that he would give them leave to build churches in his fief provided that no objection was raised by a famous Buddhist scholar-priest named Genkitsu, who was one of Ieyasu's confidential advisers and was then visiting a neighbouring monastery. Fr. Alonso de Mena naturally expected that Genkitsu would strongly advise against any such concession, but, on the contrary, he readily gave his approval and rebuffed some of his colleagues who urged that the missionaries should be rejected [7]. Nor was this the only instance of Buddhist tolerance that the friars experienced in Hizen. When they finally had to leave in November 1613, as a consequence of the general persecution, a famous old Zen hermit who lived near their church at Hamamachi, and who often paid them friendly visits, came to condole with them on the eve of their departure " y mostrava a los menos en lo exterior tanto sentimiento, que no le faltava sino llorar " [8]. Incidentally, this Bonze had also adopted the technique of his Satsuma colleague in politely evading the friars' efforts to engage him in theological disputations.

On their expulsion from Satsuma, Fr. Francisco Morales and his two remaining companions moved to Nagasaki, where they founded the Dominican church of the Rosary. Between 1609 and the beginning of the general persecution in 1613, the Dominican mission achieved its greatest extent and prosperity in Japan. In addition to the church at Nagasaki, there were three churches in Hizen, one in Kyoto, and one in Osaka. Other places in Southern Japan, such as Hirado, were visited periodically; but the Dominicans were too few in number to

---

[7] Orfanel, Historia, fls. 3-4, 9; Aduarte, Historia, Libro I, cap. 64, where the Bonze's name is given as " Gaco ", which is a transcription of the Japanese word *Gakko* (school, college), and was often applied to Genkitsu, since he had been director of the celebrated Ashikaga Gakko, or Ashikaga College (University).

[8] Orfanel, Historia, fls. 22-23; Aduarte, Historia, Libro I, cap. 75.

accept the invitation of Daté Masamune, the powerful *daimyo* of Oshu (Mutsu), to extend their mission to the northern provinces. As there were never more than ten ordained Dominicans in Japan at any given time, and as some of them were always on the move, ministering to the scattered Christian communities, there were never more than one or two friars officiating in each of the six churches before the outbreak of the general persecution in 1613 led to the concentration of all the missionaries at Nagasaki.

As indicated above, we have very little information about the missionary and conversion techniques employed by the Dominicans in Japan, in contrast to the wealth of material available in Jesuit and Franciscan sources. We know, however, that they were careful to avoid any close connection between God and Mammon, and they assured potential converts that they had no special " pull " or influence with the traders at Manila. " Mas queremos cuatro cristianos hechos puramente por Dios ", wrote Fr. Juan Rueda de los Angeles in February 1606, " que ciento por interés del mundo, que corren mucho peligro en la fe en faltando el interés que los movió a hacerse cristianos ". They also realised that some of the primitive Satsuma peasants and fishers whom they converted did not always fully understand what was involved in their conversion. For this reason, continued Rueda, " parece necesario que todos los domingos se les diga alguna cosa de catecismo, ahora sea dentro del mismo sermon, o de otra cualquiera manera "; and this, as he recognised, was one of the reasons why the friars should (and did) study the language intensively [9]. We also know that the friars made great use of *dojuku*, or native catechists, as the Jesuits and Franciscans had done before them.

Although the friars emphasized that their missionary methods differed in some ways from those of the Jesuits, they frankly acknowledged their debt to several of the works printed in the vernacular by the Jesuit press in Japan. These included an abridged version of one of the most famous works by a writer of their own Order, *The Sinner's Guide* of Fr. Luis de Granada, O. P. Among several tributes to the great popularity of this book the following by Fr. Jacinto Orfanel, O. P., is worth quoting in full. Writing of a Christian household in the village of Kibara, Bungo province, he states:

---

[9] Juan Rueda de los Angeles, O.P., letter of 24 February 1606, ed. in MD. IV, pp. 370-71, 399-400.

" Tenian estos buenos Christianos en su casa el *Guia de pecadores* del Padre fray Luis de Granada, y solian leer en él muy de ordinario hasta la Maxencia, que tambien sabia leer: y no se puede bien dezir el gran provecho que ha hecho en Iapon este libro traduzido como anda, al qual no solo estiman, y andan perdidos por él los Christianos; pero aun hasta los Gentiles gustan de leer en él muchos, y le tienen algunos en sus casas "[10].

This Japanese version was first printed at Nagasaki in 1599, in a mixture of woodblock and moveable type. The bulk of the text was in Sino-Japanese characters and *kana* syllabary, with many quotations from the Vulgate printed in Latin. It proved so popular that a second edition was apparently printed a few years later, but no copy of this has survived, and only some eight existing copies — all save one, incomplete — are recorded of the first edition. The universal appeal of *The Sinner's Guide* is shown by the fact that it also ran through two editions in contemporary England (1598 and 1614), where its translator was a Protestant preacher and its popularity likewise was not confined to Catholic readers.

This is not the place to discuss the reasons for and the antecedents of the decree promulgated by the Tokugawa *Bakufu* (*lit.* " curtain government ") or military dictatorship in January 1614, by which all the missionaries were expelled from Japan, and the profession and propagation of Roman Catholic Christianity were forbidden on pain of severe punishment. Even this decree, though applied from the beginning more seriously than previous anti-Christian decrees had been, was not enforced with the utmost rigour in all localities for the first few years, and some of the *daimyo* used harsher methods than others. Even in places directly controlled by the Bakufu, such as Kyoto and Nagasaki, the decree was not at first applied wholesale to all those who were known to be Christians, but only to certain selected — or unlucky — victims. One reason for this was that for a couple of years the authorities were preoccupied with the two Osaka campaigns which culminated in the defeat and death of Toyotomi Hideyori (4 June, 1615) and this gave the missionaries a relative breathing space. They

---

[10] Orfanel, Historia, fl. 33. For other references to the Japanese version of the *Guia de pecadores* and its popularity in Japan, cf. ibidem, fl. 42, 74; Aduarte, Historia (ed. Manila, 1640), Libro II, pp. 38, 56; MD. III, p. 190. For a bibliographical description and the location of all recorded copies, see Johannes Laures, S.J., Kirishitan Bunko. A manual of books and documents on the early Christian missions in Japan (3rd ed., Tokyo, 1957), pp. 60-62.

had all been concentrated at Nagasaki during the spring and summer of 1614, pending their deportation to Manila and Macao in three ships, which finally set sail in November. But a few of them managed to slip away in disguise before the ships left and many others disembarked when the ships had reached the open sea into some boats sent by the local Christians. Of the nine ordained Dominicans who were then in Japan and assembled with the other missionaries at Nagasaki, seven managed to evade arrest in this way. This was a relatively higher proportion than with any of the other Orders, since out of the ten Franciscans only six remained; out of three Augustinians only one; out of eighty-five Jesuits only twenty-seven; and five Japanese secular clergy out of seven. Those missionaries who had remained in hiding or else returned in disguise, naturally wore secular clothing from then on, though many of them kept the habits of their respective Orders to wear if they should be captured and martyred [11].

The return of so many missionaries in disguise had been arranged by one of the leading Japanese Christians, Murayama Toan, the *Daikwan*, or Deputy-Governor of Nagasaki, whose previous career deserves some notice. Though the Dominicans claimed that he was of *samurai* birth, it seems that he was really born at Nagoya of humble parents. He went to Nagasaki when a youth, where he was baptized by the Jesuits under the name of Antonio. Here he not only displayed a commercial acumen which enabled him to amass a large fortune, but he became famous as a *bon-viveur* and cook, particularly in European-style dishes or *Namban-ryori*. Wealthy, amusing and hospitable as he was, he soon became one of the leading citizens. He was selected as a delegate from the municipal council to Toyotomi Hideyoshi in 1592, when the latter made an attempt to incorporate Nagasaki in his own domains. His conversation, cooking, and buffoonery so pleased Hideyoshi, with whom he seems to have had a good deal in common, that the latter changed Antonio's name to Toan and made him the local tax-farmer, in return for a fixed annual payment of 25 *kwamme* of silver. Toan closely cooperated with the Jesuits in the workaday administration and commerce of Nagasaki, and all his male children were educated by

---

[11] As, for instance, Fr. Francisco Morales, O.P., did with the sanction of the official who arrested him on 15 March 1619; cf. Orfanel, Historia (p. 93): " Entro el Padre, y de alli a poco salió vestido con su habito de Religioso (porque antes estava de seglar) con tanta autoridad, y alegria de rostro, que se espantaron todos los que presentes se hallaron ".

them. When Tokugawa Ieyasu came to power, he continued to patronise Toan as Hideyoshi had done, and confirmed him in his post of deputy-governor. Toan's five sons and three daughters were all devout Christians, and one of the former, Francisco, had been ordained as a secular priest by the Jesuit Bishop of Japan in 1604 [12].

For reasons which are far from clear, Toan seems to have fallen out with his Jesuit friends and benefactors about the time of the Dominicans' arrival at Nagasaki. At any rate, he transferred his favours to the friars and became a member of the Dominican confraternity of the Rosary, as did his sons. He avoided an open breach with the Jesuits for some years, but they considered he was partly to blame for the destruction of the great ship from Macao which was attacked and sunk near Nagasaki in January 1610 [13]. However this may have been, both his wealth and his generosity to the local Christians and their European pastors over a period of many years are well attested facts from both Japanese and Western sources. Fr. Francisco Morales, O.P., was certainly not exaggerating when he recalled in 1620 that Toan "era el amparo de todas las iglesias y religiones de Nangasaqui, y en particular él y sus hijos muy aficionados a la de San Francisco y San Domingo". Morales added with engaging frankness: "No por estas limosnas y virtudes de Toán le quiero canonizar por santo; mas antes, yo concedo que con las muchas riquezas y poder que tenía andaba también distraido, mas lo bueno bien es que se diga, y lo que tuvo también es que en cosas de la fe estuvo siempre firme; y si no lo estuviera, sus hijos, que fueron en este particular muy extremados (como luego diré), le dejaran y le fueran más crueles enemigos que cuantos él tenía" [14].

Despite the fact that Murayama Toan and his family were widely known to be staunch Christians, and although they all took part in a public procession of intercession and atonement organised by the Dominicans at Nagasaki on the 9 May, 1614, no action was taken against them by the Bakufu until 1617 or 1618. At that time, however, Toan became involved in a bitter dispute with another prominent Nagasaki

---

[12] For Murayama Toan and his career cf. N. Peri, Essai sur les relations du Japon et de l'Indochine aux XVI et XVII siècles (Hanoi, 1923), pp. 55-58; C. R. Boxer, The Christian Century in Japan, 1549-1650 (California University Press, 1951), pp. 178, 273, 298, 333-34, 345, 430.

[13] Cf. C. R. Boxer, Fidalgos in the Far East. Fact and Fancy in the History of Macao, 1550-1770 (The Hague, 1948), pp. 52-62, and the sources quoted there.

[14] Undated letter (1620 or 1621) of Fr. Francisco Morales, O.P., in MD. IV (1921), pp. 156-57, 187, 220-21.

character, Heizo Suyetsugu, who had likewise been a Jesuit convert, but who had apostatised before the crisis of 1614.

It is not clear from the conflicting evidence who started the quarrel, but it was carried as far as the Shogun's council and became a famous law-case in feudal Japan. It seemed as if Heizo would lose the day (and possibly his head) but then he played his trump-card by revealing to the Bakufu that Toan's clerical son, Francisco, had been among the defenders of Osaka Castle when he was killed in the final assault, and that Toan and his family were giving aid and comfort to the missionaries who had secretly returned to Japan. These accusations, which were perfectly true, turned the scale in Heizo's favour. Toan and two of his sons were disgraced and exiled from Nagasaki, and his office of *Daikwan* was awarded to his accuser. Further than that the Bakufu did not go, " pero dejándole con su plata y hacienda, a la mujer y los demás hijos libres ", as Morales wrote in 1620[15].

The death of Ieyasu (May, 1616), and the accession to real power of his son, Hidetada, who had been the nominal Shogun since 1605, was the occasion of intensifying the persecution of Christians, both native converts and foreign missionaries, since Hidetada was even more resolved to stamp out Christianity than his father had been. The first Europeans to suffer martyrdom, Father Pedro de Asunción, O.F.M., and Father João Baptista Machado, S.I., were beheaded at Omura on the 29 April 1618, and a few weeks later Father Alonso de Navarrete, O.P., and Father Hernando de San José Ayala, O.E.S.A., suffered the same fate, as related on pp. 54 ff. *infra*. These martyrdoms coincided with the disgrace and banishment of Murayama Toan and the triumph of the apostate Heizo Suyetsugu. Toan's eldest son, André Tokuan, was still left in undisputed possession of his house and property at Nagasaki, although he was known to be a fervent Christian, and the government must have suspected that he was secretly giving aid and protection to the missionaries in hiding, as indeed he was. Fr. Francisco Morales, the Dominican superior in Japan, was lying concealed in Tokuan's house when this fact was revealed under torture on the 15 March 1619 by a Japanese catechist of Fr. Alonso de Mena, O.P., who had been caught the day before. This was the final ruin of the Mura-

---

[15] Sources quoted in notes (12) and (14) above; Fr. Francisco Morales, O.P., letter of 25 April, 1620 in MD. III (1920), p. 384; N. Murakami (ed.), The Diary of Richard Cocks, Cape-Merchant of the English Factory in Japan, 1615-1622 (2 vols., Tokyo, 1899), II, pp. 39-69 passim.

yama family, who had been such generous benefactors of the Dominican mission in Japan. Tokuan was burnt alive at Nagasaki on the 18 November 1619, " alcanzando gloriosa corona de martirio ", as Francisco de Morales reported from Omura jail. " Por el mismo tiempo ", he added, " al Toán y a su hijo Jochuán hizo llamar el Emperador [= Shogun] del destierro, y los mandó cortar la cabeza; para lo qual ellos se aparejaron como buenos cristianos con mucha oración y lección de libros devotos y muchos actos de contrición, etc. ". More of Toan's children and grandchildren, one of them only seven years old, were executed next year, and the women of the household were exiled or imprisoned. " No por esto quiero decir que Toán es mártir ", concluded Fr. Francisco Morales, " pero menos me atrevo a decir lo contrario, pues no se sabe que haya otra causa sino la dicha ". [16]

We have dealt with this tragedy at some length because the part played by the Murayama family has been underestimated or misunderstood by many writers on the history of Christianity in Japan. The testimony of Fr. Francisco Morales, O.P., who knew the family well, and who was burnt alive when André Tokuan's wife, María, was beheaded in the " Great Martyrdom " at Nagasaki on the 10 September 1622, is sufficient to dispose of the slander that Toan was " a leading Judas ", as Padre João Rodrigues Girão, S.I., called him in 1618 [17]. No doubt Toan's conduct was equivocal at times, and Richard Cocks was only repeating a widely spread opinion when he alleged that Toan " is held to be the richest man in Japan, and come up of base parentage by his subtle and crafty wit ". But without him and his " subtle and crafty

---

[16] Letter of Fr. Francisco Morales, O.P., in MD. IV (1921), pp. 220-21. Cf. also M. Anesaki, A Concordance to the history of the Kirishitan Missions (Tokyo, 1930), pp. 40-41, 139-40, for the martyrdom and genealogy of the Murayama family.

[17] " mas são tantos os Judas em Jappão, persuadidos de hum Judas principal que he Toão o qual na demanda que teve com Feizo pera lhe fazer mal, e justificar a sua causa se ajudou de Fabião, e doutros dojucus que estiverão na Igreia os quaes como ladrões de caza sabião muy bem que Padres, quantos e aonde estavão, e as cazas em que se agazalhavão em Jappão principalmente em Namgazaqui, pretendendo o mao homem fazer nos tãobem mal com isto, e bom por este caminho á sua causa contra Feizo, e dizendo desta materia mil mentiras; as quaes descobrindosse todas e suas muitas faltas, e ladroiçes, ficou tido por falso mentiroso, e ladrão, e perdeu o yaku de Nangazaqui, e corre risco de perder tãobem a vida, e tudo quanto tem " (P. João Rodrigues Girão, S.J., to P. Bartolomeu Sequeira, S.J., Macao, 12 December, 1618, *apud* António Baião (ed.), Carta Anua da Vice-Província do Japão do ano de 1604 (Coimbra, 1933), p. xi.

wit", far fewer of the missionaries would have evaded deportation in November 1614, and he ended by sacrificing everything for the sake of his religion. The Jesuit historian, Charlevoix, was being less than fair when he wrote of Murayama Toan: "Il ne fut pas longtemps sans abjurer le Christianisme: ensuite... il se porta aux plus grands excès: il fit enfin profession ouverte de l'Athéisme... Il haissoit les Jésuites, a qui il devoit tout; et comme il vit que quelques Personnes venues des Philippines n'etoient pas bien disposées en leur faveur, il se joignit à eux, se contrefit assez pour les tromper plus aisément, les servit de son crédit et de sa plume" [18].

It was precisely this bland assumption of superiority that antagonised so many people of all races and creeds against the Jesuits both then and later, in the Far East as in Europe. The insinuation that the friars — "frailes idiotas" as the Jesuits often termed them — were poor deluded fools, who were easily hoodwinked by a smooth-tongued Japanese apostate, is quite erroneous. By the time that Morales wrote his defence of Toan's loyalty, he had lived for nearly twenty years in Japan and knew as much about the Japanese as did any Jesuit, and certainly more about the Murayama family than they did. Any unprejudiced person who takes the trouble to read the Dominican defence of Murayama Toan as well as the Jesuit attacks on him, must come to the conclusion that the Jesuits' assertions of his treachery and apostacy are grossly exaggerated where they are not wholly false.

Fr. Francisco Morales, who was the founder of the Dominican mission in Japan, who was its leader for much of the time that it existed, and who was the man who suggested that a Spanish dramatist might find it a suitable theme, was certainly not a "fraile idiota", who could easily be fooled by Murayama Toan or by anyone else. He was born at Madrid in 1567, son of the licentiate Morales, "Fiscal del Consejo Real". Educated at the Convent of San Pablo de Valladolid, where he took the habit of the Friars Preacher, and the College of San Gregorio, he came out to the Philippines in 1598. Without accepting at their face value all the eulogies of his contemporary colleagues and biographers, Manzano, Orfanel and Aduarte, it is clear from his published correspondence that he was an exceptionally intelligent and attractive character, who had the gift of getting on with all conditions of men. We can believe Manzano when he tells us that Morales was

---

[18] J. Charlevoix, S.J., Histoire du Japon (ed. 1754), Livre XIV, p. 454-55, *apud* N. Peri, Essai sur les relations du Japon et de l'Indochine, p. 56 n.

" muy amado de los Portugueses que alli habitan, por su apacible condicion, mui respectado de todas las Religiones por sus letras, mui querido de todos los Iapones por su virtud, predicación, i zelo que en él veian "; and we can believe Orfanel when he tells us that at the time of Morales's arrest in Nagasaki, " era el Padre fray Francisco muy estimado en toda la ciudad por sus muchas partes y talento, que hasta los de la Xoya tenian noticia desto, y le respetavan "[19].

From 1614 onwards, the missionaries who remained in Japan, or who were subsequently smuggled into the country by Portuguese or Chinese ships, had to work in disguise and " underground ". At first they disguised themselves as Spanish or Portuguese laymen; but later, when foreign merchants were forbidden to travel in the interior, save on officially escorted trips to Yedo or Kyoto, they had to resort to Japanese costume. A Dutch account of 1629 noted that " the priests are usually concealed in holes in the earth under the floorboards of the room of the houses wherein they lie, which holes are covered over with planks and mats; others stand all day long in a small space behind the privy, in dirt and filth, wherein one would not expect to find a beast, let alone a man; others conceal themselves between two partitions or behind the wainscoting which appears to be thinner than it really is ". As the pursuit grew hotter, lepers' huts became a favourite hiding-place; " for the lepers, who are numerous in Japan, are greatly abhorred; and nobody will be easily persuaded to enter into their huts or hovels, which are very miserable and merely slight things of straw, put up to keep off the rain at night, since they go abroad to beg in the daytime "[20]. To their honour, the missionaries of all the Orders had always ministered to these leprous outcasts, who were regarded as pariahs in feudal Japan, just as they had been in feudal Europe. The Dominicans had a small leprosarium attached to their church at Kyodomari, and they

---

[19] Fr. Melchor de Manzano, O.P., Relación verdadera del insigne y excelente martyrio, que diez Religiosos de la sagrada Orden de Predicadores, padecieron en el populoso Imperio de Iapon el año pasado de 1622 (Binondoc-Manila, 1623), fls. 58-60; Orfanel, Historia, fls. 93-95; Aduarte, Historia (ed. 1640), Libro II, pp. 152-53. Confirmation from Japanese sources in M. Anesaki, Kirishitan Dendō no kōhai (Tokyo, 1930), p. 294. The *Xoya* (Japanese, *shoya*, village headman) is here used for the municipal government of Nagasaki.

[20] Cf. R. Gysbertszoon's account of the persecution of the Japanese Christians, first printed at Amsterdam in 1637, and translated into English by C. R. Boxer, A true description of the mighty kingdoms of Japan and Siam by François Caron and Joost Schouten (London, 1935), pp. 73-88.

brought the inmates with them when they moved from Satsuma to Nagasaki in 1609.

The story of the persecution of the Christians in seventeenth-century Japan has often been told, and we will confine ourselves here to mentioning a few points which are sometimes overlooked. The incidence of the persecution varied greatly at different times and places, and the persecutors sometimes revealed a curiously ambivalent attitude. The Matsura *daimyo* of Hirado, for instance, who had always been anti-Christian, and who systematically persecuted converts in their fief, yet turned a deaf ear on more than one occasion to the resident English Factor, Richard Cocks, when he reported that fugitive priests were hiding in the town. For that matter, the attitude of the English Protestants themselves was not always consistent, and they seem to have had occasional qualms of conscience about denouncing their adversaries. The famous Will Adams, who continually advised Tokugawa Ieyasu and his son to expel all the missionaries, was married with a Roman Catholic Japanese wife, and their children were brought up in that faith. Moreover, he remained on friendly personal and business terms with many Portuguese and Spaniards, while actively intriguing against these nations at the Shogun's court. Similarly, Richard Cocks, who was never backward in denouncing Roman Catholics and all their works, wrote in his Diary on the 3 June 1615:

> " I thought good to note down that a padre or Jesuit came to the English house and said his name was Tomas and a Biscayan by nation, and gave it out that he was a merchant; and others gave him the name of Captain. Yet I knew what he was, having seen him in this house before etc. He begged a little alloes of me, which I gave him, as I did the like when he was here before. For you must understand that these padres have all the gift of begging and always answer: *Sea por el amor de Dios.* This is a general note to know them by, for they cannot so counterfeit but that word will still be thrust out ".

Nor did Cocks betray the transparently disguised Fr. Tomás del Espíritu Santo Zumárraga, O.P., on this occasion, although he did not hesitate to denounce fugitive missionaries at other times, as stated above [21].

---

[21] Diary of Richard Cocks, 1615-1622 (ed. N. Murakami), Vol. I, pp. 3-4. Fr. Tomás del Espíritu Santo, O.P., born at Vitoria (Vizcaya) in 1577, entered the Dominican Order in 1594, joined the pioneer Japan mission in 1602, and was martyred at Omura, 12 September 1622. According to Manzano (Relación, 1623), he was " muy elegante y abundante en la lengua de aquel Reyno ".

The recorded number of Christians who were killed outright, tortured to death, or died of privations suffered in prison, during the period with which we are concerned was as follows:

Year		Persons
1614	...	63
1615	...	13
1616	...	13
1617	...	20
1618	...	68
1619	...	88
1620	...	17
1621	...	20
1622	...	132

It is certain that some other victims must have suffered for their faith, whose names did not find their way into the contemporary reports from which these figures are taken. But as these reports were compiled with great care and accuracy, it is unlikely that the real number of martyrs substantially exceeded these figures [22].

The Dominicans found by experience, as did the Jesuits and Franciscans, that on the whole the poor and lowly were more ready to sacrifice their lives than were their social superiors. "Todos estos Santos mártires que murieron este año", wrote Fr. Jacinto Orfanel at Nagasaki on the 28 March 1615, "eran muy penitentes, gentes de buena vida y humildes; buena disposición para recebir del Señor grandes mercedes: por falta de lo qual renegaron los demás". The Dutchman, Reyer Gysbertszoon, was also impressed by the steadfastness under torture of the Christian fishers and peasants.

"Their resolution is all the more to be admired, since they know so little of God's word, so that one might almost term it stubbornness rather than steadfastness; because (in so far as Holy Writ is concerned) they know but little, and can only read a Pater Noster and an Ave Maria, besides a few prayers to Saints. The Romish priests exhorted them not to recant, upon pain of the loss of their salvation, accompanied with many dire threats. It is indeed

---

[22] For various estimates of the number of martyrs and a discussion of the different figures, cf. C. R. Boxer, The Christian Century in Japan, pp. 354-61; J. Laures, S.J., The Catholic Church in Japan. A short history (Tokyo, 1954), pp. 177-79.

extraordinary that there are so many among them who remain steadfast to the end, and endure so many insufferable torments, in despite of their scanty knowledge of the Holy Scriptures "[23].

It may be added that both Roman Catholic and Protestant accounts of the persecution agree that a high proportion of Japanese Catholics were from the seafaring communities of Kyushu.

The missionaries, as we have said, were well aware that many of their converts knew only the rudiments of their new faith, and among the means which the Dominicans used to strengthen the courage and cohesion of their flock was the establishment of the Confraternity of Our Lady of the Rosary. They had founded this brotherhood at Nagasaki when they moved there in 1609, but Orfanel tells us that it was not until the persecution hotted up in 1616, that the friars decided to intensify their propagation of this form of devotion:

" y assi pusieron en lengua y caracteres Iapones el sumario de la Cofradía, y sus indulgencias. Y informados los Iapones de la verdad, y viendo la excelencia desta santa devocion, y las grandes indulgencias que a sus Cofrades están concedidas, comenzó una tan estraña devocion en todo el pueblo, que no avia otra cosa sino el santo Rosario, y hazer pintar imagenes del Rosario, que les fue necessario a los Padres hazer emprenta de la Imagen ".

Orfanel does not tell us whether these pictures and the explanatory text on the Confraternity were printed from wood-blocks or with movable type; but as the Jesuit mission-press had been dismantled and sent to Manila in 1614, the former would seem to be by far the most likely, though hitherto no specimens have come to light.

The most ardent propagandist of the efficacy of the cult of Our Lady of the Rosary was friar Juan de los Angeles Rueda, O.P. Born at Villasandino near Burgos, he came out to the Philippines in 1603, and was sent to Japan next year. He became exceptionally fluent in Japanese and, as his friend and biographer, Diego Aduarte, tells us:

[23] Fr. Jacinto Orfanel, O.P., letter of 28 March 1615 in MD. VI (1923), p. 252. Reyer Gysbertszoon's narrative *apud* C. R. Boxer (ed.), Caron and Schouten's description of Japan and Siam (1935), p. 80. Cf. also Richard Cocks's account of the martyrdom he had witnessed at Kyoto when 55 people were burnt alive, including little children of five or six years old, burned in their mothers' arms crying out " Jesus receive their souls " (R. Cocks to T. Wilson, Nagasaki, 10 March 1620, *apud* N. Murakami, Letters written by the English residents in Japan, 1611-1623 (Tokyo, 1900), pp. 238-39.

" Del sancto Rosario era muy devoto y tan continuo predicador de sus sanctos misterios, que los Japones le llamavan el padre del Rosario ". He founded a branch of this Confraternity in Arima, where he worked in disguise for several years. His propaganda was so successful, that in 1619 the members refused to supply the labour for building a Buddhist temple at Shimabara, as they had been ordered to do by the *daimyo's* local representative. The brethren of the Rosary met periodically for mutual religious help and discussion, held retreats and prayer meetings, organised demonstrations at martyrdoms down to 1623 (whereafter they were usually strictly forbidden); and they kept the missionaries advised of safe hiding-places, and of those believers who were in need of their ministrations [24].

At the end of 1619 or early in 1620, Fr. Juan de Rueda was sent to Manila, " vestido de Iapon con dos catanas a su usança en la cinta, para mas disfraçado llevar socorro a tan necessitada Christiandad ". In this he was unsuccessful, for reasons briefly discussed below, and he then resolved to return to Japan alone; but before he did so, he compiled two extensive treatises on the Rosary in romanised Japanese, which were printed at the Dominican press at Binondoc (a suburb of Manila) in 1622-23. In this latter year he embarked for Japan via the Ryukyu islands, which had recently been conquered by the Shimazu of Satsuma, " para desde alli con mas facilidad passar en habito de Iapon, que muchos años auia vestido, y le asentaua tan bien que engañaua a los naturales de alla ". This was the last that was heard of him for several years, until a Japanese Dominican friar on his way to Japan in 1629, who also called at the Ryukyu, heard that he had been martyred by drowning at sea off Awaguni island, having previously profaned a sacred Buddhist (or Shinto ?) grove there [25]. The date of Rueda's death is not known, but it was probably in 1623 or 1624, and he may have been the missionary involved in the conversion of one of the local officials under the circumstances related in Appendix IV, below.

---

[24] Orfanel, Historia, fls. 64-65; Aduarte, Historia, Libro II, cap. 28.

[25] Aduarte, op. et loc. cit. For the Rozario Kiroku and the Rozario no Kyō, compiled and published by Rueda at Manila in 1622-23, cf. J. Laures, S.J., Kirishitan Bunko (ed. Tokyo, 1957), pp. 117-121; Fr. J. Gayo Aragón, O.P., " Catálogo de los impresos Filipinos conservados en los archivos de la provincia del Smo. Rosario de Filipinas y de la Universidad de Santo Thomas de Manila ", (in: Unitas, Año 25, nr. 2, Manila, April-June, 1952), pp. 323-26; M. Kinoshita, " Manila-han *Rozario no kyò* ni tsuite ", in Shigaku, XII (Tokyo, 1932), pp. 107-50.

With the departure of Fr. Juan de Rueda from Japan, only three Spanish Dominicans were left at large in that country - Orfanel, Salvanés, and Diego Collado who had arrived from Manila at the end of July, 1619. Two others, Fr. Juan de Santo Domingo and Fr. Angel Ferrer Orsucci, had arrived in August 1618, but they had been arrested in December of the same year, before they had been able to do much more than begin to learn the language. A third, Fr. Luis Flores, had been seized on his way to Japan together with his Augustinian companion, Fr. Pedro de Zúñiga, when the Japanese ship in which they were travelling was intercepted by some vessels of the Anglo-Dutch " Fleet of Defence " cruising in the straits of Formosa. In order to save the Christian captain and crew from execution, Flores and Zúñiga, who were disguised as laymen, for a long time denied their identity when brought to Hirado, but they eventually confessed who they were. The indefatigable Collado, who was to prove the stormy petrel of the mission, threw himself with equal energy into missionary work, Japanese language study, and plots to release Flores and Zúñiga from their captivity at Hirado. " El Padro Fr. Diego Collado ", wrote Orfanel to the Dominican Prior at Manila on 20 March 1620, " está muy adelante en la lengua, tanto que confiesa ya a todo género de gente; y segun se da prisa, paréceme que dentro de poco me dejará a mi por popa si somos vivos. Está tan contento en esta tierra que me parece que no trocaria su buena suerte por ninguna corona de Emperador ni Rey, ni por la tiara del Sumo Pontifice " [26].

Two reinforcements for the mission, Fr. Domingo Castellet and Fr. Pedro Vásquez, reached Nagasaki in July, 1621, but their arrival was offset by the arrest of Orfanel (in April) and of Salvanés (in August) of the same year. All the arrested Dominicans were now concentrated in Suzuta jail at Omura, where they remained until they were martyred in August and September of 1622. Their life in prison, and the ways in which they contrived to communicate with the outside world are

---

[26] Orfanel to Manzano, 20 March, 1620; MD. VI, 316. For the seizure of Flores and Zúñiga by the Anglo-Dutch " Fleet of Defence ", and their subsequent misadventures at Hirado, cf. L. Riess, History of the English Factory at Hirado, 1613-1622 (Transactions of the Asiatic Society of Japan, Vol. XXVI, Yokohama, 1898), pp. 86-92, as well as the Dominican accounts by Orfanel and Aduarte, op. cit. Collado also tried to persuade his compatriots to sabotage English and Dutch shipping at Hirado. Cf. his letter of 3 March, 1622, quoted in part by C. R. Boxer, The Great Ship from Amacon. Annals of Macao and the Old Japan Trade, 1555-1640 (Lisbon, 1959), pp. 104-5, and in full on pp. 78-81 *infra*.

briefly discussed on pp. 48 ff. below, and it will suffice here to mention their tragic if triumphant end.

The first to suffer were Fr. Luis Flores and his Augustinian companion, Fr. Pedro de Zúñiga, who were burnt alive at Nagasaki on the 19 August 1622, together with Joaquín Hirayama, the Captain of the ship in which they had been taken, while thirteen of the passengers and crew were beheaded on the same occasion. On the 10 September occurred the " Great Martyrdom " near Nagasaki, when twenty-five Christians, including five European Dominicans were burnt alive, and another thirty-one believers, including two Japanese Dominican friars, were beheaded. The martyrdom was witnessed by a crowd estimated by some eye-witnesses at 60,000 people, most of them Christians of both sexes and all ages from Nagasaki and its immediate neighbourhood, who covered the surrounding hills and fields or watched from boats moored inshore. The missionaries were able to exhort those who were nearest them; and Fr. Francisco Morales told them that their spiritual leaders were now prepared to make good with deeds what they had taught with words. " Solo les advertia que si acaso el cuerpo como flaco, i ellos como hombres de carne i sangre se meneasen algun poco no lo tuviesen a flaqueça del espíritu, ni se escandaliçasen, que no seria señal de cobardia, ni falta de voluntad de padecer, sino oficio de la carne que naturalmente rehusa el tormento " [27].

The day had dawned wet and windy, though the sky cleared and the weather was fine and hot by the time that the martyrdom began about one p. m. when each of the victims meant for burning was tied loosely to his stake.

" Los Santos Religiosos, que estavan pegados al palo, atadas las manos con un cordel que de lo alto de la columna pendia, sin que el cordel ciñese pies, braços, ni cuerpo, como se usa en aquel Reino (porque pudiesen menearse o moverse, con que los infieles tomarian motivo de risa, i ocasion de irision de su poco animo i valor) recojidos en lo intimo de sus coraçones empeçaron a ofrecerse a su Criador. La leña como estava algo apartada, i humeda del agua

---

[27] Manzano, op. cit., fls. 48-56, for the earliest printed account of the " Great Martyrdom " of September, 1622, mainly derived from the eye-witness narrative of Castellet and Collado. For other contemporary and contemporaneous accounts by Dominican, Jesuit, Augustinian and Franciscan writers see Streit-Dindinger, Bibliotheca Missionum, VI (Aachen, 1929), pp. 463-97.

que por la mañana avia caido, ardia mal, i todo era humear, i aflijir a los Santos, que con un invincible animo, superior fortaleza, i nunca vista quietud se estavan tostando i ahumando ... Acabose la leña, i juntamente acabaron algunos sus vidas, despues de media hora de fuego lento, saliendo sus almas abrasadas con el fuego vivo del amor de Dios. Uvo otros que no acabaron tan presto, por ser de mas recia complexion, pues del Santo Fr. Iacinto Orfanel, dijeron las guardas que al canto del dia siguiente, le avian hallado diciendo, Jesús, Jesús, Jesús, Maria, aviendo los de mas acabado a la una i medio del dia ".

Two days later, Fr. Tomás del Espíritu Santo Zumárraga, with a Japanese Dominican friar, Mancio de Santo Tomás Chiwato, and seven other inmates of Suzuta jail were burnt alive in the mountains three miles from Omura. Their martyrdom was not attended by such publicity as the previous one, since Christians were strictly forbidden to witness it.

The two surviving Spanish Dominicans in Japan, Collado and Castellet, had been among the crowd watching the " Great Martyrdom " and at the end of the year the former left for Manila to try to obtain some reinforcements for the mission. In this he was hardly more successful than Rueda had been, although three friars disguised as laymen reached Nagasaki via Kagoshima in 1623, a fourth having been mortally wounded in a fight with Chinese pirates on the voyage. Dissatisfied with the support that he found at Manila, Collado left for Madrid and Rome to get more concrete support for the mission. During his stay in Europe, he saw a number of works through the press, including a Japanese grammar and dictionary, and a couple of memorials bitterly denouncing the Jesuits for their real or alleged obstruction of the Mendicant Orders in Japan. After much lobbying at Madrid and Rome, he procured from the Dominican Master-General and the Holy See permission to found a congregation called San Pablo, independent of the Philippine Province of the Rosary, whose members would devote themselves to the evangelisation of Japan and China. Collado returned to Manila with twenty-three Religious in June, 1635, but immediately encountered opposition from his colleagues of the Rosary Province, who claimed that he had got permission for his new Congregation (of the " Barbones " as the members were called locally) under false pretences. Among his fiercest critics was the chronicler, Fr. Diego Aduarte, now Bishop of Nueva Segovia, who denounced him, among other things, for his advocacy of the formation of a native Filipino clergy — " cosa indigna de pensarse, pero assi lo traia en su misma patente, por aver el assi informado al Reverendissimo, contra todos quantos buenos espíritus a avido en las Indias, y contra todo lo que a mostrado la experiencia, desde que ay en ellas religiones " [28]. Aduarte's continuator and biographer tells us that the Bishop's death (August, 1636) was hastened by his chagrin at Collado's attempts to found a break-away Congregation in the Far East, and he fiercely denied Collado's claim that the Province of the Rosary had unduly neglected the Japan mission. Local opposition proved too strong for the innovator in the end, and finding his Congregation dissolved and his efforts frustrated, he left again for Europe clandestinely, but was shipwrecked and drowned on the voyage. Collado's abortive attempt to found an autonomous congregation for the Dominican Japan mission closely paralleled the previous failure of Fr. Luis Sotelo, O.F.M., to found a custody (" con la advocación del Nombre de Jesús ") for Japan independent of the Franciscan Province of San Gregorio in the Philippines, and which was likewise squashed by the opposition of his colleagues at Manila in 1618-1620 [29].

Although Collado was not altogether fair in accusing the Philippine Province of not doing all it could for the support and reinforcement of the Dominican mission in Japan, the fact remains that for one reason or another, only a few friars were sent at long intervals. They were all caught, tortured, and martyred sooner rather than later, just as happened with the Jesuit, Franciscan, and Augustinian missionaries who succeeded in effecting an entry from time to time, whether they were Westerners or Asians. The last Dominican party, three Europeans and a Japanese, were martyred in September, 1637, and this was the end of the Dominican mission in feudal Japan. During its existence of less than forty years, thirty-two sons of the Philippine Province of the Rosary had sacrificed their lives in its service. Nineteen were Europeans; three were Japanese friars and ordained priests; the remainder were Japanese choir-brothers, lay-brothers, and *donados*. Apart from

---

[28] On the other hand the friars early decided that the Japanese might be admitted to Holy Orders and minister the Sacraments (Juan López, O.P., Quinta parte de la historia de Santo Domingo y de su Orden [Valladolid, 1621], f. 270).

[29] Aduarte, Historia, II, cap. 51. For Collado's writings and memorials, cf. Streit-Dindinger, VI, 534-37, where, however, item 1481 should be ascribed to the year 1626 or 1627 and not to 1633. For the reluctance of the Religious Orders in the Philippines to admit Filipinos to their ranks, cf. J. L. Phelan, The Hispanization of the Philippines. Spanish aims and Filipino Responses, 1565-1700 (Madison, 1959), pp. 84-89. For Sotelo's unsuccessful attempt to found a Franciscan mission in Japan, cf. Fr. Lorenzo Pérez, O.F.M., Apostolado y martirio del Beato Luis Sotelo en el Japón (Madrid, 1924), pp. 187-219.

these, there were seventeen tertiaries, and numerous brethren of the Rosary Congregation. Finally, it may be mentioned that the martyr who achieved a record for enduring the terrible torture of the pit (*ana-tsurushi*) without recanting was a Dominican tertiary, Sister Magdalena de la Cruz, whose sufferings lasted for thirteen and a half days (October, 1634)[30].

Unlike the Jesuits and Franciscans, the Dominicans do not seem ever to have estimated the total number of their Japanese converts, or if they did, their estimates have not come down to us. But Orfanel admitted in his *Historia* that the great majority " fueron bautizados ya desde niños por los Padres de la Compañía de Jesús ", who had preceded the Dominicans in this mission-field by over fifty years. This was natural enough, especially as the Dominicans after their expulsion from Satsuma worked chiefly in Nagasaki, Arima, Omura, Hizen and Kyoto, where the Jesuits were already strongly established save only in the fief of Saga, since Nabeshima was unfriendly to the Society, and denied them the facilities which he gave to the Dominicans in 1606. The Jesuits would have been more than human if they had not sometimes resented this intrusion into " their " mission-field, to reap where they had sown. On the other hand, they do not seem to have objected to the intrusion of the Dominicans nearly as much as they did to that of the Franciscans, perhaps because the Dominican effort was on a more modest scale. In any event, the Jesuits, though by far the most numerous of the four Orders represented in Japan during the first four decades of the seventeenth century, simply had not got enough men to cope with the existing Christian communities, quite apart from making new converts. We may therefore agree with Orfanel when he wrote: " y assi no ay duda sino que la venida de las demas Religiones a Iapon fue para general consuelo, alegria, y esfuerço de los Christianos, que los Padres de la Compañía solos no podian tanto, y la verdad que ellos predicavan y predican mucho mas confirmada queda con quatro testigos que con uno " [31].

The Jesuits argued exactly the opposite: in their opinion a diversity

---

[30] Pablo Fernández, O.P., Dominicos donde nace el sol (Barcelona, 1958), pp. 91-95.

[31] Orfanel, Historia, fls. 117-18; and López notes (op. cit., f. 265) that the first friars encountered Japanese converted by Xavier who had then been forty years without priest or religious instruction; they knew only the holy Names, Jesus and Mary.

of missionaries from different Orders would confuse the Japanese who would mistake them, with their different methods and theological principles, for devotees of different religious sects. Considerable controversy followed upon this clash of opinions and it influenced the Dominicans in the Japan mission-field by making them aware, in a unique way, of the urgent need for publicity for their work. The result of this realisation is of interest to students of Spanish literature since it led to Lope de Vega's prose work, *El triunfo de la fe en el Japón* and to the writing of the play *Los primeros mártires del Japón.* Another curious characteristic of this Dominican mission was the friars' attitude to martyrdom. We shall now consider these two aspects of the Dominicans' work.

The Jesuits had already shown themselves to be adept in the art of propaganda for their mission and had aroused the envy of the Mendicant Orders in this respect. One of their most successful ventures was the despatching of the first Japanese embassy to Europe which, in the words of Pastor, "spread the praise of the Society of Jesus throughout the world". The Fathers reinforced this by the publication of the letters sent to their Roman headquarters which appeared as the *Annuae Iaponicae* and since they brought the first news from unknown worlds they naturally enjoyed an immense success. The Jesuits were not the first to use the press to publicise their achievements, for the Dominicans and Franciscans had already published similar reports from Mexico and North Africa; but here, as elsewhere, the Jesuits gained by their rigorous systematization. St Ignatius Loyola had laid down rules that virtually made letter-writing a religious obligation for the Jesuit. The Society's primary aim in publishing these letters was to win favour and financial support for their work and to encourage their own brethren within the Order besides stimulating volunteers for the missions [32]. In this they were eminently successful; sometimes too much so. When Father Trigault arrived in Europe from Asia in 1615 and published his account of China there were so many offers from all over the continent that the Iberian patrons of the mission took fright at the prospect of a large number of foreigners entering their sphere of interest. Trigault's propaganda tour made a great impression on Germany, for instance, and there were 31 volunteers from there

---

[32] J. Correia-Afonso, S.J., Jesuit Letters and Indian History (Bombay, 1955), pp. 3-34.

alone. These however were rejected, in accordance with policy, for Germans were regularly told to go and find their "Indies" to convert within Lutheran Germany [33].

Some friars took this clever propaganda badly and saw it as the cause of the Jesuits' undoubted power at Rome. Others, however, and more positively, saw it as a stimulus and took to writing accounts of their own work to be shown to the Pope and Cardinals. Thus a Franciscan writing in 1585 from Goa to Rome urged that a *relación* of their activities in India should be shown to the Pope "por que saiba como cá ajudamos a Igreia de Deus, o que os Padres Teatinos fazem, porque nada cá fazem que o não saiba o Papa pollo seu Geral" [34]. The Dominicans made a determined effort to systematise the sending of reports to their Roman headquarters and in 1609, for instance, the Master-General of the Order sent a formal command to Japan and the Philippines demanding news of the development of Dominican work there. The friars were ordered, under pain of mortal sin, to submit an annual account to the General giving complete progress reports and statistics "y todos las demas cosas, que pueden ser de honra a Dios, consuelo a los religiosos, ornato y hermosura de nuestra religion" [35]. But earlier than this, however, the friars had shown an awareness of this need, and Aduarte tells us that in 1606 the Dominicans in Manila had decided that "se juntassen con diligencia todas las cosas memorables y dignas de ponerse en historia, que huviessen sucedido en esta provincia, y en virtud desto el padre provincial puso precepto formal a todos los religiosos de la provincia, que le escriviesse cada vno lo que en esta parte supiesse, con toda fidelidad, y verdad, y por esta via se junto algo, de lo que aqui queda referido, pero siempre es mucho lo que se queda sepultado en olvido" [36].

These good resolutions unfortunately were allowed to lapse, at least outside Japan, and in 1645 when fray Juan Bautista Morales arrived in Rome to report on the situation in the China mission he found that in Propaganda Fide they had had no news of the friars' work there for years, apart from some random notes from an Augustinian who "escriu-

---

[33] E. Lamalle, S.J., La Propagande du P. Nicolas Trigault en faveur des Missions de Chine (1616), Archivum Historicum Societatis Jesu, IX (1940), pp. 49-120.

[34] F. Lopes, O.F.M., Os Franciscanos no Oriente Portugues de 1584 a 1590, in: Studia, N. 9, January, 1962, p. 81.

[35] Aduarte, Historia, I, p. 366.

[36] Ibid., p. 327.

iendo al Señor Secretario de Propaganda, casualmente y entre renglones, le participó nuevas de nuestra mission "[37].

The Dominicans in Japan, as we have said, were very different. They took very seriously indeed the order to write and showed a laudable keenness to publish accounts of their life and activities and to enlist the aid of established writers and artists in Spain to further this propaganda. An early example of the publication of Dominican letters is the *Relacion verdadera ... de Iapón* by Melchor de Manzano O.P. (Binondoc, 1623), published, according to the preface by the Dominican provincial, to act as a " despertador a los [frailes] que están en España, esperando (que no quiero decir ociosos) viña fertil que cultivar i Minas Ricas que labrar ". The provincial goes on to say that a fuller history will follow this, " que les sirvirá de espejo en que se miren, de exemplo que les mueva i solicite, de Iardin en que se recreen, i de mesa bien proveyda de diversos manjares conque se sustenten ". This promise was indeed fulfilled by Orfanel's *Historia* of 1633 and Aduarte's of 1640[38]. Orfanel's history covered the years 1602-1620 and a supplement for 1620-22 was added by friar Diego Collado who published the work. Collado had urged Orfanel to write the book, and after the latter's arrest by the Japanese he felt it his duty to complete the work, even though this was, as he said, " poner cabo de esparto a cordon de seda y oro ". Orfanel was a shrewd choice for the task, for he was painstaking and careful and went to extraordinary lengths to make sure his version was accurate. When the history was written he sent the manuscript into prison where friars Francisco Morales, Tomás de Zumárraga and Alonso de Mena lay awaiting martyrdom, so that they could check his accuracy from their own experience; he also showed it to his fellow-

---

[37] Domingo Fernández Navarrete, Controversias antiguas y modernas de la mission de la Gran China (Madrid, 1679; printed but not published), p. 51. Selections from this work are included in the English edition of Navarrete's writings: The Travels and Controversies of friar Domingo Navarrete, ed. J. S. Cummins (London, Hakluyt Society, 1962). In 1623 Propaganda demanded annual reports from those Orders engaged in the missions, though for years this remained an unfulfilled ideal (L. Pastor, Lives of the Popes, XXVII (London, 1939)), p. 137.

[38] López's Quinta parte also goes some way towards this aim. This work, which Aduarte drew upon, reads at times almost like a newspaper printing stop-press reports. There is, for example, a strikingly modern sense of urgency about the " particulares avisos que han venido " printed at the end of the work, and which include the comment that there is nothing new out of China beyond a report (in 1621) that the Tartars have broken through the Great Wall.

prisoners after he himself had been arrested and took careful note of their comments. The final amended draft manuscript he then sent to Fray Francisco Hurtado urging him to use it, rather than the earlier version sent to him the previous year. The result, as Collado notes, was that the history had been seen by some thirty persons in all and was checked, amended and added to by them. It was not only accurate but charitable, and, where it was necessary to criticise, Orfanel did so " con mucha brevedad, y de passo, o los escusa, dorando intenciones, sin nombrar personas, ni aun de que Religion eran " remarks Collado in his prologue. Others shared this zeal and in 1620 fray Joseph de San Jacinto Salvanés wrote to the Provincial warning him that anything published about the Japanese mission was to be sent back to Japan first so that it might be proof-read and approved by the friars on the spot: " la Orden y menos Dios no tiene necesidad de alabanzas falsas ni postizas "[39].

In their letters and reports the friars show a keen awareness of the need for publicity and even in prison they were busy writing: " En esta dichosa cárcel o paraiso, vi un precepto de V. R. ", wrote fray Alonso de Mena to his Provincial in 1620, " en que mandaba que apuntasen las cosas que fuesen para gloria de Dios y honra de la Orden " and in obedience to this command he dispatched " por diferentes vias diferentes relaciones a un sustituto de V. R. que tambien me lo mandó, como forzado ". These reports were written with a view to sending them to Rome; " he enviado largas relaciones a V. R. y a sus antecesores y creo que ya V. R. las tendrá enviadas a nuestro P. General y a todos los Padres de la Orden ". Similarly fray Francisco Morales sent a report from prison. These writers did not limit their accounts to their own doings, either, but celebrated the sufferings of their converts. Fray Francisco Carrero wrote a history of the Dominican Rosary Confraternity but thought its glories deserved even more: " requerian un libro muy grande y una historia muy copiosa que algun dia saldra a luz con el favor de Dios "[40]. These *relaciones*, like the Jesuits', were thus made a religious duty, and fray Tomás Zumárraga answered his provincial by referring to an order " por obediencia " to submit an account of events in his area after the death of the Dominican proto-martyr

---

[39] Orfanel, Historia, prologue, n. p. MD. VI, 58; MD. V, 93.

[40] Orfanel, Historia, fl. 118; MD. II, 348, III, 286; F. Carrero, O.P., Triunfo del Rosario [1626], (Manila, 1868), 60.

in Japan, fray Alonso Navarrete[41]. These written reports were also backed with relics and pictures. A painting of the martyrdom of two celebrated Japanese, Cosme and Juan, was sent from Japan to the Philippines by friar Mena in 1615[42]; and the sword with which fray Alonso de Navarrete was martyred was bought from the executioner for 150 *escudos* and sent back to Spain as a relic; cloth soaked in the proto-martyr's blood was also sent to Madrid and to the Dominican priory of San Pablo de Valladolid where, at the end of the eighteenth century, it still figured among the community's treasures[43]. A "miraculous" ear of corn was sent by friar Orfanel to the Provincial in Manila (" con todo envio a V. R. dentro de ésta, espiga de trigo... ") and through him came into the hands of Lope de Vega when he was writing the *Triunfo de la fe* (" Con todo eso, me enviaron una espiga de una heredad... ")[44].

The friars had another and basic reason for publicising their work in Japan: they felt obliged to justify themselves because of Jesuit criticism of their right to be in Japan and of their behaviour while they were there. In 1585 the Jesuits got a *Motu propio* from Gregory XIII which gave them the monopoly of the Japan mission-field. The friars, alleging that the Jesuits had obtained this papal favour by underhand means, were therefore undeterred by it, and they themselves then entered Japan in the rôle of ambassadors from the Philippine government. The quarrel was complicated by nationalism, for the Jesuits worked under the Portuguese and the friars under the Spaniards, and this difference sometimes showed itself in bizarre ways. A Spanish sea-captain who attended a Mass offered by the Jesuits complained that they were unwilling to pray for King Philip of Spain in the "*memento* for the living" and that "diciéndolo al Padre Rector, respondió que devía de haver sido descuydo; y al día siguiente dixeron: *V. Regem,*

---

[41] MD. III, 90; for evidence that the friars' letters from the missions were read and appreciated at home see Aduarte, I, 59-66.

[42] MD. VI, 27.

[43] Archive of the Dominican convent of S. Pablo, Valladolid: ' Inventario de alajas, joyas y reliquias a principios de 1768 ', fol. 20 v.: " ... un pedazo de paño ... manchado con la sangre del Ve. Pe. fr. Alonso Navarrete, hijo deste convento ". L. Pagés, Histoire de la Religion chrétienne au Japon depuis 1598 jusqu'à 1651 (Paris, 1869-70), I, 366; II, 189.

[44] MD. VI, 252; Lope de Vega, ' Triunfo de la Fe en los Reinos del Japón, por los años de 1614 y 1615 ', p. 176 of " Biblioteca de autores españoles ", vol. 38, (Madrid, 1908), pp. 159-180; hereinafter referred to as BAE.

sin poder cabar contiguo, aunque les andávamos bien a los alcanzes, y que nos havían lastimado, *V. Regem nostrum Philippum* ". This unfortunate rivalry also affected the converts who began to refer to themselves as " friar-Christians " or as " Jesuit-Christians " as the case might be [45]. Both friars [46] and Jesuits [47] lamented that the situation had become like that of which the Apostle speaks, with the faithful crying out, " Ego sum Pauli; ego autem Cephae; ... ". Fr. Gabriel de Matos S.J., complained of this division among the converts: " No tratan los Christianos hechos por los frailes con los que hizieron los de la Compania " [48]. Though, on the other hand, the Jesuits seem to have preferred that it should be so. Even the distinction between the Spanish and the Portuguese forms of the Christian names given to the converts began to take on an importance of its own [49]

Nevertheless, the friars maintained that they had a right to be in Japan, especially as later Popes modified Gregory XIII's *Motu proprio* of 1585. They also, quite rightly, emphasised that there were not enough Jesuits for the work in Japan; they pointed to the province of Hizen as an example of an area which had not been properly evangelised until their arrival: " parece que se guardaba como bocado regalado para

---

[45] For some documents dealing with the question of the friars' right to be in Japan see Maggs's Catalogue 515 (1929), Bibliotheca Asiatica, Pt. III, pp. 29-44, especially the report of 1606 (pp. 33-4); Orfanel, Historia, 118. L. Pérez, O.F.M., Cartas y relaciones del Japón, III (Madrid, 1923), 255 gives the sea-captain's remark.

[46] Diego de San Francisco, O.F.M., in: Relaciones, ed. L. Pérez, O.F.M. (Madrid, 1914), p. 34: " ... los cristianos, entre los cuales, sucede lo mismo que en el tiempo de los Apostoles, que unos decían: *ego sum Pauli*; *ego autem Cephae*; *ego Christi*; asimismo dicen en Japón: yo soy de la compañía; yo soy de los frailes ".

[47] " ay en Japón lo que reprehendia S. Pablo a los de Corintho que dezian Ego sum Pauli, ego autem Apollo, ego vero Cephae... " Gabriel de Matos, S.J., " Rasones... por las quales se muestra no ser de prouecho, antes de daño la ida de los Religiosos por Nueva España y filipinas a Japón " (British Museum, C. 62-i-18, item 93, para 4).

[48] Ibidem. Sometimes they came to blows: some friar-converts went to the Jesuit bishop to be examined by him to satisfy him as to their knowledge of Christianity but the Bishop's servants held them up first, quarrelling and disputing: " Oydas estas razones por los criados del Obispo, llenos de indignación de ira, les dieron muchas puñadas y cozes, hasta que al ruido salió el Obispo y les puso en paz... viendo a los Japones las caras tintas en sangre y los vestidos hechos pedaços ... " quoted in L. Pérez, O.F.M., Cartas y relaciones del Japón, III (Madrid, 1923), p. 251.

[49] M. Anesaki, A Concordance to the history of Kirishitan Missions (Catholic Missions in Japan in the Sixteenth and Seventeenth Centuries), Supplement to vol. VI of the Proceedings of the Imperial Academy (Tokyo, 1930), p. 6.

nuestra Orden de Santo Domingo, que hasta que ella fue allá, no tuvo la predicacion del santo Evangelio libre entrada " [50]. Moreover, the Jesuits in Japan showed less discretion than did their colleagues in China, for they took part in political struggles and got themselves mistrusted by the central government. Some of the *daimyo* also turned against them and did not want them in their territories; this reinforced the friars' arguments that the Mendicants were needed in Japan to work those areas where the Jesuits had fallen from favour, or were forbidden " por particulares enemistades que ... tienen " [51]. The friars also mistrusted the Jesuits who were involved with traders and merchants, not merely because they thought this undesirable in Religious vowed to holy poverty, but also because they felt that in the long run such a stratagem would bring ruin on the mission. " Sé decir ", wrote fray Alonso de Mena to his provincial in Manila in 1609, " sé decir que esto de andar con navíos y contrataciones no lo puedo tolerar " and the reason was that " hemos pasado ogaño enfados y pesadumbres intolerables en orden a esto ".

The Jesuits, on the other hand, complained bitterly that the friars were endangering the mission by their rash behaviour and their reluctance to compromise. Some of them, said the Fathers, acted as though they were still at home in Old Castille, and when high-ranking Jesuits rebuked them for their imprudence they were said to reject these counsels and, worse, " hazian burla y no hazian caso dellas ". The Jesuits, in the words of one witness, were more discreet and when persecution broke out in the 1590s " andan los dichosos padres por las cozinas y rincones de los Christianos, con mucho secreto y resguardo " [52]. The Fathers regarded the intruding friars as poachers upon the Society's private reserves, and at one time they attempted to prevent their converts from having any dealings with friars or even to attend services conducted by them [53]. They were alleged to forbid the converts to join the Domi-

---

[50] Carrero, op. cit., 40.

[51] MD. IV, 336; G. B. Sansom, The Western World and Japan (London, 1950), p. 166.

[52] MD. IV, 336-7; 370-1; Dos Informaciones hechas en Japón, printed privately, Madrid, 24 May 1599, fols. 30 r-v.

[53] Domingo Fernández Navarrete, O.P., Controversias, 404, 447, 470-71; C. R. Boxer, The Christian Century, 418 and, for Jesuit-Franciscan rivalry in Japan, pp. 160-71, 231-47, 326, 416-8, 470-2, and the sources quoted therein. See also L. Pérez, O.F.M., Cartas y relaciones del Japón; III: Persecución y martirio de los misioneros franciscanos (Madrid, 1923), 248-56, and López, f. 266.

nicans' Rosary Confraternity and to refuse absolution to those who did so, but possibly this is an exaggerated rumour; and probably the Jesuits feared the Confraternity would be mistaken for a political organisation and alarm the government [54]. But even the most discreet Dominican historians hint at opposition to the Rosary Confraternity without identifying whence it came [55]. The Jesuits, then, not only forbade their converts to resort to friars, but they also refused to confess the friars' converts: the friars alleged that this was because they were unwilling to confess members of the friars' sodalities, but the Jesuits retorted that the real reason was the ignorance of the friars' converts, who were not properly instructed in the Faith [56].

It was against this background that the martyrdoms of 1597 took place [57]. On that occasion twenty-six Christians died: six Spanish Franciscans, seventeen Japanese converts and three Japanese Jesuits. Incredible accusations were launched against the Jesuits as a result of this. They were said to have been the prime cause of the persecution. The Rector of Nagasaki was reported to have declared that the martyred friars got what they deserved. Some friars went so far as to declare that the Jesuits paid the executioner, and an eye-witness report by Andrés de Cuaçola, a senior Government official, stated that the Jesuits had refused to intercede for the condemned friars " first, so that they should not be deprived of their martyrdom, and secondly so as not to encourage the Conbaco [Kwambaku] to hold the Jesuits to ransom and demand sums of money from them. They assured the petitioners that the sentence was immutable. What astonished the Spaniards was the fact that after the execution the Judge who martyred the Padres, sat down to a meal with the Jesuits who 'served and regaled him' ... ". It is likely that the Jesuits did not realise that the Franciscans would be martyred but had assumed they would merely be deported. The allegation that they paid the executioner is probably due to the fact that they wanted to buy weapons used in the martyrdom, or some other relics: this was quite usual. However, stories of this sort, true or not, served to accentuate the rivalry between Jesuit and friar, and this feeling was not limited to the mission but also spread back to Europe. The

---

54 Domingo Fernández Navarrete, Controversias, 404, 470-71.

55 Orfanel, Historia, ff. 21, 139; Carrero, Triunfo del Rosario, 51-2.

56 C. Bayle, S.J., in a review article in: Missionalia Hispanica, V (1948), p. 201.

57 On this see A. Millares Carlo and J. Calvo, Los protomártires del Japón (Nagasaki, 1597): ensayo biobibliográfico (México, 1954).

friars naturally celebrated the martyrdom as something praiseworthy, but the Jesuits opposed these celebrations and in Manila were even said to have ridiculed the martyrs " con representaciones mímicas ". Some Jesuits maintained that since the friars had entered Japan against the wishes of the Pope, as implied in Gregory XIII's *Motu propio*, they had therefore died excommunicate, and were not martyrs to the Faith, but to their own folly and imprudence. One preacher in Macao in 1639 declared that the martyrs had only been absolved of their excommunication at the foot of their crosses. In Seville the affair caused particular excitement and " llegó a tanto, que estuvo en bandos la ciudad y no sin riesgo de alguna sedición grave " [58]. The canonisation of the martyrs by Urban VIII in 1627 was something of a triumph and vindication for the friars. A drawing of the scene of their deaths was made for these celebrations and it was noticed that only the friars and their Japanese converts were shown crucified: the three Japanese Jesuit martyrs were not, nor was any reference made to them. In the frontispiece to Juan Francisco de San Antonio's *Chronicas* (Sampaloc, 1738-44) the martyrdom is depicted and here too only the Franciscans and laymen are shown. The only Jesuits to appear in the picture are two absolving the martyrs at the foot of their crosses, and, in the bottom right-hand corner of the picture, may be seen the Jesuit bishop observing the scene from the safety of his quarters [59]. In the canonisation celebrations in the Franciscan Church in Barcelona the Jesuit martyrs seem also to have been ignored, although the Fathers made up for this omission by " suntuosas y costosas fiestas " [60].

The friars laid great stress upon the need for martyrs in the new Church and their record in the Japan mission is remarkable; they behaved with great courage and utter selflessness, and it is worth noting that not a single European friar apostatised during the entire persecution, even under the most severe torture. So that it must be said that if they were reckless, as is alleged, they had at least the necessary courage to match their convictions. The Dominicans were especially proud of the proto-martyr of their Order in Japan, fray Alonso Navar-

---

[58] L. Pérez, O.F.M., Cartas y relaciones del Japón, III (Madrid, 1923), pp. 8, 19, 62, 170-3, 177, 207 bis, 208 bis, 252-6; Maggs's Catalogue 515 (1929), Biblioteca Asiatica, Pt. III, 5, 10, 11. Domingo Fernández Navarrete, O.P., Tratados historicos (Madrid, 1676), p. 442.

[59] E. Male, L'Art religieux après le Concile de Trente (Paris, 1951), 117-19.

[60] Memorial histórico español, XX (Madrid, 1888), 23-5.

rete, who died in 1617, and the Dominican Orfanel boasted, quite justifiably, of the record of his colleagues: " aunque en Iapón ay otras santas Religiones, son mas los Padres de Santo Domingo que están presos, que los de las demas Religiones, por aventajarse continuamente los Padres de Santo Domingo a los demas en ayudar a la Christiandad, postpuesto qualquiera proprio peligro " [61].

In 1617, when each of the four Orders working in Japan had at least one martyr to its credit the friars saw a divine mark of approbation in the fact. But the Jesuits continued to complain of the Mendicants' imprudence, and Alonso Navarrete's courage in deliberately courting death, which greatly impressed the Japanese, was denounced by some writers. Thus Charlevoix describes the " zele plus vif que prudent " of the friars, and Cordara's officially sponsored Jesuit *Historia* blames Navarrete's " excessive ardour " as the reason for the fresh outburst of persecution. The Dominicans held that Navarrete had a divine vision which induced him to seek his martyrdom and down to the 19th century showed themselves ready to spring to his defence when he was attacked by some critics: " Crétineau Joly, apasionado historiador de los Jesuitas, llama al beato Alfonso Navarrete *fanático* y *aventurero cuyo celo indiscreto mereció el desprecio y la burla de todos*. La Iglesia le ha decretado solemnemente los honores de Beato, le ha puesto en los altares; luego el fanático aventurero, indiscreto, calumniador y hasta blasfemo es Crétineau Joly ", wrote one defender [62].

It is hardly surprising, then, if Navarrete's own contemporaries saw clearly the need to defend the reputation of their proto-martyr. But even earlier than this they had approached Lope de Vega to write a prose account of their achievements in Japan. It was thus that the *Triunfo de la fee en los Reynos del Japón por los años de 1614 y 1615* came to be written in 1617.

Lope states clearly that the source material for the work had reached him from Japan and the Philippines: " Escribo los martirios no testigo de vista, que no fue mi dicha tanta, pero por relaciones de algunos padres que me las enviaron desde Manila, a efecto que en el estilo con que he nacido las publicase ", and in a letter to the Duque de Sessa, written

---

[61] Orfanel, Historia, f. 140.

[62] P. F. X. Charlevoix, S.J., Histoire et description générale du Japon (Paris, 1736) V, 502; J. Cordara, S.J., Historiae Societatis Jesu, Partis Sextae Liber II (Romae, 1750), 121; R. Martínez-Vigil, O.P., La Orden de predicadores (Madrid, 1884), p. 151.

in mid-July, 1617, he remarked, " Mi estudio estos dias ha sido una historia de unos martires, o digamos *Relaçión*, a que me ha obligado haberme escrito unos Padres desde el Japón [63]. The reference to " unos Padres " is sometimes taken automatically to mean the Jesuits [64], although this assertion may be discounted immediately. It is easy enough to follow the events, for Lope in writing his *Triunfo* relied almost entirely upon a *Relaçión* written on 28 March, 1615 by the Dominican fray Jacinto Orfanel in Japan [65]. Orfanel concludes this report with the comment that it has been written " paraque sepan de las maravillas que el señor obra por acá " and adds that he is sending a copy to the Prior of Manila " para que lo envíe a España ". The most likely contact in Madrid between Lope and the Philippine and Japan friars would be Canon Pedro Fernández Navarrete, author of the *Conservación de monarquías*, brother of the martyr fray Alonso Navarrete and first cousin of the martyr fray Alonso de Mena [66]. The Navarrete family, which was not without distinction, was proud of its martyrs, and Canon Pedro Navarrete refers in the *Conservación* to his " glorioso hermano fray Alonso Navarrete ... el protomártir de su religion en aquellas provincias " [67]. Nothing would be more natural than that when the Japan Dominicans, with whom the Canon corresponded, sought his advice about finding a publicist of renown to record their story, he should think of the greatest writer of the day, Lope de Vega, and ask him to undertake the task ' with that style with which he had been born ' [68].

---

[63] Lope de Vega, Epistolario (ed. A. G. Amezúa), III (Madrid, 1941), p. 317; and BAE, XXXVIII, p. 162.

[64] As in H. Bernard Maitre, S.J., Lope de Vega et l'Extrême-Orient, Monumenta Nipponica, IV (1941), p. 279.

[65] Published in MD. V (1922), p. 389; VI (1923), pp. 26-27, 58-9, 89-90, 123-24 217-18, 251-52.

[66] MD. VI, p. 252; Pagés, II, 187, 189, prints letters sent to the Canon in Spain by friars in Japan.

[67] Pedro Fernández Navarrete, Conservación de monarquías (Madrid, Biblioteca de autores españoles, 1920), vol. XXV, p. 539. The martyr's nephew, the marqués de la Terca, for instance, enquired in Rome for news of his uncle's process in 1672 (Dominican Archives, Rome, IV, 145, fol. 5-6).

[68] Lope de Vega, Triunfo, BAE, XXXVIII, p. 162. In English literary history there is an interesting and contemporary parallel to the case of Lope's being asked to write a work of religious propaganda. The promoters of some of the first English settlements used poets, preachers and playwrights to advertise the new lands and to make them appealing. Thus in 1622 John Donne was enlisted by the Virginia Company to preach what has been called the first missionary sermon in English in favour

Even if this conjecture as to the identity of the middle man is mistaken, there is certainly no mistake about the identity of Lope's informant as we shall show. Lope was willing to undertake the work, for he regarded himself as a martyrologist-historian: the duty of Apostolic Notaries in ages past was to write " las persecuciones de los tiranos y los gloriosos triunfos de los mártires " thus it seemed to him proper that he, a Notary Apostolic himself, should write the new martyrology. He was proud of this work and mentioned it later in *La Filomena* as evidence of the range of his literary interests: " Yo canté, finalmente, los mártires japones "[69].

Those critics who maintain that the *Triunfo* was written from Jesuit source material and to exalt Jesuit successes in Japan have apparently not reflected upon the singular fact that the work of the Society is scarcely mentioned in the essay. There is a bare *memento* of the three Japanese Jesuits who died with the Franciscans in 1597; in the opening paragraphs the Jesuits are named, with the three other Orders, as working in Japan, and there are one or two conventional asides; apart from that there is no mention of them, and this is the more conspicuous in a work which is headed by a prologue full of warm praise for " el Tito Livio Christiano ", Father Mariana. Lope could, of course, have used Jesuit material had he chosen to do so, for he knew the value of their letters from Japan [70], and would have had easy access to the *Relaciones* of Morejón and Pineyro [71]. Perhaps the answer is to be found in the fact that at the very time he was preparing the *Triunfo* Lope was having trouble with the local Jesuits who, according to him, were threatening to take his house from him. In December 1617 he complained to Sessa, " Hasta ahora no nos han quitado la cassa estos padres; que las de los lados son las que más han menester; y aunque entraron con cohetes,

---

of the colony which needed to recapture popular support. In return for this, Donne received stock in the Company and for a time he nourished the hope of becoming Secretary of the Corporation (Newes from the New-World, ed. L. B. Wright, Huntingdon Library, 1946, pp. 1-5). See also The Sermons of John Donne, ed. G. R. Potter, and E. M. Simpson, IV (Berkeley, 1959), pp. 37-8, 264-282.

[69] Lope de Vega, La Filomena, BAE, XXXVIII, pp. 483, 491.

[70] Lope de Vega, Triunfo, p. 162. On Lope's coolness towards the Jesuits, as shown in the Triunfo, see A. G. de Amezua (ed.), Epistolario de Lope de Vega, II (Madrid, 1940), p. 200.

[71] Pedro Morejón, S.J., Relación de la persecución... 1612-15 (Rome, 1615; Mexico, 1616; Saragossa, 1617); Luis Piñeyro, S.J., Relación... del Japón... 1612-15 (Madrid, 1617).

no quieren que sea a fuego y sangre ... Finalmente, cuando me quiten mi cassilla, mi quietud, mi guerteçillo y estudio, me queda V. Exa ". And if one may judge from a later letter of his he had a poor opinion of the Fathers whom he described to Sessa as " gente que, en medio de su humildad y preceptos de su instituto, tienen más tretas y modos de vivir que mercaderes de mohatras " [72]. He could, of course, be cynical about the friars too and make Voltairean asides about their explanation that the Rosary had won the battle of Lepanto [73]. But perhaps he was the more sympathetic to these friars who, like himself, were being threatened by the Jesuits. These friars, moreover, were very different from those he was criticising at home, and he knew how to distinguish between the two types, just as did his informant, Canon Pedro Navarrete. For it is to be noted that the passage in which the Canon praises the friar-martyrs of Japan comes from the section of his *Conservación de monarquías* where he denounces the excessive number of clergy in Spain. Moreover Lope read the friars' account of their trials at a time of crisis in his own personal life, for in that summer of 1617 he, a priest vowed to chastity, was daily awaiting news of the child to be born to him of ' Amarilis '. " Esta noche no he dormido, aunque me he confessado; mal haya amor que se quiere oponer al Cielo! " he wrote in a letter at that time. In such a mood of guilt and repentance he may well have found every line in the friars' *relación* from Japan was an accusation and a reproach to himself, for their story, in his own words, seemed " una afrenta de los que con tal descuido esperamos el incierto límite de nuestra vida ". It is little to be wondered at if he was moved to sincere admiration and perhaps even spoke the truth when he confessed that he had written the *Triunfo* with tears in his eyes [74].

A comparison of Orfanel's long letter from Japan and Lope's *Triunfo* shows the latter following scrupulously to his source except once or twice where he inserts material from other Dominican writers: for instance, he refers to a " relación del venerable padre fray Josef de San Jacinto " which he had used [75]. The first clue, however, to Orfanel's

---

[72] Lope de Vega, Epistolario, II, 197; III, 350; IV, 142.

[73] Ibidem, III, 320; IV, 53.

[74] Ibidem, III, 325; Triunfo, 162; J. de Entrambasaguas shows (Estudios sobre Lope de Vega, I (Madrid, 1946), 391 ff.) how Lope used the preface to the Triunfo to strike a blow in his controversy with Torres Rámila.

[75] Triunfo, 176. Or he could have supplemented Orfanel with the *relaciones* of friars Mena and Morales: details in H. Ocio y Viana, Reseña biográfica (Manila, 1891), pp. 200, 204.

identity comes when Lope writes: " el que por sus cartas me ha advertido destas relaciones, ... se partió a Arima, donde de la sangre de tantos mártires traía hecho un jaspe el hábito del español Domingo " which may be compared with Orfanel's original account: "Yo me fuí a Arima, donde fue el martirio de los santos, del cual me hallé tan cerca, que casi puedo decir que me volví salpicados los vestidos con su sangre [76]. It may be noted that though Lope's reference to the Dominican habit is useful for identifying his unnamed informant he is however mistaken, for, as we have said (p. 13), the friars were not wearing their religious habits at that time, and when Orfanel says *los vestidos* he is referring to his lay or secular costume [77]. This opening passage serves to pinpoint the difference between Lope and Orfanel, for it draws attention to the precision with which the friar wrote and reveals Lope's readiness to jump to conclusions, and to spoil the simplicity of the friar's account with " fine writing "—a mistake made worse, elsewhere, by the introduction of irrelevant classical allusions, or what Aubrey Bell has called the " brambles of erudition " [78]. These, no doubt, were inevitable since Lope hoped to please his readers (" pienso que agradará ") and this artificial style was calculated to gratify sophisticated taste.

After a brief survey of the work of the four Orders in the missions, Lope turns to Japan, " ya tan conocido de nosotros, como ignorado antiguamente, o por la noticia de sus embajadores en Roma, o por los que al Rey Católico vinieron tan deseosos de la fe, por orden de los padres de San Francisco, el año de 1615, o lo que es más cierto, por la que nos han dado con sus cartas los padres de la Compañía, buenos testigos del fruto de su predicación, y cuidado ". A brief survey of the Japanese background follows in which the Japanese are described as " gente blanca, su ingenio y memoria admirable ". He then states his precise aim in the *Triunfo*: he will relate the new persecution of the Japanese Christians during 1614-15, and in his outlines of the historical background he notes a similarity between the persecution in the Japanese islands and that in Britain. Even in this general outline there

---

[76] Ibidem, 164; MD. V. 389.

[77] See friar Orsucci's description of the friars in Japan " in abito di mercanti con la spada alla cintura... senza corona alla testa e con i barbigi lunghi " (P. T. Masetti, Lettere Edificanti scritte dai Frati Predicatori martirizzati nel Giappone [Roma, 1868], pp. 38-9).

[78] A. F. G. Bell, " Lope de Vega as a writer of Prose ", Bulletin of Spanish Studies, XII (1935), 234.

are echoes of Orfanel's account here and there, such as the mention of the fact that condemned Christians were made to parade naked through the streets and Christian women were put into the public brothels as a punishment [79].

Then follows an account of the persecution in Arima, Ariye and Kuchinotsu, and from this point Lope remains close to his source, only departing from it momentarily, perhaps to show he is not merely a copyist:

Orfanel: MD., VI, 26*:*	*Lope: BAE.,* 164-5*:*
el tiempo que duró esta persecución no fue menos terrible que la de Domiciano o Diocleciano.	Los pocos días que duró la persecución deste tirano, no pienso que fue inferior a las de Nerón y Diocleciano.
Partió, pues Safioye con multitud de soldados de varios reinos al de Arima, ...	(Safior) Acompañado pues de armas y de arrogancia, con numeroso ejército de soldados de varios reinos llegó al de Arima, ...
dando primero un tiento a los de Cuchinote...	dió un tiento a los cristianos de Cochinotzu...

Sometimes Lope misreads a date; thus he mistook Orfanel's " 17 November " for the 7th November and rather heavily underlined his error by glossing it:

MD., ibid.:	*BAE., ibid.:*
lunes a 17 de noviembre ...	séptimo dia de la octava de Todos Santos y víspera de los cuatro coronados, no sin misterio, pues siendo escultores, por no haber hecho, a petición de los romanos, las imágenes de sus fabulosos ídolos, entre los azotes de plomo dieron sus almas ...

Next in the account comes the story of the two brothers, Juan and Cosme. In this section of the essay, which follows Orfanel's very nearly, there are one or two additional items, probably taken from an account

[79] Triunfo, 162-4; MD. VI, 218.

by fray Juan de los Angeles, O.P., who knew the two martyrs personally. However, Lope may have used other *relaciones* or letters by Orfanel which have not survived or not been printed, for, it should be noted, he refers to Orfanel's writings in the plural and therefore must have had at his disposal more than the one letter of March 1615 [80]. In the main however he is following this letter as when he goes on to quote from it a miracle connected with the martyrs' relics:

Orfanel: MD., VI, 27:	*Lope: BAE., 165:*
(a Juan) le dieron crueles palos y	le dieron tantos palos,
uno en lado derecho de la frente de	que por su bendita cabeza
donde le corrió tanta sangre	corría un mar de sangre,
que le cegó el ojo	y quebrado el uno de los ojos,
y la carne quedó denegrida y él tan	puso la interior vista donde no alcan-
fatigado de este golpe que siempre se	zan las tinieblas de la tirana ira ...
entendió que le habían quebrado el	...
hueso,	...
hasta que el otro dia,	aquella venerable cabeza, que mirada
mirando su santa cabeza - (que en	después de los padres, que hoy la
nuestro poder está este precioso	tienen con digna veneración en
tesoro) - vide que está entero el hueso.	Manila, ninguna lesión muestra.

A comparison of these two passages above shows Lope following his original obediently but with some changes permitted by artistic licence, and obviously he is confused in thinking that the relic is in Manila, for Orfanel who had looked at it " el otro dia " was then in Nagasaki, where he wrote his account, although afterwards it was in fact sent to Manila [81]. Later in his *relación* Orfanel returned to the story of Cosme and Juan but Lope seems to have thought this second reference was to a different pair of brothers; also he misread Orfanel and made Cosme the first to be beheaded [82]. Moreover, Lope puts into the mouth of the martyrs speeches which are not to be found in his source. An example can be seen in the story of the torturing of Juan Kizayemon who, having been struck on the head and bleeding as a result, is made to address the judge with the words, " No soy yo el ciego, juez engañado; así vieras tú el bien que pierdes, como yo por

[80] Triunfo, 164, 170.
[81] MD. VI, 27, 217.
[82] MD. VI, 217; Triunfo, 174.

las celosías desta sangre ". Sometimes, indeed, Orfanel does quote dialogue to add to the dramatic effect of his story. Lope follows him closely in re-telling the story of the 15-year-old slave, Martin, who asks his master to grant him his freedom so that he may surrender to the judge and volunteer for martyrdom:

Orfanel: MD., VI, 58:	*Lope: BAE., 166:*
Lo cual le concedió su amo; y asi casi toda aquella noche no durmió, rezando y acudiendo a otras cosas de la casa.	Esto le concedió su amo enternecido, y así toda aquella noche no durmió un instante, antes bien la paso toda rezando las oraciones que sabía, y acudiendo á otros ministerios de la casa para dejar en orden lo que estaba a su cuenta.

Lope's version is more verbose, and nothing is gained by his additions or attempts at greater precision. The account continues:

Venido el jueves, a las nueve del día, como ya comenzasen a examinar los cristianos, lavándose la cabeza y el cuerpecito	Venido el dia, que fue jueves, como ya comenzasen el examen de los cristianos, y le alterase el ruido y confusion de las voces y de las armas, lavandose la cabeza y el cuerpecillo en el mar
para entregar limpios el alma y el cuerpo a Dios, puesto el mejor y menos remendado vestidillo que tenía se fué allá y procurando entrar dentro de aquella rueda de soldados.	para ofrecer á Dios el alma y el cuerpo limpios, puesto el mejor ó menos remendado vestidito que tenia, se fué adonde sonaba el concurso de la gente, y procuró entrar en aquella rueda de soldados que servía de muro al teatro, donde representaba la fe tan soberanas tragedias, ayudándole la esperanza hasta los postreros actos.
no pudo porque se lo impedían, pensando que iba a ver no más, como muchacho: y así el uno le daba un puntapié, otro un empellón, otro con el palo de la alabarda.	Mas como ellos pensasen que solo quería ver, como muchacho, aquel espectáculo, era con los cabos de las alabardas y con las coces resistido de todos.

Orfanel concludes the story and comments that he can only give the bare summary of many of these events and this too Lope echoes, though more wordily: " Si se hubieran de referir los tormentos que en esta dichosa ocasión padecieron innumerables mártires, parece que lo fueran (i. e. tormentos) estos discursos". Orfanel then tells how he ministered to these martyrs just before their end and Lope retells the story, without, however, revealing the friar as his source. Orfanel relates the story of Liyemon who at the moment of execution apostatised in the hope of saving his life, but the judge, an old enemy of his, ordered him to be beheaded and ignored the retraction. Though Liyemon died "con señales de contrición" he was not considered to be a martyr. Lope's version of this affair is much longer, and he either used a supplementary source or else the printed version of Orfanel's letter makes omissions at this point. It seems more likely that an additional source was consulted here for Lope also mentions, though briefly, the brothers Gaspar and Bartolomé Yatayu who are not mentioned in Orfanel's letter of March, 1615.

After this brief truancy from his source, Lope returns, and the narrative passes on to discuss the persecution at Ariye, a town about a league to the north of Arima. This was carried out by a judge called Matashiro:

Orfanel: MD., VI, 89:	*Lope: BAE., 167:*
un juez llamado Mataxiro, cruel enemigo de cristianos y de malísimas entrañas,	un nuevo Diocleciano, llamado Mata Girion, hombre de ferocísimo ingenio y duras entrañas, y á quien era abominable el Evangelio:
el cual, después de haber hecho sus diligencias, ...	el cual, despues de haber hecho las posibles diligencias ...
usó	trazó, pensó y ejecutó
de una traza diabólica ...	la mas diabólica imaginación que pudo fabricar su entendimiento ...

In the following passages Lope intersperses the account with biblical and classical allusions which are not in Orfanel. But this particular passage is interesting for it bears out, if the coincidences of the two narratives did not, the fact that Lope is relying on the friar for his information:

MD., VI, 90; 123:	*BAE, 168-169:*
Estaba el juez, este día,	Estaba el juez aquel dia
en un pueblo media legua de Ariye, llamado Sucava,	en un pueblo llamado Sucaba, media legua de Arie,

donde entonces estaba yo escondido	*donde el padre, de quien es el alma, y substancia destas relaciones, estaba escondido;*
y acabando de rezar completas; ya casi a la puesta del sol,	y cuando acababa de rezar completas,
llegaron a mí corriendo dos o tres cristianos	llegaron a él corriendo dos japones cristianos,
a decirme que allí, en la calle, acababa de cortar la cabeza a Adrián ...	que le dijeron como en aquella dichosa hora acababan de cortar la cabeza al bienaventurado martir, ...
dos horas después de muerto el Santo Adrián, ...	Dos horas despues de muerto el santo Adrian,
pasé por el lugar donde le habían cortado la cabeza;	pasó este padre por donde le habian cortado la cabeza,
y también acababa de recibir una carta del P. Fr. Juan de los Angeles ...	y allí recibió una carta del padre fray Juan de los Angeles ...

There is no doubt, then, that Orfanel was Lope's chief source, for he admits and shows it is so. A running parallel version of the two accounts from beginning to end is not necessary here, but it is hoped to publish it in a new edition of Lope's *Triunfo*. Curiously, Lope never identifies Orfanel as his source, though he refers to him in his essay as one of the friars working in Japan. One reason for this might be that the friar out of modesty had asked not to be named [83].

After telling of the persecution in Kuchinotsu, Lope concludes his account in the brief business-like manner of the Roman Martyrology (" *et alibi, aliorum plurimorum sanctorum Martyrum...* "), by naming other martyrs who died elsewhere and at different times, including those who had died in 1597. In the course of this account Lope quotes some Latin verses in honour of the martyrs and adds some of his own in Spanish and finally closes his study with a pious invocation.

Orfanel's original, like those of his colleagues printed in *Misiones Dominicanas*, makes stirring reading, and it is not difficult to see how Lope was moved by them. The style is straightforward and unpretentious; and where the scrupulous Orfanel is writing it can be taken that the story is well authenticated. Lope took his task seriously and on two occasions saw fit to censor the original in the interests of edification. Once he primly altered a reference by the friar to Japanese sexual mores

---

[83] On Orfanel's modesty see P. T. Masetti, I Martiri dell'Ordine de' Predicatori (Rome, 1868), 249-50.

so as to make the incident described less shocking to pious Spanish ears [84]. Another time, in re-telling Orfanel's story of an apparently miraculous and certainly symbolical ripening of a martyr's harvest, Lope suppressed a comment by the friar who adds that the fields of others, not martyrs, had also ripened in the same way.

The *Triunfo* is written in unequal prose and the reason is that, apart from the difficulty of deciding whether he was writing for a sophisticated or a simple audience, a doubt common to all Golden Age writers, remarks Aubrey Bell, Lope was further troubled by the need to select a style proper to his exalted subject [85]. He could have written a poetic history: " dar esta relación a las musas y hacer a Clio metrificadora " as he commented in the prologue. But he was aware that he was writing not merely history, but sacred history; that truth is the first law of history; and " la verdad siempre fue enemiga del artificio, alma de los colores poéticos, como ella de la historia, y más en las cosas de la Iglesia y del aumento del patrimonio de Jesucristo ". Yet the gaunt, homely prose of friar Orfanel was not sufficient, as the friars themselves implicitly admitted when they chose to send the *relaciones* to Madrid and asked Lope to re-write them, "a efecto que en el estilo con que he nacido las publicase [86]. There was reason for feeling particularly self-conscious about the style of the *Triunfo*, therefore, and for making sure that those who had solicited it were not disappointed when they asked him to write his best on their behalf " de las cosas de la Iglesia y del aumento del patrimonio de Jesucristo ". The theme demanded a certain grandeur, and before long he was exclaiming " Quien tuviera un estilo grandílocuo " and the less satisfactory portions of the work, the heavy sententious, obscure passages, are obviously written in an attempt to capture this grandiloquence. It is ironical in this connection to find Bell praising a passage of the *Triunfo* as an example of Lope's ability to write with discretion and restraint, and, unfortunately for his thesis, choosing as his model a paragraph which is taken almost word for word from Orfanel, " Venido el dia, que fue jueves... " (see p. 44 above).

* * *

The second aspect of the Dominican mission to Japan upon which we wish to comment concerns the friars' attitude to martyrdom. They

---

84 MD. VI, 58-9, 251; Triunfo, p. 175.

85 Bell, op. cit., 232, 234.

86 Triunfo, p. 162.

held fully the belief that the blood of martyrs is the seed of the Church, or in Lope's words, " Quien considerare los fundamentos de la Iglesia, que Jesucristo adquirió con su sangre en la de tantos mártires, desde las primeras piedras de Esteban, a las últimas líneas de su edificio, conocerá fácilmente que donde quiera que se planta este soberano arbol de la fe catolica, se ha de aumentar con sangre, como a los que produce la naturaleza el alma vegetativa con el humor del agua ". The friars' record shows that as far as they were concerned this was no mere cliché, and some consideration of this attitude is essential to the understanding of the events related in the *Triunfo*, but much more so for the appreciation of the conduct of the Dominican proto-martyr, Alonso Navarrete, and his Augustinian companion, fray Hernando de San José Ayala, whose martyrdom in June 1617 forms the central theme of the play *Los primeros mártires del Japón.*

Conditions in Japanese jails differed according to the locality, and some were enough to make the strongest quail. The best known and certainly the most horrifying description is the frequently quoted account of Yedo prison by the indomitable Franciscan, fray Diego de San Francisco [87]. Omura jail, during these years, is described in detail by the Dominican Manzano in his *Relación verdadera* which is based on letters written by the prisoners themselves. The central cage of the prison, the *jaula*, was composed of thick wooden stakes so close together that only a finger or two could be squeezed between them. This *jaula* measured approximately 18 feet by twelve and was six feet high; 34 persons were kept in it. Of these 16 were Religious and the remainder were Japanese converts. There was one small door, which was only opened to admit newcomers, and a trapdoor through which the prisoners' food was pushed. Surrounding the cage were three separate stockades of thornwood to discourage sympathisers from approaching, and the guards were changed daily to prevent any fraternisation. Moreover not even the guards were allowed to go closer than the second stockade. The diet was officially set at two daily helpings of soup (*shiru*) and some vegetables [88], but the Dominicans seem to have been given

---

[87] Ibidem, 161. Diego de San Francisco's classic account of the horrors of Yedo jail is quoted by many writers; see for instance, H. Cieslik, S.J., " The Great Martyrdom in Edo 1623 ", in: Monumenta Nipponica, X (Tokyo, 1954), 1-44; Orfanel, Historia, fls. 60-61; J. Murdoch, History of Japan, vol. II (Kobe, 1903), pp. 604-5; C. R. Boxer, The Christian Century in Japan, pp. 347-9.

[88] Cieslik, op. cit., p. 24; cf. also MD. III, 93, 94; VIII, 189.

rice and occasionally a little fish (" una sardina podrida "); the drink was warm water. Despite the severity of the conditions, their converts sometimes sought to smuggle food into the *jaula* and Manzano tells of two such who were trapped and executed, " i los dos dichosos Cofrades por el valor de dos melones vinieron a poseer el Reyno de los Cielos [89]. The prisoners' clothes were never washed and were swarming with lice. Since knives and scissors were forbidden in order to prevent suicides, their hair, beard, and nails could not be cut, and soon the prisoners looked like hermits from the desert. Writing materials were strictly forbidden but it is apparent from the number of letters that were written that the friars found their way around this prohibition in very many cases. Yet it is far from clear how these letters were written or despatched. Manzano, having commented on the difficulty of obtaining writing materials in the *jaula*, almost immediately goes on to describe how the prisoners spent part of their day in writing letters " para consolar las viudas de los Martyres. Unas escrivian a los vezinos de Nangasaqui, otras a los Españoles de Manila, paraque acudiesen a las necesidades, que en Japón pasavan muchas personas, por aver dado posada a Religiosos " [90]. Other letters went to the superiors in Manila urging the brethren there to go over to Japan to join the martyrs. Sometimes, obviously, they managed to send letters by bribing the guards. Tomás del Espíritu Santo Zumárraga, in order to express fully how severe is his prison, remarks that " not even letters " can be received or despatched, though this is then qualified by a possibility: " sino es por alguna traza " and he himself writes from prison to thank Admiral Juan Ruiz de Icoaga in Manila for a gift of 100 pesos which will enable him to bribe the messengers: " ahora es menester sobornar al que ha de meter o sacar algunas cartas ". A few months later this was still possible: " Aqui hay grande rigor y el que mete cualquiera carta es con grande peligro de la vida, y así, el dinero abre algún camino para algunas cartas "; two months later still the same friar was asking for " algunas resmas de *fanagami* que puedan servir para cartas ... un poco de tinta y plumas de Japón ". One of this friar's letters begins with the superscription, " perdone V. M. el papel; es de carcel " [91]. More puzzling still is how Orfanel managed to smuggle his manuscript history in and

---

[89] Manzano, Relación verdadera, 43-44.
[90] Orfanel, Historia, 61; 124; Manzano, 43-45.
[91] MD. II, 318; III, 30, 31, 94, 125, 156, 190, 347.

out of prison and have it checked by his colleagues as described above (pp. 30-31).

The friars, like the Jesuits, were wont to pepper these letters with Japanese words and phrases which is evidence of their affection for Japanese as well as of their knowledge of the language. Tomás del Espíritu Santo, in a short note of barely 30 lines uses no less than 13 Japanese words, and there are many more instances of this tendency [92]. At other times they resorted to the use of code words intended to deceive the Japanese, thus a priest is often called " the doctor " in a letter and his equipment for saying mass is referred to as the " medicine " [93]. For safety's sake letters were addressed as to seculars. Superiors of the Order were called " The Boss " or " The Captain "; Collado who came from Salamanca was referred to as " Señor Salmantino " and instead of being called " vuestra reverencia " was called " vuestra merced "; Fr. Diego de la Cruz was called " Cruzado " and the Third Order of St Francis was the " Tercera Escuadra ". These attempts at deception were far from subtle, and anyone reading the letters would not have had any doubt that the addressee was a Religious [94].

Severe though conditions might be, even in the appalling *jaula* of Yedo, the friars rejoiced, such was their exalted mood, and in letters from these prisons they frequently remark that they would not change places with anyone:

> " Que no trocar yo este lugar por los más soberbios palacios de los monarcas del mundo; ni las sogas y cordeles con que me amarraron por sus piedras preciosas y cadenas con ' tuson '; ni la mala y poca comida con sus opulentas mesas y preciosos manjares ... Esta cárcel escojo por *requies mea* ... Cuando me ataron la soga comenzó mi vida, entonces comencé a ser religioso... " [95].

---

[92] MD. III, p. 30. For an example of this tendency in Jesuit writers see the letters of Jeronimo de Angelis and Miguel de Carvalho in H. Cieslik, S.J., Hoku-ho Tanken-ki (Tokyo, 1961), p. 3-42.

[93] Pagés, Histoire, II, 131. To hear confessions was described as " taking the pulse ".

[94] Diego de San Francisco, Relaciones, ed. L. Pérez (Madrid, 1914), pp. 38, 84; Orfanel, Historia, fl. 164; P. T. Masetti, Lettere edificanti scritte dai Frati Predicatori Martirizzati nel Giappone (Rome, 1868), 76 n.

[95] MD. VIII, 189-90; Pagés, Histoire, II, 172. It is rather touching to find friar Orsucci, in prison awaiting martyrdom, writing a last letter in which he bids farewell to the Indians he had known in the Philippines: " ... Addio mille millione di volti, addio a tutti gl'Indiani " (Masetti, Lettere, p. 48).

For some friars prison conditions were not severe enough and they sought to add to their trials by taking the discipline; and they rejoiced so much in these sufferings which, of course, they saw as purposeful and to the honour of God, that they dreaded being released from their *jaulas*: " la peor nueva que nos podían dar, es que nos fuesemos libres a donde quisiesemos ... No faltan temores que nos han de embarcar para Manila ". Fray Alonso de Mena, writing from " esta dichosa carcel o paraiso ", expresses the fear that he and his companions may be deported and not martyred; Fray Francisco de Morales expresses a similar fear, adding, " estoy yo más contento con mi esposa, la cárcel, que algún marido con su mujer "; fray Tomás del Espíritu Santo, writing from " esto tronco o jaula " described his contentment in curious language: " es tan grande nuestro contento y alegría en esta cárcel, que me parece que todo el infierno junto no podrá causarnos tristeza, ni enfado " [96]. They managed to lead something like a religious life in their prisons; their regime in Omura, for example, was as if they were in " la más bien ordenada casa i más bien rejido convento de la Orden ". They rose at midnight to say Matins, but since they had no light to read their breviaries they used to recite the Mattins of the Little Office of Our Lady each day since they knew this by heart; this was followed by an hour of mental prayer and the discipline was taken by the " community ". At dawn the *Benedictus* was sung and in the early days, while they still had bread and wine, a Mass would be said, though later a *misa seca* in which the elements are not consecrated, had to suffice. At noon was another hour of mental prayer, and in the evening the *Salve Regina* was sung in accordance with the ancient Dominican tradition. On Saturdays the Rosary was said in common. Before sleep there was another hour of meditation based usually on a reading from Luis de Granada's *Guía de pecadores*. The remainder of the time was spent " en hablar de Dios " and their " happy lot " [97].

The converts were as devout as the friars and often spent their time

[96] MD. III, 94, 156, 285; VIII, 58; see also friar Orsucci's letter of 1620 in which he says " Il mio desiderio è di essere abbruciato vivo ... " (Masetti, Lettere, 44).

[97] Manzano, 44-5; those who, like one of the present writers, spent some years of the Pacific War of 1941-45 in a Japanese jail (as distinct from a P. O. W. Camp) will notice that in one respect at least Omura *jaula* had the advantage. The inmates were evidently permitted to talk freely with each other, and were not forced to squat in silence facing a wall, with the risk of being beaten up if they were caught by a jailer whispering to each other.

in prison in spiritual exercises preparing for death. The imprisoned priests also sought to convert other prisoners. The heroic fray Diego de San Francisco, in the midst of the unspeakable horrors of Yedo jail, converted no less than seventy of his fellow-prisoners and they, in turn, protected him from being murdered by the rest when he lay ill. Stranger still, some prisoners converted in jail were even admitted to the Dominican Order and actually studied Latin there under the friars' tuition [98].

Martyrdom was welcomed by both friar and convert and they waited each day, " esperando la dichosa sentencia de ser asados ", as Tomás del Espíritu Santo reported to his provincial in 1619 from Omura [99]. They made something like an attempt at psychological conditioning in preparation for martyrdom; for although the friars travelled and worked in lay dress they always kept a habit in readiness so that they might die in the respective robes of their Orders [100]. Similarly, the converts who joined the Rosary Confraternity had special, and elaborate, vestments which they wore to martyrdom; or else kept their best clothes aside for the occasion. Alonso de Mena describes a family in which " hasta la mujer e hijos tenían hechos sus vestidos de seda blanca para cuando las pusiesen en las cruces ". Orfanel describes the habit of the Rosary Confraternity:

> " era una toga blanca, larga hasta los pies, y encima una capita negra como muceta de obispo, y la cruz y armas de la orden, con el rosario alrededor del pecho, y como entre éstos del numero había muchos principales y ricos hacían esta ropa, quién de tercipelo, quién de damasco o tafetán, y quién no podía tanto, de manta de china, cada uno según su posibilidad. Y ahora, cuando salieron al martirio, cuatro de ellos, eran del número y tenían guardados sus hábitos, fueron con el... " [101].

The Japanese converts showed an extraordinary desire to die for their new faith: one who had been condemned to death by burning

---

[98] MD. III, 157; Manzano, Relación, 46-8, 66; Orfanel, Historia, 125-6; Pagés, II, 174. The converts' devotion (and the idea of 40,000 striving to confess to a dozen priests) made one friar compare the Mission to the church of the very Apostles themselves (López, f. 270). Later he preached upon this theme in Mexico.

[99] MD. II, 317, 319, 348, 349, 350; III, 92, 93.

[100] See page 13 above; and also MD. II, 349; Orfanel, Historia, 26, 73, 93, 124. Masetti, Lettere, 38-9.

[101] MD. II, 349; VI, 283; Carrero, Triunfo del Rosario, 151.

wrote to thank the missionary who had indirectly been the cause of his fate; another convert, Leon, was constantly repeating "*go foco ni xinitai,* esto es, deseo morir en servicio de Dios" and Orfanel reported, what was certainly true, that even children of five years of age longed to die a martyr's death. Joaquín and Tomé, whose deaths are briefly mentioned by Lope, sought to prolong their suffering. They were hanged by the feet, head downwards, from a tree, and Joaquín, who was a doctor, told Tomé to try to keep his head up so that the blood would not rush to it immediately: "conviene que lo hagas y que no desees morir presto, considerando que estos tormentos te han de servir de tener aqui el purgatorio y todos han de ser para mayor merecimiento". Later, managing to free an arm and secure a piece of rope, Joaquín began to whip himself as he hung from the tree. Such was their zeal to suffer that fray José de San Jacinto reported how converts consulted him to ask if it was legitimate to throw themselves on to the fires in which other Christians were being burnt, and thus find their own martyrdom although not yet condemned to die. The Jesuit, Organtino, describes the native Christians as hastening to martyrdom "as if to a festival", and some of the missionaries were obliged to discourage many who were over-eager to die [102]. They also had to urge some of the converts to moderate their penances and flagellations. This is understandable because the Japanese way of life with its high regard for ritual suicide predisposed the converts to martyrdom and their stoical—not to say masochistic—temperament was naturally encouraged by the Christian doctrine of the purpose of suffering, and found ready expression in the practice of physical penances. This national attitude distinguished the Japanese from many other Asian peoples that the missionaries had met, and it made conversion easier, for the Japanese, unlike the Chinese, for example, found nothing repugnant or distressing in the doctrine of the Crucifixion or the Atonement [103].

The ecstasy with which these martyrs suffered is shown clearly in Orfanel's account of how he questioned converts who had had their

---

[102] MD. IV, 30; VIII, 57, 58; G. B. Sansom, The Western World and Japan (London, 1950), 130-40. The twenty-year old Japanese friar brother Tomás del Rosario, sentenced to be beheaded, begged to be burnt alive as were the Europeans; this was refused him but he clung to the stake and had to be dragged from it. (Ocio, Reseña, 234).

[103] Sansom, 136; on religious suicide in Japan at this period see L. Delplace, S.J., Le Catholicisme au Japon (Bruxelles, 1910), II, 42-3.

fingers and toes cut off and been branded on the forehead. He, true to his inquisitive nature, asked them how they had endured such suffering and precisely what pain they had felt. One of them explained to him that there had simply been no pain at all: the cutting off of the toes and fingers had felt like a soft brushing of his hands and feet; the branding had been equally painless, for though he had heard the hissing of the brand burning into his flesh and had felt something warm on his brow, there had not been the slightest pain involved [104].

This extraordinary mood was not peculiar to the Japanese, however, and Orfanel describes how the Portuguese Captain, Domingos Jorge, the first European layman to be martyred in Japan, went to the stake in 1619. He was dressed in the rather spectacular Rosary Confraternity habit described above, " y como el hábito era de seda y él blanco y rubio, estaua muy hermoso, y todo el camino fue con una boca de risa, despidiendose de todos con un pañiçuelo blanco que llevaua en la mano... ". He was accompanied by Andrés, who " parecía un Angel con una rosa en cada mexilla con gran alegria ". As they were tied to the stake they showed great signs of joy at the prospect before them. When the fires were lit the Portuguese began to recite the *Credo*, but only reached the words *Incarnatus est* when the smoke began to suffocate him and prevented his continuing. But just before the end the bystanders saw him looking up to heaven, and it appeared to them that he was laughing as he died [105].

This wide-spread longing for martyrdom, the desire to be dissolved and made one with Christ, which was common to priest and convert alike throughout the mission, may be said to date from 1617 and the dramatic self-sacrifice of friar Alonso Navarrete O.P., and his Augustinian companion fray Hernando de San José Ayala. To the Japanese the deaths of these two must have seemed almost like a Christian form of *hara-kiri*. For some time there had been a lull in the persecution but in 1617 there was a fresh spurt of activity on the part of the authorities with the result that for the first time since 1597 some of the foreign missionaries forfeited their lives. Early in 1617, under pressure from the new Shogun (Hidetada), the feudal lord of Omura who was sympathetic to the Christians, was forced to arrest two missionaries: Father João Baptista Machado, a Portuguese Jesuit, and friar Pedro de la Asunción, a Spanish Franciscan. The *Daimyo* of Omura reported the arrest

---

[104] Orfanel, Historia, f. 46.

[105] Orfanel, Historia, f. 100.

to the Court and was ordered to execute the pair; the sentence was carried out on 21st May when the two priests were beheaded, not by the common executioner but by one of the leading *samurai*[106]. This martyrdom had the double effect of strengthening and stimulating the persecuted converts and of inspiring two other missionaries to seek a similar fate. Friar Alonso Navarrete, the Dominican Vice-Provincial, had for some time been disturbed by the fact that though the converts were being martyred, their foreign pastors, who had encouraged them to persevere unto death, had themselves escaped unharmed. Others felt some shame too when witnessing the Japanese converts' readiness to die; their zeal was such that one writer reported, " nobis quoque nativitate et patria Christianis haec Japoniorum non ita pridem ad fidem conversorum, ad vitam pro hac effundendam alacritas non levem pudorem incuteret "[107]. This, together with the need to give a further example to the persecuted and a reproach to the apostates, made Navarrete act. A few days after the martyrdom of the Jesuit and the Franciscan, Navarrete decided to offer himself openly for martyrdom. He had already given an indication of his spirit when some time earlier he had tried to snatch away some rosaries which were being burnt; on that occasion he had been severely beaten for his pains. Once decided on martyrdom, he wrote to his Dominican colleagues appointing Friar Francisco Morales in his place as Superior of the Mission and explaining his plan to revivify the Church, now unhappily dwindling under the new persecution, by shedding fresh blood: this time his own. He had, also, another reason for his decision which he did not confide to them, at least so far as we know. Among the friars in Japan there remained only one Augustinian, Hernando de San José Ayala, who had become attached to the Dominicans and was Navarrete's penitent: in Aduarte's words " casi siempre andava entre nosotros, como si fuera frayle Dominico ". To him Navarrete revealed his plan and the Augustinian agreed to accompany him, sharing his lot: " si tuviera perlado ", he declared, " por el me rigiera pero pues no le tengo, no me queda otro remedio sino ponerme en manos de V. R. a quien doy en nombre de Dios la obediencia "[108].

---

[106] Pagés, I, 350 ff.

[107] L. Froes, in De rebus Japonicis, ed. J. Hay (Antwerp, 1605), 30, 32, 322; cf. also Masetti, I Martiri, 64 n. 2.

[108] Aduarte, Historia, II, 35; Masetti, I Martiri, 66-74; Boxer, The Christian Century, 328 ff.

After two days' prayer and reflection they decided to set off together to seek death in Omura. On the way they met Morales, who, a hard-headed man, submitted the two Enthusiasts to close questioning as to their motives and the prudence of their decision. Their sensible answers showed him that they had weighed the matter before deciding and thus they convinced him; Morales gave his approval to the project and asked the two friars for their blessing. The rest of the journey to Omura was a combination of triumphal procession and mobile spiritual exercises; for the friars spent their time holding services, preaching, conducting public readings of Granada's *Guía de pecadores* and hearing confessions. As they neared their objective they changed from secular dress into their religious habits and shaved their tonsures. Finally the forces of the *Daimyo* of Omura caught up with them and they were arrested with many *kowtows* and apologies from the soldiers, some of whom were lapsed Christians themselves. For their part the friars courteously presented the officer with a hat and six wax candles *en albricias*. A number of Christians begged the honour of being arrested with the friars, but this was refused, since the soldiers explained they had no orders to arrest anyone but the two friars; they did, however, give in to the importunings of one youth, " Tomás, mancebo de poca edad que desde niño se avía criado en la iglesia de Sancto Domingo ayudando a missa ". Making an exception in his case they consented to arrest him [109]. The party set off by night in pouring rain; the friars were mobbed by enthusiastic crowds of converts who tried to kiss their habits as they passed. Navarrete's scapular and part of his habit were torn off by eager relic-hunters, and the *Daimyo* was so alarmed by the demonstrations that he ordered the friars to be removed to a small island. Even there, however, converts, including the *Daimyo's* aunt and grandmother, came to them for confession. To the aunt Navarrete gave a picture of our Lady, which he wore round his neck. In their last moments the friars wrote a number of letters, and Navarrete begged that his institute for rescuing abandoned children and orphans should be allowed to continue. They also wrote to Morales. Navarrete himself

---

[109] The servant's desire to suffer with his master is no doubt an aspect of the Japanese custom whereby the servants of a man who committed harakiri often imitated him. (A. Valignano, Historia del principio y progesso de la compañía de Jesús en las Indias Orientales (1542-64), ed. J. Wicki (Rome, 1944), 132). For other instances see Orfanel, Historia, f. 122 and Diego de San Francisco, Relaciones, ed. L. Pérez, p. 44.

wrote a highly significant letter to the Jesuit superior, pleading for charity and concord between the Orders in Japan:

" Ben si vede, P. Rettore, che vuole Dio Nostro Signore, che tutti siamo fratelli, poichè di tutti i quattro Ordini ci menano a morire in Omura, e mentre a Dio piace, non andiamo noi altri divisi, e non procuriamo che non entri uno dove l'altro ha posto il piede; questa Cristianità si trova molto in bisogno e però quegli che prima si troverà in pronto la soccorra ec. Fr. Alfonso Navarrette " (sic).

Reading between the lines here it is easy to see that they were proposing to lay down their lives for a number of causes, and one of them was that the friars should thereby earn the right to remain working in the Japan mission field. That the two friars had special reasons for seeking martyrdom is suggested by a discreet remark of the Augustinian fray Hernando which shows they were sacrificing themselves in a cause which they had decided to keep to themselves alone: " ... yo estava determinado de no dezir ninguna razon de las que nos movieron a yr ", he wrote. There is further evidence for this view in the fact that Navarrete asked the Augustinian to join him; it would have been more natural for him to urge a fellow-Dominican, such as Morales, to share his fate, but that would have left one of the Orders unrepresented. His turning to the Augustinian was, therefore, no mere accident, but design [110].

On Thursday 1st June 1617 the two were beheaded, together with a Japanese catechist, León. Their bodies were put in the coffins in which lay the two martyrs of a week earlier, Machado and Asunción; the Jesuit and Dominican were placed together in one and the Franciscan and Augustinian in another. Not surprisingly Aduarte, the Dominican chronicler, saw this as symbolic: " donde parece que el Señor quiso hazer una estrecha hermandad entre estas quatro religiones ... huuo de cada una dellas un mártir ... y como los cuerpos de los mártires estavan juntos y abraçados en los ataudes assi las religiones estuviessen unidas con vinculo de amor y paz en un mismo espíritu " [111].

This, alas, was still a little optimistic. But the self-sacrifice of

---

[110] Aduarte, Historia, II, 61; Pagés, I, 363, 365, II, 183; Masetti, I Martiri, 75; Masetti, Lettere, 2.

[111] Aduarte, II, 62-3; and Orfanel used almost the same words writing to the Augustinian Provincial in Manila (Pagés, II, 183). López was especially impressed by this symbolism around which he weaves elaborate arabesques (Quinta parte, f. 396-7).

Navarrete and Ayala had quite remarkable results in other ways. The Faith in that area had cooled considerably in recent years during the persecution, partly owing to the lack of priests. Now there came a burst of spiritual fervour throughout the whole Nagasaki area: the faithful were inflamed, the indifferent became ardent, the timid took courage, the apostates were reconciled. The new Dominican superior, Morales, threw all his available men into the zone to cope with the demand for priests, and in Aduarte's words " plantavan casi de nuevo la fe ". Friars of the other Mendicant Order, the Franciscans, now joined the Dominicans in their work. Aduarte, relating the scene, was reminded of the fervour of the ancient Church in Egypt during the time of St Antony. The priests were obliged to work ceaselessly: " ni de dia ni de noche descansavan " and such was the pressure of those demanding confession that they had to make a rule that only penitents who had not confessed for three years or more could be heard. The authorities had completely mistaken the situation, for instead of intimidating the Christians they had stirred them up: " Con la ayuda de estos religiosos y la sangre fresca de los mártires, Omura, que antes era un monte escabroso de cambrones y espinas, quedó hecho un jardin de deleytes; ya rezavan y se confessavan y tratavan de su salvacion y aun se ponian a peligro de perder la vida por la fe, y si se atrevieran los tiranos a perseguirlos, huviera muchos martires "[112]. Yet another result of the martyrdom was that even some non-Christians were now convinced that the priests were not crypto-conquistadores; and their willingness to volunteer to die for their Faith was taken as evidence of the purity of their intentions. The most striking example of the effect of their deaths was the reconciliation of the apostate Lino Tomonaga Jirobioye, deputy of the *Daimyo* of Omura. The son of Christians, the brother of a Jesuit, he had apostatized after the *Daimyo's* example and had presided at the martyrdom of the two missionaries, Machado and Asunción. Perhaps he was moved by their deaths; certainly he was impressed by the heroism of Navarrete and Ayala, and the result was his re-conversion. When acting as ruler during the *Daimyo's* absence he had aided the Christians, and for this was denounced upon the *Daimyo's* return. But Lino refused to abandon his twice-found Faith, and in November he was executed for it[113].

The friars, as well as the converts, were moved by Navarrete's action. Morales, who at first had questioned their wisdom and motives,

---

[112] Aduarte, II, 66-68; MD. III, 90; VIII, 92.

[113] López, Quinta parte, ff. 277, 392, 398-400.

was deeply impressed by their courage and by the effect of their deaths. Contemplating what seemed like a Second Spring in Omura he realized that he had witnessed something remarkable. And if friar Orfanel and the other publicity-conscious friars had felt that the persecution of 1614-15 deserved to be commemorated, Morales saw that the latest events were much more striking, for he had seen a drama, more, a Christian tragedy, and this also deserved to be perpetuated for the glory of Spain and the Dominican Order so that, in the words used of the " Great Martyrdom " of 1622, "alégrese España con su triunfo, y la Religion de Santo Domingo, celebre justamente su gloria " [114]. There was also, of course, the need to defend Navarrete's self-sacrifice from the criticisms of the Jesuits (cf. p. 37 above). The idea of a play recounting the martyrdom of Navarrete would come readily to Morales's mind, for the theatre was a highly developed and popular feature of life in the Philippines, where it was used for religious and official occasions. There, as in Europe, the theatre had had religious origins and was, in fact, started by the Jesuits, although even earlier the local Spaniards had regularly attended performances put on by the Manila Chinese, and this in spite of their being unable to understand a single word of what was said or sung on the stage. Among the first Spaniards in Manila to learn Chinese were the Dominicans who soon discovered that the Chinese plays were often improper and required censorship. Censored or not, however, they retained their attractions, and in 1638 when the local Chinese were planning an uprising in Manila it was alleged that they knowingly arranged to perform a play near one of the city gates in order to distract the citizens from noticing their designs. The Filipinos themselves were greatly addicted to the theatre; every feast-day had to have its play and even the rehearsals were packed. They had a special preference for extended serial-type plays, based on historical accounts or on novels, and which continued in daily instalments for a month or often more. Rather curiously, it has been asserted that this taste was due to the popularity of the play *La Celestina* in the colony [115]. Morales, then, with all this in mind, set himself to compose

---

[114] Quoted in J. A. Robertson, "Bibliography of Early Spanish Japanese Relations", Transactions of the Asiatic Society of Japan, XLIII(i), (Yokohama, 1915), p. 100.

[115] The remark about the influence of La Celestina was made by S. de Mas, Estado de las islas filipinas (Madrid, 1843), II, 115; see also E. H. Blair and J. A. Robertson, The Philippine Islands 1493-1898, XL (Cleveland, 1906), 246. Aduarte, I, 200; W. E. Retana, El teatro en Filipinas (Madrid, 1909), 17, 23-7, 31, 32, 44; C. Sanz, Primitivas relaciones de España con Asia (Madrid, 1958), 284-5, 289.

a long account of Navarrete's death, and this he sent to Madrid to the martyr's brother, Canon Pedro Fernández Navarrete, royal chaplain and secretary. Fray Alonso de Mena, a cousin of the Navarretes, and himself to die a martyr's death a few years later, also sent an account of the death home to Spain. Morales's letter, however, is the more important of the two, for it was this which seems to have led to a dramatist's having been approached for a play upon the theme of the martyrdom.

Morales first congratulated the Canon upon his brother's happy death, which was an honour to his house, to his Order and the Church; he enclosed a letter left with him by the martyr for his brother in Spain and also sent a drop of the martyr's blood, together with the sword which had been used at the execution and which had later been ransomed. The friars in Japan had been sufficiently moved by Navarrete's death to have a picture painted depicting the scene in all its detail, and Morales now told the Canon that this had been sent to the convent of San Pablo in Valladolid, Navarrete's mother-house, so that " there, where there are excellent artists, it may be reproduced with more art " [116]. This might be thought to be enterprising enough, but Morales was not satisfied and he continued his letter with a reference to the long account of the martyrdom which he was enclosing: " Your Reverence can have a tragedy composed upon this subject if there is anyone who feels inspired to undertake the task: it would be a subject of great edification to all " [117]. This letter is dated 12 March 1618, from Japan.

Since Lope, the greatest dramatist of the day, had already written a prose work, the *Triunfo*, upon the subject of the missions to Japan, he would be the obvious person to whom the Canon would turn for a play upon that same theme and to celebrate the martyrdom of " mi glorioso hermano ... el protomártir de su religion en aquellas provincias " [118]. In any case, it seems likely that the result of friar Morales's suggestion is the justly neglected play, *Los primeros mártires del Japón*, which has been attributed to Lope de Vega. For our study of the friars' awareness of the value of propaganda the authorship of this play is not

---

[116] Pagés, I, 366; II, 189. And see p. 32 above. One wonders whether this painting could have influenced the dramatist in his stage-directions for the final scene of the play, Los mártires.

[117] Pagés, I, 366; II, 182-90.

[118] Pedro Fernández Navarrete, Conservación de monarquías (Madrid, Biblioteca de autores españoles), vol. XXV, p. 539.

a prime concern, though in fact the play was probably not the work of Lope.

The *comedia* was subjected to a characteristically close (and somewhat testy) scrutiny by the late A. R. Nykl, who raised all the main problems connected with it, although he was not in a position to answer all of them. Nykl believed the play was by Lope and suspected, rightly, that both the prose work and the play were written in response to requests from friars; and he also discussed Morley and Bruerton's theory that the play as it stands is not by Lope alone, and he concluded that there are strong arguments against this theory. Nykl, like the other commentators, is puzzled by the title of the play, for Navarrete and his companion were not the first martyrs in Japan as was well known. Why, then, was it given the secondary title of *Los primeros mártires*? The answer is that the play, of course, is primarily about Alonso Navarrete, the Dominican protomartyr, " el protomártir de su religión en aquellas provincias ". Hence the title has nothing to do with *primeros* in the sense of *mejor*, *más notable*, as Nykl conjectured. There can be no doubt about this, because Navarrete is shown as the central martyr in the drama: the other friars in the story, although of different Orders, are shown as unhesitatingly accepting fray Alonso as their leader, and his is the dominant personality all through. He is the only friar who is specifically named (the others have only generic names representing their different Orders): moreover, the play includes not only Navarrete's brief biography but also a sketch of his physical characteristics and thus reveals knowledge on the dramatist's part which could only have come from the martyr's brother, Canon Pedro Navarrete.

Nykl also discusses the date of the play which Restori put at 1617. Nykl himself suggests 1618 as more likely, although this itself leaves unanswered another problem, for the play makes a reference to Philip IV, who came to the throne in March 1621. Now the main reason for assuming that the play was written before 1618 seems to be that a play about the martyrs of Japan was performed in Manila in December 1619, and this is taken to be *Los primeros mártires*. But this conclusion is false. First, the play about the martyrs of Japan performed in Manila in 1619 was part of nineteen days' celebration marking the arrival of a papal bull authorising devotion to the Immaculate Conception; and secondly, the play was put on by the local Franciscans. These two facts alone dispose of the idea that the play was the one attributed to Lope, for the Manila Franciscans, if they were planning to celebrate any martyrs of Japan in 1619, would think immediately of their famous six martyrs of 1597, for whose canonisation they were then strenuously working. Nor would the Franciscans have chosen a play like *Los primeros mártires* (the very title would have proved unacceptable to them) which exalted not their own Order but the Dominicans, through the figure of fray Alonso Navarrete. Moreover, if fraternal charity had inclined them to choose the " Lope " play, they would quickly have desisted, because the Dominican Order was opposed to the establishment of the doctrine and devotion of the Immaculate Conception; and during those three weeks' celebrations in Manila the Dominicans alone, of all the Religious Orders in the colony, were conspicuously absent from the festivities and, indeed, did not leave their convent once during the entire time, a fact which caused much gossip. If, therefore, the Franciscans had deliberately chosen the play attributed to Lope for that occasion, they would not have been demonstrating brotherly feeling for the Dominicans but rather showing an extraordinary insensitivity, not to say malice, at a particularly delicate moment. More evidence is provided by the Jesuits, who, in their Annual Letter of 1619-20, praise the play put on by the Franciscans. They would have found it easy to praise a play celebrating the martyrs of 1597, since among those martyrs were three Japanese Jesuits, but on the other hand, they certainly would not have praised *Los primeros mártires*, because it is remarkable for its calculated omission of all reference to the Jesuits, an omission which is one of the more mysterious features of the work. Finally, as has already been stated, the Jesuits did not approve of Navarrete's self-sacrifice which they denounced as reckless folly, and this conviction would naturally bias them against a dramatic *apologia* for the Dominican's action [119].

Indeed it is far more likely that the play was written in 1621 or later. Morales's letter suggesting a tragedy be commissioned by Canon Navarrete was written in Japan on 12 March 1618, and its arrival in Madrid would bring the first news of the martyrdom to Lope or to anyone else there. It is not possible to estimate exactly how long this letter took to reach Madrid. The yearly galleon from Manila to Aca-

---

[119] The play is included in the edition of the Obras de Lope de Vega publicadas por la Real Academia Española, V (Madrid, 1895), pp. 505-39. All references to this play herein are to these pages. A. R. Nykl, Los Primeros Mártires del Japón and Triunfo de la fe en los reinos del Japón, Modern Philology, XXII (1925), pp. 305-23; S. G. Morley and C. Bruerton, The Chronology of Lope de Vega's comedias (London, 1940), pp. 328-29; Retana, Teatro, 23-9.

pulco in Mexico left the Philippines any time after the 1st May; if Morales's letter, which had to be smuggled out of Japan first, arrived in Manila too late for the 1618 galleon, it would then have to wait for another year, that is until the summer of 1619, before starting its journey to Madrid via Mexico [120]. In any case, the letter would probably have taken two years to reach Spain, and thus at the very earliest could not have been there before the summer of 1620, and it might easily have been 1621 before the *comedia* was finished, in which case the reference to Philip IV is self-explanatory. It was certainly not unusual for news from Asia to take two years to reach Spain, or vice versa: the death of the Bishop of Japan, which took place in February 1614, was not known in Spain until the early summer of 1616; and a papal bull issued in June 1608 did not reach Japan until 1610. Besides, the news of Navarrete's death may very well have taken much longer to reach Europe since during those years (1618-20) Manila was harassed by Dutch raiding vessels and, as happened on other similar occasions, the Manila galleon might not have been able to leave port for as much as a year after its annual scheduled sailing-date. Thus the reference to Philip IV does not necessarily postulate a *refundición*. The final line of the *comedia* (' Del año que está presente '), which Restori took literally and consequently dated the play 1617, must be dismissed as poetic licence: there is enough poetic licence in this play to make the operation easy as well as necessary [121].

Moreover, if the play was written after 1621, the omission of any reference to it in *La Filomena* (1621) is also self-explanatory. Morley and Bruerton object that in the *Filomena* Lope is referring to the comedia, rather than to his prose work, because he uses the word " *cantar* " which " is a curious word to use of a prose work " [122]. Curious it may be, but there is not the slightest doubt that he does mean the prose work, for in the dedication to the Segunda Parte he names it by its name: " defiende lo que ha cantado ... *El triunfo de la fe* ", and this is evidently what he means when, a little later, he amplifies the remark:

Yo canté, finalmente,
Los mártires japones,

---

[120] The news appears to have reached Manila in June-July, 1618 (cf. López, ff. 388, 389) and an account was published in Manila 1618 (Streit, V, 435).

[121] Fr. Lorenzo Pérez, O.F.M., Apostolado y martirio del Beato Luis Sotelo en el Japón (Madrid, 1924), 251 n.; Pagés, II, 187; Morley-Bruerton, 328.

[122] Morley-Bruerton, 328.

Porque mi voz no agradeciese solo
El mar que el Duero, el Tajo, el Bétis bebe, ...

BAE, XXXVIII, 491.

Nykl's third point is that much of the material used in the prose work is also used for the background of the play. This, however, is not so, for the play shows little sign of any desire to achieve geographical or historical accuracy, apart from the presentation of the main figure, Navarrete.

When Lope sat down to write the *Triunfo* he presumably thought of writing it in verse for in the preface he remarks that " bien se pudiera dar esta relación a las Musas y hacer a Clio Metrificadora ". But he finally decided to confine himself to prose since he was writing history and " la verdad siempre fue enemiga del artificio, alma de los colores poéticos, como ella de la Historia, y mas en las cosas de la Iglesia ".

The essentials of the plot of *Los primeros mártires* are as follows:

Act. I: Tayco Soma, the " Emperor " of Japan died leaving the throne to his six year old son, Tayco. But for fifteen years the son has been imprisoned in the tower of Usaca by a usurper-Emperor, Jisonen. Tayco, ignorant of his own identity and of all life around him, grows up like a savage, dressed in skins, his only contact with the world being Alcaide, described as " un indio viejo ". When the petty king of Siguen denounces Jisonen as a usurper, the petty king of Bomura, an apostate Christian, explains that Siguen is plotting with the Christians who have placed their hopes in Tayco. Jisonen, having seen the prisoner-prince Tayco (who feigns madness at the interview), decides that the youth is no danger to his throne and allows him some freedom, as a result of which Tayco learns who he is and then falls in love with Quildora, a widow, huntress and mother of Tomás, a child convert to Christianity.

Friar Alonso Navarrete is accepted as their superior and leader by the three Orders of friars working in the Japan missionfield. (No reference is made to the Jesuits). The friars are deported but plan to return, under Navarrete, to work in disguise.

Act. II. The usurper, Jisonen, also falls in love with Quildora. Tayco's jealousy leads him to betray himself, thus arousing the usurper-Emperor's suspicions, and he is put under guard. The friars return in disguise and Navarrete comes across the Emperor molesting Quildora whereupon he goes to her aid and frees her. The thwarted Emperor, though furious, finds himself mysteriously unable to shoot Navarrete and goes off vowing vengeance. Navarrete then catechises Quildora and gives her a picture of the Crucifixion. The young Tayco, observing this, mistakenly assumes Navarrete is acting as a go-between for the Emperor. Believing the picture is of the Emperor he later snatches it from Quildora and nails it to a tree, whereupon blood spurts from the picture into his face. Tayco then promises the Unknown God that he will become a Christian if the Empire is restored to him. The rebel king of Siguen stirs up a revolt against Jisonen.

Act. III: The Franciscan is arrested and questioned as to the identity of Navarrete whose brief biography is then related. When the Emperor orders the burning of rosaries in a furnace, Navarrete appears, rushes into the flames to rescue them and is miraculously saved. Captured later, Navarrete is sentenced to death; his former housekeeper, Mangazil, brings the friars' habits, representing the three Mendicant Orders. They are executed together with the child Tomás. A rebellion, connected vaguely with the martyrdom, breaks out and the usurper Jisonen is killed. The final scene is presided over by the triumphal appearance of Navarrete, " con la cabeza en las manos y un hacha que la parte "; he is flanked by the Franciscan and the Augustinian martyrs. Tayco takes Quildora for his wife and they both promise to become Christians though it must be a secret until they are on the Imperial throne.

This plot, which is a variant of the Barlaam and Josafat story, has some, though little, connection with the reality of the situation. On the other hand, the dramatist knew what Madrid audiences demanded, and it can be argued that he was fully justified in departing from the facts since his chief aim was to arouse enthusiasm for the heroic figure of Navarrete. The introduction of the fantastic love-story would make the martyrology more palatable, and it is no worse than what happens nowadays in popular film versions of Biblical themes.

The first liberty taken is with the chronology, for the time sequence is telescoped so that the expulsion of the friars from Japan (1614) is made to precede Navarrete's death by a short time. And in putting his death in the shogunate of Ieyasu, the author has anticipated the event by at least a year, for Ieyasu died in May 1616 and the friar in June 1617. There is another error here also, for not a single European missionary was martyred under Ieyasu. Navarrete's deliberately seeking martyrdom is not properly brought out in the play, although one would have thought that this was precisely what made him unique; instead he appears rather to have been arrested and executed in the normal course of duty like any of the other missionary-martyrs. The incident in which Navarrete attempted to rescue the burning rosaries is true (see p. 55 above) though it is naturally much dramatised in the play, and the miraculous elements, of course, are not mentioned in the friars' accounts of the affair. There is no way of checking the description of friar Alonso's appearance, but the biography of him put into the mouth of the Franciscan is accurate, though incomplete. The dramatist rightly stresses Navarrete's courage, nobility and generosity, virtues which properly become the hero of a *comedia*, and indeed the Navarrete who rescues the Amazon-like Quildora from the unwelcome attentions of the Emperor might be thought more akin to the hero of a *capa y espada* drama than to a missionary. Perhaps it is significant that at this point Navarrete tells Quildora that she has been rescued by a priest of the " Dios de los españoles ". Thus the gentler side of Navarrete's character, for instance the un-Spanish love of animals which so gratified the chronicler Aduarte, is here ignored [123].

Nevertheless there is some evidence that the dramatist had read, even if he did not follow, the *relaciones* sent to Madrid by friar Morales and Navarrete's cousin, friar Mena. Once or twice the speeches of the martyrs in the play echo lines from the friars' histories. Quildora's convert son, who dies with the martyrs, was a real person (see p. 56 above) who acted as mass-server for the friars, and in the play he refers to this: " cómo ayudaré yo a misa ? " is his question when the friars are deported. However, the chronicles make no mention of his mother, and in any case Quildora is a quite fantastic figure. The dramatist sometimes shows himself informed about conditions in the mission. This is particularly true, for example, where he makes the King of Bomura declare that the priests can be caught more easily through the confessional; that this was so is borne out by the statement of fray José de San Jacinto, who explained how he himself was arrested as he was hearing confessions, for he mistook the approaching soldiers for more penitents and thus, off his guard temporarily, was trapped [124]. There is surely sly irony—at least it is unconscious humour—in the picture of Navarrete's arrest, for the friar's first request on hearing the sentence is for writing materials (*recado para escribir*). The dramatist, like the modern reader of these letters written from Japanese jails, must have

---

[123] Aduarte, II, 64, 66. For the connection between this play and the Barlaam and Josafat story see Lope de Vega, Barlaán y Josafat, ed. J. F. Montesinos in Teatro antiguo español, VIII (Madrid, 1935), pp. 189, 191, 202 ff., 219, 229, 235-6, 239.

[124] MD. VIII, 154; Pagés, I, 364, II, 363; Primeros Mártires, 531a, 537b.

wondered at the freedom and readiness with which the condemned martyrs fell to writing, and were able to 'post' their splendid letters. The author also shows he was aware of the friars' custom of arranging to die in their religious habits and thus has Navarrete call for his after his arrest.

As we have seen (p. 56 above) Navarrete was visited after his arrest by the grandmother and aunt of the *Daimyo* of Omura and to the latter, Marina, the martyr presented a picture of our Lady. The dramatist took up this detail and used it in the second act, with some changes, where it is made to influence Tayco and leads to his conversion.

A striking characteristic of the play is the insistence upon the Spanish aspect of the friars' enterprise in Japan. Presumably this also was a bid to win popular sympathy. Thus there are references to:

"el Dios de los españoles"; "la religión de España";
"la ley de los españoles"; "sacerdotes españoles";
"la sangre de españoles inocentes"; "estos muertos españoles";
"el Imperio español",

and there are others besides these [125]. This emphasis reflects exactly the mood of the earlier anonymous *romance*:

"Pues en Japón y en la China
se espera otro nuevo estado
con que para siempre sea
el nombre de Dios loado;
y así nuestro rey invicto
quiere estar siempre ocupado
en sembrar por todo el orbe
el Evangelio sagrado,
y con este santo celo
todo lo tiene allanado" [126].

For although the idea of conquering China and Japan had had to be rejected, it was still hoped that they might be conquered spiritually, and it was widely believed in Spain that this task was reserved by God for the Spaniards. This nationalistic undertow running through the

---

[125] Primeros Mártires, 509a, 520b, 521b, 527a, 530a, 538b, 539a.

[126] Quoted in F. Díaz-Plaja, Verso y prosa de la historia española (Madrid, 1958), 156.

play may well explain why all reference to the Jesuits was deliberately omitted. For the Jesuits were either Portuguese or worked in most of the Orient under Portuguese sponsorship, even at this time when the two crowns in Iberia were united. Nevertheless, the omission is remarkable when one considers the achievements of the Fathers of the Society in Japan and when it is remembered that a Jesuit, Father Machado, was martyred at the same time as Navarrete: hence the emphasis by the friars upon the fact that God had chosen a martyr from each of the four Orders. On the other hand, however, the Jesuit Machado was, rather inconveniently, a Portuguese, and thus the author may have preferred to ignore him in the interests of simplicity and to avoid any depressing qualifications to his theme. Still, he might have allowed a Jesuit to be represented in the final *cuadro* of the play, or, when the *gracioso* appears bringing the martyrs' habits (" Sale Mangazil con habito negro [Augustinian], escapulario blanco [Dominican], y capilla de francisco " [Franciscan]), the traditional Jesuit biretta might have been included. As it stands, the play gives the impression that Japan was evangelised exclusively by Spanish Mendicant friars; and this was indeed to write for the groundlings, since the educated among the audience would have been aware of the Jesuits' well-publicised work in the East. It is interesting to recall here that Lope's *Triunfo* also virtually ignores the Jesuit contribution to the Japan mission.

One reason for believing that the play is not by Lope is that there are many factual divergences between the essay and the drama. Thus, as Nykl pointed out, though Japan is presented in the *Triunfo* as a cold land, in the play it has become the haunt of parrots and alligators; in the prose work it is a sterile land: in the play it is " Japón hermoso, campo ameno, de variedad y de hermosura lleno ", a land of " ejércitos de flores " which " nos da sus frutos, Piadosamente cortés; Produce las plantas bellas ". Though in the *Triunfo* Lope had correctly counted the provinces or petty kingdoms of feudal Japan as sixty-six, in the play the dramatist names seventy-four petty kings. The Japanese in the prose work are described as being white, but in the play they have become " indios ", and Navarrete, when planning to return in disguise to continue his work, is made to say, " estemos disimulados como indios " [127]. More understandable are the mistakes due to simple igno-

---

[127] Primeros Mártires, 507 (stage directions), 509b, 516a; Nykl, 314, 315, 320. The description of the Japanese as " indios " is explained by the fact that Japan was regarded as part of the " Indies ". In fact the Japanese were inconveniently white

rance, such as making the Emperor present diamonds to Quildora when in fact the Japanese despised diamonds; nor would the Emperor of Japan be likely to refer to Venus, Diana and their nymphs, although this, perhaps, given contemporary taste, was inevitable in a *comedia*. Tayco, the prince-prisoner of the play, was actually Hideyori, son of Toyotomi Hideyoshi, who died in 1598 after leaving the five year old prince in the care of a regency under Ieyasu. The Regent gradually took control of the government, and the prince grew up for the next fifteen years in Osaka Castle, an immense construction, the greatest and strongest fortress in the empire, with a defence force of some 90,000 men. His life, therefore, was in no way similar to the description of it in the play, and the young Hideyori was far from being the semi-savage, dressed in skins, who " como muerto vive " in the play. Ieyasu (the Jisonen of the *comedia*) attacked Osaka castle in 1614 and finally overcame all resistance there in the summer of 1615. Hideyori committed suicide and consequently Ieyasu remained supreme. The Christians, and especially the Dominicans, had put their hope in Hideyori, though there is little evidence that they would have fared any better had he survived and conquered Ieyasu. The dramatist, in converting him to Christianity, allowing him to defeat Ieyasu and making him Emperor of Japan, had abandoned any pretence at reality and was indulging in fantasy; or else he was expressing Christian hopes of what might yet be, for after the battle of Osaka, Orfanel reported that the young prince's fate was not known, though it was thought he might have escaped down river by boat. At best, the dramatist was writing history as it should have been, where Lope's prose work kept fairly closely to the facts supplied to him.

Some confusion surrounds the figure of the villain of the piece, the petty king of " Bomura ", more properly Omura. The persecutor of the Christians in the *Triunfo* was, correctly, named as Sahioye who was the moving force behind the persecutions in Arima, Ariye, and Kuchinotsu in 1614-15. The play, as we have said, transposed the martyrdom of Navarrete from 1617 to this earlier period, but instead

---

and Orfanel, who was swarthy, found it hard to pass himself off in disguise for that reason (Aduarte, II, 140). Valignano, the celebrated Jesuit writer and policy-maker for the missions, warned that the Japanese were not to be called ' niggers ' (J. F. Schütte, S.J., Valignanos Missionsgrundsätze für Japan, Bd. I (Rome, 1951), 325, 422). López, in his *Quinta parte*, refers to the Japanese as ' Indios '; see, for example, ff. 266, 268.

of retaining the historical figure of Sahioye it also transposed the Prince of Omura, making him the persecutor. Omura was in fact an apostate, though it is doubtful if he was as anti-Christian as Sahioye, for he had Christian relatives and was evidently unwilling to order the execution of the first two of the four missionary-martyrs of 1617, hesitating until definite orders came to him from the Court. In the case of Navarrete and Ayala he had no alternative but to execute them since they demanded nothing less than martyrdom. Nor did Omura press Ieyasu to banish the missionaries, as he is made to do in the play; moreover, though he renegued out of political ambition, different and differing reasons are given in the play: in Act I he declares that " por conocer nuevos dioses Dejé la ley que ellos siguen ", though a few lines later his reason is that a missionary condemned his importuning a woman who was the wife of one of his vassals; in the second act he says " ¿ No es Nerea la que me mata de amores y por quien dejé la ley del español que persigo ? ".

Such confusions betray a distracted hasty writer; and there are others: the King of Amanqui later appears as Amarque; the king of Siguen rebels against Jisonen but a little later is absent-mindedly shown accompanying the Emperor. The guardian of the prince-prisoner during his years in Osaka Castle is a " indio viejo " who is not named in the cast but in the play itself has no less than three names: Gualemo, Polemo, and Lepolemo. Navarrete's housekeeper, Gaspar, who surrendered to the friar's captors and who was himself martyred, is shown in the play as Manganzil, a pagan and the clown of the plot.

* * *

The play, then. though rough and rude, is not without interest, and if it was ever performed it would have served its purpose fully, that is, to make the name of fray Alonso Navarrete, the Dominican protomartyr of Japan, known in the market-place. Even if it were never performed and this purpose remained unfulfilled, it still remains as a tribute, of a sort, to a remarkable man and to those of his colleagues who felt the need to honour his courage and devotion in a modern way [128].

---

[128] We are indebted to Professor A. A. Parker of London University, and to Professor E. M. Wilson of Cambridge, for reading the portion of this paper which deals with Lope de Vega and for their helpful criticism and comments.

APPENDIX I

List of European Dominican Missionaries Working in Japan (1602-1622)

	Arrived	Arrested (or left)	Martyred
Francisco Morales	5 July 1602	15 March 1619	10 Sept. 1622
Alonso de Mena	5 July 1602	14 March 1619	10 Sept. 1622
Tomás del Espíritu Santo Zumárraga	5 July 1602	July 1617	12 Sept. 1622
Tomás Hernández	5 July 1602	returned to Manila in 1605	
Juan de la Abadía (lay brother)	5 July 1602	returned to Manila in 1605	
Juan de los Angeles Rueda	1604	returned to Manila 1620	in Ryukyu, 1623 or 1624
Jacinto Orfanel	June 1607	25 April 1621	10 Sept. 1622
José de San Jacinto Salvanés	June 1607	17 August 1621	10 Sept. 1622
Juan de San Jacinto (lay brother)	June 1607	returned to Manila before 1614	
Juan de Santo Tomás	July 1609	returned to Manila before 1614	
Antonio de San Vicente (lay brother)	July 1609	returned to Manila before 1614	
Alonso de Navarrete	August 1611	May 1617	1 June 1617
Domingo de Valderrama	August 1611	returned to Manila before 1614	
Baltasar Fort	Aug. or Sept. 1612	» » »	Nov. 1614
Juan de Santo Domingo	August 1618	13 Dec. 1618	19 March 1619
Angel Ferrer Orsucci	August 1618	13 Dec. 1618	10 Sept. 1622
Diego Collado	July 1619	left in Nov. 1622	
Luis Flores (Frarin)	July 1620 (as a prisoner of the Dutch)		20 Aug. 1622
Pedro Vásquez	July 1621	April 1623	25 Aug. 1624
Domingo Castellet	July 1621	15 June 1628	8 Sept. 1628

In addition to the above twenty friars who are mentioned by Aduarte, Orfanel, and other emporary chroniclers, the following were in Japan for short periods before 1622, according Iilario Ocio y Viana, Reseña biográfica de los Religiosos de la Provincia de Filipinas, -1650 (Manila, 1891):

Antonio Zamudio de la Madre de Dios (lay brother), assigned to Nagasaki in 1610.
Tomás Gutiérrez, assigned to Satsuma in 1608.
Lorenzo Porras, arrived in 1612, and returned to Manila in Nov. 1614.
Antonio Gutiérrez, allegedly in Japan at some unspecified date.
Domingo González, allegedly in Japan at some unspecified date.
Juan Bautista Cano, arrived August 1618 (intended for Korea), left Dec. 1618.
Diego Rivabellosa, arrived August 1618 (intended for Korea), left Dec. 1618.

The last two hardly count in any event, as they were intended for the Korean mission only spent a few months at Nagasaki before returning to Manila.

II

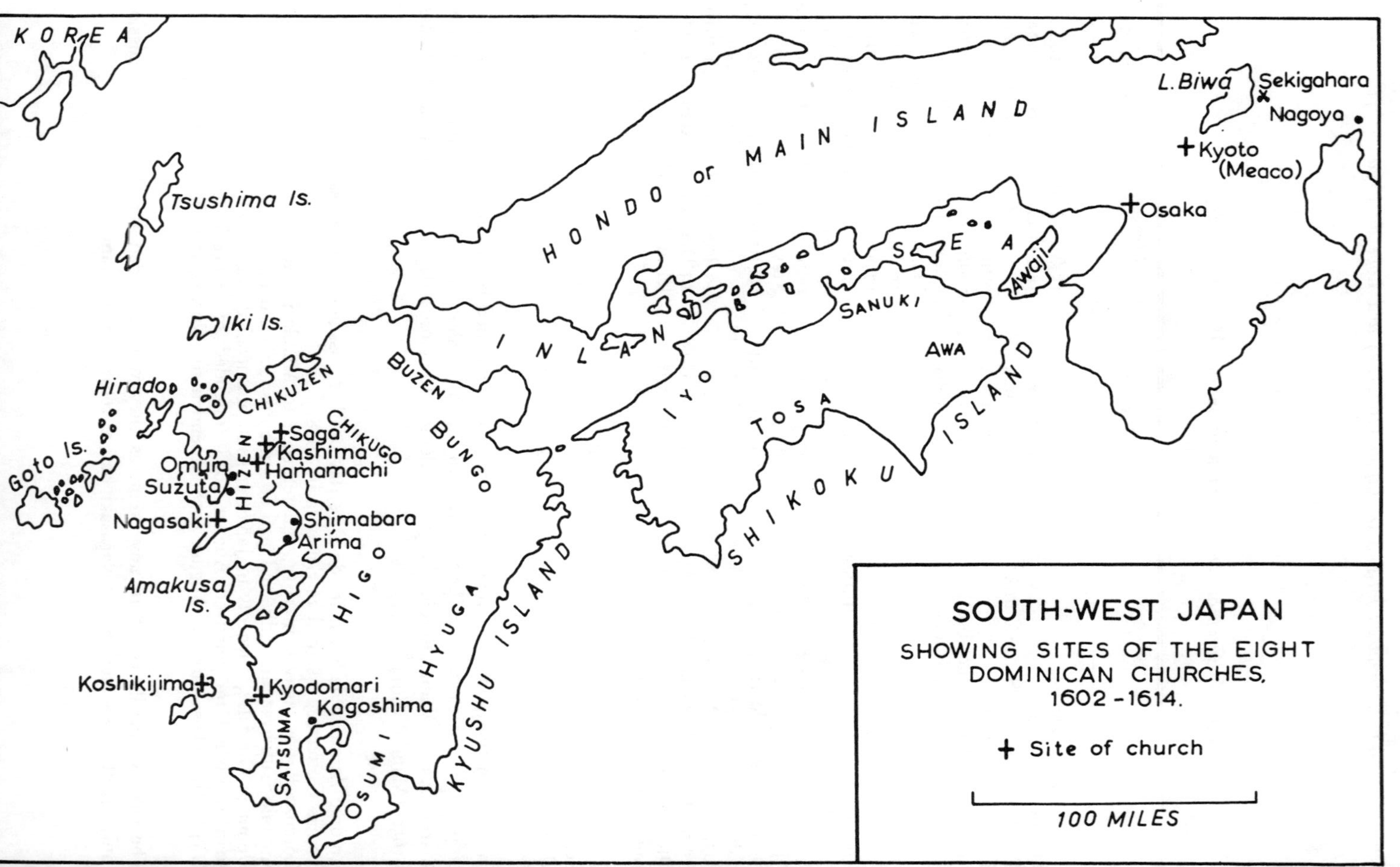

KOREA
Tsushima Is.
HONDO or MAIN ISLAND
L. Biwa
Sekigahara
Nagoya
Kyoto
(Meaco)
Osaka
INLAND SEA
Awaji
SANUKI
AWA
IYO
TOSA
SHIKOKU ISLAND
Iki Is.
Hirado
CHIKUZEN
BUZEN
BUNGO
CHIKUGO
HIZEN
Saga
Kashima
Hamamachi
Omura
Suzuta
Goto Is.
Nagasaki
Shimabara
Arima
HIGO
Amakusa
Is.
HYUGA
KYUSHU ISLAND
Koshikijima
Kyodomari
Kagoshima
SATSUMA
OSUMI
SOUTH-WEST JAPAN
SHOWING SITES OF THE EIGHT DOMINICAN CHURCHES, 1602 - 1614.
+ Site of church
100 MILES

APPENDIX II

List of the Dominican Churches in Japan (1602-1614)

1. N. S. del Rosario, Koshikijima, Satsuma, October 1602 - May 1606.
2. N. S. del Rosario, Kyodomari, Satsuma, July 1606 - May 1609.
3. N. S. del Rosario y Santo Domingo, Nagasaki, July 1609 - 28 October 1614.
4. N. S. del Rosario, Hamamachi, Saga, 1606 - 8 October 1613.
5. San Vicente, Kashima, Saga, 1607 or 1608-1613.
6. San Pablo, Saga, 1607 or 1608.
7. N. S. del Rosario, Kyoto, 25 January 1610-1613.
8. Santo Domingo, Osaka, 6 July 1610-1613.

APPENDIX III

Carta del Beato Alonso de Mena, O. P., al P. Provincial y Padres Definidores de la Provincia; 20 de Nov. de 1606. — From: Misiones Dominicanas, IV (1921) pp. 336-7.

Sea siempre con vuestras reverencias: Parecióme que era buena ocasión la que hoy se ofrece del Capítulo, para dar cuenta de las cosas que por estos Reinos pasan, así en lo que tocan a la conversión, como en otras cosas, y aunque ya VV. RR. tendrán por otras vias larga noticia de lo que hay, pero por cumplir mi oficio, daré breve relación.

Y lo primero digo, que es muy grande el provecho que por aquí se hace cada día y mucho más lo que se espera de hacer con la ayuda de Dios, así bautizando y predicando, como confesando y animando muchos de los cristianos que ya están hechos, que son muy muchos y muy esparcidos por todo el Japón, y muchos en partes donde nunca Padres de la Compañía llegan, porque son muy pocos dichos Padres, y tienen mucho en que entender, o porque los señores no permiten que Padres de la Compañía entren en sus tierras, por particulares enemistades que con ellos tienen; de los cuales hay algunos y muchos, aun de los mismos cristianos, que tienen más afición a otros religiosos que no a los de la Compañía como cada día vemos por experiencia. Pero como quiera que para estar en Japón es menester tener contentos a estos señores, los cuales todo su deseo es que vengan aquí navíos de españoles como de otros japoneses a contratar a sus puertos. Lo cual pretenden hacer por medio de religiosos, porque casi todos los japoneses que tratan de navíos o los más son cristianos; es mucho enfado y moina para los religiosos, porque cualquiera cosa que les suceda mal a los mercaderes, dicen que los Padres les persuadieron ir allí y que si fueran a otra parte que hicieran y acontecieran... No sé si les persuadiría todo el mundo a que no tenemos parte en ellos y en las mercaderías; digo cierto que hemos pasado ogaño enfados y pesadumbres intolerables en orden a ésto. VV. RR. lo miren lo que les parece, por que lo que entiendo es que si no andamos así, no hay que tratar de estar en Japón, a lo que entendemos.

Las cosas de por allá no se pueden guardar en algunas cosas tan puntualmente como allá, por cuanto andamos entre gentiles. El año pasado, envió el Padre Provincial unas ordenaciones para que acá se guardasen; con ellas parece que está todo lo que se puede hacer bueno ...

Lo que por acá hay de nuevo es que un señor muy principal, que es uno de los señores nobles que hay en Japón cristianos, llamado Vomurandono y nombre de cristiano D. Sancho, ha renegado o está en hacerlo y mandado que en su tierra que es una parte del reino de Fijen, llamado Vomura, se cierren las iglesias, y muchos de los principales han renegado ya; él está en la Corte del Emperador, y ahora esperan que venga; aún no ha echado los Padres por algunos respetos. Dícese que en viniendo de la corte donde está, puede ser que los eche, y dado que consienta estén en su reino, es como digo, por algunos respetos. La causa de aborrecerlos si fuera por reprenderles algun vicio fuera gran cosa, pero no es por eso, sino porque el Emperador le ha quitado un pedazo de tierra que tenía junto a Nangasaqui, que es la ciudad donde están los Padres con más poder y el señor Obispo.

Dirán VV. RR. qué culpa tenían los Padres? a esto respondo que el que gobierna a Nangasaqui es un cristiano, el cual fué puesto por el Emperador con traza de los Padres, con lo cual cuanto en aquella ciudad se hace es todo ordenado por los Padres y, a dicho de todos, el gobernador tiene el nombre y los Padres lo hacen todo.

Al presente, que esta escribo, estamos el P. Fr. Tomás y yo en tierras de este señor, donde hemos andado de una parte a otra, animando a unos y a otros confesando, para si acaso sucediere alguna persecución; ya la cristiandad tienen mucha afición todos, y todos echan la culpa a los Padres en común; harto los hemos escusado.

También hemos ido el P. Fr. Tomás y yo estos días a un reino que llaman Firando, donde el señor es grande enemigo de la cristiandad y no permite que ningún Padre, ni de paso, esté en su reino, aunque hay muchos cristianos. Estuvimos catorce días escondidos, donde fué cosa extraordinaria los muchos cristianos que acudían a confesarse de noche, que estábamos hasta las doce de la noche confesando y nos levantábamos a las tres o las cuatro a decir misa donde siempre acudía muchísima gente. Es cosa extraordinaria el grande amor que nos mostraron y las limosnas que nos dieron; hízose mucho provecho, las confesiones de muchos años; y animando a perseverar en la fe, que hacen harto los pobres según son los trabajos que tienen.

No hay otra cosa de que avisar, sino pedir a VV. RR. miren con mucha atención las cosas de esta cristiandad; yo tan aficionado soy como cualquiera y así he venido tres veces a esta tierra y trabajado lo que he podido. Mas sé decir a VV. RR. que esto de andar con navíos y contrataciones no lo puedo tolerar, fuera de que, como todos saben, yo al presente estoy enfermo y con enfermedad trabajosa. Salí de ahí el año pasado y así pido por amor de Dios que me den licencia para irme a curar; en particular pido encarecidamente que lo que toca en negocio de hacerme prelado vuestras RR. no traten nada, porque lo contrario me concierne mucho, y yo tengo muy grande experiencia de ello, y no tengo salud ni fuerzas para ello, y así pido por amor de Dios que VV. RR. me consuelen.

Con esto Dios dé a VV. RR. su santo amor y gracia como este menor hijo de esta santa provincia desea.

Fr. Alonso de Mena

De Vomura, a 20 de noviembre de 1606.

APPENDIX IV

Extract from a letter of Fr. Alban, O.F.M. Cap., Catholic Mission Okinawa, 21 February, 1953; to C. R. Boxer, University of London.

" In the heat of a recent discovery I have made while on the island of Ishigaki in Yaeyama Gunto, the southernmost of the Ryukyu Island groups, I have decided to consult you for information that may give me the story I want.

The " discovery " was the account of the governmental execution of a certain " bugyo " — I presume he would be called — named Motto Miyara (no kashira) Ishigaki Eisho. The execution — burning at the stake — took place in the last year of the rule of Hidetada, that is, in 1622.

This Ishigaki Eisho was a wealthy samurai owning vast property in Ishigaki Jima and conducting a widespread trading business. Having once been stranded on the shores of China, he had stayed long enough to learn both Chinese and Spanish — the latter from a missionary.

A " nam-ban-sen " (" Southern-Barbarian-Ship " — would this designation indicate the ship to be Portuguese or Spanish according to the differentiation referred to on p. 293 of your Christian Century in Japan?) being forced into the harbor of Ishigaki City (which may at the time have been called Miyara City), a Christian missionary-passenger of the ship lived in the city for the period required for repair of the damaged ship.

During this time Ishigaki Eisho served as interpreter between his people and the missionary. In the secrecy of the Ishigaki family's ancestral mausoleum outside the city, the missionary taught the Christian Faith to Ishigaki Eisho and his two younger brothers. There the three were baptized.

Nothing further is recounted of the missionary. But according to the account of Ishigaki Eisho's descendants (of whom there are some two thousand now living on these islands), the three Ishigaki brothers were reported to Shoho, the king at Shuri, Okinawa. Investigators were immediately dispatched to Ishigaki Jima. They took the Ishigaki brothers back to Shuri, where they underwent a trial before the highest court (" saiko saiban "). Eisho profferred a defence of their Faith, which served only to seal the verdict of guilt. One brother was beheaded; the other exiled to a small island of the southern gunto. Eisho, as the most responsible for the transgression, was sentenced to burning at the stake. Even to this day, once a year the descendants of Ishigaki Eisho gather at the family mausoleum and conduct the memorial services they know — the Buddhist — in honour of the man whose nobility is a matter of pride for every inhabitant of Yaeyama. The Ishigaki family crest, still extant, shows the sign for " God " surrounding a Christian crown.

The story, Ishigaki City's Elder Historian told me, was never written into official published records, lest the example of so illustrious a native spread the Christian Idea. But it has been handed down in the family through the succeeding years ... ".

APPENDIX V

Memorial y arbitrio que presentan algunos religiosos que andan en Japon a los consejos de su Magestad el Rey de España, nuestro señor, que residen en corte. — British Museum C. 62-i-18(91).

No pudiendo sufrir los daños que vienen y los grandes peligros que instan a la honrra de Dios y de el Rey nr. sr. y a la fee catholica de el poder que tienen por estas partes los herejes cosarios Holandeses y Ingleses, y de la poca preparacion de parte de los vasallos de su magd. el Rey nro. sr. asi en las partes de la India y China, como en Luçon, no solo para echar a los herejes de por aqui; sino aun para defenderse así, y a los que de ellos se amparan; todo lo qual parece resulta de el poco concepto que en España de esto se tiene, por no saber quiças su Magd. el Rey nro. Sr. y sus reales consejos la verdad de lo que pasa y lo que esto importa. Movidos de el zelo de la honrra de Dios, y de vasallos leales de su Magd., por poder dar relacion de vista, disfraçados algunos (y el portador que es el p. fr. Diego Collado entre ellos) en habito de españoles seglares nos emos ido a meter entre los dichos Holandeses y Ingleses en el puerto de firado aqui en Japon y vistoles sus galeones de guerra contandoles las pieças de artillería y procurandoles sacar sus intentos en particular de algunos catholicos que por desgracia andan entre ellos; son pues lo primero impedir el trato de la China con Luçon; y tomarle para si; y con esto salir con otras cosas y para esto sustentan aora de compañía diez galeones de guerra que van todos los años [129], y aora actualmte. estan esperando en la costa de China y en la boca de Manila a los Chinas que vienen al trato con los Españoles, impidiendoles la entrada y robando a los que cogen, paraque molestados con estas obras, y incitados con promesas que les hacen; vengan a ir con el trato a sus fatorias de Jacatra y otras partes; y quede Manila perdida sin el en particular que de camino esperan los dichos herejes las naos que vienen de nueva España; y aun llegaron ya a pelear con una avra dos años [130]; y si las cogen, quedan rematadas las islas Philipinas, sin poderse valer ni sustentar a si, ni socorrer a Maluco, que sin socorro de Manila no se puede sustentar, ni Manila socorrerle sino le llega conque de Nueva España.

Estos galeones de los herejes estan desde Noviembre hasta Julio en la boca de Manila, embocadero y costa, y despues se vienen a recoger y rehazer de todo a Japon y en el camino roban lo que encuentran. Son fuertes en par-

---

[129] A reference to the Anglo-Dutch annual " Fleet of Defence ", which functioned in the China Sea with Hirado as its base, between August 1620 and July 1622.

[130] The Acapulco galleon *S. Nicolás* on 25 July, 1620; cf. W. L. Schurz, The Manila Galleon (New York, 1939), p. 348.

ticular los de los ingleses, de ingenios de guerra y de 34 a 42 pieças de artillería de 10 hasta 18 libras de vala, las mas de hierro. Y la gente que tienen es poca para tan grandes naos, y tanta artillería; en particular que enferma mucha de ella el tiempo que estan en la boca de Manila; Pero como en Manila no ai ya galeones ni se dan maña de haberlos con facilidad; aunque aya gte. y artillería no sirve de nada; y se estan los herejes a los ojos de los españoles todos los años con los daños y peligros dichos: y assi es necessario que venga socorro de España de galeones a Manila que con la ayuda de gte. y artillería de Manila y buenos soldados por cabeça destruyan de una vez esta potencia de los herejes y mientras se ordena, se puede probar a quemarles los dichos galeones, o cortarles las amarras en tiempo que se pierdan en firando que sera facil como dira el portador, si ai quien se ponga a ello por su ley y rey, que no seran los españoles que por aqui andan segun an mostrado en cosas que pedian menos brio [131].

Mas porque los dichos herejes no an de escarmentar como se a visto ya por experiencia dos vezes que en Manila les an vencido y destruido en parte [132] por tener concepto de la gran importancia que les es salir con sus sobredichos intentos; y assi se an de procurar juntar otra vez y vezes, y nunca an de desistir, es menester tambien formar los españoles gran concepto de ello y conservar siempre galeones en Manila para salirles luego al encuentro y dar entrada a los navios de Chinas y a los que vienen de nueva España a Manila y poder sustentar a Luçon y socorrer al Maluco, y aun se podra tratar de ganarle echando los Holandeses de alli; aunq para esto es menester mas fuerça; Pero si se hiziera fuera de gran provecho a su Magd. Tiniendo la entrada de Manila segura, importara mucho se abra el viaje de Macan para Manila y no vengan los Portugueses de Macan a Japon, que para los de Manila y para los mismos Portugueses de Macan y para su Magd sera mucho mejor y con esto an de venir los Japones a cesar o a floxar mucho de la persecucion que hazen a la Christiandad porque buelvan los Portugueses al trato con ellos, y en particular si con esto se pusieran y fortificaran los Españoles en Isla Hermosa [133] que es por donde necessariamte pasan todos los navios que van y vienen de Japon (que sera facil) se podía, tiniendo alli navios y galeras, lo uno hazer mal a los herejes que pasasen a Japon a recogerse, y por bastimentos para Jacatra y otras partes y para el Maluco; y de camino se les tendría tomado el lugar que ellos pretenden si les echan de Japon (que no tienen otro donde

[131] This allegation was quite unjustified, as the naval victories won by the Spaniards in the Philippines against the Dutch (who usually enjoyed a numerical superiority in ships and men), between 1610 and 1646, clearly proved.

[132] In the battles of the Playa Honda (25 April 1610, and 14 April 1617).

[133] As they did in 1626 in North Formosa (Kelung and Tamsui), two years after the Dutch had established themselves at Fort Zeelandia in the Southwest of that island.

poderse recoger en tal caso) y lo otro (si pareciese) se podia a su tiempo por via de su Magd. por escrito y un embaxador de pecho, desengañar al Rey de Japon de el mal concepto que tiene de nr̃a. ley y Rey y requerirle por los agravios que nos a hecho, que sino dexaua la persecucion no avian de dexar entrar ni salir navio en Japon; que junto con no venir los Portugueses de Macan al trato, les avia de obligar a quitar la persecucion y quedar solo amigos de los españoles, que de los Holandeses no les viene provecho: y sino les echan, o cierran la puerta, es por temer que sean de poner en isla hermosa y no dexar salir ni entrar navio en Japon. Esto es necessario por lo arriba dicho y aun para Macan mientras sustentan el trato con Japon, porque como entran y salen a un tiempo con los herejes en Japon, siempre es con grande riesgo; y ya por medio milagro sean escapado huyendo debaxo de los vaupreses de sus galeones por ser mas ligeras las galeotas de los Portugueses[134]; pero para eso, trataban ya ogaño los herejes de hazer embarcaciones tan ligeras para poder les dar caça.

Si se haze lo dicho, se a de mandar se encarguen los officios y galeones, no por favor como suelen a vezes a quien lo echa a perder, sino a quien lo haga como debe con gran zelo de la honrra de su Dios Ley y Rey.

La India en opinion de los que por aca bien sienten, esta perdida en materia de govierno y milicia y apoderados los Holandeses de mucho de ella y de sus Reynos circumvezinos por no tratar las cabeças de ella tanto de ser soldados y poner a los Portugueses en esto y hazerles obedecer, y mirar por la honrra de España; como de ganar dinero para si sin mirar por el bien comun y en particular que por no adunarse con los castellanos, ni ayudar a los de Manila quando es menester y pudieran, dan muestras que haran qualquiera cosa[135]. Tienen los herejes intento de tomar a Malaca ayudados de

---

[134] Presumably a reference to the narrow escape of the *São Bartolomeu* on the 28 July 1620; cf. C. R. Boxer, The Great Ship from Amacon (Lisboa, 1959), pp. 314-15.

[135] A common complaint of the Spaniards, as instanced by Fr. Diego Aduarte, O.P., who wrote from Manila (26 June 1598): " Y es çierto que por via de los Portugueses, qui ni la Fee ni la Corona Real se augmenten mucho, porque ellos se pagan con solos los puertos que tienen para assegurar la mar para sus contrataciones " (Archivo Ibero-Americano, vol. XXXVIII, pp. 455-58). For Luso-Spanish cooperation — or lack of it — against the Dutch in the Eastern Seas at this period; cf. A. Botelho de Sousa, Subsídios para a história militar marítima da India, 1585-1650 (4 vols., Lisboa, 1930-56), vols II (1605-1617), and III (1618-1635), passim. Some of the Portuguese were equally critical of their own countrymen in India. Ruy Freyre de Andrade wrote to the Crown from Ormuz on the 12 February 1621, that the King should ensure " aja armadas em forma e comprimento a suas instrucçõis, a que qua se não dá effeito, tratando as pessoas a quem toca a execusão, de anteporem particulares, e comveniensias proprias a toda a materia por grave que seja do serviso de Sua Magestade que anda mui distraido, pedindo castiguo de tantas exurbitansias, e maos exemplos... " (British Museum, Egerton MSS, 1131, fl. 16).

el Rey de Dachen [136] y si pueden, por guerra, engaños o sobornos entrar en Macan: y irse fortificando mas y tomando fatorias por coger los tratos de la India y China; que no deben de ser poco provechosos, pues por ellos andan los herejes tan cuidadosos y dizen no se han de cansar, ni reparar en gastos: y assi es menester poner cabeças de gran gobierno y brio en la India y Macan y darles socorro.

Antes solían estar los Holandeses en Bantan, mas aora tienen ya guerra con el Rey de alli, y assi estan alli cerca en Jacatra, que es su principal fatoria en estas partes, parece que si los españoles tratasen de ayudar al Rey de Bantan para echar a los herejes de Jacatra, lo llevaría bien, assi el, como el de Jacatra que le tienen retirado, y podrían con esto tener los españoles el trato de alli de la pimienta [137].

En resolución si se quiere sustentar y augmentar lo que su magd. tiene en estas partes, y quebrar los braços a los herejes para las guerras de flandes y otras partes, y darselos a la Christiandad y corona de España, es menester hazer mas caso de las cosas de por aca, y tratar mas de veras de remediarlas que hasta aqui, y esto sentimos como que por aver estado antes en Philipinas y estar aora en Japon; lo vemos, y sabemos todo lo que aca pasa y avisamos como vasallos de su magd. con el portador, que dara mas larga relacion si es menester. De Japon y Março 3 de 1622 años.

(s) fr dio. collado vic. pl.
de Sto dgo en Japon.

fr Pedro de Sta. Cata. Mr.
fr Domingo castellet
fr Antonio de san Buenaventura,
comiss. por la Prov.de S. Greg. p. discalziatis.

---

136 Achin or Acheh, the Muslim kingdom in North Sumatra.

137 Cf. J. Bastin, The Changing Balance of the early Southeast Asian Pepper Trade (Kuala Lumpur, 1960), for the importance of Bantam in the pepper-trade at this period.

APPENDIX VI

Relacion del socorro de Armada que es necessario para la conservación de los Estados de su Magestad, en la India Oriental, y Islas Philipinas. — *British Museum C 62-i-18(75).*

Señor.

Fray Diego Collado de la Orden de Santo Domingo, dize, Que por tener experiencia de muchos años de las cosas de Philipinas, Iapon, y Maluco, y aver visto agora lo que en la India passa, Da quenta a V. Magestad de lo que siente (en Dios y en su conciencia) con zelo solo de la gloria de Dios, y de la conservacion y augmento de los Reales Estados de V. M. cuyo humilde vassallo es.

Lo primero, puede assentar V. Magestad, que no es Rey ni señor de la navegación de la India Oriental, de las Islas Philipinas, ni de Maluco, ni tiene que esperar V. M. provecho ninguno de todas estas partes, sino se pone el remedio que abaxo diré. Porque demas de aver perdido ya V. M. (por traycion de algunos particulares vassallos) la fortaleza de Ormus que era la primera llave de la India[138]: y correr gran peligro la de Malaca, que es la segunda, si la cerca el Holandes, con ayuda del Rey de Achen, como pretende; y estar tambien los Olandeses con grandes esperanças (no obstante que no les salio bien la primera prueba que hizieron de venir a entrar en Macan el año passado de veinte y dos)[139] de fortificarse en aquella plaça (con que quedaran destruydas Philipinas, y la India) con solo lo que agora passa, tiene V. M. poco mas del nombre de Rey y señor destas partes, y el provecho y señorio verdadero es de los Olandeses y Ingleses: porque ellos son señores del mar, sin serlo los vasallos de V. M. de navegar, ni de la China a Manila, ni de Manila a Maluco, ni de aqui a la India, ni en la India de unas partes a otras, ni a la China, ni della a Manila, ni Iapon, ni de Malaca a parte ninguna, ni de otra parte a Malaca, sino con notable peligro, que es milagro quando se escapa alguna embarcacion de manos de los dichos Hereges, por ponerse en todos los sitios, passos, estrechos, y embocaderos que ay en estas partes. Y vinendo el Suplicante con otros compañeros de Manila a Malaca, les corrieron doze naos suyas en diferentes lugares y tiempos: y ellos tienen todo el trato y ganancia de ropas, clauo, pimienta, canela, nuez, y massa,

---

[138] Cf. Luciano Cordeiro, Como se perdeu Ormuz. Processo inédito do século XVII (Lisboa, 1896); Documentacão Ultramarina Portuguesa, II (Lisboa, 1962), 274-461.

[139] Cf. C. R. Boxer, Fidalgos in the Far East. Fact and fancy in the history of Macao, 1550-1770 (The Hague, 1948), pp. 72-92, for the defeat of the Dutch at Macao, on the 24 June, 1622.

pedrería, y drogas de la India, fuera de lo que roban y cogen a los Chinas, y a los Españoles vassallos de V. M. Y como son señores de la mar y lo corren y navegan todo, les es necessario a todos estos moradores de los Reynos circumvezinos, ser amigos de los Holandeses y tener trato con ellos, por ser señores de sus haziendas, y poderse aprovechar dellas, vendiendoselas a los dichos Hereges, y por poder navegar y tener comunicacion por mar con sus vezinos[140]: y V. Magestad no tiene nada de trato, ni las Aduanas rinden nada, ni se puede sustentar la India, sino que forçosamente la avran de venir a dexar sus vasallos de V. M. porque no se pueden sustentar sino con el trato, y faltando esse por lo dicho, sin otra guerra, les sera necessario dexarla, y Philipinas, y Maluco se ha de ver en mucho aprieto, Maluco por no tener de donde le venga socorro sino de Manila, y Manila por no poder socorrer a Maluco, ni sustentarse a si sin el trato de China, y comercio con Nueva España, que tambien corre notable peligro, por ponerse los Enemigos al paso por donde vienen las Naos de allà, que si las cogen, todo queda por tierra. Y assi es necessario que se ponga remedio eficaz, y que se les quite este poder a los Enemigos, por ser tan contra la reputation de las armas de V. M. el perder lo que sus antepassados ganaron, y de tanto provecho para el augmento de su Real Corona, el ser verdadero señor de la India, Philipinas, y Islas Malucas, y de lo que destas partes se saca.

Assentado pues en esto, y que insta la brevedad deste remedio, porque los Enemigos no se fortalezcan mas en las fortalezas que agora tienen, y tomando otras y metiendose en alguna de las que agora son de V. M. y enriqueziendo mas con las pressas de la China, y India, y con los tratos que en essas partes traen: y enflaqueziendo las fuerças de V. M. con los gastos ordinarios que se hazen en procurarse sustentar en las fuerças de V. M. de Maluco y otras, sin entregarlas a los Olandeses, sin otro provecho ninguno.

Lo segundo, suponga V. M. que no ay fuerça en las Philipinas, ni en la India para quitar la que los Olandeses tienen, ni en mar, ni en tierra. Porque dexado que no se juntará el poco poder de la India con el de Manila, sin particular orden y riguroso mandato de V. M. y embiando de aca quien lo junte con poderes suficientes, aun dado que se juntara, es muy poco, no solo para echar los Olandeses de sus fuerças, y del mar (que es como su casa en estas partes) sino aun para defenderse dellos. Porque en la India ay pocos Galeones, y no ay gente de mar, ni artilleros, y los soldados Portugueses, estan tan mal acostumbrados, que ni ay entre ellos obediencia, ni rastro de milicia: aunque esto deve de ser, porque ni les pagan, estiman, ni castigan, ni tienen Capitanes que traten ni les hagan tratar de milicia[141]. En Manila tampoco ay

---

140 Cf. M. A. P. Meilink-Roelofszoon, Asian Trade and European Influence in the Indonesian archipelago between 1500 and 1630 (The Hague, 1962), pp. 173-294.

141 Cf. Francisco Rodrigues da Silveira, " Reformação da milicia e governo

Galeones y los artilleros y marineros son pocos, y quando mucho avra para armar quatro o seis Galeones, que sera a lo sumo a que se podra estender el poder de Manila. De suerte que junta la potencia de la India, y Philipinas quando se juntassen, a lo sumo serían diez o doze Galeones, que es nada contra el poder de los Enemigos.

Y asi se ha de resolver V. Magestad, de hazer el gasto de una vez, y emprender echar los Hereges de estas partes, assi de sus fortalezas, como del mar, embiando fuerça de España de Galeones, que por lo menos lleguen a veinte y quatro, nuevos, fuertes, y bien artillados y pertrechados de belame y xarcias dobladas, y de cables y anclas, con doblados artilleros y marineros, y con provision para dos años, y que vayan en ellos General, Capitanes, y soldados diestros, y salgan de España a buen tiempo, y con secreto, de suerte que no se puedan prevenir los Enemigos, sino que si se huviere de yr la Armada de V. M. por la India, que será lo mejor, se vaya derecha a la principal Fortaleza de los Olandeses, que es Iacatra [142], teniendo avisado de antemano al Virrey de la India, que tenga junto su poder para el tiempo en que se pudiere juntar con ella, sin que se sepa para donde es, echando voz que es para otra parte de los Reynos de los Moros, y que haga la mayor provision que pudiere de bastimentos. Y avisando tambien a Manila, que se prevenga de Galeones y galeras, y bastimentos, y espere la orden de V. Magestad. Y si huviere de ir la dicha Armada por el Estrecho de Magallanes, que vaya derecha a Maluco, donde señalando tiempo al Governador de Manila, se juntara con ella, para yr destruyendo por alli al Enemigo. Y teniendo prevenida la potencia de la India, para el tiempo, y lugar en que se ha de juntar con la Armada y fuerça de Manila. Y en todo acontecimiento ha de embiar V. M. un Fator suyo con carta, y algun presente al Rey de Macasar, que es muy amigo de V. M. y su Reyno es muy proveydo [143]: y otro a Iapon, que son las partes de donde puede aver mas provision para socorro de la dicha Armada: y por donde quiera que se comiençe a perseguir a los Olandeses, se han de procurar assolar por mar y tierra, sinque quede rastro dellos en todo este Oriente, apoderandose V. M. de todas sus fortalezas, y del trato todo de estas partes. Que haziendose assi, quedará V. M. Rey y señor absoluto de todo, y los Reyes de todo este Oriente volverán a ser aliados de V. M. como antes, y ayudaran (por querer mal a los Olandeses, que si agora los siguen, es por la fuerça que tienen, y viendo

---

do Estado da India Oriental", MS. of 1634 (British Museum, Additional MSS. 25419), copious extracts from which were published by A. de S. S. Costa Lobo, Memorias de um soldado da India (Lisboa, 1877), and which confirms Fr. Diego Collado's allegations.

[142] Batavia, as the Dutch called Jacarta after their capture of it in 1619.

[143] For the relations of Macassar with the Iberians and the Dutch at this period, cf., M. A. Meilink-Roelofszoon, Asian Trade and European Influence, 1500-1630, pp. 163-64.

que los Españoles no tienen ninguna) a echarlos de sus Reynos, como ellos mismos lo dizen.

A esto me ha obligado el zelo del servicio de Dios y de V. M. que nuestro Señor nos guarde.

APPENDIX VII

Letter of fray Francisco Morales O.P., to the Provincial Chapter in Manila written from Japan on 24 March 1604. Juan López, O.P., Quinta parte de la historia de Santo Domingo y de su orden de predicadores, Valladolid, 1621, ff. 268 verso-269 verso.

" Para esta tierra lo que es menester nos negocien Vuestras Reverencias por allà, es algun dinero para podernos sustentar y hazer casas, y yglesias, y vestirnos pobremente conforme al estilo de la provincia. Querriamos hazer un hospital para pobres, dandoles de comer y curandolos y ayudando a los que piden limosna a nuestras puertas (que de ordinario es esta gente pobrissima) y para caminos; que la variedad de casos desta tierra nos obliga a hazer muchos viajes a Nangasaqui, y a Meaco, y otras partes; que aunque se hazen las jornadas a pie y con muy poco gasto, es menester para ellas algun socorro, y para sustentar algunos niños à quien enseñamos Gramatica, conque a su tiempos puedan ayudar. Esta es la cosa mas importante; porque es impossible passar nosotros, ni hazer el fruto que desseamos, sin ayuda de los naturales. Esto no podra ser, si no los criamos desde niños conforme a la dotrina de santo Tomás que tanto importa introduzirla en todos los Reynos donde entrare la Fè, y mas en estos del Iapon, que están muy dispuestos para recibir heregias[144]; porque algunas sectas de los Gentiles parece que se ajustan con algunas cosas de nuestra Fè; y para conocer quan diferente es la una dotrina de la otra, y la una luz de la otra, es menester lengua y dotrina. La lengua aprenden a los pechos de sus madres. La buena dotrina la han de enseñar los frayles. Para estos gastos es menester dineros. Quando no se pudiere proveer, no por esso se ha de alçar mano de la labor. Toda la dificultad está en los principios, que con el tiempo fiamos en el Señor que las cosas tomaran otro assiento mejor; porque adelante los Christianos acudiran al remedio de nuestras necessidades, y de los naturales de Stiuma [*sic; i. e.* Satsuma]. No

---

[144] This is obviously a reference to the Jesuits' teaching of Probabilism, for a little later in the letter Morales complains that " en Manila, y en otras partes han començado a enseñarse doctrinas nuevas, y han corrido las mares; lo que pocos años atras se predicó y escrivio en los Reynos de Castilla, y en toda España, calificando las confessiones hechas por escrito, en que el santo Padre Clemente Octavio dio ya su censura; y otras doctrinas, que por acá no se tienen por muy acertadas. De todo esto dio muy larga cuenta el Padre fray Juan de Ormaça en una carta que llegó a Valladolid, fecha en Manila, diziendo el cuydado con que la Orden avia salido a contradezir las nuevas dotrinas " (López, f. 269). The introduction of this new theory, still disputed in Europe, into a mission as complex as that of China and Japan, could not fail to cause dismay among the friars.

estamos tan desamparados, que no nos ayan dado en vezes mas de cien pesos en dinero, y mas de sesenta fardos de arroz. De un pueblo ha mandado el Rey señalar diez hombres que vengan a servirnos al uso de la tierra. Lo que importa sobre todo es, que nos embien religiosos de buen espiritu, que con esto todas las cosas tendrán buen sucesso. ... No se puede encarecer lo mucho que importa que el rigor de nuestra provincia y el buen exemplo se vaya continuando en estas partes: que en esto está librado todo buen sucesso en materia de conversiones; y faltando esto, faltará todo lo que la Orden pretende, en cumplimiento de lo que avemos professado. Aqui procuramos guardar las constituciones de la Orden, y dessa santa provincia [145]; pero en casos, con las circumstancias que aqui diré, sujetandolas a la censura de Vs. Reverencias. El dormir en tabla, no se ha hecho hasta agora; que aun para esso no hay comodidad. Dormimos en unas esteras de pajas que acá se usan [146]; que por ser dobladas, es mas blando que tablas. Ahi va la muestra dellas. Vean Vs. Reverencias si las podremos usar en lugar de tablas, y en avisandonos, lo que ordenaren se hará con mucha puntualidad. En lo que es no comer, ni bever entre dia, no se puede aqui guardar tan puntualmente la constitucion, por ser uso desta tierra, en viniendo o yendo a visitar, dar de bever un poco de agua cozida con una yerva que llaman Cha, y se beve tomando un bocadillo, que es como conserva del tamaño de una avellana. Assi lo avemos hecho hasta agora, porque es mas cerimonia que otra cosa [147]. Con todo esso vean V. Reverencias si merece correccion, y nos la embien. Lo que es andar a pie, se guarda, aunque con mucho trabajo, por ser tierra fragosissima. En las yglesias no puede aver la diferencia de ornamentos que dize nuestro Ordinario, que la pobreza no da lugar a esso. Tenemos necesidad de una sobrepelliz, y una sobremesa en que poner el recaudo del baptismo; que por los caminos no ay pilas para bautizar, y sino se haze con alguna decencia, lo tienen en poco. Embiennos Rosarios, Agnus, Reliquias bien adereçadas, que hazen por acà mucho al caso para acariciar y aficionar a los recien bautizados. Es menester que los que aqui vinieren, se acomoden con el estilo de los naturales, en todo lo que no parare perjuyzio a nuestro modo de vivir: y que los que vinieren, sean habiles, que puedan aprender las lenguas: porque esta es dificultosissima. Que sean letrados. Sobre todo es menester que traygan gran paciencia: no piensen que

---

[145] These were printed shortly after Morales wrote this letter, under the title of Ordinationes Generales provintiae Sanctissimi Rosarii (Binondoc, per Ioannem de Vera chinã Christianum. Cum licentia, 1604), the permission for publication being signed at Manila on the 24 June, 1604, by Fr. Miguel Martín de San Jacinto, prior-provincial of the Dominican Province of the Philippines.

[146] tatami in Japanese.

[147] The Jesuits took the same line. Cf. G. Schütte, S.J. (ed.), Il Cerimoniale per i missionari del Giappone. " Advertimentos e avisos acerca dos costumes e catangues de Jappão " di Alexandro Valignano, S.J., Importante documento circa i methodi di adattamento nella Missione giapponese del secolo XVI (Roma, 1946).

porque se dize (y con razon) que está ya la mies blanqueando, que no ay mas que llegar y coger. Es aqui el trato de los ministros con personas de muy diferente natural, y al fin gentiles que no han de quebrar en la costumbre en que se han criado, sino es con mucha dificultad y contradicciones que ofrece su conversion de sus Bonços. Es el demonio el que con todas fuerças procura impedir la conversion de las almas. Aqui dizen vino primero el santo Francisco Xavier y despues dos o tres vezes Padres de la Compañía que vista la obstinacion y dureza desta gente los han dexado. A la potencia de Dios y a su divino braço no ay resistencia; y la perseverancia todo lo alcança...

ADDITIONAL NOTES

For a recent treatment of aspects of 'The Christian Century in Japan', see George Elison, Deus Destroyed: The Image of Christianity in Early Modern Japan, (Cambridge, Mass., 1973).

P. 15 n. 15: On Cocks see Michael Cooper, SJ., 'The Second Englishman in Japan: Richard Cocks', Transactions of the Asiatic Society of Japan, Third Series, XVII (1982), pp. 121-159.

III

PALAFOX, CHINA AND THE CHINESE RITES CONTROVERSY

It was perhaps inevitable that Bishop Juan de Palafox y Mendoza, given his hostility to the Jesuits, should have been interested in the famous Chinese Rites Controversy involving the missionaries of the Society of Jesus in China. This bitter quarrel began early in the 17th century, continued well into the 18th, and had strong repercussions not only upon the fate of the Jesuits, but also upon the course of European ideas, since it served to bring China to the attention of the theologians, philosophers, economists and politicians of Europe and led to the *rêve chinois* which constituted one of the few moments of Romantic relief in Neo-Classical Europe.[1]

[1] There are many accounts of this controversy available, particularly from the Jesuit standpoint; for example that of PASTOR GUTIÉRREZ, SJ., in *Missionalia Hispanica,* III (1946), 511-73. The most scholarly Dominican presentation is the closely documented study by Dr. BENNO BIERMANN, OP., *Die Anfänge der Neueren Dominikanermission in China,* (Münster in Westfalen, 1927). On the Franciscan side there are the documents edited in *Archivum Franciscanum Historicum,* vols. IV and IX, and in *Sinica Franciscana,* vols. II-V, besides the work of ANTONIO S. ROSSO, OFM., *Apostolic Legations to China in the Eighteenth Century* (South Pasadena, 1948). The friars' viewpoint is also presented in the Introduction to *The Travels and Controversies of Friar Domingo Navarrete,* edited by J. S. Cummins, (London, Hakluyt Society, 1961). A brief but uncommitted account is given by G. ROMMERSKIRCHEN, OMI., in *Enciclopedia Cattolica* (Vatican City, 1954), s. v. *Riti*; a popular account, which however is not always reliable on details, is that of DOM COLUMBA CARY-ELWES, OSB., *China and the Cross* (London, 1957). There are further bibliographies in H. CORDIER, *Bibliotheca Sinica* (Paris, 1905-24) cols. 869-926; 3125-6; and in R. STREIT, OMI., *Bibliotheca Missionum,* V, VII (Aachen, 1929-31). For some of the intellectual results of the meeting of China and Europe, see V. PINOT, *La Chine et la Formation de l'Esprit Philosophique en France (1640-1740),* (Paris, 1932).

This present paper is limited to Palafox's intervention which came at the beginning and, perhaps, most crucial stage of the long debate. The controversy proper began in the 1630s when Franciscan and Dominican friars managed, despite Jesuit opposition, to enter the China mission-field which for some years had been a monopoly of the Society of Jesus. The newcomers professed themselves appalled and scandalised by what they found in China. They alleged, for instance, that the Jesuit missionaries allowed their Chinese converts to retain superstitious, possibly even idolatrous, practices such as the veneration of Confucius and their ancestors. The friars furthermore asserted that the Jesuits there were preaching an impure form of Christianity; that not only did the Fathers themselves refuse to have any dealings or discussions with the friars, but that they even carried their policy to the point of forbidding their converts to confess to the friars, whom the Jesuits seem to have treated almost as though they were the propagators of a different religion. It was also reported, and this was certainly true, that the Jesuits, despite papal rulings to the contrary, were still striving to retain their old monopoly of the China mission and that they were resorting to quite extraordinary means to rid themselves of such friars as did manage to enter China after penetrating this early and somewhat surprising form of the "Bamboo Curtain".[2]

In Europe such damaging reports might well have been dismissed as fantastic but, unfortunately, they had been preceded by similar complaints from Japan where the Jesuits had made their converts sign affidavits that they would not have recourse to friars, and,

[2] The Dominican, Juan Bautista Morales, for example, "étonné et scandalisé des pratiques de certains jésuites en Chine avait demandé en vain des explications..." (H. Bernard-Maitre, SJ., *Histoire universelle des Missions catholiques*, II (Paris, 1957), 341); see also Pastor Gutiérrez, SJ., *op cit.*, 558-60; D. A. Mortier, OP., *Histoire des Maîtres Généraux*, (Paris, 1914), VII, 282; Biermann, OP., *op. cit.*, 33, 39, 42, 46; and for contemporary accounts see Domingo Fernández Navarrete OP., *Controversias antiguas y modernas de la mission de la gran China* (Madrid, 1679), 469, 474, 511, 538, 541, 542 (this work was printed but never published; relevant passages from it are included in Navarrete's *Travels and Controversies* edited Cummins); and the letters in *Archivum Franciscanum Historicum*, e.g. IV (1911), 54-56; IX (1916), 200, and *Sinica Franciscana*, II, 413.

allegedly, had forbidden the rosary to their Christians, presumably on the ground that it was considered a particularly Dominican devotion. Modern editors find a problem here, for though many of these allegations are scarcely credible, yet they cannot declare that so many friars, making sworn statements *in verbo sacerdotis*, are perjurers.[3]

The Jesuits, of course, had their reasons for adopting a special approach to the China mission. They maintained, after careful study and much heart-searching, that the Rites of which the friars complained were not in fact idolatrous, and that perhaps they were not even superstitious.[4] In any case the Fathers hoped eventually to purge these practices of any superstitious accretions and, in time, to christianise them. They were also sincerely convinced that they themselves were alone suited to the China mission because it raised delicate problems and demanded peculiarly skilled men. They believed that if the friars, "with their ignorance and imprudent zeal", were allowed into the Empire they would upset and confuse the converts there, would stir up persecution and destroy the mission.[5] Possibly this opinion was justified and the danger may indeed have been real, but in the manner of their reaction and tone of their complaints the Jesuits can only be called indiscreet.

Allegations of the Jesuits' lack of cooperation and reports of their thinly disguised contempt for their Mendicant colleagues soon spread widely and rapidly and their reluctance to allow friars into China naturally served to increase suspicion and resentment.[6] Nationalistic feelings were also involved because the Jesuits worked under the aegis of Portuguese and the friars under the Spanish *Patronato*. Moreover, the traditional rivalry between the Jesuit and Domi-

[3] C. R. Boxer, *The Christian Century in Japan, 1549-1650* (London, 1951), 418; *Arch. Fran. Historicum*, IV, 55-6; Navarrete, *Controversias*, 404, 470; [Noel Alexandre, OP.,] *Apologie des Dominicains, Missionnaires de la Chine* (Cologne, 1699), 136.

[4] Biermann, 170; *Fonti Ricciane*, ed. P.M.D'Elia, SJ., I (Rome, 1942), 118.

[5] Biermann, 59, 61-2; Gutiérrez, 530.

[6] Gutiérrez, 559, 568; Biermann, 55.

nicans increased ill-feeling and the friars did not forget slighting remarks such as Father Diego Morales's description of them as "unos frayles moços [que] no quisieron tomar el consejo que los de la Compañía les dieron". And when the Jesuit Patriarch, Affonso Mendes, complained to Propaganda Fide that "estos Frayles Idiotas, con sus imprudencias, van echando a perder la Mission", he earned himself a number of heavy-handed rebukes from irritated Mendicants. For the friars could see no reason why any Jesuit should set himself up to preach at a Dominican "como si estuviera con los niños de la escuela" and if the Jesuits believed that they alone were fitted to convert the Chinese Empire, the friars had other opinions. The Franciscan Antonio de Santa María wrote in 1637 of the "manifiesta providencia de Dios al permitir que entraran en China los dominicos y franciscanos, para que así como S. Francisco y Sto. Domingo fueron llamados por Dios, para el reparo de la ruina que amenazaba en el siglo XIII en la sociedad, así sus hijos han sido elegidos por Dios, para reparar los falsos cimientos sobre que se edificaba la Religión cristiana en China". From the beginning of the quarrel, therefore, strong and deep-seated emotions were called into play, and by 1652, when a Jesuit Vice-Provincial wrote to Santa María apologising for his earlier treatment of the friars, it was already too late: the damage had been done and by then each side saw itself as called upon to perform the will of God and rectify the errors of the opposite faction.[7]

Bishop Palafox, like many others, seems to have found no difficulty in believing the friars' reports about the Jesuits and his notorious and highly emotional letter of 1649 to the Pope shows how agitated he was by what he had heard of the China mission from a friar eye-witness. "Toda la Iglesia de la China gime y se queja, Padre Santísimo: clama altamente, que no ha sido instruida, sino engañada por los mismos Jesuitas, en los rudimentos de nuestra purísima fe que la han enseñado; y huérfana, sin jurisdicción eclesiástica, se duele al ver escondida la Cruz de nuestro Salvador, autorizados los ritos gentílicos, y corrompidos, más bien que intro-

[7] NAVARRETE, *Controversias*, 32, 150-51, 400, 408, 467; *Arch. Fran. Hist.*, IV, 52; R. MARTÍNEZ-VIGIL, *La Orden de Predicadores* (Madrid, 1884), 378; *Sinica Fran.*, II, 413.

ducidos los que son verdaderamente cristianos: ... Dios y Belial en una misma mesa, en un mismo altar y en los mismos sacrificios; y finalmente, mira con pena incomparable venerar los ídolos bajo la apariencia del cristianismo, o por mejor decir, mancharse la pureza de nuestra santísima fé, bajo la sombra del paganismo".

This summary of the complex situation is obviously hasty and exaggerated. Palafox, to his credit, later warned his readers of this by reminding them that the letter had been written in a time of stress, when, involved in a dispute with the Mexican Jesuits, he was "algo congojado de las sinrazones que, a mi parecer, habían hecho aquellos Padres contra mi Dignidad, y persona; y así, de ella no se ha de hacer más caso que lo que pesaren sus razones. Pero yo confieso que la encomendé a Dios primero, y que no entiendo que escribí sino aquello que juzgaba que era servicio suyo".[8] In view of this, it is interesting to find that Palafox wrote another letter (see appendix below) upon the thorny subject of the Rites Controversy, a letter which is calmer in tone and against which he has no warnings to make.

Palafox's interest in China had other roots. He felt particularly responsible for the mission there, since he held that he as Bishop of Puebla, was one of the nearest Bishops to the "Middle Kingdom" — a claim that would have been vigorously contested by a number of prelates had they come to hear of it.[9] Consequently, he kept himself informed of the mission, and of Chinese affairs in general, by means of reports which he received twice-yearly, and it was chiefly upon the basis of these that he wrote his history of the Tartar invasion of China. As early as 1647 he had two large volumes of documents concerning the Rites Controversy. His interest increased after 1646 when he met fray Juan Bautista Morales, OP., who arrived in Mexico that year with a party of friars bound for the Philippines and, ultimately, the China mission.[10]

[8] PALAFOX, *Obras* (Madrid, 1762), XI, 111, 559; *Cartas* (México, 1841), 87, 342.

[9] PALAFOX, *Obras*, XI, 111, 114; *Cartas*, 87, 91.

[10] C. DE ST. VINCENT, OP., *La vie du grand Apôtre de la Chine, le vénérable père Jean-Batiste de Moralès* (Cologne, 1701); PALAFOX, *Obras*, X, 273, 391; XI, 213; *Cartas*, 72, 88-9, 231.

Friar Morales had already been in China some years earlier and after an unsatisfactory interview with the Jesuit Vice-Provincial had tried vainly to persuade the Jesuits to join him and his friar colleagues in a general discussion of their different evangelical techniques and their differing interpretations of the native Rites. When this was refused the friars next appealed to the Jesuits in Macao, then to those in Manila, and finally, in despair, decided to report to Rome and ask guidance there.[11] The Jesuits' refusal to discuss their differences with the friars was a fatal decision for, in a sense, peace between the two groups was impossible from then onwards. The Jesuits, however, had no alternative but to avoid entering into formal discussions with the friars since to do so would appear to be a tacit admission of the friars' right to be in China —a right which the Fathers were not prepared to concede. Yet had the Jesuits at this juncture cooperated with the newly-arrived Mendicants, removed their suspicions by welcoming them as allies in a common cause, and abandoned the claim that China was the exclusive monopoly of the Society of Jesus, they might more easily have convinced the friars of the legality and desirability of their methods. Had this

[11] "Il [Morales] n'en obtient une fois de plus que des excuses polies et se résout à aller en personne plaider sa cause à Rome" (Henri Bernard-Maitre, SJ., "Un Dossier bibliographique de la fin du XVIIe siècle sur la Question des Termes Chinois", in *Recherches de Science Religieuse*, XXXVI (1949), 52), and "L'on doit reconnaître qu' en cette délicate affaire, les deux [friars] missionaires de Manille se comportèrent très correctement. Après avoir vainement essayé d'obtenir satisfaction, pour leurs doutes, de leurs voisins jésuites, ils portèrent la cause aux supérieurs ecclésiastiques de Macao" (Bernard-Maitre, SJ., *Histoire universelle*, II, 35, 341). Earlier Jesuit writers, however, tended to take a more severe view of this procedure: "ritus gentis Europaeo oculo considerans, miris scrupulis agitari coepere ... omnia ad Europaeam consuetudinem exigens ... nihil proinde mirum, si praejudiciis occupatus ... primus bellum ritibus Sinicis indixit [P. Morales OP.]" (George Pray, SJ., *Historia Controversiarum de Ritibus Sinicis* (Budapest, 1789), 18-19, 61. On the friars' abortive interview with the Jesuit Vice-Provincial, see Rosso, *op. cit.*, 110 and *Apologie des Dominicains*, 130-31. As a result of the meeting with the friars, Father Francisco Furtado SJ. later wrote his *Informatio antiquissima* but this failed to satisfy the friars' doubts (Biermann, 63-4) and indeed, according to Navarrete *(Controversias*, 329, 331, 335-39), served only to give rise to more and greater doubts in their minds.

happened, history would have a different story to tell. But another reason why the Jesuits evaded cooperation with the friars was that they were themselves sending a representative, Father Alvaro Semedo, to Rome and they hoped that his negotiations there would justify their procedure and entirely obviate any need for discussions with the friars. The Jesuits, then, were obliged to play for time; and the friars, on their side, had no alternative but to refer the matter to Rome.

Unfortunately for all concerned, although the Jesuits in China steadily declined to enter into discussions with the friars, an impetuous and not very well-informed Jesuit in the Philippines, Father Bartolomé Roboredo, took it upon himself to write a treatise in which he admitted the essentials of the friars' thesis, namely, that the Rites permitted to the Chinese Christians were in fact superstitious. He declared that the Chinese were polytheists but that the Christian converts could be excused for taking part in the Rites because their inner intentions were pure. The Jesuits were later to disown this as misguided and inaccurate, but in the meantime, and in the absence of any more official policy-statement, Roboredo's work not unnaturally came to be regarded as representative of Jesuit policy in China. Friar Juan Bautista Morales would have found other Jesuits confusing too. Father Alexandre de Rhodes, for example, who had served in Tonking and Macao, was as forthright as any friar on the question of the nature of the Chinese Rites: "Un de leurs faux Dieux, est un certain Confucius... Il n'est pas croyable, combien ils ont de respect pour lui; nous avons peine, de persuader aux Chréstiens qui se convertissent de ne fleschir pas les genoux devant ses statuës, qu'ils ont quasi tous dans leurs maisons, et ceux qui ont fait courir le bruit, que les jesuites permettent cette idolâtrie à leurs Néophytes, me permettront de leur dire qu'ils sont très malinformés."[12]

Friar Morales arrived in Rome in 1643 where the Secretary of Propaganda Fide, Francesco Ingoli, showed him a Jesuit letter receiv-

[12] Bernard-Maitre, SJ., *Dossier*, 51; Biermann, OP., 169, 175; Navarrete, *Controversias*, 79-85, 335, 337, 484-505. Baltasar de Santa Cruz, OP., *Historia de la Provincia del Santo Rosario de Filipinas* (Saragossa, 1693), 23-26. A. de Rhodes, SJ., *Divers voyages et missions* (Paris, 1653), 54.

ed there earlier. This document denounced the friars in China as "idiotas e imprudentes", a view that cannot have failed to incense the Dominican. Granted an interview with the aged Urban VIII, Morales explained that he had come to submit certain doubts concerning the China mission. At this the pope drew himself up and, striking the arm of his chair, cried out, "Heresy, heresy, to the inquisition", for he had heard earlier of the problems in Morales's mind and seems to have already reached a decision about them. Possibly he had been influenced in the friars' favour by the Jesuit Semedo's *Relatione* (Rome, 1643) which, with its chapters on sects, superstitions and sacrifices of China, must have gone far in cautions Roman eyes to confirm much of what Morales had to say about religion in the "Middle Kingdom". However, in his official written report Morales was careful not to make any specific accusations against the Jesuits and limited himself to submitting queries about proper procedure in the China mission. A commision was accordingly appointed to investigate Morales's question and give rulings upon them.[13]

Meantime the Dominican himself went on to Spain where he gathered together a group of volunteers for the missions. Among these, whom he qualified as the "cream of the Province" in a letter to Propaganda, was a 28-year old professor of theology, fray Domingo Fernández Navarrete, from San Gregorio, Valladolid. This man was later to distinguish himself as the foremost opponent of the Jesuit "mandarin-missionaries". The group reached Mexico in August 1646 where they waited for a ship to take them to Manila, but since no Galleon came in 1647 they were obliged to wait until April 1648 and thus were in Mexico for the climax of the clash between Palafox and the Jesuits, or what Navarrete described as "aquel torbellino y tormenta desecha contra el Sr. Obispo". Palafox, as Bishop of Puebla, had clashed with the local Jesuits in a dispute involving the payment of tithes, and following on this had forbidden them to preach or hear confessions until they had given him proof that they had the necessary faculties. The Jesuits, holding this was improper, refused

[13] British Museum, *Add.* MSS 16933, f. 248-9; 256; Navarrete, *Controversias,* 421; Santa Cruz, 403-36; Rosso, 112; Biermann, 66; St. Vincent, 60-4; *Histoire des differens entre les missionaires* (Nancy, 1735), 152-3.

to comply. Both parties then lost all sense of proportion and what began as a legalistic wrangle, a clash between episcopal authority and institutional privileges, rapidly degenerated into a personal issue with passion and vanity swaying those concerned. So that whoever was wrong in the beginning, it may be said that no one could be excused in the end. The Bishop held that all his troubles had come upon him as a result of his zeal and his defence of the decrees of Trent; and the Jesuits held that they were obliged to defend the privileges and reputation of their Order. Within a short time both sides were firmly entrenched in their respective positions and peppered each other with noisy threats and unseemly, but otherwise harmless, pronouncements of excommunication. In brief, the affair was conducted with a vigorous, pre-Reformation lack of inhibitions. Eventually however, both sides were exhorted from Rome to compose their differences and tempers, and the Jesuits were reprimanded by their Father General for their conduct in the matter. The quarrel was rather painfully patched up and Palafox recalled to Spain under something of a cloud.[14]

But the business was far from concluded. Indeed the rights and wrongs of the actual incident were almost unimportant in comparison with its consequences, for the dispute, the most scandalous in the history of the American church, raised echoes which were heard both in Europe and Asia and continued for more than a century after its originators were dead, so that, in time, Palafox became the symbol of hostility to the Society of Jesus. In the 18th century a proposal to canonise the Bishop was eagerly exploited by the Jesuits' enemies, while the Fathers, interpreting this as an indirect blow to their prestige, strenuously contested the project. Typical Jesuit misgiving on this score may be seen in the words of Father José Isla who was well

[14] NAVARRETE, *Tratados historicos, politicos, ethicos y religiosos de la Monarchia de China* (Madrid, 1676), 296; *Controversias*, 616, 625; NAVARRETE, *Travels*, ed. Cummins. For Father-General Carafa's rebuke to his Mexican subjects, first published in Mexico City as a *pliego suelto in* 1888, see GENARO GARCÍA, *Documentos inéditos o muy raros para la historia de México*, VII (1906), 90-4. There is a trenchant presentation of the Jesuit view of the dispute in F. J. ALEGRE, SJ., *Historia de la Provincia de la Compañía de Jesús de Nueva España*, edited E. J. Burrus, SJ., and F. Zubillaga, SJ., vol. III (Rome, 1959).

aware of the dangers of the time, was anxious to strike a blow for the Society against all comers ("ni pazes ni treguas con los enemigos de la Iglesia y de mi Religión") and was prepared to write in its defence "otra obrita que dejase muy atras la Historia de Fr. Gerundio"— a promise unfortunately not fulfilled. Father Isla denounced the attempt to raise Palafox to the altars, seeing it as made "para desacreditar á los Jesuitas por todos caminos, y hacer verosímiles las calumnias presentes, canonizando las pasadas", and he praised the Order —his own— "que avia hecho un gran servicio á la Yglesia en oponerse á la Canonización de un cierto siervo de Dios mas admirable, que imitable." In 1761 the matter looked serious enough and he feared that a certain Religious Order, discreetly unidentified, would already have its triunphant sermons for the beatification prepared and circulated. In 1778 the affair looked desperate: "Dadole ha que ha de ser canonizado cierto Obispo (cuio Catholicismo fue mui dudoso) aunque el Spiritu Santo no quiera: Si lo fuere sera dichosa la Puta que le parió". Obviously, therefore, few prospective *beati* can ever have found themselves with so many voluntary and devoted "Devil's Advocates" as did Palafox, and his unfortunate shade had a halo alternately thrust upon it, or swiftly plucked away again, according to the allegiance of whatever faction was predominant for the moment. The situation was not without its humorous side, especially, as Menéndez Pelayo noted, the spectacle of free-thinkers loudly begging Rome for a new Saint.[15]

[15] On the difficulty of writing objectively about Palafox, a figure constantly surrounded by passion and exaggeration, see JUSTO ZARAGOZA, "Influencia del Obispo Don Juan de Palafox y Mendoza, en los destinos de la América española", in *Revista contemporánea,* XXV (Jan-Feb 1880), 258; and V. RICO GONZÁLEZ, *Historiadores Mexicanos del Siglo XVIII* (México, 1949), 131-205. For background to the struggle over the beatification process compare R. HERR, *The Eighteenth-Century Revolution in Spain* (Princeton, 1958), and M. DANVILA, *Reinado de Carlos III* (Madrid, 1893), II, 255-70. MENÉNDEZ PELAYO *Heterodoxos,* V (Santander, 1947), 157, and Pastor, *Lives of the Popes,* XXXVIII (London, 1951), 136-7 see the projected canonisation as part of the plot to destroy the Jesuits; others attribute the failure of the proposed attempt to Jesuit machinations, thus implying that even after the suppression of the Society in 1773 they were still influential: see GENARO GARCÍA, *Don Juan de Palafox y Mendoza* (México, 1918), 294; and compare V. RODRÍGUEZ CASADO, "Iglesia y estado", in

Nothing of this could, of course, be foreseen in 1647 but nevertheless the Palafox affair made a profound impression upon the friars travelling with Morales to the Philippines. Domingo Navarrete, for one, never forgot those dramatic events and thirty years later, in another argument, when refuting Jesuit claims that it was "una de las cosas más agenas de la Compañía usar de medios violentos", he contented himself by answering that Palafox could witness how true or not that statement was.[16] Bishop Palafox, in the midst of his battle with the Mexican Jesuits, must have found congenial company in fray Juan Bautista Morales, for the friar was unique in that he had first-hand experience of the state of the China mission and could answer all Palafox's questions. He was, wrote the Bishop to Innocent X, "muy docto y muy zeloso propagador de la fé católica en la China, por cuya causa ha sido cruelísimamente azotado y perseguido, á ejemplo de los primitivos mártires". To these assets fray Juan added a hatred of the Jesuits that was little short of morbid. His view of the Fathers in general was plain and simple: to him they were "herejes i destruidores de la Iglesia de Dios" whom the Dominicans had

Estudios americanos, I, (1948), 31-33 and G. Decorme, SJ.; "P. Juan Francisco López, SJ. ... en Roma se dice que fue el, quien dio el golpe de muerte a la causa de Palafox." *(La obra de los Jesuitas mexicanos durante la época colonial* (México, 1941), I, 187). Another, earlier, attempt at beatifying Palafox was thwarted by the Jesuit General Tirso González who, apparently, circulated the Spanish bishops and also wrote to the King complaining of Palafox's relations with the Jansenists, "con quienes este Prelado mantuvo estrechas correspondencias, comunicándoles sus escritos contra la Compañía y recibiendo y alabando lo que los Herejes dibulgaban contra ella" (British Museum *Egerton MSS.*, 452, f. 17; 447, f. 123-29. For an even earlier linking of Palafox's possible canonisation and the suppression of the Society of Jesus, see the letter of Rodrigo Serrano y Trillo, of 30 October 1659, written upon hearing the news of the Bishop's death *(Biblioteca de autores españoles*, LXII, 95-110). This letter forecasts much of what was to happen later and warns those who then rejoiced at Palafox's death that they would rue it if he should come to be canonised; see in particular the passage beginning "¡Dios te libre de ser asolada, Compañía! ..."(p. 100). For Isla and Palafox, see J| F. de Isla, *Cartas inéditas*, ed. L. Fernández, SJ. (Madrid, 1957), 58, 151, 304, 305, 343, 361; and further references at *ib.* 32, 37, 40, 89, 307; 309; see also R. Esquerra Abadía, "Obras y papeles perdidos del Padre Isla", in *Estudios dedicados a Menéndez Pidal*, VII (i), (Madrid, 1957), 429-30.

[16] Navarrete, *Controversias*, 468.

been chosen to oppose: "solo emos quedado los Dominicos para pelear i tener controversias perpetuas con los Padres Jesuitas. Dios nos de paciencia i fortaleça para poder resistir contra lo potente del mundo. Noaquerido Dios, queio tengo poder en la iglesia, quesi lo tubiera ia estubieran acabados los Padres Jesuitas, y sientolo asi, porque endias de la vida no adeaver Paz en la yglesia de Dios, mientras estos benditos Padres estubieren de por medio".[17] More particularly Morales was now afraid that Jesuit intrigues in the papal nunciature in Madrid would prevent the arrival of the decree answering the doubts he had submitted to Rome. He had decided not to wait in Europe for this document but had entrusted the task of receiving it, and bringing it to the missions, to fray Vittorio Riccio, one of his Italian volunteers.[18]

Bishop Palafox and friar Morales, therefore, had plenty to discuss when they met. The Bishop showed the friar a treatise written by a namesake, Father Diego Morales, SJ., Rector of San José in Manila, defending the Society's policy in China. Fray Juan and his group of friar-missionaries carefully studied this work and, since it showed the sort of defence the Jesuits would probably put forward, copies were made of it. Friar Morales also wrote a reply to it which he left with Palafox and at the same time he wrote to Propaganda Fide warning them of the Jesuits' latest move.[19]

Domingo Navarrete, like fray Juan Bautista Morales, had a warm affection and admiration for Bishop Palafox and his reference to him as a "Prelado a todas luzes grande, y tantas, que jamás podrá ninguno obscurecerlas, ni aun disminuir sus resplandores; hizonos grandes cariños, y siempre se nos mostró padre amoroso", was considered fit to include in the eulogies printed in the 18th-century edition of Palafox's works.[20] Navarrete and Palafox had much in com-

[17] Morales to Ingoli from San Jacinto Hospice, Mexico, on 7 March 1647 (Archive of Propaganda Fide, Rome, *Scrit. rif. Con. Gen.*, v. 145, f. 311). Palafox, *Obras*, XI, 112; *Cartas*, 89.

[18] J. M. González, OP., *Un misionero diplomático: La vida del P. V. Riccio* (Madrid, 1955), 9.

[19] Arch. of Prop. Fide, Rome, *Scrit. rif. Cong. Gen.*, vol. 145, ff. 297, 311; British Museum, *Add. MSS.*, 16933 f. 260; Navarrete, *Controversias*, 79, 332, 468; Palafox, *Obras*, XI, 112; Bernard-Maitre, SJ., *Dossier*, 52, 77.

[20] Navarrete, *Tratados*, 295; and also *Controversias*, 468-9, 474, 616, 625.

mon. Both were learned, studious, zealous and possessed of tremendous energy —that Spanish energy which is as rare as it is excessive. Both were especially interested in educational problems: Palafox, for example, drew up admirable statutes for the University of Mexico, thus ending the confusion which in the past had hampered progress there; and it was probably Navarrete who, a few years later, persuaded the Philippine Dominicans to adopt those same statutes for their new University of Santo Tomás, in Manila.[21] Both men had firm ideas about just treatment for the Indians of America and the Philippines, and both considered the Indians to be people of high quality. Indeed Palafox was said to consider them superior to Europeans in intelligence. Later, when he was back once more in Spain, Palafox remembered them in his farewell Pastoral Letter to his former diocese of Puebla: "encomiendo a todos la blandura, y la piedad con los Indios... Son obedientes, mansos, humildes, utiles... si tienen imperfecciones, son hombres como nosotros, y las defienden menos y con menor malicia las platican entre sí. Tengo por señal de predestinado el amor a essos pobres..." And Navarrete for his part, still fresh from brooding over Las Casas's manuscripts in San Gregorio College in Valladolid, thought that "the Indians' only crime was to have been born"; claimed boldly that "en ocasiones me introduzco à Abogado de los Indios de Philipinas, como otros muchos hã hecho por los de la America", and he roundly criticised Spanish misdeeds in this respect. This zeal was later to cause him to be denounced by a Jesuit critic for confirming the allegations of Las Casas, whose misguided zeal "ha desacreditado en el Mundo a la Nación Española".[22]

Both Palafox and Navarrete wrote histories of China (1650 and 1676, respectively) which were also implicit criticisms of Spain, so

[21] C. Crivelli, SJ., article "Mexico" in *Catholic Encyclopedia*, X (New York, 1911). P. A. Santamaría, OP., *Documentos históricos de la universidad de Sto. Tomás de Manila*, (Manila, 1937), 81-3.

[22] Palafox, *Obras*, III (i), 384; X, 518-9; Navarrete, *Tratados*, "Advertencias", no pag. On Palafox's devotion to the Indians see M. Cuevas, SJ., *Historia de la Iglesia en México*, III (Tlalpan, 1924), 285 and M. M. Martínez, OP., "El Obispo Palafox y el indio mexicano" in *Revista de Indias*, XX (Ap-jun, 1960), 83-94. For Jesuit criticism of Navarrete's attitude towards the Indians see [J. Cortés Osorio, SJ.] *Reparos historiales* (Pamplona, 1677), 22.

that it is little wonder that the Spanish Jesuits, looking for reasons to denounce both authors, should have listed lack of patriotism among their faults.[23] Navarrete spent twelve years in China altogether, but Palafox was never there, as his critics used to stress in order to discredit him: "I have taken nothing from Palafox. A man who wrote the History of China in Mexico on information sent him from the Philippines, could not be a sound guide to follow."[24] The histories by Palafox and Navarrete are among the earliest contributions to the 18th-century *rêve chinois* and are the two most considerable examples of this literary cult to be found in Spanish. Both works enjoyed a certain reputation outside Spain: Palafox's history, for instance, served Elkanhah Settle for his play on China, and Navarrete's book, which was even more widely translated, was quoted by Voltaire and Quesnay and provided reading matter for Leibnitz.[25]

Palafox was more critical in his appreciation of China but nevertheless he, like Navarrete, considered that the "Middle Kingdom",

[23] Palafox, *Obras*, XI, 323, 326; [Cortés Osorio] *Reparos*, e.g. 15, 16, 22, 44, 46. But such accusations were common for "después de Mariana, hasta nuestro siglo, apenas ha habido un español ejemplar a quien los necios que nunca hicieron nada no hayan acusado, entre aplausos de la plebe, de extranjerización" (G. Marañón, *Las ideas biológicas del P. Feijoo* (Madrid, 1934), 264).

[24] P. J. D'Orleans, SJ., *History of the Two Tartar Conquerors of China* (London, Hakluyt Society, 1854), iv; a similar criticism is made, clearly directed at Palafox, in the preface of F. de Rougemont, SJ., *Relaçam do estado politico e espirital do Imperio da China* (Lisbon, 1672). Basically, this stricture might have been levelled against Father Du Halde's monumental work. But, in fact, Palafox was not entirely dependent on letters for his information about China for he could, and did, question travelling missionaries, such as Morales, with direct knowledge of China or the Chinese. Doubtless, also, Palafox, with his great intellectual curiosity and interest in China, would have interrogated some of the Chinese who had reached Mexico and with whom he would easily have had contact (R. Konetzke, *Colección de documentos para la historia de la formación social de Hispanoamérica, 1493-1810* (Madrid, 1958), II (i), 291, and *Thomas Gage's Travels*, edited J. E. S. Thompson (Norman, 1958), 68).

[25] G. Langbaine, *Momus Triumphans* (London, 1688), 24; Ch'ien Chung-shu, "China in the English Literature of the Seventeenth Century" in the *Quarterly Bulletin of Chinese Bibliography* (English edition), New Series, I (1940), 376-79; and J. S. Cummins, "Fray Domingo Navarrete: a Source for Quesnay", in *Bulletin of Hispanic Studies*, XXXVI (1959), 37-50.

with its admirable system of government and high moral standards, was a model for Europe and Christendom. He pointedly warned those who believed themselves superior to the Chinese to look more closely and they would see that, on the contrary, they had much to learn from them. Navarrete and he agreed that all history has lessons to teach; but for them the history of China was more than a mere lesson: it was a veritable sermon. Both writers praised the benevolent despots of China who were depicted as excelling the kings of Europe in their care for their people. Palafox, having praised the Emperor of China and his Ministers, added, "¡Y estos son los barbaros de la Asia. Assi fueran en muchas cosas los politicos de Europa!" Navarrete filled in the detail: there were, he declared, Emperors in China who were fit to be likened to St. Ferdinand himself, to St. Louis, or "el Papa más santo del mundo". It was a striking comparison for a rigorous Spanish friar to make, but apparently not only Emperors and their councillors were remarkable for their devotion to the welfare of the Empire, for even the lowliest servants of the "Dragon Throne" showed courage in speaking up for the common good whenever it was necessary, sometimes daring to make criticisms that in Europe "would not be permitted to a royal confessor or a preacher in the Chapel Royal." Navarrete, clearly, had not the slightest doubt that the Chinese, idolaters though they might be, were become the "Doctors of the Faithful".

Just before Palafox wrote his history the Chinese Empire had been conquered by the Tartars and this event was next shown to have suitable lessons for those Spaniards who were keen enough to see them because now China, too, could be said to have its King Roderick and its Cid Campeador. Both Palafox and Navarrete were troubled by the decline of their own country and both were anxious to use China in order to open the eyes of those who had them closed. Thus Palafox, describing the fall of the Ming Empire, added with meaning, "no murió el Imperio de incurable, sino de no curado". There was still time to help Spain: "no hay más diferencia del buen Gobernador al que no lo es, que ver el uno las desdichas antes que lleguen, y el otro después de sucedidas". Palafox repeatedly distinguishes between the Chinese and their new Tartar masters; and the distinction is made not in order to criticise the latter, but to praise them even more than the Chinese themselves. Admittedly they were invaders, but at least they tried to justify their action and showed "más escrupulos de los que se usan a veces alla en nuestra Europa; y con todo esto se llaman estos allá Barbaros y aquellos se llaman Politicos". Thus the very Tartars were presented as a source of shame to Europe, for their unity of action before the task of conquering China was very different from the situation in Europe where the Christian Kings were so distrustful of each other that they could not unite to fight the Turk: "No puedo leer estas cosas", admitted Palafox, "y ver lo que pasa entre los Europeos y los Christianos . . .¡y que estos son Christianos, y los Tártaros, Idolatras, y que estos son politicos y los Tártaros son Barbaros! O, ¡confunda Dios tan barbaras politicas!"[26] The Tartars, too, were quick to act for the welfare of the community where necessary. Palafox gives an example and adds, "estos si que son socorros de la Tartaria, y no los socorros de España, que se pierden los gastos, y no se logran los intentos; porque de ordinario llegan pocos días despues que se perdío la plaza, o la facción, que había de ser socorrida. Perdoneme mi Patria, que el mucho amor que la tengo. . . me obliga á que no disimule este sentimiento". Navarrete, for his part, was fascinated by everything that he saw in China from tailors' needles to the Great Wall; everything there seemed to him to be better than in Spain, and Chinese ingenuity seemed to know no bounds: "con quatro gotas de agua, y otros tantos palos hazen un molino de papel, y otros instrumentos, y por acá es necessario un mundo de cosas".[27]

The moral qualities of the Tartars were equally impressive. By some coincidence they seemed to have nearly all the virtues that the ascetic treatise-writers recommend. They were not hypocrites for example: "No se usa entre ellos el besar las manos, que desean ver cortadas. . . Sin duda que se ha pasado de Europa á la Tartaria el Rey Saturno y sus tiempos". Palafox's Tartars were similar to the long-dead Castilians held up for admirations and imitation by Quevedo, for, among other things, they preferred not sweet but martial music and never drank to excess, even though misguided courtesy

[26] Palafox, *Obras*, X, 34, 286, 287, 291, 293, 319, 337, 405-6, 414-17.
[27] Palafox, *ib.*, 368; Navarrete, *Tratados*, 340.

might seem sometimes to demand it: "más se precia, dicen, entre nosotros la salud, el juicio, y la razón que la cortesía." Although they were hearty trenchermen they were praiseworthy even at table for not even there did they cease to be philosophers. "¿Qué hicieran", wondered Palafox, "si demás de la ley natural de la razón, tuvieran otras Leyes divinas, y humanas que les prohibieran la embriaguez, como las tienen los Catholicos?" Half a century later this disturbing problem of natural goodness in non-Christian peoples, and the so-called "argument from the Chinese", were to cause much heart-burning among the theologians and to bring delight to the Deists whose theories the people of the "Middle Flowery Kingdom" seemed to be proving. Palafox and Navarrete, however, were unaware of this and felt scarcely any to moderate their enthusiasm for this extraordinary country, itself another New World, where even the women were exemplary and as modest as enclosed nuns. Only rarely does Navarrete limit Chinese virtuosity and virtues to "quanto ay de tejas abaxo."[28]

But, naturally, what interested the Bishop above all else was the state of the missions in China. It was imperative that the Chinese should be properly instructed in the Catholic faith, a task which might be presumed to be the easier in a people apparently inclined by nature towards virtue. All the more lamentable, therefore, was what Palafox believed to be, and denounced as, the false step taken by the Jesuit missionaries. As a result of his meeting with friar Morales, Palafox found himself in a position to intervene in the controversy and, moreover, considered it his duty to do so since literature discussing the subject was reaching Mexico and giving rise to talk. Palafox's opportunity came after 13th September 1646 when friar Vittorio Riccio arrived in Mexico from Rome, bringing with him the papal decree answering the questions submitted by Morales. This decree, issued by Innocent X, was addressed to "each and every one of the missionaries of whatsoever

[28] Navarrete, *ib.*, 32, 90; Palafox, *Obras*, X, 330, 441; 432-34. Palafox's view of China is much less gloomy than his view of Europe for which see J. M. Jover "El sentimiento de Europa en la España del xvii", *Hispania*, IX (1949), 276-8.

Order", and to this were added the pointed words, "including the Society of Jesus."[29] The decree contented itself with answering Morales's questions, *inaudita altera parte,* and as such it constituted a triumph for the Mendicants since it condemned the Chinese Rites as they had been described by the friars and as admitted by the Jesuit, Roboredo.[30] By implication, therefore, it also condemned the Jesuits who countenanced the practice of such Rites by their Chinese converts. On closer examination, however, Morales saw with alarm that the decree had not been passed by the Consejo de Indias and was consequently liable to be rejected on a technicality at the instigation of the Jesuits. Morales lived in perpetual fear that the Fathers would find an "escapatoria" through which to ignore the papal ruling and he now turned to Palafox for help and advice. This was a natural move for him to make since Palafox ("gran varon, i de gran virtud i celo Apostolico . . .me ha hecho muchos fabores"), besides being the local Bishop and an experienced administrator, was a personal friend. As a result of Morale's appeal Palafox addressed a letter to Philip IV which shows careful thought and acute insight into the nature of the problems involved in the dispute.[31]

[29] The phrase "etiam Societatis Iesu" has no special value and is no more than a Curia cliché, according to A. BROU, SJ., *Les Jésuites de la Légende* (Paris, 1906-7), II, 55; but not all Jesuit writers agree with this: see for instance, C. DE ROCHEMONTEIX, SJ., *Les Jésuites et la Nouvelle-France au XVII siècle* (Paris, 1895), I, xliii.

[30] ". . . la pratique des Jésuites de Chine, telle qu'elle avait été avouée par Roboredo, ne pouvait être que condamnée. . ." (BERNARD-MAITRE, SJ., *Dossier,* 53).

[31] Morales's fears that the Jesuits would resist this and other decrees were fully justified, for the Jesuits held tenaciously to their opinions for another century, and the Chinese Rites were "assailed with equal unsuccess by one pope after another" *(Encyclopaedia Britannica,* 11th editn., s. v. "Jesuits"); for although the Rites Controversy shows that, contrary to popular belief, the Holy See is not always ruled by Jesuits, "Alas, it also shows that the Holy See has not always been implicitly obeyed by Jesuits" (J. RICKABY, SJ., "Clement XI and the Chinese Rites", in *The Month,* LXXIII, 76), and "Certains pensent même que Rome eut l'impression que la Compaigne 'ne savait plus obéir'." (ABBÉ E. JARRY, in *Histoire de L'Église,* by E. Préclin and E. Jarry, XIX (París, 1955), 192.

On behalf of the friars Palafox called upon his Catholic Majesty to intervene in a struggle which was daily worsening and he expressed surprise that the King should not have heard more of this important matter, especially since the controversy was already some twelve years old and he himself had known of it for three or four years. It was, he declared, the King's duty to know of the controversy, for the Faith was part of his royal heritage and many of the missionaries were his subjects; furthermore, if the truth were not properly taught it would be a stain upon the Catholic Monarchy, for the heretics of Europe could then simultaneously accuse the Church of spreading error and Spain of aiding and abetting it. They were the sort of arguments likely to impress a Spanish King. And Palafox, even at that early date, seems to have realised the importance of this controversy which he rightly qualified as "una de las mayores controuersias en materia de fe, y de conuersion de Almas, que puede ofrecerse en la Iglessia de Dios". He reported to the King that the Jesuits were said to be keeping back the doctrine of the Crucifixion from the Chinese, and were preaching only Christ Glorified, because the people found "dureça en adorar a un hombre crucificado".[32] He also alleged that they were holding back the teaching of the "Precepts of the Church" such as injunctions to attend Mass regularly, to abstain from meat weekly and to confess and receive annually. These, however, were minor points. Much worse, according to the Bishop's informants, the Jesuits were permitting their converts to perform Rites "contrarias a la pureza de

[32] Of course, the Jesuits could not have kept back the preaching of the Crucifixion completely, but they tended to relegate it to the later period of religious instruction since they believed that it offended Chinese susceptibilities; in the early years of the mission they also kept the Cross out of sight in their churches lest it be mocked by Chinese pagans. This caution naturally gave a bad impression to the friars (GUTIÉRREZ, SJ., 554-58, 565; *Arch. Fran. Histor.* VIII, 582 ff.) and it was one of the points, raised by Morales in Rome, to which the answer was given in the decree of 1645: "Censerunt [the Holy Office Qualifiers], Nulla prudentia, aut praetextu differendam esse Doctrinam Passionis Christi post Baptismum, sed omninò praemittendam... Censerunt etiam conveniens esse, ut in Ecclesijs Imagines habeantur Christi Crucifixi, & ideò curandum, ut quoad opportunè fieri potest exponantur" (NAVARRETE, *Tratados*, 458). The subject is discussed in Biermann, 200 ff.

la fe christiana, que no admite temperamentos en su verdad y misterios". A synopsis of the controversies up to that date then followed, together with a warning that the struggle between the two opposing parties was worsening, and that knowledge of it was spreading where it ought not to, with the consequent risk of bad example and precedent.

Palafox then goes on to note that so far there has been no intervention in the quarrel by either the King or his ministers, although action by them seemed urgently needed. Then follow a number of points to support this opinion. The Bishop foresaw another difficulty, and warned that nationalism would widen the division between the missionaries, for the China Jesuits traditionally paid allegiance to Portugal, which had just (1640) broken free from Spanish domination, whereas the friars were Spaniards. False patriotism would thus add to a pastoral and technical difference: "conque vendra a crecer la disputa Dogmatica sobre la oppossicion natural de las Naciones y de las voluntades, y a hacerse mas implacable."

Finally, seizing a golden opportunity to talk of matters near his heart, and nearer home, Palafox concluded his report by pointing out that it was dangerous, in his opinion, to leave one religious Order alone in a mission-field. Just as the Jesuits, or so he believed, were guilty of unorthodox behaviour in China so, too, might be those friars who had now been alone in New Mexico for some fifty years, without the benefit of a reproving episcopal eye. It had, he said, been assumed for long enough that all was well in China and only the comparatively recent reports of the friars had drawn attention to the state of affairs there; might not the same be true of New Mexico and Sinaloa, he asked. For Palafox, China was more than a local tragedy; it was a terrifying portent and he, for his part, never for a moment forgot that he was both a secular priest and Bishop.

In the Rites Controversy, Palafox sided entirely with the Mendicants. He is, consequently, open to accusations of rashness and of allowing himself, metaphorically speaking a blind-man in these matters, to be guided by those who were themselves at best but one-eyed; of listening too readily and trusting too willingly to allegations based on expediency rather than experience; of plying his indefatigable pen too glibly in a cause which he never understood but was satisfied to twist to his own purposes. Now, he was not impartial, but he could also have been accused of failing in his duty if he had ignored the appeals of Morales, and turned a deaf ear to apparently unassailable evidence, proffered *in verbo sacerdotis* by an eye-witness of the China scene. Morales must have been convincing, for, it should be remembered, he had managed to secure himself a favourable hearing in Rome itself and had impressed two Popes, apart from the fact that he could point to Father Roboredo's work which apparently corroborated much of his evidence.

Palafox agreed with the friars, and incidentally with Propaganda Fide itself, that nothing must be done that would interfere with non-religious custom among the new peoples encountered by the missionaries. But the great problem lay in deciding what was religious rite and what was merely civic ceremony. And this problem was all the more complex in China where, often enough, even the Chinese themselves did not seem to know the distinction. Moreover, the Jesuit missionaries there were divided among themselves on these issues and their differences and hesitations reinforced the doubts of the less adventurous friars. Even Father Longobardi, chosen as superior of the Jesuits' China mission by Matteo Ricci himself, had dissented from Ricci on some points and had written a treatise setting forth his reasons for so doing, a treatise which, in the interests of unity in the Jesuit ranks, was later burnt by order of the Vice-Provincial in a sort of domestic *auto-da-fe*. And the famous João Rodriguez, whose linguistic ability earned him the nickname of "the Interpreter", was another Jesuit who opposed some of Father Matteo Ricci's theories. These divergences of opinion could only increase the friars' doubts about the propriety of Jesuit methods in China. Yet a speedy resolution of all these doubts seemed particularly necessary in those early years when it was widely, but wrongly, believed that the Tartar invasion of China would make the work of conversion the easier. Fray Juan Bautista, for instance, informed Propaganda Fide that the Emperor of China had been slain, that there were no less than three claimants to the

"Dragon Throne", that the Empire was in a state of chaos and, all in all, "buena ocasion es esta para los Pescadores de Christo quando el Rio anda rebuelto."[33]

Fray Domingo Navarrete learnt much from Palafox. In particular, one of the Bishop's comments is to be found repeated by him: both noted that the first Jesuit missionaries in China had not been persecuted whereas the first friars were. To their somewhat pessimistic minds this suggested that the Jesuits must have over-compromised, since persecution must, they held, always attend the preaching of the Faith in the beginning. Persecution, it was thought, might well follow the promulgation of the papal decree that Morales was taking out to China; but if that happened it was to be welcomed, "que será en su genero menor daño que dexarles de dar pura e incontaminada la Leche y sustento de la Dotrina Euangelica." Palafox used this curious argument later to the Pope: China seemed quiet and peaceful, but "me ha parecido siempre esta profunda paz, que hay entre christianos y gentiles, muy sospechosa y triste, aunque a ellos les parezca muy segura y dulce." In keeping with this logic he found consolation in the friar-missionaries' sufferings which he read as evidence of their irreproachable orthodoxy: "senti en mi un gran consuelo, y concebi una grande esperanza del establecimiento de la fe en aquella tierra." Palafox's attitude shows that the tendency to equate persecution with progress (a derivation of the classical "Blood of the martyrs is the seed of the Church" approach), and to suspect that accommodation led to apathy, was not exclusive to the friars.[34]

[33] PALAFOX, *Obras*, X, 392, 442. On the fate of Longobardi's offending thesis see BERNARD-MAITRE, SJ. *(Dossier*, 47) and for Rodriguez see LOUIS PFISTER, SJ., who in his *Notices biographiques et bibliographiques*, II (Shangai, 1934), 23*, describes him as an "adversaire irréductible de l'usage introduit par le P. Ricci". The difference here was mainly about the Term question and the friars did not fail to notice this disagreement among the Fathers (S. VINCENT, *Vie de Morales*, 55). Morales to Ingoli, from Mexico, 21 November 1646, Archive of Prop. Fide, Rome, *Scrit. rif. Cong. Gen.* vol. 145, fol. 300.

[34] For an ironical Jesuit view of two friars who arrived in Peking in 1637 thirsting for martyrdom, see Father Schall's letter in *Arch Fran. Hist.*, IV, 53-4; VIII, 588-89. On the other hand the European friars had a magnificent record

Palafox never forgot China, nor did he trust the Jesuits there with what appeared to him to be their Jacob-like voices and their Esau-like hands. Despite their cleverness, he concluded that they had gravely misjudged the situation; the Fishermen had themselves been caught: "non ad fidei regulas Magistri Neophytos, sed Neophyty ad Idolatriae partes, & nefarios ritus & cultum Magistros alliciant, attrahant, & deducant, ita ut non a Piscatore piscis, sed a pisce Piscator capi videatur."[35] Even after his return to Spain from Mexico he kept in touch with the friar-missionaries in China and sent them alms.[36] Finally, in 1657, "hallándome yo ya cerca de los 60 años de edad, y cada dia aguardando la muerte", he left instructions with his executor about the disposition of his papers concerning the China mission, which still troubled him, for "todavia queda por hacer lo más dificultoso, que es dar a entender a los Neofitos de aquellas tan dilatadas conversiones lo contrario de lo que les han enseñado sus Maestros [*the Jesuits*], y que esso lo hagan los mismos Maestros que lo enseñaron, pues de otra manera no bastaran." The papers he left were, he believed, "importantísimos para en caso que en algun Concilio se tratase de estos puntos, que son tan universales al bien de las almas y su conversion: y también para que se vea hasta donde se llega a opinar en estas materias, pues aunque al entrar la fe en cualquier Provincia puede haber algún género de temperamentos, pero no tales ni de esta calidad."[37]

So far as I know, the full text of this letter of Bishop Palafox to Philip IV on behalf of Juan Bautista Morales has not been published previously. Yet it is of interest because it shows the unity of thought and collaboration between the Bishop and friars. The document also shows Palafox's concern over what seemed to him the greatest practical problem of all, namely, how persuade the Jesuits' Chinese converts ultimately to accept Catholicism without the adjustments and privileges that the Fathers were permitting

of bravery and not a single one of them apostatised either in China or Japan even in face of torture and death (BOXER, *op. cit.*, 447). PALAFOX, *Cartas*, 91.

[35] PALAFOX, *Obras*, XI, 113, 185.

[36] E. g. the letter of Fray Buenaventura Ibáñez, OFM, from Amoy in September 1654 refers to such help *(Sinica Franciscana*, III (1936), 37).

[37] PALAFOX, *Obras*, XI, 556, 561-2; *Cartas*, 339, 345.

them. Like the Mendicants, Palafox saw the urgent need to turn the neophytes into adult Catholics who could nourish their new-found faith on the crusty bread of ecclesiastic legislation; like the Mendicants he too feared lest under Jesuit nurturing these new Christians would never pass beyond the stage of spiritual infancy and a diet of 'pap and milk'. Their critics in general feared that those Fathers who tolerated the Chinese Rites and approved the novelties of the China mission, were dazzled, perhaps even hypnotised, by their own brilliance and were, consequently, being over-optimistic about the outcome. To their critics, these Jesuits seemed to believe that all such problems would be solved if only the China mission-field could be kept as a Jesuit monopoly and free from friars. No one can doubt the Jesuits' sincerity and breadth of vision, but, as a modern Jesuit writer shows, some of the fears entertained by the more hesitant Jesuits, by the friars, and by Palafox, were not unreasonable: "Los jesuítas corrían, a no dudarlo, peligro de quedar indefinidamente estancados en el estado inicial e 'infantil'..."[38]

There was also the danger that one day the church established in China by the "mandarin-missionaries" would fall into schism rather than yield up the privileges conceded to it in those early years, and Palafox, with his typically Spanish sensitivity towards "new Christians", realised this keenly. And if the Jesuits were sincere, their critics were not less so. Again and again Palafox shows that he genuinely feared for the salvation of the Chinese converts who were practicing the Rites, this was the "punto tan graue, y en que consiste la saluación de aquellas Almas, y aun la de sus Operarios y Maestros". It was for these reasons, as well as because of his suspicion and hostility towards the Jesuits, that Palafox felt impelled to enter the Rites Controversy on the friars' behalf.

The letter to the King is dated 15th August 1646. This however must be an error because if it were correct it would mean that the letter had been written by the Bishop within three days of the main group of friars' arrival in Mexico and some weeks before the arrival of friar Vittorio Riccio with the papal decree. But this

[38] Gutiérrez, 570.

is impossible for Riccio's arrival is referred to within the body of the letter and Riccio himself states elsewhere that he arrived in Mexico in September 1646.[39] Moreover, the whole point of Palafox's letter turns upon the decree which Riccio brought with him in September, which Palafox has been shown and which he now wants to strengthen with the backing of the Consejo de Indias. The letter may, therefore, have been written in August 1647. This supposition is supported by the reference within the letter itself to "el año passado de 1646" and by the superscription of the Consejo clerks in Madrid which is dated November 1647. Had the letter been written in 1646 this last date suggests that it had taken sixteen months to reach the Consejo. This, though of course not impossible, is unlikely. If the letter was, in fact, written in August 1647 it suggests that Palafox may have stayed for some time with the Dominicans in their priory of San Jacinto when he was thought to be in the mountains taking refuge from the Mexican Jesuits, preferring the "scorpions and serpents", as he rather dramatically puts it, to the Fathers in his diocese.[40]

39 "Con buonissima salute giunsi in qa. nuova Spagna li 13 de 7bre dell' Anno 46 doppo due mesi di ottima navigne." (Riccio to Propaganda Fide, Arch. Prop. Fide, *Scrit. rif. Con. Gen.* vol. 145, f. 310). He had sailed from Cadiz on 12 July 1646 in the fleet under Lorenzo Fernández de Córdoba (H. AND P. CHAUNU, *Séville et l'Atlantique (1504-1650)*, V, (Paris, 1956), 460.

40 PALAFOX, *Obras*, XI, 70. Other copies of this letter are recorded as being in the Archive of Propaganda Fide, Rome, at S. A. 193, f. 35-42, and in the Biblioteca Nacional, Madrid, Sec. de MSS., vol. 8512 (antig. X-157) but I was unable to find them there myself. The Madrid copy was apparently dated 1647.

PALAFOX INFORMS THE KING OF THE CHINESE RITES CONTROVERSY

(*Source* - Archivo General de Indias (Seville): Leg. *Filipinas 86*).

†

Angeles. A su Magd. 1646

El S.Obpo. Vissitador. 15 Agto.

S(eñor) s(obre) la reduzion de la China, y modo de enseñanca de los religiosos de Sto. Dgo,frco,y la conpa. con (illegible) de fray Juan de Morales y un quaderno impresso.

Para el fiscal.

en 24 de mco 1645 se concedieron al dho fray Juo de Morales dominico 24 Religiosos de su orden y tres legos a costa de su Mgd.para filipinas; de donde el abia venido a bolber con ellos por su vicario general cuyo expediente viene aqui y no se halla otra raçon.

El Obispo Vissitor.refiere a VMd. la mayor. controuersia que en materias de fe se ha ofrecido ni puede ofrecer en la Iglessia de Dios en las Prouincias de China entre los Religiosos Dominicos y Franciscos de vna parte, y los de la Compañia de la otra, en razon de la forma de enseñar y reducir los nueumte. christianos lo que se les oculta de la fe, y lo que mezclan esta con las Idolatrias de los Gentiles; y lo que en el punto destas controuersias se ha de seruir de ordenar V.M. ——

En el consso. el 31 de 8tre. de 1647.

reconozcase si por los religiosos de sto domingo se presentaron en el Co.algunos breues o decretos de la congregacion de Propaganda y si lo ay o razon que se allare cerca desto se junte con los papeles que se citan en esta carta y ella y todos se lleven al Sr. fiscal para que lo vea con todo lo que remite el Sr. don Juo. tocante a este punto.

†

El fiscal — dice que faltan de traher con estos papeles una apologia que el Sr don Juan de Palafox dice en esta carta que remite — pide se busque en la Secretaría y se le trayga para responder. Madrid. 5 de nobiembre de 1647. No hay en la secra. mas de lo que se ha traydo.

†

Señor, Aunque en todas materias es justo que se halle V.M. informado de las que fuesen graues, y dignas de su noticia y de su Rl Consejo, quando influyen en el estado ecclessiastico, o politico, y en Prouincias tan remotas; pero la que represento a V.M. en esta carta, es de las mayores que se pueden ofrecer a su sto. y christiano zelo, y a la atencion con que está a la conuersion de las Almas, assi destas Prouincias como de todas las demas de su Monarchia; y aunque ha tres, o quatro años que ha llegado a mi noticia y conssideracion, he suspendido el auisarla a V.M. juzgando que por otra parte la podria tener entendida, hasta aora que por los accidentes que han sobrevenido me consta de lo contrario, y assi veo que se puede ganar mucho en darla a V.M. y por el contrario perderse, sino se le diesse, y por lo menos no preuenirse lo que conuenga a la caussa publica, y seruicio de Dios, y de V.M. y mas solicitado de los mismos que son partes formales en esto.

En las Prouincias de China a cuyas Missiones/es fuerça que se vaya aora por la Corona de Castilla por las Religiones de Santo Domingo, y S.Francisco despues de la rebelion de Portugal en quanto a los Missioneros que embia V.M. a ellas, y van desde Philipinas haciendo su viaje aesta Nueua España, y de aqui a aquellas Islas, se ha ofrecido de doze años a esta parte poco mas o menos, vna de las mayores controuersias en materia de fe, y de conuersion de Almas, que puede ofrecerse en la Iglessia de Dios, y ha sido entre los Religiosos Dominicos, y Franciscos y vna parte, y los de la Compañia de Jesus de la otra.

Porque hauiendo llegado las dos Religiones de San Francisco y Sto Domingo a China cinquenta años despues que la de la Compañia de Jesus, hallaron segun affirman, que en la Dotrina conque edifican, enseñan e instruyen a aquellos nueuamente christianos chinos, o neofitos los Padres de la Compañia, se les dexaban de manifestar por ellos los misterios dolorosos de Christo Nño.Sor. y su Imagen de Christo Crucificado: Las cargas y obligaciones del derecho possitiuo y obligacion de ayunar: oyr Missa los dias de fiesta, conffessar y comulgar cada año vna vez; y la abstinencia de comer carne en los dias determinados porla Iglessia sin limitacion alguna, como se ha hecho enestas Indias Occidentales, permitiendoles ritos/de Gentilidad a sus Christianos, y asistir a sus Templos e Idolatrias con los Gentiles, y otras cossas deste genero, contrarias a la pureza dela fe christiana, que no admite temperamentos en su verd. y misterios, dando aesto color conque no se retardassen los Gentiles, por la obseruancia destos preceptos y conocimiento destas verdades, de entrar en nra Sagrada Religion. Hallando dureça en adorar a un hombre crucificado, y padecer en ella la penalidad de mas preceptos que los del Decalogo, y assi noseles mostraban las Imagenes de Chisto bien nro enla Cruz, ni las tenian en las Iglessias, y les permitian y toleraban los ritos Gentilicos, por via de culto politico, y les aligeraban dela carga del derecho possitiuo, en la obseruancia de ayunos, fiestas, y abstinencia, como V.M. verá en las Apologias que vltimamente de Philipinas han remitido aestas Prouincias, que son las que me han puesto en mayor cuydado desta materia, por verla tan publicamente disputada, no se halle oculta solo a V.M. ni asu Supremo Consejo, quando aqui corren estas Apologias, y hablandose en algunas dellas con V.M.

Uiendo esto las Religiones referidas Dominicos y Franciscos, escriuieron vn papel en Philipinas probando que todo esto era contra lo establecido por/la Iglessia, Sagrados Canones, Decretos Apostolicos y Conciliares, y la sana, y segura Dotrina de los Santos y que ni aquellas Almas quedaban bien instruydas, ni eran bien gouernadas, y enseñadas, y que sin el expresso conocimiento deste misterio, y con el culto exterior que hacian a los Idolos, y sin obseruancia del derecho possitiuo, limitado a lo mas a loque obseruan los Indios enla America, no podian saluarse aquellos Gentiles, y esta Apologia corrio tanbien en las Islas y yo tengo copia della con los demas papeles.

Por parte dela Compañia a todo esto se respondio en las mismas Philipinas por el Padre Bartholome Roboredo satisfaciendo con razones y con authoridades al papel destas dos Religiones, negando algunas cossas en el hecho, y conffessando otras, y probando que se podia hazer lo que obraba, de la manera, y por las razones que referian en esta respuesta; Pero deste papel replicaron los Dominicos, manifestando su nombre el Prouincial del Rosario de aquella Prouincia fr Domingo Goncalez, Varon muy docto y Mistico, censurando solo aquello que conffessaban los Padres de la Compañía, que en sustancia es lo referido arriba, y probando con muchos lugares la contraria Dotrina, y affirmando que solo defendian las Religiones este punto por el remedio de aquella Chistiandad. En respuesta de lo qual por los/Padres de la Compañia se escriuio vn tratado muy largo fundando lo contrario desto, que yo copio, hauiendomelo dado para ello el Padre Juan de Bueras Prouincial de la Compañia de Jesus, y es el Autor el Pe. Diego de Morales, Rector del Collegio de San Joseph de Manila, y es harto erudito discurso en quanto he leydo aunque no califico, hasta lo que conuence en el punto principal desta question, y mas con las addiciones quele ha hecho deste libro fr Juan Bautista de Morales, como varon tan experimentado, zelosso, y docto, y que ha visto, y tocado con las manos lo practico de la conuersion de China y parece que tiene grande fuerca en sus discursos, y quese acercan en todo a lo determinado por la santa Sede, contra lo enseñado, y defendido por la Compañia.

Los Padres Dominicos viendo esto, y que publicamente se deffendia opinion tan nueua en materia de conuersiones, y misterios de fe, y que hauiendo intentado quese deçidiesse en Philipinas, se hauia remitido a Roma, embiaron porla India Oriental al Padre fr Juan Bautista de Morales Religioso muy practico y zeloso (como se conoce en la determinacion) y quese hauia ocupado enla conuersion de China muchos años, y muy erudito en/aquella lengua, y que hauia padecido por la fe en los Tribunales de los Gentiles, y disputado esta question conlos Padres de la Compañía, y trabesando este Religiosso toda la Persia, Babilonia, y el Asia, vino allegar a Venecia, y de alli passo a Roma, donde reduciendo a puntos, y dudas materia tan graue, porque no dixessen los Padres de la Compañia que les acussaban sus conuersiones, pidio a la Beatitud. de Urbano VIII. declaracion destas dudas, y proposiciones; el Pontifize (segun este Religioso me ha referido) lo remitio ala Congregacion de Inquission. y despues se passó ala de Propaganda fide, y hauiendose nombrado Calificadores sobre estos puntos, declararon en fabor de lo que las Religiones de S.Franco.y Sto Domingo enseñan y defienden, en casi todas las dudas, y la Junta dio Decreto, para que assi se enseñasse, y su Santidad lo confirmo, y porque el tiempo le instaba para boluer a España a pedir Religiossos a V.Md. en su Consejo delas Indias, dexando vno desus compañeros en Roma, a sacar los despachos, hubo de salir de aquella corte sin ellos, y me ha dexado la calificacion de las personas nombradas, y los otros dos Decretos, dize quelos aguarda, porq. no tubo tiempo, para sacar los despachos dela resolucion.

Boluio este Religioso fr. Juan Bautista, Dominico/de Roma a España, y pidio sujetos en el Consejo para Philippinas el año pasado de 46, y V.Md. muy justamente selos ha dado, porque la Prouincia del Santo Rosario en aquel Reyno, es el consuelo de todos los buenos, y sumamente obseruante y reformada, y de alli acuden con grande espiritu a las Missiones de China; y hauiendo llegado conla Armada de Barlobento General D.Juan de Urbina, llegó poco despues la flota General Don Lorenço de Cordoba, y en ella Religiosso que trae las declaraciones de Roma.

Hauiendo reciuidolas el Pe.fr Juan Bautista Vicario genl. destas Missiones, hallo que nose hauian pressentado en el Consejo, con lo qual le parecio darme quenta de todo como a Consejero de V. Md. para que yo se la diesse, dexandome originales las dhas declaraciones, para que yo las remitiesse a V.M. con el memorial inclusso, que con esta tanbien remito.

Entre tanto que este Religiosso hiço su viaje, y saco estas declaraciones de Roma, y ha trydo estos operarios, ha ydo creciendo en Philipinas, esta controuersia, y aunque hauia ya llegado a estas Prouincias, y yo tenia noticia della, y hecho vn bolumen de los papeles de vna parte, y otra/por ser materia graue, ydigna dela attencion de vn Prelado y Ministro, y lo remitiré conla flota a V.Md. porsi huuiere de tratarse della; Pero agora ha venido otra Apologia de aquellas Prouincias que habla con V.M. en nombre del Procurador de la Prouincia de San Gregorio de la Orden de S.Francisco de los Descalzos, llamado fr Antonio de Santa María, que queda original en mi poder, y de la qual remito copia a V.Md. en que pone toda la question, y a mi me han remitido de Mexico vna, y es muy verisimil que corran otras, por estos y otros Reynos, conque se va dilatando y dibulgando esta diferencia sobradamente donde no es menester, y puede caussar la diuersidad de opiniones, y disputas en materias tan asentadas, contrarios affectos, alo que conuiene al seruicio de Dios, y de V.Md. y mas en Prouincias donde actualmente se estan descubriendo nueuas conuersiones por las mismas Religiones que tienen la duda como sonlas del Nueuo Mexico y Sinaloa, la vna encomendada a los Padres Franciscos, y la otra a los de la Compañia y estas son las noticias que aqui he podido tener de materia tan graue e importante al servicio de Dios, y de V.Md.

Y siendo ella tan graue, y de tal calidad, y que ni en/Philippinas, ni aqui, ni en Roma veo interuencion ni noticia de V.M. ni desus Ministros, hallo que no deue ocultarse, ni despreciarse; antes merece los reparos siguientes.

El primero: Que de controuersias tan grandes en sus Reynos y de su estado, y progressos, es bien que sea sabidor V.M. a quien principalmente esta encomendada la fe, enestas, y en aquellas Prouincias assi por su esclarecida Religion, heredada con su propia y serenissima sangre, como porla Sede Apostolica; pues aunque los Neofitos de cuya perfecta conuersion se trata, son vasallos del gran Crino, pero los Maestros y Operarios, lo son de V.Md. assi por la Corona de Castilla, como porla de Portugal y es justo que de Corona tan sta. y tan Catholica, como la de V.Md. salga la Dotrina como la Corona y que V.Md. y su Consejo sepan, y entiendan quales, que Dogmas, y que Fe enseña, y sobre que son las dudas que mueben a controuersias y Apologias publicas en Philippinas, y en la Nueua España; y q.desto, si fuere necessario, se dé noticia al Inquisidor Genl. paraque pues está rebelde la Corona de Portugal, se atienda con orden de V.Md. sobre todo, preuiniendo quanto la materia y su grauedad ofrecieren en el seruio. de Dios, y de V.Md.

El segundo es: Que siendo assi que estos Decretos queaora remito a V.Md. hauian de venir passados por el Consejo, si han de tener la fuerça que conuiene en punto tan graue, y en que consiste la saluacion de aquellas Almas, y aun la de sus Operarios y Maestros, es forçosso que los tenga V.M. entendidos con la misma materia y caussa que aello se dio; pues certissimo es que no ha de poder conseguirse su execucion sino es saliendo la proteccion Rl a defender los Decretos santos de la Iglessia, y assi se ha acostumbrado en ella, y lo ha hecho siempre la Corona de V.Md. obligando aque se enseñe comose decreta y mas siendo todos los que han de propagar la fe, Vasallos de V.Md. y que van de essas Prouincias a aquellas, y estando estas controuersias tan encendidas entre tres Religiones grauissimas y santissimas, que cada vna ha de lleuar adelante su intento, y la de la Compañia que va mas a perder (en alguna manera) de su credito y opinion por declararse implicitamente con estos Decretos de su Santidad, no estar bien instruydos tan gran numero de Neofitos en China, y hauer trauajado tanto tiempo en vano, formando vna manera de Iglessia y conuersion singular, y nunca vista de Christianos, que mas parecen Gentiles, o de Gentiles, que no parecen christianos; siendo assi que de mudarse ahora la forma de la conuersion/y alumbrarles con los misterios que ygnoraban y cargarles los preceptos possitiuos que no tenian, es verisimil se despierten persecuciones en China, y reclamen y se deffiendan aun los mismos Christianos y retrocedan de la fe, que será en su genero menor daño que dexarles de dar pura e incontaminada la Leche y sustento de la Dotrina Euangelica, sino seles da pura como se affirma y defiende porlos Dominicos y franciscos con publicas Apologias; Y aunque las dos Religiones son mas en numero que los Padres de la Compañia pero en China, es mayor el poder destos vltimos, que de los primeros, porque lo fueron en la conuersion, y si alli no ay vniformidad en los Maestros y V.Md. no se sirue de procurarlo y asegurarlo con mandar que vnos y otros executen y guarden estos decretos de Roma, o losque la santa sede ordenare, no solamente no ha de hauer fruto en la conuersion de las Almas, sino que puede resultar gran nota a la Corona Rl de VdMd. a vista de tantos Herejes como ay en aquel Archipielago, calumniando que alli se enseñan por Vasallos de V.Md. Dogmas contrarios a la fe Catholica y que no se predica a Christo cruzificado que es nro remedio y origen de toda nuestra gracia y redencion, y que se toleran Idolatrias formales, y que no se guarda el derecho possitiuo, ayunos, fiestas,/abstinencia, y penitencia, y otras cossas deste genero que han de nacer, y nacen de las mismas declaraciones dudas y questiones.

A que se añadc, lo que influye por nra miseria aun para lo espiritual, las controuersias politicas y diferencias de naciones, y que siendo Portugueses por la mayor parte los Religiosos de la Compañia que han hecho aquella conuersion de China, por hauerse gouernado por la Corona de Portugal, y por el contrario Castellanos los que V.Md. embia para Philipinas, y aquella Corona oy rebelde, es muycontingente que no se sujeten aun mismo dictamen, o con grandes inconuenientes y dificultad, y mas siendo rebeldes a V.Md. los de Portugal, y leales a V.Md. los vnos, y otros de Castilla, conque vendra a crecer la disputa Dogmatica sobre la oppossicion natural de las Naciones, y delas voluntades, ya hacerse mas implacable.

El tercero reparo es: Que luego que estas declaraciones se han hecho, y por quien puede hacerlas que es la Sede Apostolica; seria el enseñar contra ellas, y no asegurar V.Md. que se executen y cumplan por los Operarios, y Missioneros, punto y omission muy escrupulossa; porque pagando V.M. como paga porla Corona de Castilla y embiando algunos Operarios a su costa aestas conuersiones, como a las de Philipinas se halla obligado V.Md. a que estos vayan a enseñar la pura, y verdadera Dotrina, porq lo contrario bien se ve que sería concurrir y cooperar con estos socorros a la ruyna y perdicion de aquellas Almas, tan ageno del Christiano zelo, e intento de V.M. y su Supremo Consejo, y assi es justo que viendose en tan gran Senado estas questiones, y declaraciones, y el estado de la materia, y con la noticia dela Rl Persona de V.Md. si fuere necessario, se despache zedula y orden, y la dé, a los que pasaren a sus expensas a la gran China, o en qualquiera otra manera a los que fueren Vasallos de V.Md. inxiriendo las declaraciones en ella, si fuere necessario, pues estan resueltas por forma de dudas, que en estas questiones guarden la orden que tiene dada la Sede Apostolica, y Congregacion de Propaganda, y con esta Fe, enseñen, y no contra ella.

Al quarto: que siendo tambien esta materia tan graue, y en puntosde fe, en los quales no conuiene que en Prouincias de V.M. aya dudas algunas sino ue sea cierto y claro aquello que deuemos creer y mas en lo que toca a lo Dogmatico, y sobre si se ha de ocultar a Christo bien nro crucificado de las/Iglesias, o predicarlo solamente Gloriosso, y si enlos Templos de los Gentiles, se puede mezclar el culto Divino, con el Idolatra y profano, y si se ha de guardar el derecho possitiuo, o no, y otras deste genero que V.M. mandará ver por la Apologia cuya copia remito, entretanto quese embian todas las demas que son en gran numero, y yran con la flota, es bien que V.M. y su Consejo tengan entendido el estado desta question, porque no vaya creciendo sobrado con la emulación de los que la sustentan, y despertandosse en sus Reynos, Dotrinas nueuas, y no necessarias, antes bien nocibas, quando porla bondad Diuina esta tan asentada la fe en ellos, y las differencias, y disputas deste genero, siempre es conueniente quese preuengan por los Principes y Reyes, antes que se enciendan mas, por hauer resultado tantos inconuenientes delo contrario en todas Naciones. Y enquanto alas proposiciones y questiones, y su calificacion, y censura, supuesto que vienen calificadas de Roma, donde se ha mirado conel espiritu, erudicion, y zelo que acostumbra siempre su Santa Sede a quien vnicamente tocan estas decissiones, y oyendo a los Padres de la Compañia, bien se ve que no deja/discurso a Ministro alguno de V.M. y que son santissimas, y dignissimas de ser abracadas y enseñadas.

Solamente porque de vnos cassos se deue deducir tal vez escarmiento, experiencia, y atencion aotros me hallo obligado a representar a V.M. y a su Supremo Consejo el daño grande que caussa o puede caussar, que toda vna Christianidad se fie solo de vna Religion, o proffession por mucho tiempo, como se haze oy en las Prouincias de Synaloa a la Compañia y en las del Nueuo Mexico a la de S.francisco, que ha mas de cinquenta años quelas tienen solos, sin aueriguar por lo menos tal vez dela manera quese obra y enseña, embiando V.M. quien lo visite, o nombrando Obispos a estas dos Prouincias, pidiendo assi a su Santidad paraque en ellas zelen, velen, y vean lo que pasa como en todas las de la Christiandad, pues se conoce en la question pressente que hasta que llegaron a China las dos Religiones de San Francisco, y santo Domingo, con licencia del Pontifize, y vieron lo que obraba la Compañia cinquenta años despues de su conuersion, se ha gouernado aquella Iglesia con vna fe tan incierta, y/dudossa, que han llegado dos Religiones tan graues y santas, a dudar, firmar, affirmar y defender, no solo que nose saluan los dicipulos sino que corren riesgo los Maestros, siendo estos, Hijos de vna Religion como la dela Compañia de Jesus, Seminario de toda virtud, y erudicion, y vemos que ha salido condenado por estas declaraciones del Pontifize, y Congregacion de Propaganda la forma desta conuersion delos dela Compañia, y q se ordene que en todo se enmiende, que es punto bien notable, y digno de ponderación, para enseñarnos quanto conuiene procurar que se siga enquanto se pueda el establecimiento comun y vniversal dela Iglessia en los Operarios de conuersiones nueuas, dexando libre su exercicio, y que entren de diuersas professiones a seruir al Señor, aunque al principio todos traygan vna forma exterior de habito, porque no aya estanco delas conuersiones, y que assimismo aya Obispos, y se siga la forma Regular y ordinaria, pues todos estos inconuenientes, y peligrossas Dotrinas dela conuersion de China se escussaran, si las puertas del Euangelio hubieran estado abiertas a todas suertes de estados, proffessiones, y/Religiones, y con Prelados vnas vezes destas, otras de aquellas, otras del clero que con vna santa emulacion y zelo promueban a que se obre porlos vnos, y por los otros con seguridad de Dotrina, y de exemplo: Y es cierto,(Señor), que en lo interior de Sinaloa y menos en el Nueuo Mexico, no ha entrado hasta el dia de oy Obispo ninguno, y quando mucho han llegado a los primeros Pueblos los que estan mas vezinos, conque nose sabe el estado que tienen las Almas en la Fe, aunque se ha de suponer que será el mejor, porlo que deue creerse de Religiones tan santas; Pero no sé si con esto se satisfaze a la conciencia d V.M. de tener tantos años sin Prelado, ni Obispo aquellas Prouincias, y sinque aya quien lo reconozca, y vea, que no sean las mismas partes; Pues lo mismo se creya de China y han sucedído estos accidentes, questiones decretos, e inconuenientes, hasta que entraron estas dos santas Religiones en ella/aquien es de creer, que el zelo despertaria a dessear y procurar lo mejor.V.Md. mandará entodo lo que fuere seruido en materia tan graue y grauissima como la conuersion de las Almas, y pureza de Dotrina Euangelica, promulgada por Vasallos de V.Md. cuya catholica Persona guarde Dios como la Christiandad ha menester. Angeles el 15 de Agosto de 1646.-

(s) El obpo de la Puebla de los Angeles.

duppdo.

ADDITIONAL NOTES

There is an energetic survey of Palafox's clash with the Mexican Jesuits - the scandal of the American colonial Church - in the Jesuit Father R. Olaechea's 'Algunas precisiones en torno al venerable Juan de Palafox', Montalbán, V (1976), pp. 1053-1131. For a summary of known material on the life of Palafox, deriving from a commemorative conference held at Osma in 1959, see Francisco Sánchez-Castañer (who has made the Bishop his concern), Juan de Palafox, virrey de Nueva España (Zaragoza, 1964); and see also his article on Palafox's beatification process in Revista de Indias, 31 (1971), pp. 183-200.

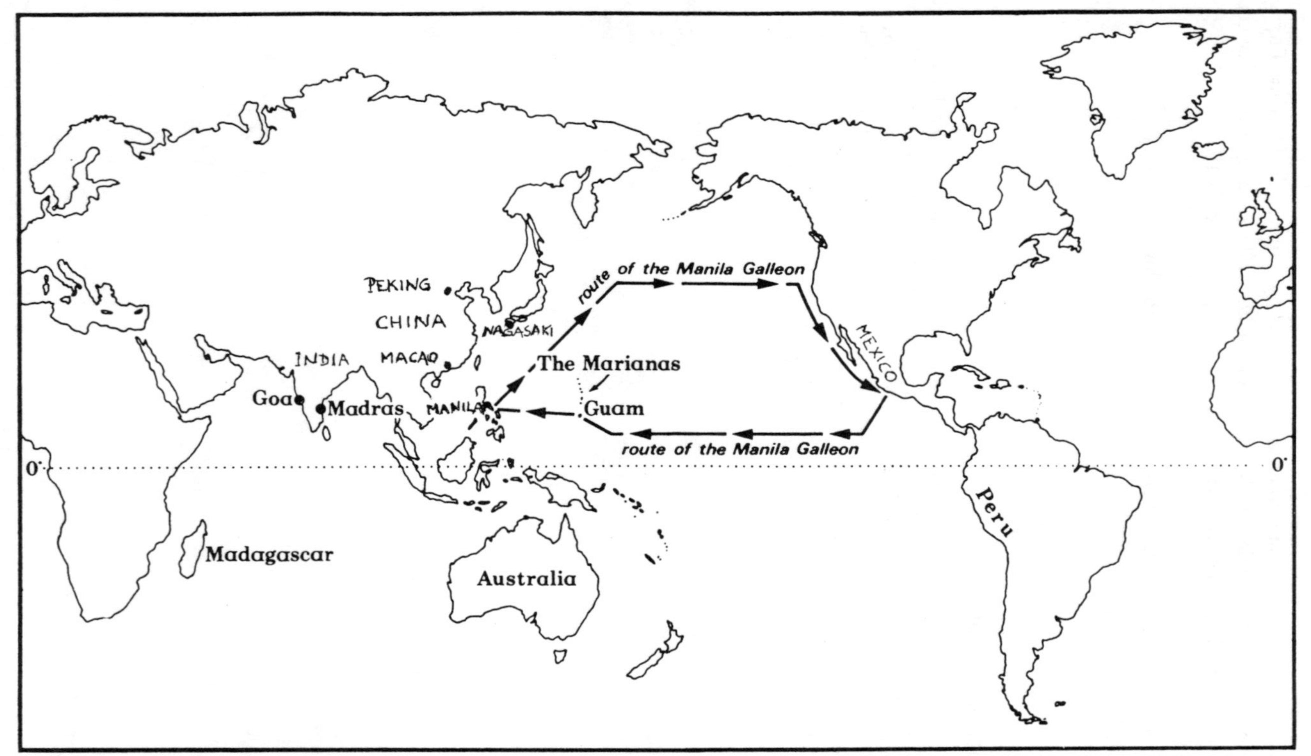

PEKING
CHINA
NAGASAKI
INDIA
MACAO
Goa
Madras
MANILA
The Marianas
Guam
route of the Manila Galleon
MEXICO
route of the Manila Galleon
0°
0°
Peru
Madagascar
Australia

IV

LABOR IN THE COLONIAL PHILIPPINES: THE *DISCURSO PARENÉTICO* OF GÓMEZ DE ESPINOSA

In collaboration with Nicholas P. Cushner

LABOR IN THE PHILIPPINES

The stabilization of Spain's empire in America depended in great part upon the utilization of native labor. Mines, haciendas, cattle ranches and estates required laborers and when it was found that the Indian was unsuitable for sustained work and the population was actually diminishing, the African slave trade supplied the required hands. In Spain's outpost in the Pacific, the Philippines, native labor was not required to stabilize the colony. There were no mines and relatively few haciendas and cattle ranches. But labor was needed for the shipyards constructing the galleons which crossed the Pacific to Acapulco, for public works projects, for building and maintaining churches and for personal services rendered to crown and ecclesiastical officials.[1] Labor in the Philippines, then, while not essential to the existence of the Pacific colony, was nevertheless of paramount importance to its relatively smooth functioning.

The first permanent Spanish settlement in the Philippines was made in 1565 on the Island of Cebu. In 1571 Manila was founded and became the capital of the archipelago. To both Cebu and Manila the colonial labor practices which had developed in Mexico and Peru were transferred. The *encomienda* and *repartimiento* became standard institutions in the Philippines with little or no opposition from the native peoples. When opposition did manifest itself. it was not directed so much against these institutions of labor and tribute, but rather against

1. Cf. Nicholas P. Cushner, *Spain in the Philippines. From Conquest to Revolution* (Manila, Tokyo, Rutland, 1971), esp. Ch. 5, "Tributes and Labor."

particular abuses connected with their practice. One can almost say that the concepts of forced labor and taxation were accepted quite readily by Filipinos, as being a corollary of conquest possibly because of their prevalence in the pre-hispanic Philippines. Slavery to and labor service performed for the chiefly classes of pre-hispanic society had been accepted institutions. When the Spanish conqueror demanded like services, there was no objection.

When the Spaniards arrived in the Philippines in 1565 they found a social organization more or less uniform throughout the archipelago. The shores of Manila Bay, around Laguna de Bay, and what is now the province of Bulacan, were inhabited by Tagalogs. The Pampangos were established west of the Tagalogs and north of Manila Bay, separated by the Pampanga River. The northern margin of the Central Plain of Luzon, along Lingayen, was occupied by Pangasinans. The group occupying the islands between Luzon to the north and the island of Mindanao to the south was called the Visayans. In general the Muslims occupied Mindanao. The basic political unit of all of these peoples was the *barangay*, a kinship group consisting of thirty to fifty families. Barangays sometimes joined to form sizeable villages.

The social organization of the Tagalogs and Visayans differed slightly.[2] The barangay of central Luzon was a community of free men (*maharlika*), bound together by blood relationship under a chief (*datu*). The *maharlika* had dependents who were either serfs (*aliping namamahay*) or slaves (*aliping sagigilid*). The *aliping namamahay* owned private property (but not his own land) which he could pass to his heirs. This belonged to the *datu* or *maharlika*. For the *datu* and *maharlika* he also provided labor services, e.g. constructing houses or planting fields. The full slave, *aliping sagigilid*, was a household dependent, acquired

2. What follows is based mainly on Juan de Plasencia, O.F.M., "Customs of the Tagalogs," in Emma Blair and James A. Robertson, *The Philippine Islands, 1493—1898* (hereinafter cited BR) (Cleveland, 1903—1909), VII, 174—175; and F. Landa Jocano, "The Philippines at Spanish Contact: An Essay in Ethno-history," in *Brown Heritage*, ed. A. Manuud (Quezon City, 1968), p. 51.

by capture in a war or through non-payment of a debt.[3] In the Visayan Islands the political and economic class positions were similar. They could be represented as follows:

Selected Symbols of Political and Economic Class Position in the Pre-Spanish Eastern Bisayas[4]

	Political			*Economic*				
Classes	*Symbols*		*Statuses*	*Symbols*				*Classes*
	Trib.	*Serv.*		*Hse.*	*Prop.*	*Earn*	*Share*	
I. Chiefly								I. Fully Independent
A. High chiefs	No	No	Datu 1 Datu 2					
			Datu 3	Yes	Yes	Yes	No	
B. Low chiefs		Yes	Tumao					
II. Non-chiefly A. Freedmen			Timawa					
B. Bondsmen	Yes	Yes	Gintubo	Yes	Yes	Yes	Yes	II. Partly Dependent
C. Part slaves					Part	Part	Part	
D. Full slaves	No	No	Bihag, etc.	No	No	No	All	III. Fully Dependent

Abbreviations: Prop. — has right of private property; Hse. — can live in and own his own house; Earn — the fruits of his labor accrue to himself; share — must regularly give part or all of his earnings to another in recognition of attachment and indebtedness to him; Trib. — pays tribute to Datu; Serv. — does service (corvee) when called on by Datu 1 or 2.

3. Debt slavery becomes more understandable when one recalls that the barangay existed on a subsistence economy, i.e. only enough of the staple crop was grown which was required for the barangay's consumption and

It is clear from the above outline that native Filipino society was accustomed to offer labor service and tribute to the barangay heads. It might well have been this pre-hispanic practice which disposed Filipinos to accept without protest the Spanish demand for tribute and labor.

Spanish colonial policy dictated that where possible the social structures of the conquered peoples in America and the Philippines be retained. In the archipelago this meant that the *datus* were incorporated as colonial officials, not holding absolute authority, but now responsible to the Spanish governor (*alcalde mayor*) of the province. The *datus* function was changed. He became a colonial tax collector who retained a measure of his prior distinction by receiving the title, *cabeza de barangay*. He became the hinge or buffer between Spaniards and Filipinos, between the conquerors and conquered.[5] The position was a sensitive one. It afforded almost unlimited opportunities for bribery and oppression of his fellow Filipinos, but he was rarely rebuked by his colonial masters. The Spaniards were content because the cabeza assumed into the colonial bureaucracy, insured control over the masses. The cabeza on his part was content because he still exercised authority over passive subjects.[6]

for seed for the next planting. There was no surplus. Hence, borrowed rice was in effect seed rice. It was thought just that the borrower should return not only the quantity borrowed but a quantity bearing some relationship to what the rice would have produced had it been planted. Inability to do so justified a lien on services. The practice was probably extended to other commodities. For other reasons for slavery, see Pedro Chirino, *Relaciõn de las Islas Filipinas* (Rome, 1604), Ch. 46.

4. Frank Lynch, S.J., "Tempo and Mode in Social Mobility," unpublished paper given at the Second Biennial Conference of International Association of Historians of Asia, Taipei, 6—9 October 1962.

5. It is interesting to note how the Aztec aristocracy of Mexico was absorbed into the lower echelons of the Spanish Bureaucracy to act as a buffer between the conquerors and the conquered. See Charles Gibson, "The Aztec Aristocracy in Colonial Mexico," *Comparative Studies in Society and History*, II (1960), 169—196; and the same author's *The Aztecs under Spanish Rule: A History of the Indians of the Valley of Mexico, 1519—1810* (Stanford, 1964).

6. In the nineteenth century the functions of the cabeza de barangay became more complicated. But by this time the barangay ceased being a

The labor demanded of the colonial Filipino population was referred to in general as *servicios personales*, personal services, required for the king (*servicios personales reales*) and for private individuals or religious corporations. As early as 1574 a cedula of Philip II prohibited the use of native rowers if it involved them moving from one island to another. They were to be paid a just wage for their work.[7] Apparently the abuse continued, because the Synod of Manila, convened in 1582, devoted an entire section to the Forced Labor of the Indians.[8] Here again the chief abuse seems to have been the government use of Filipinos as rowers. Cutting timber for the galleons was also a source of unjust treatment. Both of these types of work kept Filipino males from their farms and families for unreasonably long periods of time. The Synod went so far as to recommend that restitution be made to individuals so unjustly treated.

Almost twenty years later Philip III voiced the same admonition. Late in 1601 the king objected to the "poor treatment, oppression and forced services" of the Indians. Farm work, building construction, guarding cattle, and domestic service was to stop. Indian labor could only be used if the Indians gathered in a public place, were asked if they wanted to work on specific projects and if they were offered just wages.[9]

Woodcutting and shipyard labor were especially onorous for forced laborers. Levies of workers were drafted from the provinces of Tondo, Bulacan and Tayabas by the *alcalde mayor* of the province. These gangs sometimes reached six or eight thousand men. They would be forced to leave their homes and farms for at least a month and trek into the mountains where the *molave* and *banaba* was found. The hardship involved was

kinship unit, and had become merely a political unit of society. This was in great part due to increased mobility of the population. See Manuel Azcárraga y Palermo, *La reforma del municipio indigena* (Madrid, 1871).

7. 7 November 1574, Archivo General de Indias (hereinafter cited AGI), Filipinas, 339, Tomo I, fol. 58.

8. The Actas of the Synod have recently been published. "Actas del Primer Sinodo de Manila, 1582—1586," *Philippiniana Sacra* (Manila), IV (1969), 425—537.

9. 24 November 1601, AGI, Indifferente, 428.

so great that workers often sought substitutes, paying them the "princely" sum of ten pesos. Some sold themselves into slavery in order to raise the money to pay for a substitute. The *alcalde mayor* frequently added more men than were necessary for the levy, and he reaped a handsome profit from those able to pay their way out. The local *gobernadorcillo* (an elected Filipino town magistrate) came in for a share of the profits by running a general store where all the workers were forced to purchase their daily needs. In the shipyards working conditions were primitive and what was perhaps worse, salaries were rarely paid. In 1619, Captain Sebastián de Pineda reported that the wood-cutters of Cavite were receiving seven and eight reals a month as well as the daily food ration. The more skilled received ten to twelve reals a month. The maestros — those who laid out, prepared and made the masts, topmasts, and yards — were paid three or four pesos as well as double rations of fish and rice. But when Pineda wrote his account, workers' wages had not been paid for five years.[10]

In the early seventeenth century the religious orders began to emerge as chief violators of regulations regarding *servicios personales.* Natives found it convenient to wander from crown encomiendas and take up residence in towns adjoining monasteries, thus making themselves liable for work in the monastery or church. This annoyed crown officials, because the treasury income from encomiendas was reduced. The religious also had the practice of using *tanores* who once a week provided fish (on Fridays) and baked bread. They received no pay for this service. Philip III objected. "We order that the governor and captain general, the audiencia and other ministers of justice forbid this personal service." Two years later Philip repeated the cedula and added that if religious wanted fish on Fridays, they were to pay for it.[11]

Individual religious were also guilty of unjust exactions and harsh treatment of the natives. In some villages the priests

10. AGI, Filipinas, 30.

11. *Recopilación de Leyes de los Reynos de las Indias* (1791), Book VI, Title 12, Law 43.

would requisition chickens, eggs and rice and pay for them at a price far below the market value.[12] Illegal buying and selling was also charged against some religious, especially Augustinians.[13] Not only religious, but also *alcalde mayores* and Filipino *gobernadorcillos* were accused of similar practices.

By 1649, the patience of Filipino workers had worn thin. Governor Diego Fajardo attempted to collect woodcutters from the Visayan Islands, over the violent protests of missionaries and natives. Fajardo insisted and the stalemate was broken only when Juan Sumoroy led a group of Filipinos in revolt on the island of Palapag. Sumoroy was finally defeated and executed in July 1650. Pampanga province was the scene of another revolt in 1660, caused by demands for woodcutters. About 330 natives fled their towns shouting for liberty from tributed, *vandalas* and personal services.[14] The uprising spread to the provinces of Ilocos and Cagayan. Five encomenderos, two Dominican missionaries, two Augustinians, an *Alcalde mayor* and an *alguacil* were killed. Government forces, led by Sebastián Rayo Doria, quelled the revolt. 134 Filipino rebels were condemned to death, 70 to the galleys, 99 to work in the port of Cavite and 59 were assigned to domestic work in colleges and hospitals.

It is against this background that the *Discurso Parenético* was

12. For some accusations see, Philip III to Governor Fajardo, Madrid, 2 June 1639, AGI, Filipinas, 100; AGI, Filipinas, 339, Tomo 3, Fols. 64—65, Tomo 5, fols. 18—21; also the cedula of 5 March 1653, AGI, Filipinas, 74, ramo 7, no. 232.

13. The Jesuits and Dominicans were frequent targets of criticism for their activity in the Galleon Trade. Unfortunately there is no account, scholarly or otherwise, of how the religious orders financed their missionary activity and social welfare programs. Much of the money which was made from haciendas, trading and bequests was used to finance schools, hospitals, orphanages and mission stations. One would like to know what proportion of the profits made from various commercial activity was ploughed back into the mission, or forwarded to Spain or Rome. If the Jesuit reductions of Paraguay are a valid indication, the proportion of profits used with the missions must have been high. See Magnus Morner, *The Political and Economic Activities of the Jesuits in the La Plata Region: The Hapsburg Era* (Stockholm, 1953).

14. Governor Sabiano Manrique de Lara to Philip IV, Manila, 20 July 1661, AGI, Filipinas, 9.

written and was meant to be read. But its effect was negligible. Despite cedulas from the king, protests from missionaries, and revolts by Filipinos, the cause of the unrest remained through the eighteenth and nineteenth centuries. In the nineteenth century the law stated that every able-bodied male was obliged to render forty days service to the state or pay three pesos.[15] In 1882 this service was reduced to fifteen days or three pesos, a regulation which continued to the end of Spanish colonial regime.

THE AUTHOR, GÓMEZ DE ESPINOSA

In 1657 a high-court judge in Manila, Salvador Gómez de Espinosa y Estrada, a man of more zeal than foresight, took it upon himself to publish a statement of his views on the abuses committed against Filipinos by some of the local clergy and officials. This work, called the *Discurso parenético* (Admonitory address), was meant primarily as a gloss upon the body of royal decrees that had been issued for the proper administration of the colonies. In his *Discurso*, Gómez de Espinosa criticized some of the friar missionaries, accusing them of ill-treating and exploiting the native Filipinos in their care. These comments had a remarkable effect, for the friars reacted with something near to panic. Abusive sermons denounced the author, the book was withdrawn, and both were delated to the Inquisition on a number of charges. Some attempt was made to defend Gómez, notably by Jesuits, who seem not to have been included in his strictures.

This extremely rare work merits republication, for though the Philippine Islands had no one to match Bartolomé Las Casas* in indignation, yet the *Discurso parenético* reminds us that there were always some Spaniards concerned for the spiritual and temporal welfare of their colonial subjects.

Since the denunciations and accusations made in the *Discurso* mainly touch upon the subject of native labor and the system

15. There were, of course, exemptions, due to age, health or other justifying reasons.

* Read: Bartolomé de Las Casas.

of *servicio personal*, some comment on the background is necessary.

Little is known of the life or career of Gómez de Espinosa. He had a doctorate from the University of Salamanca where he hoped to get a chair in Law. In 1650, apparently to his own surprise, he was named *oidor* for Manila.[16] He was given official permission to depart, taking two servants, four daggers, four harquebusses, his household goods and books. There is no mention of any family. On his way to the Philippines he stayed over in Mexico, where in April 1652 he is recorded as having acted as substitute *visitador-general* on behalf of Pedro de Gálvez. At that same time he complained that he was unable to pay his fare to the Philippines, although the galleon was waiting to leave; as a result, in September 1652, the Viceroy was ordered to advance him a year's salary to enable him to travel.[17] He reached the Islands late in July 1653 on board the *San Francisco Xavier* which also brought a new governor, Sabiniano Manrique de Lara; a new Archbishop of Manila, Miguel Millan de Poblete, together with Rodrigo de Cardenas, O.P., Bishop of New Segovia, as well as two groups of missionaries: one of Jesuits and another of Augustinian Recollects.[18] Also on board was a civil service colleague, Juan de Bolivar y Santa Cruz, later to be the innocent cause of many of Gómez's troubles.

In Manila Gómez de Espinosa immediately set to work on the traditional *residencia* into the conduct of the out-going Governor of the Islands, Diego de Fajardo. A Dominican historian was later to complain that Gómez threw himself too peremptorily into matters of government about which he did not know enough, and that he "went about passing sentences and issuing manifestoes, more as a result of his erudition than from any necessity for it."[19] On the other hand, the new governor, Manrique de Lara, wrote to the king in praise of him,

16. AGI, Filipinas, 347, tomo III, fol. 304r, dated 2 March 1650.

17. Archivo General de la Nación (Mexico), (hereinafter cited AGN), Hacienda, 600, No. 9.

18. José Montero y Vidal, *Historia general de Filipinas*, I (Madrid, 1887), 293.

19. Baltasar de Santa Cruz, O.P., in BR XXXVII, 103.

describing him as "one of the best officers in the colonial service, and the governor's right hand man."[20]

By 1658, however, after the publication of his *Discurso*, Manila suddenly seemed to Gómez to be a particularly disagreeable place and he petitioned the king to remove him from "so many calumnies, injustices, and persecutions" to some more "gentle climate." After five years' work in Manila, he was promoted (10 April 1658) to the post of high-court judge of Guatemala. Shortly after his arrival there, he died. Nothing else is known about him other than that in 1658 he was sending money to an heir and that he had a brother called Lorenzo.[21]

Gómez de Espinosa was moved to write his *Discurso* partly in response to a request from the attorney-general of the colony, Bolivar y Santa Cruz, who, in addition to his other duties, was also the official "*Protector de los indios.*"[22] In this role he had urged that the Filipinos should be freed from having to render personal service to the Spaniards.[23]

Bolivar and Gómez seem to have been similar in character: idealistic rather than realistic, both sought to apply the letter of law, at a time which others might have judged inopportune. The appearance of the *Discurso* in 1657 might be judged especially provocative, since Bolivar had only just emerged from a battle with the regular clergy. Soon after his arrival he attempted to enforce strictly the Royal Patronage privileges which gave the king (and by extension, his viceroy) the right to select priests for parish work. This alienated the Religious Orders

20. AGI, Filipinas, 22, dated July 19, 1654.

21. AGI, Filipinas, 23, ramo 2, No. 29; Escribania de Camara, 410, fols. 1, 2; Ernesto Schafer, *El consejo real y supremo de las Indias,* II (Seville, 1947), 476. But the chronicler Baltasar de Santa Cruz, O.P., (quoted J. T. Medina, *La imprenta en Manila* (Santiago de Chile, 1896, p. 52) says Gómez died in Manila and was buried in Santo Domingo priory.

22. For some details of Bolivar's career see Schafer, *El Consejo,* II, 496, 521, 523; AGI, Escribanía de Camara, 410, fol. 124. In 1656 he also petitioned to be moved from the Philippines, but instead was promoted to *oidor* in place of Gómez de Espinosa in 1658; in the following year he was appointed *oidor* of Guadalajara, but in 1664 he was still in Manila (AGI, Filipinas, 22; AGN, Hacienda, 600, No. 115).

23. AGI, Filipinas, 23, ramo 2, no. 1.

to such an extent that they threatened to resign from their parishes and up-country stations. The seriousness of this threat is obvious when it is remembered that there were in the Philippines 252 religious centres staffed by 254 priests of the Religious Orders and only 54 secular priests to replace them if they withdrew their services. Clearly the Orders could not be forced to act against their will. Eventually, after a battle that lasted two years, an uneasy peace was restored: the Manila *audiencia* was obliged to recognise the reality of the position and referred the matter to the *Consejo de Indias* in Spain. It is interesting to note that when the *audiencia* took this decision a minority, dissenting, report was submitted by Gómez de Espinosa.[24]

The *Discurso*, therefore, is not the only work to come from the pen of Gómez de Espinosa. In 1653, for instance, he published a statement on the proper measures to be taken on the king of Tidore's action in helping the rebels of Terrenate.[26] The following year he published two works: the first discussed the need for trade with the kingdom of Tonkin (trade with China had been lessened owing to the Tartar invasion, and trade with Macao had been cut off by the revolt of the Portuguese in 1640); the second handed down a judgement defining the legal powers of Captain-general of the Philippines in military affairs.[27] In 1655 he published a survey of the history of the Philippine *audiencia* and its jurisdiction.[28] A work which he himself refers to occasionally in the *Discurso parenético* is his *Dictamen polĩtico sobre la traslación del puerto de Cavite al de Lampon*

24. H. de la Costa, S.J., *The Jesuits in the Philippines* (Cambridge, Mass., 1961), 423—28. The report is published in F. Colín, *Labor evangélica*, ed. P. Pastells (Barcelona, 1904), III, 728—9; and for another bureaucratic intervention, see *ibid.*, 802.

25. J. Gayo Aragón, O.P., "Catálogo de los impresos filipinos conservados en los archivos de la Provincia del Sto. Rosario de Filipinas y de la Universidad de Sto. Tomás de Manila," *Unitas*, Ano 25, No. 2, April-June, 1952, 334—5; J. T. Medina, *La imprenta en Manila* (Santiago de Chile, 1896), 80.

26. Gayo Aragón, 335—6, 336—7; Medina, 49.

27. Gayo Aragón, 337—8.

28. Medina, 51.

(Manila, 1656).[29] Another, unknown work, which was referred to in his *residencia* was a treatise upon the proper method for appointing interim governors to the Philippines in cases of necessity. This also was alleged to be full of accusations against the Spanish residents of Manila. None of these, however, had the resounding results of the *Discurso parenético*, though all seem to be almost as rare.[30]

The only known copies of the *Discurso* are a printed copy in the archives of the priory of Santo Domingo, Quezon City, Philippines, a copy in the printed book section of the Archive of the Indies, Seville, upon which our edition is based;[31] a copy in the Archivo General de la Nación, Mexico City, and an incomplete manuscript copy in the Jesuit archives in Rome,[32] not seen by us.

THE DISCURSO PARENÉTICO

A major factor in the writing of the *Discurso parenético* was the general economic state of the colony by the middle of the seventeenth century. A contemporary of Gómez, fray Domingo Navarrete, O.P., looking back to the golden days of old, lamented the "the Islands now differ from their former state as much as does the painted portrait from the sitter." In 1655, Bolivar himself reported to the king that the public debt owed to the Filipinos for requisitioned foodstuffs and drafted labor was immense. The official accounts for 1655 showed a debt of 150,000 *pesos;* and it was requested that this deficit be met from the Mexican treasury, since nonpayment was causing great distress among the Filipinos.[33] Quite clearly, payments to the natives for services and requisitioned goods had in reality ceased to be made. By 1657, the year of the *Discurso*, the total amount

29. AGI, Escribanía de camara 410, fols. 74v—75r.

30. Retana (*Origenes de la imprenta en Filipinas*, Madrid, 1911), p. 66. Comments on the rarity of all Philippine books before 1640: works printed between 1593—1640 he defines as incunables, both for their antiquity and scarcity.

31. Medina, 51.

32. Costa, 667.

33. AGI, Filipinas, 22: account signed 17, July 1655 by Juan Rodriguez Ximeno.

owed by the colonial administration had reached 1,000,125 silver *pesos*, which represented an enormous amount in purchasing power. This situation is partly explained by the fact that the finances of the colony depended upon the galleon trade which in the previous twenty years had been greatly reduced, leaving the Islands in a most precarious financial position.[34]

In passing, it may be noted that not only the natives were suffering: for instance, the pay of soldiers and naval personnel were several years in arrears: "at present there are soldiers in Manila who go barefoot, and without swords, and some are dying of hunger."[35] Nevertheless, the primary concern of Gómez de Espinosa's *Discurso* was to protest at the situation of the Filipinos, and to suggest improving their lot. The core of the *Discurso parenético* was a demand for the suppression of the Filipinos' obligatory service both to individuals and to the administration. Chapter One discusses the general question of personal service by the Filipinos; Chapter Two, the longest, consists of 103 paragraphs on personal service in particular; Chapter Three discusses other types of obligatory service; Chapter Four deals with tax and tribute collectors and other officials; Chapter Five discusses the native chiefs and their role within the colonial administration; Chapter Six makes suggestions for the solution of the problems discussed; the last chapter deals with the services demanded by the Crown.

The *Discurso* opens by surveying the royal attitude to the Filipinos as shown in earlier decrees and letters. After this review the author turns from the past to the present. Urging the need to obey the royal orders, he warns that he will come down to specific cases, and foresees that he will arouse controversy. He claimed that he was writing under pressure because of his many other duties, but he clearly took time to present an orderly and authoritative case, and went to the trouble of

34. Costa, 413–5. See Fr. Magino Sola's "Memorial on the condition of the Philippines in 1652" in BR, XXXVI, 49–52; and W. L. Schurz, *The Manila Galleon* (New York, 1939), 49–51, 187–8.

35. Magino Sola, p. 49; Fr. Domingo Navarrete, *Travels and Controversies* II (Cambridge, Eng., 1962), 393.

translating into Latin all the marginal notes, even those quotations from his own writings. The style of the *Discurso* is baroque, the tone is calm, though there is an occasional note of sarcasm. There are few figures of speech, beyond references to the *audiencia* as "the political doctor for the ills" of the Islands, or as the "new Moses leading the Israelites out of Egypt."

The opening pages quote Instructions of the Viceroys of Mexico and Peru, and royal *cédulas* on the question of Indian labor; the author also quotes an emotionally worded letter of the Conde de Lemos, President of the Consejo de Indias, sent on 28 May 1609 to Juan de Silva, Governor of the Philippines. The purpose of this section of the *Discurso* is to show official concern for the freedom and welfare of the natives throughout the colonies, who are to be as free as men anywhere. The opening shots bring Gómez de Espinosa into direct accusations against some of the friar missionaries. He discusses the missionaries' past record as defenders of the Indians and reminds his readers that a friar, Bishop Domingo de Salazar, had been the first official *Protector de los indios* in the Philippines, though the office is now held by Bolivar as attorney-general. A passing reference to the Religious Orders as being the "flying squads of the Church Militant" is a vain attempt at escaping criticism, as is his insistence that he is condemning a minority of individuals, and not any particular organization.

It is worth recalling that the Spanish state, though it paid for the transport of missionaries to the colony, left them to fend for themselves, by and large, when they were established there.[36] This meant that the clergy were dependent upon charity. Gómez is anxious to show that he appreciates this; what he is denouncing is extortion and greed on the part of a minority of missionaries and officials. Their demands drive some Filipinos to take refuge in the hills, or to sell their very clothes and household goods to satisfy their masters' requirements. One of the practices he sharply denounces was admittedly rare, but certainly odious: this was the *Pasalamat.* Originally this had been a voluntary

36. John Leddy Phelan, *The Hispanization of the Philippines: Spanish Aims and Filipino Responses 1565—1700* (Madison, 1959), 103.

thank-offering of rice, but according to Gómez it had degenerated into a flat demand by some missionaries for an amount stipulated by them at their whim. This leads into a passage on clerical interference in the drawing up of their wills by Filipinos. At this point, also, there come two paragraphs of pointed praise of Saint Augustine: "the light and blazing torch of the Church, the very prototype of the religious life," whose extreme, almost morbid, hatred of money had earned him the rebuke of contemporaries. This eulogy of the founder of the Augustinian Order can have had only one purpose: to remind the Augustinians of the standards from which many people felt they had declined.[37]

Phelan makes the point that the majority of Religious were conscientious, and that the "spectacular vices of the minority ought not to obscure the less dramatic virtues of the majority," yet the Augustinians, he declares, were notable offenders.[38] There was an outburst of complaints against them from 1599 onwards.[39] In 1598, in a letter to the king, Bishop Benavides lamented the low standard of the Augustinians, which he blamed partly on the Mexican creole members of the Order in the Philippines.[40] They did, of course, defend themselves[41] and were sometimes praised[42] but it is clear that Gómez de Espinosa was not alone in his denunciations, although he is careful not to

37. Phelan, *Hispanization*, 36, discusses the problem and offers an explanation for the state of decline among the Augustinians; see his maps at 172—6.

38. Phelan, *Hispanization*. 37—9.

39. Isacio R. Rodriguez, O.S.A., *Historia de la provincia agustiniana del Smo. Nombre de Jesus de Filipinas I* (Manila, 1965), 359; typical complaints are those to be found in documents in AGI, 74, ramo 7, no. 232; Filipinas 74, ramo 4, No. 120; Filipinas 329, tomo. 3, ff. 122—3; Filipinas 330, tomo 5, ff. 16—18; Filipinas 8, ramo 2, No. 45.

40. Quoted in Morga, *Sucesos de las islas filipinas*, ed. W. E. Retana (Madrid, 1909), 434—7.

41. The Recollects, as the last-comers to the Islands, inherited missions in the remotest and most difficult areas: they were "in war zones, where they had to have arms always to hand, and many of them had been murdered." AGI, Filipinas, 80.

42. For instance, by the Archbishop to the King in 1660, AGI, Filipinas 81, ramo 6, No. 225.

single out any particular Order. At this point in the *Discurso* comes another reminder that his comments do not apply to conscientious and pious missionaries. This leads to one of the sharper accusations levelled against the missionaries by Gómez: their demands for extortionate fees for the administration of the sacraments to their native converts.[43] Here again it is not the practice, but the excess, that Gómez denounces. He praises those devout shepherds who strip themselves to clothe their flocks, and berates those others who strip the natives to clothe themselves: those who are not pastors but plagues upon the community. Gómez is especially critical of those priests guilty of overcharging for burial fees: an Indian who dies rich has no family of his own, for the missionaries inherit from him; but if he is poor he needs a family to raise the money for his funeral, if he is not to remain unburied; this is the opposite of what happens elsewhere in the world where the poor lack relatives, but not debts, and the rich lack debts, but not relatives. Indulging in word play and irony at this point, Gómez remarks that some, seeing all this, are surprised that the friaries are not built of silver: but such people should realize that the money goes not to the convents but to the conventuals.[44]

Another question dealt with is the punishment of natives by their priests, some of whom had their own parish stocks and even private prisons. They were accused of whipping the natives and of exceeding the forty strokes permitted by Deuteronomy. Such harshness is simply not needed, maintained Gómez, since the most striking characteristic of the Filipino is his gentleness and ready obedience. The Faith is to be introduced with sweetness not severity, for though sticks may bend necks they

43. This would not apply to the Jesuits or Dominicans, neither of whom, at this time, charged "stole fees," Costa, 479, 667; Phelan, *Hispanization*, 103.

44. Similar complaints were made by others. In 1630 the Governor reported to the King that a fray Pedro Garcia had died leaving 20,000 *pesos;* and a companion of his left 12,000 *pesos* made from the parishes in their care. AGI, Filipinas 8, ramo 2, No. 45. The missionary career of the renegade English Dominican, Thomas Gage, who of course was not typical, but was not unique either, is an example of the possibilities open to an unscrupulous cleric. See also Morga, *Sucesos*, ed. Retana, 436.

do not win hearts; moreover, trials and sufferings ought to be borne by the preachers, not the preached. The missionaries, as professionals, might well have resented this particular piece of catechizing, but there is more here than appears on the surface. Gómez, as a convinced regalist, was determined to keep the temporal and spiritual jurisdictions separate, and not to allow the clergy to intrude into the political and civil sphere, no matter how slightly.

Gómez de Espinosa does not limit himself to criticism of the clergy and officials. He recalls the adage that nothing is worse for the Indian than the Indians themselves, by which he refers to the former chieftains who have become petty employees in the colonial government, particularly as tribute collectors in the remoter areas.

In one of the later passages of the *Discurso*, the author insists that the Filipinos must not be forced to work on church feast days, and he quotes the relevant royal *cédulas* on this. The feast days in the Philippines, which were shared by Spaniard, Filipino and slave alike, were the following:

every Sunday in the year;
January 1 — the Circumcision;
January 6 — the Epiphany;
February 2 — the Purification;
March 25 — the Annunciation;
April — Easter Sunday;
May — the Ascension;
June — Whit-Sunday;
June — Corpus Christi;
June — 29 — SS. Peter and Paul;
August 15 — the Assumption;
September 8 — the Birthday of Our Lady;
December 25 — Christmas Day.[45]

Finally, drawing his *Discurso* to a conclusion, Gómez makes recommendations, and quotes further royal decrees to support his case. Personal services must not be demanded from the Indians; the requisition of goods must be abandoned; all native

45. Diego de Bobadilla, S.J., "Casos morales," Libro II, Manila, 1629; MS in the Jesuit archive of San Cugat del Valles, Barcelona, Spain. This also gives the feast days which were exclusive to Spaniards, and the fast days which the Filipinos had to observe.

labor must be paid for in cash, before witnesses, and according to a wage scale fixed by the central administration; and the hierarchy must determine "stole fees" for the administration of the sacraments.

The *Discurso* closes with an appeal to the *audiencia*, to which it is addressed, to consider his remarks, and to remedy the harm being done: his only aim has been the welfare of the Filipinos: if their position is improved he will count his labors rewarded.

Like the majority of writers of the age Gómez de Espinosa felt the need to make frequent quotations from the classics, the scriptures, the Fathers, and contemporary authorities. His innumerable sources, which he quotes in the margins, having first translated them into Latin, have not been cited in our edition since they serve little purpose now. They include, among many others, references to Seneca, Tacitus, Cicero, Ovid, Plato, Themistocles, Plutarch, Homer; St. Augustine, St. Jerome; Erasmus, More's *Utopia;* Juan de Torquemada's *Monarchia indiana*, López de Gómara's *Historia general*, fray Juan de Plasencia, author of a study of Tagalog society,[46] Antonio de Morga's *Sucesos de las islas filipinas*, fray Antonio de San Roman's *Historia de la India oriental*, fray Miguel Agia's *Servidumbres personales de los indios*, Antonio de Herrera's *Historia de las Indias occidentales*, the *Virtudes del indio* of Bishop Juan de Palafox y Mendoza, fray Antonio de Remesal's *Historia de . . . Guatemala*, Domingo de Soto, and the *Destruccion de las Indias* of Bishop Las Casas. This is to mention but a few of the authors cited as evidence or backing for his views.

Apart from the royal and viceregal orders and the Conde de Lemos's letter to Governor don Juan de Silva, all of which he is paraphrasing throughout the *Discurso*, the most frequently quoted authorities are José de Acosta's *De procuranda Indorum salute*, Juan de Matienzo's *Gobierno del Perú*, and the most important of all, Juan de Solorzano Pereira's two works, the *De indiarum jure* and the *Política indiana*.

The extraordinary range of quotations suggests that Gómez de Espinosa must have had a large library, and no doubt he was

46. For Plasencia see Phelan, *Hispanization*, 178—9.

able to call upon the library resources of the Jesuits, with whom he was on friendly terms.

Like his colleague, Bolivar, Gómez de Espinosa was a confirmed regalist, maintaining the supremacy of the sovereign in temporal and ecclesiastical affairs.[47] The attitude is presented in its most emphatic form in the opening pages of the *Discurso* where the King is described as the Vicar of God in temporal matters.[48] Of course, it was understood by the regalists that though the King had irrevocable sovereignty in temporal and ecclesiastical, even spiritual matters, he had none in the purely sacramental order. The leading exponent of regalism was Solórzano Pereira, the jurist quoted and warmly praised by Gómez de Espinosa as having brought light and enlightenment to the government and administrators of the Philippine Islands, who till then had been living in "dense darkness, and gloomy shadows."

The regalists based themselves on Alexander VI's having imposed upon the Spanish Kings the duty to send missionaries to the New World. This duty was deemed to imply some apostolic authority: the Kings were held to represent the Pope, and their royal *cedulas* to have "a certain force even in spiritual matters in virtue of the apostolic delegation."[49] Gómez de Espinosa finds precedents for this situation: in St. Peter, who sent St. Mark to Egypt; in St. Clement, who sent St. Dionysius the Areopagite to Gaul; in St. Gregory, who sent Augustine to England; in Gregory the Second, who sent Boniface to Germany. And so Gómez feels able to emphasize the equation between royal decrees with papal briefs, and insists that whoever opposes the royal power is resisting the divine ordinances. On the other

47. Bolivar had already clashed with the Augustinians in 1652—56 when he maintained that the King, as universal patron of the Church, had the right, through his representatives, to appoint catechists (*doctrineros*) (AGI, Filipinas 81, ramo 4, No. 132).

48. In his support he quotes Proverbs, XVI: "A divine sentence is in the lips of the King: his mouth transgresseth not in judgment."

49. We have here followed the account of the significance of Spanish regalism given by H. de la Costa, S.J., in *Asia and the Philippines* (Manila, 1967), 40 ff.

hand, it is stressed that the Pope has no temporal power in the colonies, for Christ had said that His kingdom was not of this world. Basically, however, in the Church Militant there are two supreme dignities: the papal and the royal; the former is the greater since it holds sway in the ecclesiastical and spiritual; the latter dominates in the temporal and earthly. Yet it follows that the pontifical power resigned part of its ecclesiastical rights when it imposed apostolic duties upon the Spanish kings.

Gómez de Espinosa took all this very literally and applied it to details. When some of the friars demanded contributions from their parishioners for the celebration of certain feasts, this was described by Gómez as an abuse and an unjust gabelle, since only the king had the right to impose such a demand, even for a religious festival. This also explains the frequent quarrels in Spanish colonial society about precedence on public occasions. The maintenance of regalist rights made it necessary to define by royal decree exactly who had preference as between Prelates, Governors and Presidents in processions and other ceremonies, or whether an Archbishop had the right to a canopy during divine services if the President were attending. Thus in 1609 it was formally decreed that prelates had precedence in religious ceremonies inside their churches, even though the Governor be present, but outside the church the Archbishops had to yield to the chief government authority, even though he were of less rank than Governor. These were considered important points and in this section of his work Gómez de Espinosa fills his margins with such an enthusiastic battery of authorities that he himself comments on it.

REACTIONS TO THE DISCURSO

Such sentiments, not to mention the accusations that went with them, were bound to raise resentment. The first reaction, however, was one of praise, though it may well have been arranged in advance as an attempt to counter any criticism. This initial approval came from a Jesuit, Father Francisco Combés, a theologian and historian, who taught in the Jesuit University of

Manila.[50] He begins by praising Gomez's concern and compassion for the Filipinos, whose state is equated with that of the Jews in Egypt: 'there are plenty of Pharoahs to defend evil, but few voices speak out for the ill-treated. In the past, of course, there had been others who spoke in favor of the natives, but to little effect. Gómez is described as the first to raise openly the banner of protest, backed by his office: his voice may be alone, but the sentiments he expresses are shared by many.

Combés then indulges in some baroque word-play interpreting the significance of the surname Espinosa: royal counsellors and judges are like fragrant roses; Espinosa's *Discurso* is a rose, but it is not without its thorns (*espinas*), for his message is severe, though the teaching behind the thorns is sweet. His first name, Salvador, is similarly interpreted. Combés quotes the Book of Judges (III, 9) on how the children of Israel, suffering under the tyrannical King of Mesopotamia, cried out unto the Lord, and He "raised up a Salvator who did deliver them." The passage is quoted in the Vulgate Latin, but instead of "Israel" Combés proposes the word "Luzon" be read: "judicavit Israel (digamos *Luzoniam gentem*) et liberavit eos." And when Gómez came from Salamanca to Manila it was like the coming of another Joseph, another Daniel, a Salvator-Savior for the natives. Combés concluded his eulogy of the *Discurso parenético* by recalling the depopulation of the Caribbean Islands and by hinting that Spanish cruelty could cause a similar disaster in the Philippines.

Less enthusiastic, however, was the Bishop of Nueva Segovia, Rodrigo de Cardenas, O.P., whom Gómez had singled out for praise in this treatise, and to whom he had sent a copy upon publication.[51] Though the Bishop, like Father Combés, did not

50. There is a copy of his eulogy in AGI Biblioteca 309/7. A contemporary Jesuit historian also finds in the *Discurso* a "judicious restraint" and a "circumstantial ring to some of his evidence" even though Gómez may not be "altogether objective and uncommitted" (Costa, *Jesuits*, 477–78).

51. There is a copy of Cardenas's reply in the Lilly Library, Bloomington, Indiana: Phillipps MS. 8493. There is also a copy in AGN, Inquisición, 458, fl. 432. According to Costa (477–78; 667) it is printed in Valentín

quarrel with the main burden of the *Discurso*, nevertheless he regarded the book as defamatory of those very Religious who were striving to improve the Filipinos' lot. He felt it would have been better to write privately to the relevant authorities, rather than to publish details of any wrong-doing, for he greatly feared that the *Discurso* would be used by the enemies both of Spain and of the Church, namely, the English, the Dutch and the Muslims. And the Japanese and Chinese would look on the Religious who sought to evangelize their lands as mere exploiters in search of fresh opportunities. The Bishop was clearly not impressed by Fr. Combés' eulogy of the book, and he forecast that it would be banned by the Inquisition.

Other reactions were violent. No doubt they were inspired partly by an exaggerated fear that the *Discurso* would not only harm the whole Asian missionary enterprise, but would also discourage potential volunteers for the Philippines. The main attack on the essay came in the form of a sermon preached on 5 February 1658 by a Franciscan, Francisco Solier.[52] He had seen Father Combés' eulogy, for he made sarcastic remarks about the new Joseph and Savior who had come to bring liberty to the Filipinos. Solier complained that if, as a result of this dangerous treatise, the "indios" lost respect for their priests, then they would also lose what little faith they had. He declared that during the eighty years since Religious had come out to the Islands the devil had been vainly trying to destroy the new Church there; now he would achieve that aim through the medium of the "new Joseph," who was in reality the determined enemy of that Church. If his essay were published in Spain and elsewhere, warned the preacher, it would do the devil's work for him. Fr. Solier reminded his congregation that if the parish priests, weary of such insults, abandoned their posts, it would mean the collapse of the missions. The devil, he added, had

Marín y Morales, *Ensayo de una sintesis de los trabajos realizados por las corporaciones religiosas españolas de Filipinas*, II (Madrid, 1901), 823—27. The letter is dated 13 February, 1658.

52. There is a synopsis of it in the Lilly Library: Phillips MS. 21529, fls. 109—10.

already made a start on this work through the former Governor, Corcuera,[53] and now Gómez had come to complete it. Solier admitted that the Filipinos were sometimes oppressed, for some *alcaldes mayores* were guilty, but these were isolated cases and insignificant in comparison with the real trials borne by the natives which included the use of *papel sellado* and the *media anata.* These were afflictions common to the whole Spanish monarchy, both in Spain and the colonies. But the Filipinos were suffering another trial, particular to themselves: the *Vandala.*[54] Then followed a brief description of the lot of the Filipinos, who were often over-worked and unpaid, sometimes so weak from hunger that the very tools fell from their feeble hands, and often driven to drunkenness as a relief from their sufferings. Without their priests to support them in these trials the natives would utterly despair and take to the hills in flight.

The sermon was preached in honor of the martyrs of Japan, and it ended with an invocation: "O holy martyrs, I pray that you, as patrons of these Islands, may protect them. You want us missionaries to imitate you in your sufferings, just as you in turn imitated Christ in being crucified. Christ was crucified between two thieves; you were not; but we are indeed crucified between Ministers of Justice. You suffered in the midst of Japanese heathen, but we in the midst of Christians, which is a greater form of martyrdom."

This sermon against Gómez de Espinosa produced a reply in the form of an anonymous and undated *Carta apologéttica.*[55]

53. Sebastián Hurtado de Corcuera (1635—44) was unpopular with the friars. See Nicholas P. Cushner, *Spain in the Philippines.* From Conquest to Revolution (Manila, Tokyo, Rutland), 1971, 159—166.

54. *Papel Sellado* (stamped paper) was required for the transaction of all official business. The *media anata* was a tax used frequently by Philip IV and his successor. It was a tax equivalent to half of the first year's salary imposed on the recipient of any public office, whether permanent or temporary. The *vandala* was the compulsory sale of products to the government. Since only occasional token payments were made in return, the *vandala* was really a burdensome and extralegal form of taxation: see Phelan, *Hispanization,* 99 ff.

55. The MS. is in the Lilly Library: Phillipps MS. 21529, fols. 111—135v: it appears to be incomplete.

There is a marginal note on the front page which suggests that it was the work of Fr. Combés: "De aqueste papel quien es el Autor pregunta Europa, el no es de proa ni popa, y asi sera de combes." This is probable, though its style differs from the convuluted baroque of the earlier *Encomio* written by Combés. The *Carta apologettica* is neither particularly interesting nor significant, and its verbosity makes it heavy reading. The author makes the point that Solier's abusive sermon would make him guilty of sin, were he not saved by his obvious ignorance. The author then discourses on the dangers of rabble-rousing sermons, such as that which led to the death of over four thousand "new Christians" in Portugal during the reign of King Manuel; similar rashness during the recent Catalan revolt is recalled, and the author congratulates the citizens of Manila for their level-headedness in the face of what he sees as Fr. Solier's invitation to violence.[56] The anonymous writer tried to turn the tables on Solier by accusing him of disloyalty, and warned that it is always dangerous to raise the cry of "Long live the King and down with bad government."[57] A deft blow is struck when the writer expresses surprise that a Franciscan should feel that Gómez's criticisms could apply to him, or to this Order. "How much more prudent were the Jesuits, who, in publishing their praise of the Discurso, showed that its strictures did not apply to them." Gómez de Espinosa is defended from the charge of scandal-mongering by the observation that his work only comments on certain royal decrees: the matter therefore is already public. Moreover a reminder of their duty is needed by those unlettered priests (rare though they are) for whom a definition

56. In Lisbon in 1506 two Dominicans incited the mob to riot. Not only Portuguese were guilty, for German, Dutch and French sailors from ships in the harbour also joined in. Three days of rioting led to the deaths of between 2,000 and 4,000 "new Christians." King Manuel had the two preachers garroted and burnt; their priory was closed down. There is a vivid account in Cecil Roth's *History of the Marranos* (Philadelphia, 1947), 64 ff. For the reference to Catalonia see J. H. Elliott, *The Revolt of the Catalans* (Cambridge, 1963).

57. According to one account this was a war-cry raised by Catalan rebels who in 1640 entered Barcelona shouting "Long live the King! Death to traitors! Down with bad government!" Elliott, 429.

of their duties is timely. The anonymous author claims that it is no answer to claim that Gómez should have taken his case privately to the Archbishop. Using Solier's own example, the writer declared that that prelate would pass through a period of persecution in Japan rather than suffer the reactions of some of the Religious in the Islands should be try to enforce discipline on them.

Gómez's advocate next turns to the allegation that the *Discurso* is a mere bid for publicity. This is countered by the assertion that only one hundred and forty copies were printed, barely enough to supply the necessary authorities. Before the sermon there had been little public interest in the work. But since Solier's sermon the book had been in great demand by everyone, though normally in Manila "there is little interest in books."

Among the flurry of papers, for and against the *Discurso*, there is yet another: the *Apologia contra el Parenético.*[58] This, again, is anonymous, but is probably by a Dominican. It is not an impressive piece of work. It combines the usual mixture of heavy baroque learning with personal abuse, and far-fetched comparisons of Gómez de Espinosa with Mahomet and with Henry VIII of England. The author of the Apologia was clearly disturbed by Gómez's regalism: "the theological error of the *Discurso* lies in its intolerable and scandalous attempt to impose laws upon the ecclesiastical state." Similarly, Gómez is criticised for claiming that the King was infallible in his choice of ministers. The author of the *Apologia* was an elitist who saw the natives as "perpetual children" and as such believed that they could quite properly be forcibly compelled by their spiritual fathers, the missionaries, to attend catechism, etc.[59] Yet, like

58. There is an incomplete copy in the Dominican archives, in the priory of Santo Domingo, Quezon City, Philippines; part of it is in an unclassified volume of documents; part of the continuation of the *Apologia* is in another volume, the "Historia civil de Filipinas," tomo 5, documento No. 5. There is also a partial copy in Barcelona University library, MS. 1013, fols. 381—393.

59. This attitude could work in the natives' favor. In confession they were to be given the benefit of the doubt, and treated with greater

Gómez's other critics, he was aware that injustices existed, though he too attributed them to the *alcaldes mayors*, not to the friars.

Inevitably the critic returned to the common theme, and accused Gómez of harmful revelations, and of revealing skeletons "with the key of his tongue." This clearly disturbed many of Gómez's readers. Spaniards were understandably troubled by the *leyenda negra* to which Las Casas's *Destrucción de las Indias* had contributed so powerfully. Gómez had cited that work and was seen to be following in the same treacherous tradition; indeed the author of the *Apologia* lamented that Gómez de Espinosa could do more harm than Las Casas,[60] for his *Discurso* would provide fresh ammunition from a new area for the Dutch in their propaganda war against the Church. The Dutch had already shown their ability to use such material, and in Japan had discredited the missionaires by presenting them as spies sent ahead by the Spanish King to prepare the ground for subsequent invasion. The *Parenético* might be read in Macassar, in China, and in Siam. But no one would travel from there to judge the truth of Gómez's allegations and accusations: rather they would be readily accepted and his accusations applied to the missionaries in general.

A long passage in the *Apologia* described the trials of missionary life in the remoter, up-country areas, and it reveals the frustrations that many priests must have felt in dealing with their converts: in effect, this is a plea for understanding, and is an attempted justification of those who demand the right to inflict paternal punishments upon their flock of childlike natives.

The author includes a rebuke to P. Francisco Combés for his

leniency than were Spaniards ("Dudas que consultaron . . . acerca de las confesiones de los indios" [17th century hand], Dominican archives, Quezon City, tomo 296. And the natives' alleged spiritual infancy largely exempted them from the attentions of the Inquisition.

60. This was a hopelessly exaggerated reaction if it was meant to be taken literally. But just at this time Cromwell had authorized the publication of an English version of Las Casas's *Brevísima* under the title of *The Tears of the Indians* in order to whip up public opinion in favor of his "Western Design" upon the island of Santo Domingo.

praise of the *Discurso* : it seemed to him to be a case of the blind leading the blind. He then concludes with a passage very reminiscent of the *Sueños* of Francisco de Quevedo. He relates a dream he had had just before the publication of the *Discurso* : he saw, in this vision, a *junta* of devils plotting the overthrow of the Church in the Philippines. For this purpose they needed a human instrument. They began to consider various possibilities until finally the devil of Ambition rose up and suggested that the assembly should take a hint from the ninth chapter of the Book of Judges, where the trees are described as choosing one of themselves as a leader. In turn, the fig, the olive and the vine, all refused the office, saying they were not prepared to risk everything for the sake of ambition. But the thorny bramble, when it was offered the leadership, accepted with alacrity, crying out "Now let fire come out of the bramble, and devour the cedars of Lebanon." This rather clumsy bit of word play (Espinosa-spina-thorn-bramble) was meant to offset Combés's earlier interpretation of Espinosa's work in flowery figures of speech. (The cedars of Lebanon, of course, are the missionaries whom Gómez with the devil's help was destroying.) Another parallel is drawn from Judges IX, where Gómez is equated with Abimelech whose ambition drove him to murder his seventy brothers (the missionaries again).

The *Apologia* ends with an apparently unfulfilled promise that it will be printed and published shortly.

Meanwhile, the agitation among the Religious continued, and on 1 July 1658, after a meeting in the Archbishop's Palace, three friars laid a formal complaint before fray Francisco de Paula, O.P., Commissary of the local branch of the Inquisition, whose headquarters was in Mexico. The three delators demanded the prohibition of the *Discurso* and the punishing of its author. After a preliminary inquiry eighty-six copies of the book were impounded. On the twenty-second of the same month Gómez de Espinosa himself wrote to the Mexican Inquisition to excuse himself, and to explain his now delicate position. In the hope of restoring calmness he stated that he had submitted all the relevant papers in the case to the Prior of Santo Domingo, fray

Juan de los Angeles, O.P., and had given him a list of all those persons who had copies of the offending book in their possession.[61] At the same time Fr. Francisco de Paula submitted his side of the story to his superiors in Mexico. He declared that the book, which had spread to Cagayan, Cebu, and Ternate, was a cause of scandal, a libel on the ecclesiastical state, and unsound in dogma; he could not understand how it had been approved by P. Combés and others. Fr. de Paula believed that at least one hundred and fifty copies had been printed, though he thought there might well be still more. Of these Gómez de Espinosa was said to have retained fifty in his possession. Finally he declared it was urgent to suppress the book which might otherwise reach Spain.[62]

These reports reached Mexico City in March 1659. The case was studied by three Inquisitors who referred it to five Qualifiers for their opinion. In the interest of impartiality care was taken that these should not be members of Religious Orders which had missions in the Philippines. The Qualifiers acted quickly. One of them found the book "unworthy to be read by Christian eyes"; a second thought that the book should either be recalled or else amended. A third, however, was more lenient: fray Juan de Herrera, a Mercedarian, thought that since it only pointed to the excesses of a few it need not be recalled. Further, it could only fall into the hands of those foreigners who, through their contacts with natives, were already aware of the abuses denounced. But it was essential to order the Bishops to prohibit all discussion of the book in the pulpit, though the book should be allowed to circulate, and the author's papers should be returned to him.

A discalced Carmelite, fray Pedro de San Simón, was similarly favorable, though he found it wrong to say, as did the *Discurso*, that the king could not err. But there was nothing against the Faith in the work, the language was moderate, and there was no attempt to wound any individual. To point out abuses was not

61. AGN, Inquisición, 458, fols. 428—34; and AGI, Filipinas, 23, ramo 2, No. 29.

62. AGN, Inquisición, 458, fols. 426—7.

only licit, but obligatory, and was traditional in the history of the Church; the Qualifier referred to other writers who had condemned abuses: Solórzano Pereira, José de Acosta, fray Luis de Morena, O.P., Bishop Las Casas and Bishop Palafox. He believed that if there had been scandal in Manila it had "not been given, but taken." Nevertheless after all this the Qualifier suddenly somersaulted and recommended that because the Manila Religious were so disturbed by it the book should be withdrawn. This was to be done quietly, and without the apparatus or ceremony of an Inquisitorial denunciation with all its consequent publicity. The fifth Qualifier, Dr. Francisco de Siles, of Mexico Cathedral, was largely in agreement with this opinion: the book should be withdrawn, but in secret.[63]

The Inquisitors acted upon this advice. On 24 March 1659 they decreed that the *Discurso* be quietly recalled, for though it was true that his Majesty had ordered that excesses be prohibited, yet these were matters for the government and not for the common people. Hence the whole matter was to be dropped and not discussed in sermons or elsewhere. All was to be done "in deep secrecy and with prudence." Gómez de Espinosa was to be informed that even if all he had written were true, yet in the interests of peace it should not be published abroad. He should realize that the unofficial withdrawal of his book was also done out of consideration for his official and public position.[64]

But in Manila action had already been taken. A group of friars, led by an Augustinian, fray Alonso Quixano, had apparently convinced Gómez de Espinosa of the error of his ways, and that the *Discurso* must be destroyed. As a result as many copies as possible were recovered and all were burnt in the orchard of one of the Manila priories, probably in Santo Domingo.[65]

Worn out by the uproar and without waiting for the result of the Inquisition enquiry in Mexico City, Gómez wrote to the

63. AGN, Inquisición, 458, fols. 492—501.
64. AGN, Inquisición, 458, fols. 501—2.
65. AGI, Escribanía de Camara, 410, fol. 119.

King on 22 July 1658 asking for a transfer on the grounds that his health was now irrevocably broken and that he was an object of hatred to the friars, who would never be satisfied as to his good intentions.[66] To the very end he maintained that he had only done his duty in bringing out the intentions of the royal decrees quoted in his *Discurso*: "the printed word perpetuates, whereas the sound of a proclamation goes with the wind." This plea was eventually received in Madrid where the Council of the Indies, forgetful that it had already transferred Gómez, and unaware that he had since died, reiterated its previous orders for the fair treatment of the natives, and sent its grateful thanks to him for his careful vigilance, urging him to continue as he had begun.[67]

The *Discurso* continued to rankle, and Gómez was posthumously rebuked by later chroniclers.[68] At least one other lifted some phrases from his work,[69] and he served as an inspiration to one of his successors, *oidor* Fernando de Escano, who was also denounced: "lacking in judgment and experience . . . he undertook to follow the opinions of Gómez de Espinosa . . . and to subscribe to his manifestoes [such] as the *Parenético* . . . he came to repentance when the shot was already fired, and much damage done thereby."[70]

Upon Gómez's posting to Guatemala his *residencia* was ordered to be conducted in the usual manner.[71] There were twenty-five witnesses, each of whom had to answer a set of seventeen

66. AGI, Filipinas, 23, ramo 2, no. 29. Although he could not know it he had already been promoted in April of that year to the *audiencia* of Guatemala, AGI, Escribanía de Camara, 410. The despatch was then on its way to him.

67. AGI, Filipinas, 23, ramo 3, no. 37.

68. Fray Baltasar de Santa Cruz, O.P., in Blair and Robertson, XXXVII, 103; Juan de la Concepcion, O.R.S.A., according to J. T. Medina, *La Imprenta,* 52, who also (61—2) cites an anonymous refutation of 1671.

69. Fray Domingo Navarrete, O.P., *Tratados históricos* (Madrid, 1676), at para. 5 of his "Advertencias a estos Tratados." Navarrete had known Gómez in Manila, but wrongly describes him (p. 324) as a "creole of Vera Cruz."

70. Casimiro Díaz, O.S.A., in BR. XLII, 120—121.

71. AGI, Escribania de Camara, 410, fols. 1—136. The Exercise was delayed owing to a threat of a Chinese invasion, and then later by the

questions. Some of them had heard of the *Discurso parenético*, and the seventh witness, Captain Marcos Pestano Gordezuela, recalled that on its appearance it had been nicknamed "peneeretico" (near heretical) by some of the clergy. A few mild complaints were made against Gómez, and so his executor, General Sebastián Rayo Doria, nominated his defendants: Captains Juan López Pérez, Juan Tirado, Diego de Palencia, Sargento-mayor Joseph de Gongora and General Phelipe Ugalde y Ayala. Rayo Doria declared that the *Discurso* had not effectively been impounded since he and others still had copies. Nor was it true, he believed, that the Holy Office had recalled the book, but what had happened was that Gómez himself had surrendered such copies as he had.

Judgment was assessed on 29 June 1664: Gómez was found to have been "worthy of all the graces and favors that his Majesty might care to show to his heirs now in New Spain," and he was pronounced to have been a "good minister of the crown, a faithful and loyal servant of the King in every way."

The rarity of the *Discurso parenético* is a tribute to the diligence of those who felt themselves offended by it,just as the uprising of 1660 is evidence that the admonitions and exhortations of Gómez de Espinosa were timely.[72] The lessons were slowly learned. Twenty years later, in 1680, the chiefs of Pampanga complained that the "many royal decrees issued for their welfare, both general and particular," were still being ignored, and as a result they found themselves" more in the state of slaves than subjects of your Majesty."[73]

José Rizal, precursor of the Philippine Revolution of 1896, complained in his turn that the Filipinos suffered injustices during the colonial period, and that, unlike the American Indians, they had no Bishop Las Casas to advertise their woes. However, Gómez de Espinosa's work, as we have previously said, serves

death of the official delegated to conduct the *residencia*. Eventually it was held in 1664 by Francisco Pascual de Panno.

72. The rising seemed at the time to threaten complete ruin to the colony. See the accounts (and bibliography) in BR, XXXVIII, 139–215.

73. Pastells transcripts, LVIII, fol. 15.

as a reminder that there were Spaniards ready to protest on behalf of the underprivileged colonial subjects and to show concern for them, even at the cost of their own comfort, peace and security.

TEXT DISCURSO PARENETICO

1. De los Servicios Personales y Reales en Universal

1. Empezando desde luego a deszifrar el concepto, siento que debe Vuestra Señoría en punto rigurosísimo de justicia y términos estrechísimos de conciencia mandar cumplir y guardar esta cédula precisa e indispensablemente; y en consequencia extinguir generalmente todos y cualesquiera servicios reales y personales que hacen los naturales de estas Islas a los padres doctrinantes, alcaldes mayores, y a las demás personas de la calidad, estado, o preeminencia, que sean prelados ordinarios, o regulares, súbditos, superiores, o inferiores, ministros políticos o militares, sin excepción ni reservación alguna.

2. Lo 1. así porque lo manda su magestad, cuya real voluntad se a de executar por sus ministros y vasallos con ciega promptitude y humilde rendimiento. La obediencia, dijo Sinesio obispo de Ptolemaida, es vida, la inobediencia muerte.

3. Opónense estos servicios diametralmente a la libertad natural en que nacieron los indios, y en que el rey les manda conservar, induciendo o introduciendo esta esclavitud, la violencia y tiranía de los que libran los intereses de sus conveniencias en la compulsión y servidumbre de estos miserables y no hay razón (como refiere la cédula referida) que justifique tan intolerable servidumbre.

4. La libertad definió el derecho una facultad natural para hazer uno lo que quisiere. Si estos infelizes no hacen lo que quieren, sino antes les apremian a hazer lo que no quieren, infiérese que no tienen el goze de ella; y que están en captividad perpetua, de que la piedad de Vuestra Señoría los debe redimir; pues las cédulas reales que se presentan por su parte son los títulos y cartas de su libertad, con que el rey nuestro señor los ampara y defiende de tantos enemigos, que se la turban y oprimen.

5. Y débese considerar que los dos polos en que consiste, se funda y sustenta la monarchía de las Indias, son el primero los religiosos cultos, y reverentes veneraciones a las materias eclesiásticas, personas sagradas; atención, y asistencia a las administraciones legítimas y funciones sacramentales por ministros idoneos, asistentes, y residentes. El 2. la protección, libertad, alivio, y desagravios de los indios; y reconociendo sus magestades la suma importancia de este negocio, lo recomiendan, encarecen, y exageran apretadísimamente a sus virreyes, governadores, y magistrados, en quien descarga con la obligación la conciencia.

6. La instrucción de los virreyes del Peru [Capitulo] 47, folio 13, ibi: *grandes son los agravios y daños que según se tiene entendido, padecen los indios en sus personas y haciendas; siendo oprimidos de los españoles, frayles, clérigos y corregidores para todo el género de trabajos, en que pueden desfrutarlos para sus aprovechamientos, sin que de su parte hay a resistencia, ni defensa, sujetándose a todo lo que se les ordena, como gente tan miserable; y las justicias, que debían ampararlos, y no consentir, que sean agraviados, ni trabajados intolerablemente, no lo hacen; porque no tienen noticia de sus daños; lo cual no se puede, ni debe creer, que pues están obligados a saberlo, y remediarlo, lo que es mas cierto, los suelen tolerar, y consienten por sus particulares fines, respetos, y provechos. Todo lo cual demás de ser contra toda razón moral, y política, ley Divina y humana, es asimismo contra la conservación que tanto se debe procurar de esos reynos, y provincias. La cual por no ser de lo que menos depende la conservación de los naturales de ellas, mirando en lo mucho, que importa esto, y que no basta para su remedio lo que tengo proveydo, y ordenado por muchas cédulas, por no averse cumplido, y executado, como fuera justo: o encargo, y mando, junteys luego todas dichas cédulas que están proveídas cerca de esto, para que de nuevo las hagais pregonar, y publicar; y las audiencias y governadores, y vos por vuestra parte, y las justicias por la suya, hagan lo mismo, teniendo tan grande, y vigilante cuidado de esto, que con el que de vos confio, cesen en lo por venir los agravios, y clamores pasados etc. de lo cual espero, que tendreis tan especial cuidado, que después del gobierno espiritual, será esto en lo que primero, y principalmente proveereis cuanto convenga al bien, y conservación de los dichos naturales.*

7. En la del virrey de Mexico, Capitulo 17. folio 7, ibi: *una de las cosas, en que aveis de tener mayor cuidado, es del buen tratamiento de los naturales, por ser de la que depende la segura conservación de esos reynos, y provincias, como lo entendereis por las cédulas que se han despachado, para su buen tratamiento, y moderación, con que se a de usar de sus servicios, y trabajos de que han de ser premiados, y gratificados suficientemente. Y porque sin embargo del cuidado, con que se a proveydo hay nuevas quexas de sus malos tratamientos, y de que son demasiadamente agraviados, y trabajados con los servicios personales, y otras cosas; lo cual es causa de que se vayan consumiendo, y acabando; de manera, que sino se remediase, como conviene, no quedaría ninguno, para remedio de ello, e ordenado lo que alla vereys en los despachos, etc.*

8. Y el Señor Conde de Lemos en una carta, que escribió al señor Don Juan de Silva, siendo presidente del Real y Supremo Consejo de las Indias (remetiendo la cédula, que está en los autos) su fecha en Madrid a 28 de mayo de 1609: *Y a fe, que si en las Indias se usara tanto el ahorcar, como en estos reynos, que los indios multiplicaran más, y vivieran con más contento, y libertad. Cosa es, que me ha pasado por pensamiento, pedir a su magestad, que me de algún corregimiento de esas provincias, para servir a vuestra md. de verdugo, y justiciar en su nombre media dozena de vellacos. Pero este movimiento se sosiega, considerando esta materia en manos de vuestra md. cuyo valor, y prudencia a de ser parte, para que de*

una vez se le de la forma, y asiento, que conviene; y tanto es hay más menester, cuanto más peligra esa monarchía de que no se venga al suelo dentro de muy pocos años; porque su ruina será infalible, sino se reparasen las vejaciones, que los indios padecen; y se aplacase por este medio la Ira de Dios.

9. Y en cédula dirigida a esta real audiencia de 13 de mayo de 1609 se manda instantísimamente que aunque los indios no pidan sus agravios, se acuda de oficio promptamente al remedio. ibi: *Y porque no es justo dar lugar a que los indios reciban ningún daño, ni vejaciones, os mando, que executeys, lo que en esto os esta ordenado, y que pongays remedio en estos agravios, aunque los indios no lo pidan.*

10. Y en otra despachada al Señor Don Alonso Faxardo, gobiernando estas Islas, su data en Madrid a 9 de agosto de 1621. *Sobre lo que decis del buen tratamiento de los naturales, y de las cargas, y males, que les siguen, está muy bien, y procurareys, que con las obras se verifique, lo que sentis de ello, descargándolos, consolándolos, y animándolos con buenas obras, equidad, y administración de justicia; tomando sus causas de oficio contra los mayores, y poderosos, que los doctrinan; con que siendo esto servicio de Nuestro Señor, y buen gobierno, es eficacísimo exemplo, y medio, para que los demas Naturales de esas Islas se reduzgan, e incorporen en la iglesia católica, y a mi gobierno. Y así pues lo teneis también entendido, procurareys se execute, viviendo con el desvelo, a que obliga la materia, informándo os por todas vías de lo que se haze, y del fructo, que de ello se sigue.*

11. Otras cuatro razones no menos vivas representa el señor Conde de Lemos en la carta referida en el numero 8, ibi: *También se hacen estos repartimientos, para cortes de maderas, navegación de Caracoas, y otros efectos de esta calidad; y pudiéndose excusar, conviene infinito, que se escusen; porque de aqui resultan cuatro efectos de grandísima importancia. Lo primero, que Dios no se ofenda, y se aplaque, perdonándonos los delictos, y negligencias, que asta aquí se han cometido en deservicio suyo, y perjuicio de los pobres indios. Lo segundo, que la religión, y gobierno de su magestad cobre el crédito que han perdido en esas naciones Barbaras, y de esta suerte se halle mas franco el paso, para la extensión del Evangelio. Lo tercero, que los indios vasallos no se vayan acabando, antes multipliquen mucho. Lo cuarto, que vivan contentos en la obediencia y vasallage de su magestad, sin apetecer, ni procurar mudanza de estado.*

12. Y de aquí es, que como las primeras instrucciones se enderezan a aliviar y consolar a estos desamparados fidelísimos vasallos, se imponga ley precisa a su defensa y conservación. El más principal capítulo que se articula en las residencias y visitas es éste, la misma cédula despachada al Señor Don Juan de Silva clausula la decisión: *Y quiero, que sea caso de residencia cualquiera omisión de mis gobiernadores, y las demás justicias, y ministros, a cuyo cargo estuviere en parte, o en todo la observancia, y cumplimiento de esta cédula.*

13. Y en la Provisión, que se libró, para que yo se la tomase al señor Don Diego Fajardo del tiempo que gobiernó estas islas, data en Madrid a 17 de Junio de 1651, se me pone obligación forzosa a indagarlo, por estas

formales palabras. *Y sabeis si los susodichos han entendido y tratado como debían, y eran obligados las cosas del servicio de Dios, y mias; especialmente en la conversión y buen tratamiento de los indios.* Y en la comisión de visita de esta real audiencia, que se cometió al señor Don Francisco de Rojas y Oñate, su fecha en Madrid a 20 de junio de 1611, ibi: *Y de que manera han entendido, usado y tratado de las cosas del servicio de Dios Nuestro Señor y mío; especialmente en lo tocante a la conservación de los naturales de aquellas islas y buen tratamiento de ellos; y si les han hecho, o consentido hacer algunos agravios.*

14. Y este es el más grato, generoso, y heroico servicio que pueden hacer los ministros a su rey; y en que confiadamente ciertos pueden esperar de su real magnificencia ventajosos y elevados premios. Pondera Fray Juan de Torquemada a las palabras del Título de Virrey de la Nueva España de Don Luis de Velasco el segundo (cuyas esclarecidas prendas le merecieron el honor de Marqués de Salinas, y Presidencia del Consejo Supremo de las Indias) en que expresando la católica majestad del señor rey Phelipe 2, los motivos que le persuadieron a condecorarle con aquella gran dignidad, que entre otros fueron los servicios de su padre Don Luis de Velasco el Primero, en que presumidamente brilla con mayores resplandores. Es que su padre siendo virrey de la misma Nueva España moderó los excesivos tributos que los indios pagaban; y que quitó los servicios personales y los Tamemes, que se cargaban, de que morían muchos y recibían daños intolerables.

15. De donde se reconoce cuanto pesa y piensa el catolicísimo zelo y augistísima [sic.] religión de los serenísimos reyes de España; el cuidado, amparo, protección, y desvelo de la conservación, desahogo y libertad de los indios.

16. El Señor Conde de Lemos, en la carta referida al señor Don Juan de Silva, confirma esta hypóthesis; donde encargando mucho la ejecución de esta cédula de servicios personales, concluye con estas palabras: *Y este seguro que serán los más lúcidos y valientes servicios que pueda representar a Dios y al Rey. Yo he querido tener alguna parte en ellos, y por eso he sido largo en la materia. Guarde Nuestro Señor a vuestra merced etc.*

17. Y no se puede admirar que su majestad con vínculos eficacísimos obligue, solicite, y exorte a sus ministros se ocupen y vigilantemente se dediquen todos al alivio, augmento y propagación de los Naturales; y aplique, y dicte tan repetidos y proporcionados medios y remedios a males tan mortales, contagiosos, y pestilentes; porque fuera de que está obligado de precepto y derecho divino a estas activas y vivas diligencias, según prueba y comprueba el Señor Obispo de Chiapa Don Fray Bartolomé de las Cassas, o Cassaus en la disputa o controversia contra el Doctor Ginés de Sepúlveda en el Corollario primero, Viene a ser escarmiento de los sucesos trágicos y funestos de los naturales de las Islas de Barlovento, que se pacificaron en tiempo de los católicos reyes Don Fernando y Doña Ysabel, que ocupados en mayores materias y faltos de verdaderas noticias, no pudieron proveer en tiempo los órdenes y descretos convenientes a la preservación de los indios, y a la reformación y castigo de los excesos, que se cometieron. Fray Juan de Torquemada en su *Monarchía Indiana,* tom. 3. lib. 17. c. 19. El Señor Obispo de Chiapa en la relación de la *Destruicción*

de las Indias; con que cobró fuerzas la relajación, los consumió, y aniquiló la avaricia de manera que brevemente no quedaron ni aún las tristes memorias de haber sido; sin más culpa, que haber nacido, como escribió de los innocentes la pluma delgada de Chrysólogo.

18. Mas se podía extrañar que tanto número de cédulas expedidas en su favor, Santísimas en su decisión, suavísimas en su disposición, benignísimas en su dirección, que no solo imperan, pero enseñan, pues indican los motivos; y devieran tener conseguido el provecho, y causado los efectos que procuran, de ninguna manera hayan fructificado; sino que la malicia humana ha prevalecido contra la observancia; la sin razón, contra la razón, vistiéndose de disculpas: y valiéndose unas veces de la fuerza, otras de la calumnia, y otras del poder para frustrarlas, solicitando que falten medios a la execución; turbando, y oscureciendo la verdad, y echando todos los cuidados sobre cualquiera majistrado o ministro, que trate de enmendar, y no quiera componerse con la transgresión: y así los indios después de muchas veces redimidos se quedan en eterno captiverio, y perpetua servidumbre, cuando en todos basta una redención para quedar absolutamente libres. Y lo que en otros fuéra remisión, indulto, y previlegio [sic], en ellos son tribulaciones, angustias, y persecuciones.

19. A esto se suele oponer vulgarmente y responder frequentemente que es costumbre antiquísima, practicada inconcusamente en estas provincias, aprobada por los señores gobernadores y ministros que las han regido; que no se han de introducir novedades; y que como el cuerpo humano no sufre repentinas mutaciones ni el místico en su estado, en que son peligrosísimas las inovaciones. Y así repreende un gran político a Apio, que el principio de su tiranía pretendió establecer con mudanzas de que ha de estar muy lejos, quien desea acertar la política de gobernar.

20. Y así como al principio de las enfermedades naturales se han de recetar las medicinas eficazes, que entonces obran con poca o ninguna resistencia; pero cuando ya los humores se han esforzado, y no puede vencerlos el arte, se suspende la curación, así en los achaques morales, al principio se deben aplicar los remedios: pero cuando han crecido, aumentádose y radicado en el cuerpo místico, mejor dictamen es el sufrimiento y tolerancia; porque muchas veces solo será a vivar incendios; y cuando se solicita a pagar llamas se dará material a nuevos fuegos, pesando más los daños que los remedios; y irritándose con el movimiento los humores predominantes, se criarán otros, o mayores, o peores que los primeros. La enmienda de costumbres es empeño de gran dificultad, cercado de peligros, señidos de riesgos, estrechado de odios, y sitiado de calumnias.

21. Bien me ajusto al aforismo político dictante, que mejor es renovar que innovar la república: pero no es novedad reducir las acciones torcidas a sus reglas; no es novedad captivar los excesos, prenderlos y rendirlos a leyes y derechos; no es novedad guardar las cédulas, órdenes, e instrucciones reales, volviendo a su lugar lo que anda extraviado, y fuera de sus rectas constituciones; no es novedad dirigir el agua a los canales, y conductos, por donde el rey quiere que corra; no es novedad suprimir abusos introducidos, antes es santa restitución de lo malo a lo bueno, restauración a la antiguedad, remoción de novedades, desórdenes, daños, e inconvenientes.

Las materias de estado no se juzgan por afectos especiales sino por razones comunes. No se ha de dar nombre de novedad a lo que nos está mal, que se renueve, ni de restitución a lo que nos está bien, que no se practican: no se ha de mirar la conveniencia como virtud, ni a la descomodidad como vicio.

22. Las costumbres que se oponen al derecho Divino, natural, y Positivo, son irracionales, detestables, execrables, y corruptelas, que se han de extirpar y destruir, como ofensivas y nutritivas de pecados y escándalos.

23. Y de lo que injusta y tiránicamente se ha obrado contra la voluntad real y contra las direcciones que repetidamente ha expedido, no es deducible argumento; pues nunca se atiende a lo que se practica sino a lo que según razon, leyes, y justicia es practicable.

24. Y los temporales o tiranos abusos de alguna provincia, región o reyno, no mudan el derecho que con prudencial acuerdo y desvelo cuidadoso se estableció y constituyó, así para ellos como para las demás comprendidas en su decisión y determinación.

25. De donde nace que las costumbres depravadas, que introdujo la insolencia y sustentó la impiedad, hacen con el uso que pecados gravísimos y horrendos, parezcan a la vista humana leves, ligeros, y aún lícitos y honestos, como llora, y lamenta el grande Augustine en su *Enchiridión.*

26. Y Cristo Nuestro Señor, cuyas acciones deben ser instrucción de las nuestras, reprendió severamente a los fariseos la transgresión de las leyes por la observancia de las tradiciones, costumbres, y estilos.

27. Y que esta costumbre (de que hablamos) introducida en los servicios personales sea depravada y opuesta a todo derecho a la libertad, conservación, justicia, razón, al buen gobierno y direcciones políticas, es demonstración matemática, y se comprueba con el cap. de Instrucción ilustrado en el numero 6. ibi: *todo lo cual demás de ser contra toda razón moral, y política, ley Divina, y Humana, es asimismo contra la conservación, que tanto se debe procurar de esos Reynos, y Provincias;* y en la del Señor Don Juan de Silva, que voy parafraseando, ibi: *a cuya causa no hay razón, que justifique tan grande servidumbre;* e ibi: *Y todo lo que no fuere preciso para su conservación, pesa menos que la libertad de los indios.*

28. Y la de 26 de mayo de 1609: *Como cosa, que tanto deseo, e importa dar principio a esta reformación tan necesaria para el buen gobierno y conservación de esas provincias, alivio y libertad de los indios.* Y en el cap. 30: *Porque aunque esto sea de alguna descomodidad para los españoles, pesa mas la libertad, y conservación de los indios.* Y la de 1601: *Y deseando yo acudir al remedio de ello, para que los indios vivan con entera libertad de vasallos míos: et ibi: de manera, que no vivan los indios oprimidos con nota y ocupación de esclavos.*

29. Y últimamente la majestad católica del rey nuestro señor Don Phelipe 4, (Dios le guarde) advertido con su soberana providencia que estas cédulas no se guardaban, ni executaban, mandó su real clemencia despachar novísimamente la del año de 1628, con dos renglones añadidos de su augustísima letra y escritos de su poderosa mano, que pueden estimar más los indios que la libertad, aunque sea inestimable, y sin precio preciosa. Dicen pues aquellas gloriosas e inmortales palabras: *Quiero me*

deys satisfación a mi, y al mundo del modo de tratar esos mis vasallos; y de no hacerlo, con que en respuesta de esta carta, vea yo executados exemplares castigos, en los que huvieren excedido en esta parte, me daré por deservido: y aseguroos, que aunque no lo remedieys lo tenga de remediar, y mandar os hacer cargo de las más leves omisiones en esto por ser contra Dios, y contra mí; y en total destruicción de esos reynos, cuyos naturales estimo, quiero sean tratados; como lo merecen vasallos, que tanto sirven a la monarchía, y tanto la an engrandecido, y ilustrado.

30. Y los vestigios de los mayores entonces se deben seguir, cuando no se extraviaron del bueno y recto modo de obrar: ni a las decisiones de los senados se atiende cuando la razón y el derecho dictan lo contrario.

31. Ni es argumento concluyente que por que los señores gobernadores antecedentes en los tiempos pretéritos, no executaron las cédulas, no se daban cumplir en los presentes. No sería culpa, que en derecho nunca se presume, sino se prueba, y más en personas de tantas y tan superiores obligaciones; y en caso que lo fuese, un delicto no se escusa con otro. Al Señor Don Juan de Silva le halló la cédula engolfado en funciones militares, entre el estrépitu ruidoso de las armas; tenía aquel espíritu belicoso divertido en los marciales exercicios, desearía desembarazarse para la prompta obediencia: fructuó en el pielago de sus más floridas esperanzas; truncóle la parca cruel en el prado de sus más amenas confianzas. Sus succesores en el cuidado mayor de otras ocupaciones, ni llegarían a comprender lo que padecen los indios, ni a considerar la necesidad del remedio„ ni la obligación del rescripto; y quizás se hallarían asistidos de los instrumentos y sujetos, que les causan las quejas, lágrimas, y gemidos, e impedirían se oyesen los clamores: y como entonces no había amanecido a este nuevo obe el sol resplandeciente del señor Don Juan de Solórzano, que le ha iluminado con los rayos de sus noticias, se vivía en densas tinieblas y sombras oscuras. A la soledad del señor Don Diego Fajardo no pudieron penetrar estas luces; guardó Dios la gloria de esta empresa al zelo piadoso de vuestra señoría como a Moyses la redención de los israelitas en Egipto, a quienes los compara en términos terminantes. De estos servicios, D. Juan de Solórzano en la *Política* c. 5. Vers. y los podremos fol. 86.

32. Y aunque los hebreos verdadera y propriamente no eran esclavos en aquel cautiverio; pero respeto de las tareas, servicios, obsequios, y contribuciones que les cargaban; y las asperezas, y crueldades con que eran exercitados, los llama muchas veces absolutamente esclavos la escritura.

33. Menos consecuencia puede ser que los ministros antiguos no solicitasen el alivio ni procurasen la execución. Lo 1. porque ninguno jura en el introito de su oficio seguir los dictámenes de sus antecesores, ni hacerlo que ellos, sino guardar las cédulas, leyes, y ordenanzas. Lo 2, porque no les tocan las materias de gobernación: precisamente deben a la obligacción de sus ocupaciones cuando les consultaren este linage de materias, advertirlas prohbiciones que hubiere, e instar en el cumplimiento de los rescriptos con activas influencias; y sino se admiten las noticias, no resistir, sino suspender. Las Audiencias, y Chancillería Reales, representan la persona Real en lo concerniente a la administración de lusticia Commuta-

tiva, que es la esfera de su poder; los Vireyes y Governadores en la distributiva, materias Políticas, y Provisionales.

34. Siempre la presumpción asiste, y auxilia a los Magistrados, y Ministros, de que proceden a justadamente, y que cumplieron rectamente con las leyes de su oficio: porque conviene assi a la autoridad, y causa publica; al credito, y decoro de quien los nombra, y elige.

35. Bien puede ser, que se hallen personas mas doctas, mas prudentes, mas zelosas, mas justificadas, y mas puras, que los Ministros; pero no mas escogidas de Dios, para la ocupacion: quiere les asistir con particular providencia, y especial auxilio, como a instrumentos, que organizo a la distribucion de Justicia: no contrae en otros, ygualmente este favor; pues no los elevo a la dignidad, ni les sostituyo el poder, ni delego la jurisdiccion, mediante la eleccion, y nombramiento del Rey; cuyos labios profetizá; cuyos juicios no son errables; porque en lo temporal es Vicario de Dios en la tierra.

36. Esto supuesto, es forcoso discurir individualmente en la especie destos servicios Reales, y Personales, sintiendo infinito, que el hallar me necesitado por tantos títulos a mirar por el servicio de Dios, y del Rey, desaogo de los Naturales, y de tantos inconvenientes, como pueden resultar de dexar los remedios de mala calidad, y mas atrevidos los daños, me obligue a entrar en lo sagrado de las Religiones, hablando de algunos Doctrinantes Regulares, y seculares; de quienes, y de los Alcaldes mayores son frequentes las quejas de agravios, y repetidos los clamores de vejaciones, y molestias.

37. Y como quiera, que estan tan unidos los danos con las causas, que los producen, que son inseparables, e imprescindibles, no es possible dexar de romper este embarazo, conque me expongo à calumnias criminalisimas, y a la ira sangrienta de los interesantes: pero quien obra por acertar, y no por contemplar, a de despreciar estas cosas, y proponer la verdad, aunque sea acosta de persecuciones. Ocasiones ay, en que es gloria, o deuda el peligrar; porque es necesario dexar el oficio, o tolerar las propriedades de su exercicio: y quien no tiene valor, para defender asta morir, aunque sea amenazado de grandes riesgos, el servicio de Dios, y del Rey, no solicite las plazas, ni procure los puestos.

38. Y asi enseña elegantemente Seneca, que el que temiere los odios populares, errara los medios, y no acertara con los fines: Y Don Juan Antonio de Vera en el Embajador disc. 1. fol. 84. Que quien los quiere satisfacer a todos, no gana a ninguno; y no se puede consultar lo suave, sino lo onesto; y mas quando amenaza peligro a lo público; y de las noticias pende el remedio de males comunes, que prevenidos, pueden facilmente corregirse, y tolerados con la disimulacion, navegar apresurados a la asolacion: entonces deve el Ministro, el Consejero representar los vivamente, aunque conozca los riesgos, que puede padecer, como clamaba el gran Temistocles en la Cedemonia, donde avia ley Capital contra el que consultase, no probando luego con evidencia la utilidad.

39. Decir la verdad, y mas quando conviene, es obligacion, y necesidad, como torpeza, y delicto decir loque no lo es, o suprimir, y callar loque lo es; y ambas convienen a los Ministros, que no deven por su oficio

lisongear con el silencio los excesos, quando cunviene declararlos, ni disiimularles el nombre, ni hacerles sombra con el vano pretexto de incredulidad: y no solo aquien haze precision el oficio, mas ni a otro qualquiera, aquien lo justo, y honesto debiese algun reconocimiento, se puede imputar a mala voluntad publicar con la detestacion, lo que no se puede disimular sin peligro de complicidad. Y en ese sentir habla San Augustin, y el Senador, Marco Aurelio Casiodoro.

40. Mal podra curar el Medico al doliento sino le refieren las causas, estado, circunstancias, y accidentes de la enfermedad, para poder advertido reconocer perfectamente la molicia del achaque, y acertar con las indicaciones en la aplicacion de las medecinas. V. S. es el Medico Politico de las dolencias de estas islas sino le representan con verdad pura los males que padecen, y las causas instrumentales, que inmediatamente los producen, no podra recetar los remedios precisos a la curacion. Mandame, que le descifre mi sentimiento: ni puede Faltar mi obediencia, ni puedo arbitrar sobre sus preceptos. Acción era mas gustosa, para escusada que para admitida; pues esfuerza lastimar a tantos compreendidos: y quando siempre e procurado acreditar, y no ofender; templar, y no encéder, me hallo enterminos esticchos, ò de condenar me con Dios, y con el Rey, si suprimo la verdad; ò de hacer me odioso con los ombres, si ponderare, como debo, las noticias, que es loque altercaba Chrysippo, referido por Stobeo, para eximir se del Magistrado: si rigiere mal, ofendo a los Dioces, y si bien a los ombres: y mas a lo umano el gran Alfonso de Alburquerque en sus ultimos alientos: mal con el Rey por amor de los hombres, y mal con los ombres, por amor del Rey.

41. Pero los Vasallos, y Ministros de grandes obligaciones, y amor a su Rey, no solo andeservir le aspirando a los premios, sino aventurando los puestos, y exponiendose a calumnias por su servicio; y mas quien pusiere los ojos en Dios, y en su obligacion, y en que se remedie lo publico, y no en la gratificacion, y aplausos vanos del vulgo.

2. De los Servicios Personales en Especial

1. Entro confesando como verdad Católica, que las sagradas Religiones son esquadrones volantes del exercito militante de la iglesia; que an plantado los Reales de Cristo S.N. en la Barbaridad de tantas naciones Gentilicas, y Paganas; que an arbolado los Estandartes de la Fee en los ultimos fines del Orbe; que an resonado los ecos dulces, y voces armonicas del Evangelio en toda la circunferencia, de la tierra; que an encendido, y alumbrado como luces del Cielo, con resplandecientes antorcas en las manos, las tenebrosas, y obscuras tinieblas de la ciega Idolatria; que instruyen, y promueven con ardiente celo, e infatigable cuydado en la Religion, y culto verdadero a los recien convertidos; que ansido, son, y seran la proteccion, auxilio, amparo, y conservacion de los Indios, como testifica con muchas autoridades, y testimonios, Fray Juan de Torquemada en sus tres tomos de la *Monarchia Indiana*, y especialmente en el tercero tomo, y en el lib. 17. c. 21. se lamenta tristemente, de que después que las Órdenes Sanctísimas de San Francisco, Santo Domingo, y San Augustín se dejaron de

unir, y confederar para tratar y dar noticias a su Magestad sobre el alivio de los naturales les faltó el remedio; y que todas las cédulas que se despacharon, para corregir los excesos que se cometían contra ellos y ésta de los servicios personales, se debieron al desvelo, solicitud, y agencia de estas celantes religiones.

2. Con que estos abusos, que preconizan las insinuaciones clamorosas de los naturales, ni se atribuyen a todas las religiones de esta región; ni a todos los regulares, sino a algunos, que son muy pocos, y no desacreditan a una religión ni provincia entera: ni pueden deslustrar su grandeza, ni eclipsar sus resplandores las imperfecciones de quatro, o seis religiosos; ni al estado eclesiástico el descuido de particulares clérigos: así como la Apostasía, y traición de Iudas, dice San Gerónimo, no obscureció, ni destruyó la fe viva de los Apóstoles.

3. Pero tampoco es negable que de estos pocos, sean solos los que fueren, comunmente se divulga, que son las causas instrumentales de sus fatigas, como más absolutos en el poder y menos resistidos de la obediencia: y sería mucho de admirar de sujetos, que han profesado el alto y verdadero espíritu de la pobreza evangélica desapropriada de todo lo que mira a intereses temporales, que tan diametralmente se opone a su santo habito, e instituto; y que despreciaron el polvo y ceniza de las comodidades del siglo, renunciando espontáneamente sus riquezas vanas, para quedar libres, y desasidos a seguir las celestiales y eternas; que se desterraron de sus Patrias, navegando cinco mil leguas a seguir y a imitar a Cristo desnudo en la Cruz, y a rubricar con la Sangre la fee católica, que predican, anelando al Martirio, que permitan, y den ocasión, a que se de a entender, que se olvidan de esta obligación, como ponderó especiosamente Innocencio tercero, que no acaba bastantemente de estrañarlo en los Monges Cantuarienses; y a que se diga, que se dejan vencer (en perjuicio y de pauperación de los indios) de la codicia, fiera insaciable, causa productiva de todos los vicios, inductiva de todos los males, privativa de todos los bienes; extensiva y sin término en lo finito, porque aspira, y anela a lo infinito.

4. Y que debiendo, como Varones Apostólicos, buscar las personas y no las haciendas, se les atribuyan que pervierten este orden y que solicitan las haciendas y no las personas contra la doctrina de San Pablo y del voto de la pobreza que es el muro propugnáculo y columna de las religiones.

5. Y dejo de explayarme en la exornación, porque viene a sobrar la materia; y como sólo miro a cumplir, me causa congoja el ponderar; y no he querido excusarlo en todo, por parecerme que podría ser que fructificase, entendido en favor de los naturales que son los que padecen los rigorosos efectos de la relajación, que es el fin que pretendo; no acusando las personas la celebridad de las fiestas, en que se quejan, de que les hacen contribuir a los indios violentamente, a medio real, y a real, y a dos; siendo ley del tributo y arancel, que regula a cantidad, la voluntad libre del Padre doctrinante; y que al paso de la avaricia se lamentan que crece la multiplicidad, y que se hace de la devoción piadosa, conveniencia, y grangería reprobada.

7. Y es dignísimo de ponderación que la pompa festiva consta de doce velas; el aire de las trompetas y viento de las chirimias; de enrramadas

de hojas, palmas, y flores, que forman y adornan los mismos indios: y para funciones de esta calidad sea segura que hacen una de capitación-tan exorbitante, y una gabella tan injusta, quando sólo en el rey, como Supremo Señor, reside la autoridad potestativa de imponer tributos, como regalia inerente en la magestad real; y Cristo enseñó a pagar, no a cargar tributos, siendo dueño soberano del universo, y de los que le habitan, e ilustran.

8. Y no puede parecer creible, pues no ignoran que estas fiestas, sacrificios y victimas no son acceptables a Dios, ni le aplacan sino le irritan; no le agradan, sino le ofenden, porque son ofrendas arrancadas de la substancia de los pobres, como si a un padre le ofreciesen a su hijo únicamente amado en sacrificio, quanto dolor sintiera si se le victimaran, y le hicieran holocausto de su cuerpo.

9. El verdadero y propio culto de los agrados de Dios es la voluntad propicia y el ánimo prompto. Los teólogos enseñan que no hay mérito donde no hay arbitrio libre; si a estas expensas y celebraciones concurren, como se afirma vulgarmente los indios violentos, y se las hazen pagar con impresión y fuerza de substanciando los de su poca y miserable sangre para satisfacer la exación, y muchas vezes se hallan obligados a vender las pobres alajas y ropa que tienen, antes les influira horror y aborrecimiento que devoción, inclinación, ni afecto; conque no sólo tendrán mérito sino demérito grave.

10. Entre otras cédulas, que irá exornando en que se repreende y reprueban estas injustas contribuciones y desórdenes es la de II de diciembre de 1613 que prescribe la forma con que se han de inquirir y averiguar. ibi. *Porque deseando algunos de los nuestros presidentes, o governadores, en conformidad de lo que está ordenado, libertar a los indios de las continuas derramas, y contribuciones de dinero, especies, y servicios personales, á que les obligan algunos ministros eclesiásticos, que los doctrinan, y administran los Sacramentos; en que suelen ser grandes los excessos, que se hazen, les parece que conste de ellos por informaciones, para darnos quenta de todo, imbiándonoslas: a que los Fiscales de nuestras Audiencias, como protectores, o los que lo son de los dichos indios salen pidiendo, que se reciban; y aviéndose hecho algunas en diferentes partes, se alla hacerse las dichas derramdas con mucha libertad, y exorbitancia, sin que se ponga remedio alguno, y alcanzádolo a saber los prelados de las religiones, en lugar de proceder al castigo, que merezen los que tal hazen, los ayudan, y amparan, buscando caminos y medios, para empatarlo todo; por dezir, no se puede hazer información contra ningún eclesiástico, sin incurrir en la censura de la bulla de la Cena: y declarando con esto por públicos excomulgados a los ministros de justicia, por cuya mano se hazen dichas informaciones; y causan con esto muy grande escándalo; no siendo lo que así escribe, para actuar, ni proceder contra el eclesiástico, sino sólo para informarnos de ello; averse dado el orden y mandamiento, para hazer Informaciones sin especificar, ni señalar persona religiosa, ni eclesiástica, sino sólo, para que se averiguen las dichas derramdas, y por cuya orden, y mandato se hazen, a que esfuerza declarar el testigo, en entrando con su deposición, quien, y como la a hechado. Y porque parece, que los dichos*

Presidentes, y gouernadores proceden en esto, como son obligados; y que es justo, que así ellos, como los prelados eclesiásticos vivan con cuydado de la protección, y amparo de los dichos indios. Rogamos, y encargamos a los dichos prelados, que en lo que les toca, procuren por su parte, que no reciban agravio, ni vejación; cumpliendo siempre lo dispuesto, y ordenado en su favor; y que en los casos excusen usar de censuras, pues no es proceder contra eclesiásticos hacer diligencia, para informarnos de lo que pasa.

11. Quéjanse del abuso de las limosnas en especie de arroz, en tiempo de las cosechas, que en algunas provincias llaman *PASALAMAT*. Refierese (no sé que sea cierto) que algunos padres doctrinantes de los pocos, que hay menos ajustados, se ponen a las puertas del templo, y van preguntando a cada indio, quanto ofrece de limosna? Responde obligado del miedo, o reverencial, o coactivo, que cinco cavanes. Replica anda: que me engañas, da diez; y manda asentar este número a los fiscales imaginarios que tienen: y de esta forma se va continuando en todos; y cobrase ejecutivamente, con prelación y anterioridad a todo lo demás. El pobre indio como ha de satisfacer el tributo a su magestad, o a su encomendero; a de contribuir a la bandala indispensablemente, y a de vender alguna porción, para vestirse en el discurso del año, se halla salido, y sin tener con que alimentarse; y despechado, o se retira en fuga a los montes, ó solicita otros medios, y remedios, para no perecer de hambre, y el usual, y más onesto suele ser, irse al mismo padre doctrinante, que se le presta. Dale, suponen, que un caban, que tiene de valor entonces un peso. Recíbelo con calidad, de satisfacerlo, a como valiere en la cosecha, que ordinariamente es, quatro cabanes al peso. Estos paga el indio con mucha puntialidad; en que se imputa, ay grandísimas grangerías; a demás de las que quieren decir, que suele aver en el crecimiento de las medidas y otras inteligencias.

12. Excesos son, que no pueden presumirse de religiosos y eclesiásticos en quien inspira la pureza del estado sacerdotal: y así e sabido de cierto, que se hallan muchos y aún los más que todo el arroz con que el rey nuestro señor les asiste, que son cien cabanes, y el synodo de otros cien pesos, y las obvenciones lícitas de los partidos, liberalmente lo distribuyen de limosna en los indios pobres, y necesitados; ocurriendo con piedad de padres a las aflicciones, y miserias de sus hijos espirituales.

13. Porque reconocen muy bien, que los intereses, á que anelan los desreglados, redundan en descrédito, y ofensa de la predicación evangélica. San Pablo, por excusar estos daños, se valía para sus alimentos, y de sus discípulos, del trabajo corporal de sus manos.

14. Y aunque pudiera recivir los precisos de aquellos, a quien predicaba, y enseñaba el Evangelio, sin subvenciones de los emperadores, antes perseguido de sus potencias; con todo eso por evitar el escandalo, padecía las incomodidades, por no hazerse molesto, y gravoso: y esto no era tomar, sino recibir, y en caso de precisa necesidad, y por el trabajo y ocupación no gratificada de los príncipes: y si en algún caso pudiera dispensarse, fue en la suma pobreza de los apóstoles; pero como la exaltación deste gran edificio de la iglesia, se fundó sobre los profundos cimientos de la pauperación, de que Christo Señor Nuestro fue la piedra

fundamental: *Petra autem erat Christus.* Y el que dio el primero, y mayor exemplo, para necessaria imitación de sus discípulos, no pudo nunca padecer falencia esta regla.

15. Ni son de menor calidad otras contribuciones que á título de limosnas se promulga, que suelen algunos repartir con no menos repugnancia y resistencia de los indios para fábricas, edificios, reparos, huertas, ornamentos, retablos, monumentos sin otro límite, forma ni poder que la voluntad no aligada a leyes de razón, ni regulada a direcciones de justicia natural, como si se pudiese medir en otro que Dios, el poder por la voluntad por ser la suma bondad.

16. Y estas no podían ser erogaciones libres sino exaciones apremiadas, no limosnas voluntarias sino exorciones violentas. La limosna según el Doctor Angélico es lo que se dá por amor de Dios al necesitado de compasión; si ésta se dá por temor de impresión y no de compasión siguiente que no puede ser limosna, porque según los dialécticos la definición se a de convertir con el definido.

17. En el católico sólo urge la compulsión de dar limosna por deuda legal aun de la hazienda que necesita para el estado y conservación de su persona y familia como no la aya menester para sublevar la propia y natural quando el próximo la padeciere extrema, porque ésta prefiere y pesa mas que la que se tiene solamente para sustentar el estado y calidad, y en este caso los bienes son comunes y así se entiende la autoridad de la Ambrosia de Milán y otros doctores y maestros.

18. Otro caso es aunque más controvertido entre los autores que fluctuando en encontradas opiniones unos lo niegan y otros lo afirman. Quando se tiene superabundancia de bienes y hazienda de suerte que excede a lo que necesita el decoro y ostentación del estado, calidad y puestos que entonces está obligado el superabundante a subvenir a los pobres aunque no esten extremados en la iropia, y se comprueva de San Lucas, donde Cristo Señor Nuestro sin mencionar la extrema manda, que quien se hallare con dos tunicas, de la una el que no la tiene, pues a él le sobra lo que al otro falta: y lo mismo en las viandas.

19. En lo que todos convienen sin disputa, es, que en esta segunda parte, quando se conceda, solo será obligación del precepto en el fuero interior de la conciencia, pero no en el exterior, de manera que no puede el juez coactivamente, como en la primera compeler al exuberante a dar Limosna, que solo la última, y extrema tiene el goze de este privilegio por derecho divino, y natural non *iure actionis* sed *officio judici.*

20. Como se ajuste extrema necesidad en la una parte, y copia superflua en la de los indios, tendré por lícita, onesta, y justa la exacción, pero en el entretanto é de estar en la verdad de las cosas, que es inmutable, y ni la metaphísica, ni la intención, que se toma, ni la materia, que se supone, ni las fábricas del entendimiento, ni el transcurso del tiempo, ni los patrocinios de theólogos, ni los privilegios de las regiones, la pueden prescribir, variar, impugnar, expugnar, ni contrastar: el trez veses Tulio de Africa encomiado por el mayor de los oradores Fray Hortensio Felix, que nació humano pero vecino del cielo.

21. Así pondera el Señor Conde de Lemos en la carta ilustrada tantas

vezes lo que la Theología se estiende en las Indias en estos servicios reales, y personales de los naturales. Y por cierto Señor (escribe aquella cristiana pluma) que yo me espanto mucho del desahogo, y seguridad con que algunos Ministros de mas, y menos porte an pasado por estos escrúpulos, y deficultades, no advirtiendo la crueldad, y violencia, con que los indios son tratados, sin embargo, que son libres, como las demás naciones, y que la grandeza, y costumbre de los repartimientos solo se justifica en las cosas, que miraren precisamente a la conservación desas provincias, y presupuestas las condiciones, que van expresadas en la cédula de su magestad, todas las quales son precisas, para que se haga lícita la compulsión de los indios, y así lo piden el derecho, y theología de Europa, no sé yo, como en las Indias ay otras leyes, y letras, que alarguen mas la licencia, y facultad de nuestro Imperio, pero como quiera que sea, es terrible la insolencia de nuestros españoles, y grande el descuido, que los Ministros de su Magestad an tenido en castigar sus desórdenes.

22. Y segun la disposición de la cedula dada en Monzón de Aragón a 2. de agosto de 1533. los naturales solamente deben asistir a los reparos, y reedificaciones de los templos con su trabajo, e industria personal, y no más. Luego no se les puede afligir en suma pobreza con erogaciones pecunarias.

23. También se debe extinguir el repartimiento, que se dice, les hazen algunos de los Padres Doctrinantes Regulares, y Seculares y Alcaldes Mayores de embarcaciones tripuladas de barigas, que son indios de boga, ó buenas boyas (si es que se pueden nominar así los que reman involuntarios) y otros muchos de respecto, para recambiar el peso de la ocupación, que llaman de esquipazón, dirigidas al expediente de sus inteligencias, sin satisfacerles el jornal, que merece exercicio tan penoso, mas que con la ración de arroz, y dos reales en dinero, aunque la duración de los viajes sea de meses enteros.

24. Quéxanse de que los viernes, y sabados, quatro temporas, y quaresmas les obligan a que les den pescado, y guebos, con que para el gasto de cada día destos están señaladas dos casas, que contribuyen a dos reales, el uno para peces, y el otro para guebos. Y sino asisten puntualmente a la exación, les castigan rigurosamente, y viene a tocarle cinco o seys vezes en el año á cada del pueblo, segun el número de naturales, que le habitan. Y asimismo se hazen repartimientos de gallinas, y pollos para los gastos ordinarios, y extraordinarios de Huespedes, y visitas de los superiores.

25. Y ésto está proibido por toda razón, y derecho por el Santo Concilio Mexicano lib. 2. titulo 2. Canone. 1. que está mandado observar en estas Islas por Bulla de la Beatitud de Urbano 8. expedida en el tercer año de su Pontificado a 11 de marco de 1626. hasta tanto, que se celebre el Manilense, cuya copia en forma probante esta en el Archivo desta Catedral. Y el motivo, que expresa su Santidad es, que quando se formó aquella synodo era esta iglesia sufraganea de la de México, conque despues de erigida en Metropoli se debe regir por las leyes, reglas, y estatutos de la iglesia de quien se dividió, desmembró, y separó, según lo enseña el derecho en reynos, o provincias unidas, o divididas de otros, hasta tanto que las construya proprias, y especiales.

26. Y porque no se entendiese, que el concilio ablaba solamente en los parrocos seculares, en el canon final declara comprehenderse en todos los regulares, que se ocupan en estas funciones doctrinales, y sacramentales, no sólo en lo resuelto en aquel título, sino en los demás decretos synodales de la sagrada congregación provincial, y quede asentada esta proposición para las autoridades, que en adelante alegare en este discurso parenético, porque no puedan acogerse a immunidad de exempción.

27. Piden eficaz remedio las compulsiones de indios, que por sus órdenes azen los governadorcillos, para que les condusgan agua, leña, sacate, y otros forrages, siendo así, que por provisión real desta audiencia inserta una cédula de su magestad, y por el capítulo 16. de las ordenancas de govierno tienen dos indios, que llaman Tanores diputados á estos ministerios con proibición de poder divertirlos á otros.

28. Y las que suelen azer, para cortes, y arrastros de maderas, que llaman *elas,* para construir champanes, caracoas, loangas, bancas, y otros linages de embarcaciones de mas o menos porte, en que transportan las negociaciones, é inteligencias.

29. Débese proibir asimismo el abuso de obligar a las Dalagas, que son indias, que no an tomado estado, y se tienen por doncellas, a rozar, y deserbar los patios, regar las uertas, las semillas sembradas, barrer las iglesias, a traer flores, y ramos, para adornarlas, y a yr de pueblo en pueblo a conducir el arroz, que llaman pasalamat (que es la limosna de que e ablado en el numero 11.) para coacervarlo en los Tambobos, que son los troxes de receptáculo, sin embargo de que tienen dos sacristanes privilegiados de las cargas públicas, para servicio, y asistencia de los templos, sin los Baintaos o Bagontaos. Y tambien las obligan, y a las mugeres de los Timauas, que son indios libres, aunque descendientes de los esclavos, que ubo en el Gentilisimo, a que pilen arroz palay, y a que laben toda la ropa del convento o casa.

30. Y encarecen, que obligan a los que tienen esclavos, aunque sea uno solo, a que los sabados los embien a misa, y en oyendola, les azen trabajar en estos, y otros oficios de suerte, que este día es el padre doctrinante dueño absoluto dellos.

31. Exageran, que tan poco se libran destas opresiones los Bagontaos, que son los jovenes ó muchachos. Y que aunque un indio tenga tres, quatro, ó mas ijos, todos los retienen, y ocupan en su servicio, sin permitir, que alguno ayude, y asista a sus padres, como parece pedía la razón natural. Y sería cosa dura e inhumana, que a los padres privasen de los obsequios filiales sin más causa, que la comodidad temporal; y así se á de mandar, y declarar no tener obligación de servirles, sino de acudir a la doctrina, y cathechesi; y en concluyendo con estos actos, que se buelvan libremente a sus casas.

32. Algunos de los padres doctrinantes, y de los alcaldes mayores hacen otro género de repartimientos gravosos, y excesivos entre los naturales, violentándoles a que les contribuyan mantas, talingas, paños de manos, colchas, manteles, medias de seda, y algodón; cera, algalia, cachumba, arróz, aceyte de cocos, lompotes, y otros texidos, y todos los demás frutos industriales, y naturales que producen las provincias; no

sólo en las que residen, sino aún en las más distantes; sin indultar su ambiciosa cudicia ni aún las cebollas, y ajos. Y que tienen mananguetes, esto es indios, que se ocupan en beneficiar la tuba, para confeccionar della el vino de cocos, o de nipa; en que se tiene negociación considerable. Y a las hijas de los Indios Principales Dalagas doncellas, costuras de camisas, calzones, albas, pañuelos, y lo demás; sin que les paguen la ocupación, precio, y valor: o quando por ventura la satisfacen, es en tan poca cantidad, que es como si fuera nada.

33. Estas exaciones bien se reconocen, que son proibidas por todo derecho. En el Concilio Mexicano expresamente se veda con graves penas; y en el Canon último declara compreenderse los Padres regulares doctrinantes, aunque lo tenía presupuesto en general en otro, como lo adverti, y asente en el numero 25.

34. Y San Gerónimo lastimado de los muchos males, que proceden destas causas, añade: que desde, que la avericia se introduxo en algunos de los eclesiásticos, como en el imperio Romano, pereció la ley de sacerdote, y la visión de propheta: que es vaticinio de Isaias, que se descifra, en que muchos sacerdotes hacen fracción de las leyes, y pierden la gracia de profetizar: porque todas las virtudes marchita la codicia, y eclipsa el interés.

35. Y todos los excesos ponderados se hallan prevenidos, y mandados remediar en las cédulas de su magestad católica. En la de San Lorenço de 18. de junio de 1594. dirigida a Gomez Perez Dasmariñas gobernante estas islas. ibi. "Decis, que en lo que toca a servicios, y esquipazones, proceden los religiosos con tanta libertad, y soltura en oprimir a los indios, y servirse dellos, como de esclavos, sin pagarles: que es cosa de mucho dolor, y digna de remedio; y tanto mas por el modo, que tienen para apoderarse de su libertad, sin dexarles elección en ninguna cosa. Y porque a los religiosos solos les toca la dotrina de los indios, y procurar, que sean relevados de sus trabajos, y no acrecentárselos con semejante opresión, dareys orden, en que los dichos religiosos no se sirvan de los indios, sino fuere en casos, y cosas muy necesarias; y entonces pagándoles lo que merecieren por sus jornales: que yo les escribo en esta conformidad la carta que va aqui, la qual les dareys, y a entender, que esto se a de cumplir precisamente."

La de 21 de Febrero de 1600, ibi: Presidente, y Oidores de mi Audiencia Real de la Ciudad de Manila de las Islas Filipinas, por relaciones, que é tenido é entendido lo mucho, que conviene para la conservación de esa tierra, composición de las cosas, que causan su ruina, y la de los naturales atajar las codicias, y contrataciones, que andan entre los sacerdotes doctrinantes, y los corregidores, anteponiendo ésto al bien común, y execución de las ordenanzas, y de los synodos, por donde les esta tan proibido; y atendiendo sólo a sus aprovechamientos, con medios de mal exemplo para los indios, y grandes molestias, que reciben, con que andan afligidos, y apurados: y como quiera, que en diferentes tiempos, y por diversas cédulas, y ordenanzas reales esta proibido a los ministros de Justicia; y sacerdotes tratar, y contratar; y el hazerlo, es del inconveniente, que se dexa entender, y tan perjudicial, y penoso para los indios; no veo que se a remediado ni escusado, como conviniera: y por que no se debe dar lugar a esto, os encargo y mando, que con el cuydado, y diligencia posible, pongays en lo suso dicho el remedio, que piden estos excesos, y los daños, que dellos resultan en lo espiritual, y temporal, de manera que tenga efecto; para que con el se atajen, y escusen estas contrataciones, y codicias de los ministros de justicia, y eclesiásticos: y en las residencias, que se tomaren a los corregidores, hareys que se averiguen, y castiguen con rigor los excesos, que en ésto uviere; y a los prelados escribo, que en lo que les toca, hagan lo mismo; y de lo que resultare, me avisareys etc.

36. La de Madrid de 29 de mayo de 1620. que esta original en el Archivo desta muy noble y leal ciudad, cuya contextura, dice: "Presidente, y Oydores de mi Real Audiencia de Manila, de las Islas Filipinas, é sido informado ay grandes excesos en algunos Religiosos, en hazer repartimientos a los Indios, para obras suyas; y les toman las gallinas, y otros bastimentos a menos precio, para comer ellos, y para sus grangerias haciéndoles agravios, y vexaciones y que conviene poner remedio en ello, mandando, que no se sirvan de los indios, sin pagarles lo que merecen; y que sin licencia de vos el mi governador, no se echen repartimientos, ni les hagan hazer obras. Y haviéndose visto en mi consejo real de las Indias, e tenido por bien de mandar la presente, por la qual os mando, trateys en esa audiencia, y acuérdolo sobre dicho; y por lo que toca a mi Patronazgo Real, mi fiscal della pida lo que convenga, de manera que cesen estas imposiciones, y agravios; y los visitadores, y corregidores de partidos tengan particular cuydado de proibirlos, y remuevan a los que fueren culpados. Y en razón de lo contenido en esta mi cédula, despachareys orden a los dichos religiosos, para que por ningun caso, hagan semejantes vexaciones contra sus feligreses. Y esto mismo encargo al Arçobispo, y obispo de esas islas, y a los provinciales de las órdenes dellas."

37. Y la repetida del Señor Don Juan de Silva, sobre estos servicios personales, y reales, de que se pide entero cumplimiento en sus finales clausulas. ibi. "Y a los obispos, y provinciales de las órdenes, ruego y encargo, que anden con la misma atención sobre el castigo de las culpas desta calidad, que suelen cometer los doctrineros, y otras personas eclesiásticas."

38. Ni podrán los que proceden con inadvertencias, quexarse que el rey nuestro señor, con geminados rescriptos mande contenerlos en sus excesos, antes deberán culpas sus acciones, excusando aun leves motivos, que puedan ocasionar, a que se piense menos bien de sus obligaciones; y reconocer, que todas tienen una misma raíz en las demostraciones de la avaricia, que se resiste a los remedios, que se defiende en los daños, que impetuosamente empeña en mayores precipicios. Elegantemente lo persuade la razón, y razones del venerable varón Joseph de Acosta.

39. Allá en el tiempo de San Gerónimo promulgaron los emperadores Valentiniano, Valente, y Graciano la ley 20. del título de los Obispos, y clérigos en el código Teodosiano, en que reprimían la cudicia de los eclesiásticos seculares, y monachales de aquel siglo; y el piadosísimo doctor gime lastimado, no la constitución, sino la causa; aprueba la herida, encomia la medicina, abomina la enfermedad, la proclama provida, se

vera; pero llora, que ni aún proibida se refrene: y quando por los fidei conmisos se defrauda el derecho, como si fuesen mas superiores, y urgentes las decisiones imperiales, que los preceptos de Cristo, tememos las leyes, y despreciamos el Evangelio.

40. Y aunque todas las cédulas reales, que e referido compreenden a los clérigos, ay otra especialísima expedida en Madrid a 18. de Febrero de 1588. dirigida a esta Real Audiencia cuyo tenor se sigue a la letra: "Presidente y Oidores de mi Audiencia Real de las Islas Filipinas, aviendo entendido, que muchos clérigos de esas Islas son tratantes, y mercaderes; de que resulta mal exemplo, y derogación de la estimación, en que deben ser tenidos, por razón de su dignidad, y otros muchos inconvenientes, escribo a los prelados desas Islas encargándoles, que provean, y den orden como los dichos clérigos no puedan ser factores de los encomenderos, ni de otras personas; ni tratar, ni contratar por si, ni por interpositas; y que castiguen con rigor a los que izieren lo contrario; y ocurran a esa Audiencia para que los ayudeys, siendo necesario, advirtiéndoles, de como os escribo sobre ello. Y por que conviene que lo que acerca desto les escribo se guarde, y cumpla, os mando que si para azerlo os pidieren favor y ayuda se le deys como conviniere; y que tengays mucha quenta, y cuydado de procurar, que la dicha orden se guarde, y execute, y de avisarme de como se guarda."

41. Y este rescripto es conforme al concilio mexicano, y el limense, lo proibió con graves penas, y censuras, de que apelaron algunos clerigos, alegando, que eran muy rigurosas, y que siempre les trayan turbadas las conciencias. Y porque en aquellas tierras son muy ordinarias, y necesarias estas contrataciones, y negociación, no se puede pasar ni vivir sin ellas: pero sin embargo, después de averse examinado, y ventilado en la sagrada Congregación de Cardenales, a quien se cometió la revisión, y confirmación del Synodo; y aviendo precedido informes del supremo consejo de las Indias, y de los embaxadores del rey en Roma, se tuvieron, y declararon por justas, y convenientes; por ser tan dañosas al estado clerical, a los indios, y a su conversión; y por otras razones, que lata, y gravemente se expresan, y ponderan en la Bula con firmante, que está puesta al principio del mismo concilio.

42. Los encarecimientos, que se azen de las exorbitancias en los testamentos de los naturales, los creo como posibles; pero no quiero escribirlos como ciertos. Dízese, que apenas está enfermo el indio, quando le conpelen a otorgarle a su arbitrio, y disposición, impresionando al testador, que mande a la Iglesia, el retablo, y al Padre; y en estos legados se consume la pobre hazienda, y substancia, quedando ex eredados los ijos, quando son erederos por todos derechos. San Pablo dixo es ijo, luego eredero. Para cumplimiento destos legados impíos, se venden luego executivamente las tierras, nipales, esclavos, y demas alaxas del difunto. Los miserables ijos, por recuperar lo que fue de su mayores, redimen su vexación comprándolo: empeñanse, para toda su vida; con que la pasan arrastrados, y perseguidos de acreedores, y deudas.

43. El testamento se difine: una sentencia iusta de la propria voluntad de lo que después de su muerte, quiere el testador, que se haga. Y si esto

fuese infalible, el desafuero corrompería la definición real, e imperial; y vendría a ser una sentencia injusta de agena voluntad, de lo que después de su muerte no quiere el testador, que se haga.

44. Quando es indubitable principio, que requiere libérrima voluntad: y aún quando los padres las dexaban voluntariamente libres a las iglesias, ex eredando, y quitándolas a los ijos, las repudiaba el gran Dotor Augustino, Luz, y Antorcha resplandeciente de la Iglesia, idea de santidad y prototypo de religión, en el sermon 49. el que quisiere (escribe con pluma de Angel) ex eredando a su ijo, instituir por eredera a la iglesia, solicite otro, que la reciba no a Augustino; y espero que estando Dios propicio, no se a de hallar quien la acepte.

45. Y era tanta la aversión, odio, y aborrecimiento, que tenia el dinero esta Sagrada Mitra de Hyppona, que refiere Cesar Baronio, que le censuraban, y acusaban el extremo de su perfección, quexandose de que los fieles se retrayan de instituir a las iglesias, por no querer admitirlas; y que esto redundaba en daño de los pobres; y que se hallo estrechado de hazer defensa pública a la calumnia, y defender el dictamen con los exemplos santísimos de Aurelio Obispo de Cartago, y de otros purísimos prelados: y ésto procedía en adquisiciones voluntarias, que sentiría en las violentas, y oprimidas?

46. Y de la ubérrima libertad, que piden los testamentos, procede, que aunque los indios mayores de edad se pueden, y deben restituir, y dezir de nulidad contra los contratos, que celebraren, sino se hallaren paccionados con autoridad de justicia, y expreso consentimiento de sus protectores generales, ó de los especiales, que se les suelen nombrar en semejantes casos; y que de más desto, ayan precedido treynta pregones en treynta días, para las ventas de bienes rayzes, y de nueve en nyeve para los muebles, o semoventes, como disponen las cédulas expresas de los años de 1540, de 1571 y de 1572. Y aún la primera requiere influencias de un señor ministro togado de la real audiencia, donde residiere: lo qual, y la solemnidad formal de los pregones en las cosas, que no excedieren del valor de treynta pesos, esta derogado por la última; y la precisión de intervención de sus protectores, en términos terminantes la extiende el ilustrísimo arçobispo de México Don Feliciano de Vega a todos los autos judiciales, y extrajudiciales, que se actuaren.

47. En las facciones testamentarias no tienen mano, ni interposición, sino es que se entienda que uvo alguna falsedad; porque en la materia de testar gozan la plenitud de libertad, que concede el derecho, y aun con mayores circunstancias y calidades que los rústicos, que necesitan de cinco testigos; y ay quien defienda que an de ser rogados, y vezinos; y en los de los indios está recebido general, y comunmente, que no necesiten de otorgarse ante escrivanos, ni testigos rogados, ni vezinos: sino que sea suficiente, que los forme uno de sus governadores; y que concurran dos, o tres testigos varones, o hembras, de los que comodamente se hallaren. Y comprobado ésto después ante juez competente, que se persuada de la armonía, y organización, que lleba luces de verdad, vale, y pasa por testamento solemne, y exequible.

48. Y por cédula de su magestad despachada en el Pardo a 6. de abril

de 1588 dirigida a esta real audiencia se proiben estos legados, y erencias, ibi. "Presidente, y Oidores de mi real audiencia, que reside en la ciudad de Manila de las Islas Filipinas. Yo é sido informado, que muchas vezes acaece, que quando algún indio rico está enfermo, y le va a confesar el religioso, ó clérigo, a cuyo cargo está su doctrina, procura, y da orden como haga testamento; y que en él le dexe a él, o a la iglesia, toda, o la mayor parte de su hazienda, aunque tengan erederos forçosos; y que con los indios ladinos sacristanes, que tienen en las dichas iglesias, que por la mayor parte son criados suyos, embían a hazer prevenciones con los dichos enfermos, y a que les persuadan a ello; y que quando la justicia lo viene a entender, ya el difunto está enterrado, y el cura o la iglesia apoderado en la hazienda; y que por este camino que dan muchos pobres defraudados de las erencias, que les pertenecen, sin saber, ni poder ir a seguir su justicia. Y porque mi voluntad, es que se ponga remedio en ello, os mando que proveays y deys orden como los dichos indios no reciban agravio en la sobre dicho, y tengan libertad en sus disposiciones sin permitir, que se les hagan semejantes violencias: y de lo que proveyeredes, me avisareys. Fecha en el Pardo, etc."

49. Deste rescripto aze generosa mencion el Señor Don Juan de Solórzano en su Política lib. 2. c. 28. Vers. pero es digna de notar fol. 238. y enseña que tambien sería justo, que los protectores cuydasen de su execución, y pidiesen lo que conveniese a sus promptos efectos.

50. Tienense por gravosísimas las obvenciones, y subvenciones, que se suelen llebar por los entierros, casamientos, baptismos, y demás funciones sacramentales, y eclesiásticas. No ignoro, antes lo ensalzo; y encomio, que muchas de las religiones, y muchos de los regulares de todas no solo no persiben estos emolumentos, sino antes les supeditan la cera, y demas necesario al funeral, y ritual de los baptismos, y matrimonios. Siempre e advertido, que no se compreenden en este discurso parenético los varones apostólicos observantes, justos y santos, que se desnudan por vestir á los naturales, que ayunan por sustentarlos; sino los que uviere relaxados, que por vestirse, y enriquecerse, desnudan, y desuellan a los indios; que por comer, los azen ayunar. Estos no seran curas, sino enfermedades de las provincias; no salud, sino peste de los partidos; no pastores, sino lobos, Idolos los llamó Dios por Zacarias; y en Ezeciel, llora infelices a los que se apacientan de las ovejas, contra la ley pastoral, en que los pastores apacientan las manadas, no las manadas a los pastores; desfructan las vtilidades, despoxan lo mas lúcido, desuellan la grey encomendada de Christo Señor nuestro. Y así los que se allaren complicados en los desórdenes, e implicados en los abusos, reconozcan la culpa, y enmienden la vida; y no se quexen de las medicinas, que se aplicaren, ni de la curación, que solicitan las vozes lastimosas de los aflixidos: que pretender procediendo con inadvertencia, que obren los rumores con modestia, el clamor con templanza, con temor las noticias, con lentitud los remedios, con omisión las execuciones y sin resolución, ni valor los ministros, es mas facil de desear, que de conseguir. Tarde o nunca se remediaran los inconvenientes, sino tuviesen libertad los expedientes; y mucho mejor será sufrir los remedios que morir de los males.

51. Bolviendo a enebrar la tesis, si el tal indio muere sin hazienda,

con que satisfacer el funeral, an de contribuir los parientes, o se a de sepultar el cadaver: obligados de la necesidad, y orror pactan las impensas, y contribuyen para la Cruz, la capa presviteral, el acetre, el sacristán, los cantores, el doble de campanas, la sepultura. De suerte, que avido quien admire, que los conventos no se fabriquen de plata; y dizen que se engaña el que lo piensa, que las subvenciones, o obvenciones no son para los conventos, sino para los conventuales.

52. Si el indio difunto es rico, no tiene parientes, que les sucedan; porque lo eredan los padres doctrinantes: si es pobre, forçosamente los á de aver, para que paguen los gastos funerarios; al contrario de lo que corre en el mundo que siempre faltan deudos, y no deudas a los pobres, y sobran a los ricos. Y así donde se vieron con hazienda estimados, y aplaudidos los padres, los ijos, y nietos se lamentan arruinados, arrastrados, y despreciados; y uyendo de si mismos se destierran de sus patrias, y vagan en las agenas.

53. En las cédulas de su magestad se previenen estos casos funestos. En la escrita a Gómez Perez Dasmariñas governante estas Islas, su fecha en Madrid a 11 de junio de 1594. en el cap. 10. ibi. "Pide también el obispo, que en el tasar de los réditos, que a los beneficiados se an de dar, se tenga atención a que los naturales desas islas, no están en costumbre de pagar derechos por los entierros, y casamientos, ni por otros ministerios eclesiásticos. Lo qual dize proveyo así por ciertos respectos, y que en los pueblos que estan a cargo de los religiosos, que quieren azer lo que deben, se a guardado esta orden precisamente; como quiera, que los dichos religiosos, sin poderlo el remediar, no an querido pasar por ello, sino que llevan excesivos derechos por casarlos, y darles sepultura. Y porque el obispo a dado razón por donde parece, que ésto conviene mucho, os mando deys orden en que en todo el distrito de ese govierno se guarde inviolablemente esta costumbre, así por los clérigos, como por todos los religiosos. Y en quanto a la tasa de los réditos de lo que se a de dar a los dichos beneficiados, se os comete a vos juntamente con el obispo, etc."

54. Y este capítulo se inserto en otra despachada al Señor Don Francisco Tello de Sandoval en Toledo a 25 de mayo de 1596. c. 8. ibi. "Pidio también el obispo, que en el tasar de los réditos, que se uviesen de dar a los beneficiados de pueblos de indios, se tuviese consideración a que los dichos indios no estaban en costumbre de pagar derechos de los entierros, casamientos, ni por otros ministerios eclesiásticos; y que se ordenase, que todos los religiosos, que tuviesen cargo y administración de doctrina, no llevasen los dichos derechos, como tampoco lo llebavan los clérigos, por averselo mandado el asi con censuras. Y por averme parecido muy bien, proveí, y ordené, que esta costumbre se guardase inviolablemente, assí por los clérigos, como por los religiosos en todo aquel districto, como lo vereys por la cédula, que en esta conformidad se despachó; la qual hareys guardar, y cumplir; y de lo que desto resultare me avisareys con particularidad.

55. Y otras innumerables, que están en el 1. tomo de las impresas pág. 91. que deseando templar la avaricia, mandan se les señalen estipendios; y que contentos con ellos, segun el Evangelio, se abstengan de llebar

derechos: de que tambien tubo reminiscencia, la illustrísima mitra de México, y el Concilio Limense 3. que con graves penas, y censuras proibe llevar toda especie de oblaciones, que no sean spontáneas. Y el Concilio Mexicano solo les dispensa aquellas, que en derecho estuviesen estatuidas.

56. Y por otro rescripto general de 6. de mayo de 1614. se resuelbe, que no lleven de derechos de entierros, matrimonios, baptismos etc. Sino conforme a la tasa, y declaración de los prelados ordinarios.

57. Y puesto que en la asinagción de los synodos se atendió, a que no avían de percebir estas subvenciones; y con esta inspeción se les constituyó el que gozan, justo será, que lo cumplan de su parte: pero en caso, que parezcan a V.S. inescusables, según el estado de las materias, accidentes, y circunstancias del tiempo, se a de servir de mandar despachar mandamientos de ruego, y encargo a los illustrísimos, y reverendísimos Señores Prelados destas provincias, para que cada uno en su diócesi forme aranceles regulados a los sagrados cánones, y santas disposiciones de los Concilios Tridentino, y Mexicano, y los remitan a la real audiencia, que los auxilie, y coadyuve la execución, o los modifique en el exceso, segun la dotrina del Señor Don Juan Solórzano, cuyas palabras copiaré por la importancia, y escrúpulo de la juridición ibi. "Y no solo se pueden interponer las audiencias reales en moderar estos derechos (ablo antecedentemente de las esportulas de notarios, y officiales de los tribunales ecclesiásticos) sino aún tambien en los entierros, y funerales, y en los matrimoniales, y otros semejantes, y aun en atajar el abuso de los doctrineros, que hacen, que los indios les hagan ofrendas forciblemente, como se dispone en una cédula del año 1556. y por otra de Madrid a 20. de diciembre del de 1608. se les encarga, que tambien hagan moderar las procuraciones, y collectas, que los Visitadores eclesiásticos lleban, y cobran en sus visitas. Todo lo qual como dice Bobadilla lib. 2. c. 18. n. 229 se funda en que los reyes pueden proibir, que los eclesiásticos no graven a sus súbditos, y vasallos, con imposiciones, y contribuciones ilícitas; y mandar a los prelados, que enbien ante ellos, y sus consejos los aranzeles de los tribunales eclesiásticos: de que tenemos también otra ley recopilada que es la 27. del título 25. libro 4. Recopilación. Y el cap. 41. de las Cortes de Madrid, del año de 1593. Y dixe otras cosas en el lib. 4. c. 8. desta Política, que se pueden tener en este por repetidas." Hasta aquí este eruditisimo barón.

58. La ley 29. que pulsa, para que se practique en el caso, y se inserte la claúsula, y penasen los despachos de los Alcaldes mayores, a cuyo cuydado se a de encomendar la observancia, dice así. "Y entretanto, porque consentir, que se lleven derechos demasiados es imposición illícita, que no se debe consentir se llebe a nuestros subditos, y naturales; mandamos a los del nuestro consejo, que den las cartas, y provisiones necesarias para los prelados y sus provisores, y juezes eclesiásticos, que en lo determinado por los aranzeles del reyno, guárdenlo en ellas contenido; y en lo que no estuviere determinado, manden traer ante sí los aranzeles del juzgado eclesiástico, para que platicado con los prelados, que para ello fueren diputados, se de buena orden, como convenga; y conforme aquello se moderen, y fagan como se an moderado, y raçonables. Y mandamos, que de aquí adelante se ponga en las provisiones de los corregimientos, y

otros oficios de nuestros reynos, que los dichos corregidores, asistentes, y sus tenientes, y otras qualesquier justicias, so pena de privación de los oficios, y de perdimiento del salario, embien relación en cada un año, si los dichos prelados, y juezes eclesiásticos guárdanlo aquí contenido en el llevar de los derechos.

59. Mas podía embarazar la aplicación de remedio a los testamentos; y el que se me ofrece proporcionado es, que se guarde el Concilio Mexicano en el Canon. 3. del título 10. lib. 3. en cuyos márgenes se citan las leyes 6 y 10. del título 4. lib. 5. de la recopilación dize pues aquel sagrado decreto trasumptado. "Quando algún indio muriere con testamento, se executen los legados, y sufragios, que dispuso; y en caso que tenga eredero necesario, estos legados, y sufragios no an de exceder la quinta parte; porque está proibido en derecho; pero si muriese ab intestato, se guarde lo proveido, en el antecedente (que establece, que si dexare bastantes bienes. se le celebre el día de su deposición una Vigilia, y Misa, y un Novenario en su Parrochia) Manda la Santa Synodo, que de qualquiera manera, que muera, o con testamento, o abintestato, el Parrocho, ora sea regular, o secular no tome nada de sus bienes, aunque sea con pretexto de distribuir en suffragios la quinta parte por el alma del difunto; pena al cura clerical de pagar otro tanto a la fábrica, de lo que intercepto de los bienes del muerto, y al religioso del castigo praescripto en el Tridentino Sessión. 25. c. 11. de Reformatione."

60. Este es el Canon, con que parece quedarían bastantemente prevenidos los daños; porque los indios destas provincias, rara vez, o nunca podrán morir sin erederos forçosos, segun sus costumbres nacionales, que estan mandadas guardar, como no repugnen á la ley natural, y evangélica por muchas cédulas, en especial, por la de 6. de agosto de 1555. Y por la ordenanza 80. desta real audiencia, ibi. "Mando que el dicho mi presidente, y oidores tengan mucho cuydado de no dar lugar, que en los pleytos entre indios, ó con ellos, se hagan procesos ordinarios, ni aya largas; sino que summariamente sean determinados, guardando sus usos, y costumbres, no siendo claramente injustos: y los dichos mis oidores tengan cuydado que esto mismo se guarde por los Juezes inferiores." Si no tienen hijo ligitimo, ni natural, les eredan precisamente los ascendientes; y en su defecto los parientes mas cercanos, según y con las distincciones, que refiere el Padre Fray Juan de Plasencia Religioso de la Seráfica Orden de San Francisco, en una relación, que hizo de las costumbres de los naturales al Señor Doctor Santiago de Vera, presidente, governador, y capitán general, que fué destas Islas, el año de 1599. Y el Señor Doctor Morga, aunque de paso, Sucesos de Filipinas c. 8.

61. Otro abuso se representa en los graves castigos, que suelen executar algunos en los indios, azotándolos cruelmente, cortando el pelo a las mugeres; prendiéndolos en cepos, y bretes, en cárceles privadas, que constituyen, para este efecto; teniendo para Ministros destas funciones, fiscales mayores, y menores, con jurisdición, y exercicio, que les confieren de su propria, y absoluta potestad; y que se ingieren en las elecciones de los governadores, y otros ministros pedaneos de las provincias, y pueblos, compeliendo a los eligentes, que voten por el que gustan salga con el

oficio; quitando la libertad, que piden estos actos: y dan exempciones (que vulgarmente llaman Reservas) de tributos a los indios, de las encomiendas de su magestad, y de particulares; con que quedan excusados, y relevados de pagarlos.

62. Aun allá en el Deuteronomia mandaba Dios, que los azotes de los esclavos no llegasen a más de quarenta; porque no cayese muerto a los pies de quien tenía tan crueles las manos. Y esto significó San Pablo, que aviéndole azotado cinco vezes los judios, no llegaron a 40. los azotes, sino que se quedavan en los 39. porque eran tan superticiosos en su ley, que por no exceder, no la cumplían enteramente; pues, que será quando á ombres se dan no 39. sino ciento, y más azotes; y no en observancia, sino en transgresión de leyes.

63. Deseo saber con que autoridad, y potestad se exercen estos actos de mero, mixto imperio en vasallos libres de su magestad católica del rey, que es la fuente perenne, y origen perpetuo de la jurisdición en lo temporal. En ninguna manera la tienen; antes esta su real voluntad constantemente opuesta, y contraria en sus cédulas rescriptos, y direcciones. Instrucción del Virrey del Peru. c. 5. 7. fol. 18. La del de México c. 5. 2. fol. 15. B. ibi: "Y assimismo se tiene entendido, que reciben muchos agravios de los religiosos, y clérigos, que los doctrinan; y particularmente en que los prenden, y castigar por qualquier caso liviano; y algunas vezes porque no acuden a sus grangerías, y servicios personales, como ellos querrían. Y como quiera, que esto les está proibido, porque no se cumple, como devía, os mando no permitays, ni deys lugar a que los curas clérigos, ni frayles, a cuyo cargo fuere la doctrina tengan carceles, alguaciles, ni fiscales; ni hagan cosa, que sea en perjuicio de los indios."

64. Y la cédula despachada á Gómez Perez Dasmariñas, su fecha en Madrid a 11 de junio de 1594. ibi. "Gómez Perez Dasmariñas mi governador, y capitan general de las Islas Filipinas o personas a cuyo cargo fuere su govierno. Porque é sido informado, que los religiosos, que residen en esas Islas, ocupados en la doctrina, y conversión de los indios, se embarazan en cosas, que no les pertenecen, os mando, no deys lugar a que tengan cárceles, ni prisiones ni prendan ni condenen; sino fueren aquellos, que tubieren comisión del Obispo, para las cosas, en que la pudiere dar, conforme a derecho; ni pongan, ni tengan fiscales, sino los que el obispo les señalare; ni lleven derechos de entierros, ni matrimonios, ni baptismos, sino conforma la tasa, y declaración del obispo etc." Y después el año 1614. se despachó sobre cédula, inserta la referida al señor Don Juan de Silva: y por otra de 1624. se buelven a mandar guardar con esta conformidad. ibi. "Suplico me mandase, se executase lo dispuesto en dicha cédula de 11. de julio de 614. arriba inserta; y que en su conformidad, el dicho arçobispo, y obispo pongan, y nombren los dichos fiscales, como les pertenece conforme a derecho; y el conocer judicialmente de los delictos, y causas de los dichos indios; y no a los religiosos, que los prenden, castigan como les parece. Y visto por los del dicho mi consejo de las Indias, fué acordado, que devía mandar dar, esta mi cédula, por la qual quiero, y es mi voluntad, se guarden, cumplan, y executen las sobre dichas cédulas arriba insertas de 11 de junio del dicho año de 594. 6 de mayo de

614. según, y como en ellas se contiene, y declara; sin embargo de lo contenido en dichas cédulas de 16 de Marco de dicho año de 614. para que el dicho Arcobispo no innovase de la costumbre, que avía en el nombramiento de fiscales, y el dicho governador informase; que siendo necessario, las doy por ningunas, y de ningún valor, ni efecto. Y mando al Presidente, y Oidores de mi audiencia real de las dichas Islas, que contra lo contenido en esta mi cédula no vayan, ni pasen, ni consientan ir, ni pasar en ningún tiempo, por ninguna manera, antes den el favor, y ayuda, que para su execución, y cumplimiento fuere necessario: que yo lo tengo asi por bien. Fecha en Madrid a treinta de agosto de 1624. años."

65. Y por otra su fecha en Madrid a 23. de otubre de 1639. se mandan guardar las referidas con insercion especial de cada una; y concluye ibi: "Y porque no halla el dicho arçobispo otro remedio, sino ocurrir a mi real clemencia, me a suplicado, que para que el estado eclesiástico no este tan abatido en aquellas partes, mande se cumplan las cédulas que están dadas en razón de que no puedan tener fiscales los doctrineros, sino los que nombraren los ordinarios, con ningún pretexto ni insignias. Y abiéndose visto en mi consejo real de las Indias, teniendo consideración a todo lo que el dicho arçobispo representa; é tenido por bien de dar la presente; por la qual mando, que las cédulas, o sobre cédulas aquí insertas se guarden, y cumplan precisa, puntual, e inviolablemente, según y como por ellas se contiene, ordena, declara, y manda; sin interpretarlas, ni ir contra su tenor y forma en manera alguna; sin embargo de qualquiera orden, que aya en contrario; que assí es mi voluntad: Y así mismo mando al presidente, y oidores de la dicha mi Audiencia las guarden, y hagan guardar, y cumplir, y executar en todo, y por todo, según y como por ellas se dispone; con apercebimiento, que de no guardarse así, me daré por deservido. Fecha en Madrid a 23 de octubre de 1639 años."

66. Y por esta real audiencia se an despachado provisiones reales, insertas las cédulas referidas, para que en su execución los padres doctrinantes no nombren ni elixan fiscales; y sin embargo ay algunos, que en in obediencia, rebeldía, contumacia, y aun desprecio de tantos tan geminados, y repetidos rescriptos, los crian, mantienen, y conservan con titulos de mayores, y menores; y haziendo, que usen, y exerzan jurisdicción eclesiástica, y temporal: teniendo obligaciónes tan precisas, y urgentes de obedecer las cédulas de su magestad. Lo primero por la de vasallos: que la religión ni el sacerdocio no destruye, sino perficiona la subjeción; y quien resiste a la real potestad, a las ordinaciones de Dios resiste, y repugna. El onor se deve por la excellencia; el temor, por la potestad; la obediencia, por la governación dominativa. Lo 2. por capellanes beneficiados de su soberana grandeza, que á tantas expensas los conduze; á confiar lo doctrina de sus súbditos; donde los alimenta, y substenta de su azienda, y patrimonio. Lo 2. porque los rescriptos reales tienen fuerza de breves apostólicos en las Indias, como enseña Fray Antonio Remesal. lib. 8. de la Historia de Guatimala c. 12. pag. 417. Y el S.D. Juan de Solórzano.

67. De algunos se refiere, que alteran los nombres de fiscales, y los titulan, zeladores; y que en lugar de la bara alta negra, que avían de usar por insignia del oficio, la transmutan en bastones cortos; como si las leyes

le constituyesen a los nombres, y no a las cosas; o como sino iziese fraude a su decisión, quien dexando salvas las palabras; violase su sentencia, mente, animo, é intencion; y no pecase mas, el que simulando obediencias, la fraudase, que no quien directa, y claramente la quebrantase, y contraviniese.

68. En la sobre cédula citada del año de 1639. se previene estos fraudes ibi. "Y se les abrió puerta a todos los Doctrineros, para que puedan tener fiscales, dándoles licencia, no lo pudiendo azer, para que tengan indios con bastones pequeños para el servicio de la iglesia: que esto es lo mismo, que si tuvieran bara alta de fiscal: porque los indios no obedecen sino a estos, que nombran los doctrineros, tengan la insignia que quisieren; y todo contra lo que está mandado por cédulas reales, para que con ningún pretexto, ni achaque puedan tener fiscales.

69. Y por auto del Señor Sebastián Hurtado de Corcuera, su fecha en esta ciudad a 29. de octubre de 1636, que a la letra dize. "Sebastian Hurtado de Corcuera etc. Por quanto por diferentes cédulas tiene su magestad mandado, que los religiosos doctrineros destas islas no nombren fiscales, ni tengan cárceles, prisiones, ni cepos, ni hagan actos de jurisdición, ne perjuicio de la que tienen los arçobispos de estas Islas; a quien privativamente pertenece el dicho nombramiento de fiscales, y el conocer de las causas eclesiásticas, de los naturales, y demás sus feligreses, y domiciliarios; sobre lo qual por esta real audiencia están mandadas despachar provisiones reales, dirigidas a los Alcaldes mayores, y Corregidores de las Provincias, y partidos destas Islas; insertas las dichas Reales cédulas, y encargándoles su execucion, y cumplimiento; poniendo penas a los que por nombramiento de los dichos religiosos doctrineros, truxeren baras, bastones, o otra insignia con nombre de fiscales, o mayordomos, o con qualquier otro color, o pretexto; lo qual conviene se guarde, y cumpla según, y en la forma, que en las dichas reales cédulas se contiene. Por tanto por la presente ordeno, y mando a todos, y a cada uno de los dichos alcaldes mayores, y corregidores, que luego que con la dicha real provisión sean requeridos, guarden, y cumplan su tenor; y si contra el intentaren alguna cosa los dichos religiosos, o estuvieren rebeldes en el cumplimiento de la real voluntad, me den luego aviso dello, para que por sus prelados, se les de el castigo conveniente; pues no por eso se les impide el acudir a todo lo que pertenece a la doctrina, y administración de Sacramentos de los dichos naturales; para lo qual se pueden, y deven servir de los fiscales, y ministros, que les nombraren, y señalaren los dichos arçobispos, y obispos. Y para en quanto a evitar pecados públicos, borracheras, amancebamientos, y qualesquiera otros, que toquen a la jurisdicción secular, o sean mixtifori, lo pueden remediar los dichos alcaldes mayores, y corregidores, y los governadores de los pueblos, donde ellos no estuvieren presentes, prendiendo los culpados, y remitiéndoselos, para que los castiguen. Y en la misma forma en los casos, que fueren mere eclesiásticos, se podrán prender los culpados, y remitirlos a su juez, sin dar lugar a que en los unos casos, ni en los otros se entremetan los dichos religiosos doctrineros, ni usen de jurisdiccion; y me embiará testimonio auténtico cada uno de los dichos alcaldes mayores, y corregidores cada quatro meses, según en otro orden les tengo mandado me le imbien, de como guardan, y cumplen los órdenes,

que les tengo dados; y so las penas en ella contenidas. Fecha en Manila etc."

70. Con que parece que a esta luz queda irefragablemente comprovado, que no tienen mero, y mixto imperio comunicado de su magestad, sino que antes lo tiene exactísimamente proibido.

71. Del sumo pontifice menos; porque ninguno da lo que no tiene; y en su santísima persona, no reside la jurisdicción temporal, que llaman cuchillo material, por lo menos directamente en acto, y exercicio; y por lo mas, indirectamente en solo abito, y potencia: que es á lo último, que se extienden los autores, que asisten con mayor fineca a la iglesia; porque la potestad dominativa, y jurisdicional precisamente se halla en los reyes, principales soberanos, como la suprema espiritual en el Papa cabeca de la iglesia, y sucesor de San Pedro, Clavero mayor del cielo.

71. Y aunque es muy disputable entre los doctores la questión, de si Cristo Señor Nuestro en quanto ombre quiso ser, o fuese rey temporal del Orbe, y exerciese la dominacion y jurisdicción suprema del Mundo, por juro de eredad, ó por derecho de elección, según lo que refirio por San Juan, que su reyno no era de este mundo.

73. La mas común, y cierta es, que Cristo en quanto ombre, no tubo, ni quiso reyno temporal proprio, y umano, o de inferior orden, como es el que formalmente tienen los reyes y príncipes; pero eminentemente dominó otro más excelente, y superior, conferido de Dios plena, y absolutamente sobre todo lo criado, por el don de unión; por el qual *ex natura rei,* fue constituido cabeça de los ángeles, y de los ombres: porque esto lo pedía, y requería la dignidad, y grandeza de Cristo ombre.

74. Pero esta potestad no se transfirió en San Pedro, ni en sus sucesores; porque es infalible, que los dones que en Cristo se confideran excelente, y eminentemente; no sólo los que miran á lo natural, y temporal; pero aun quando conciernen a la potestad eclesiástica, y espiritual, no se transmutaron en el pontífice, como la facultad de instituir Sacramentos, obrar milagros, por propria virtud; y en otros exemplos, que ostenta Santo Tomás, si es que fue suyo el tratado de Regimine Principis.

75. Y en estos principios, y especialmente en la decisión de Innocencio, en el cap. Sollita. 6. de Maioritate, et obedientia; en que sentidamente increpa al emperador de Constantinopla, (que según Jacobo de Valdés en el libro, que escrivió, de la dignidad de los reynos, y reyes de España c. 18. n. 16. se llamava Constantino; y juzgo sería yerro de las prensas: porque en tiempo, que floreció aquel pontífice, no imperó ninguno deste nombre, sino Henrico 6. Filipo, Oton. 4. y Federico 2. como refiere Onufrio Panvinio en sus Commentarios fol. 375) de que al patriarca de aquella santa sede, le daba al lado siniestro inferior lugar del que se le debía, por la grandeza de su dignidad: que aunque los emperadores, y cesares deben preferir en los actos seculares temporales; pero no en los eclesiásticos, y espirituales, en que los pontífices, debaxo de cuyo nombre se compreenden los patriarcas, arçobispos, y obispos, tienen prelación, anterioridad, y jurisdicción privativa.

76. Y para comprobación de su intento, le trae el lugar del Génesis c. 1. que asi como Dios crió dos lumbreras lucientes en el firmamento de

los cielos; una de suprema magnitud, que presidiese al día; otra menor, que regentase la noche: ambas grandes; pero una mayor que otra; assí en el firmamento de la iglesia militante instituyó dos dignidades grandes, y superiores, la pontifical, y la real: pero aquella preside al día, esto es a lo eclesiástico, y espiritual; y assí es mayor, que la que govierna lo temporal, y carnal; y tanta diferencia hace aquella á esta, quando el sol a la luna, por lo ventajoso, que es lo espiritual, y sagrado, á lo secular, y profano.

77. En estos principios, digo, que me parece se fundaría la cédula de 28. de henero de 1609. que prescrive la dirección de las precedencias entre los prelados, governadores, y presidentes, ibi. "Como quiera que esta ordenado, que los arçobispos, y obispos prefieran en la iglesia, y actos eclesiásticos a los nuestros presidentes, aunque sean governadores, declaramos, que aunque no lo sean, los dichos presidentes an de preferir en los actos públicos a los dichos arçobispos, v obispos fuera de la iglesia, y en actos seculares. Y así mandamos lo hagan; y que todas las vezes, que concurrieren con los dichos prelados fuera de la iglesia, y de los dichos actos eclesiásticos, tomen el lado derecho como governadores de la tierra, y personas que tan inmediatamente representan la nuestra."

78. Y la de 4. de noviembre de 1612. ibi. "Porque se a dudado si a de tener dosel el arçobispo de Manila en la iglesia, asi quando estuviere haciendo actos pontificales, como no los haciendo en presencia de nuestro governador della, declaramos que le pueda tener, y tenga en la forma que lo manda, y ordena el ceremonial Romano, aunque el governador se halle presente. Y en quanto a si le an de llevar al dicho arçobispo la falda alçada, declaramos que en las procesiones, y actos eclesiásticos al arçobispo le lleven la falda, aunque asista en ellos el governador, y audiencia; pero que vaya solamente con el criado, que se la llevare. Y quando fuere a las casas reales, se la lleven asta la puerta del aposento, donde estuviere el dicho governador, y allí se la suelten, y buelvan a tomar quando salga."

79. De donde tambien infiero, que supuesto, que el summo pontífice tiene en los fieles la dominación suprema espiritual, y no la temporal directa, sino indirecta en acto, y potencia, en quanto conduce a los fines sobre naturales, en la forma, que se a explicado. En los Infieles, gentiles, bárbaros idólatras, así los que asisten en reynos cristianos, y católicos, como en los suyos proprios, no tiene una, ni otra. Y consequentemente no puede, ni deve conocer, juzgar, disponer, ó determinar sus negocios, y causas; sino que precisamente tiene derecho, y facultad para azerles predicar el Evangelio, y que no impidan en sus tierras la promulgación, ni proiban a sus súbditos, que la recivan, ó les impresionen á que la nieguen después de la profesión, y baptismo; ó en otra manera injurien, u ofendan a la religión cristiana.

80. Porque la potestad gubernativa, ó política espiritual compete al Papa, en quanto cabeza de la iglesia; y tiene las vezes de Cristo Señor Nuestro en su cuerpo mixtico, que es la misma iglesia militante, como confiesan todos los católicos: y así esta facultad la exerce en los ombres, como miembros, y partes de aquel cuerpo, mediante el baptismo, por donde renacen, y se constituyen fieles, y se incorporan con Cristo su cabeza.

81. Pruévase de San Pablo, á quien explica San Gerónimo, que por razón de aquellos crímines se corrija, y enmiende a los cristianos; pero a los que no lo son, y estan fuera de los límites sagrados de la iglesia, se dexe, y libre el castigo, y vindicta a Dios.
82. Y de San Juan en el cap. final. Donde Cristo mandó a San Pedro, que apacentase sus ovejas, que todos los padres de la iglesia interpretan de los fieles: que los infieles no lo son de su rebaño. Enséñanlo con extremada erudición las púrpuras eminentes de Roberto Bellarmino, y Cesar Baronios, y otros muchos, que illustraran los márgenes copiosamente fecundos.
83. Y así Cristo Señor Nuestro solo ordeno a sus Apóstoles, que enseñasen, y baptizasen a todas las gentes: palabras, que no son coactivas, ni dominativas, sino institutorias, y denunciativas del Sagrado Baptismo.
84. Y se puede exornar tambien con la cédula real de 21. de febrero de 1631. años, dirigida al Señor Don Juan Niño de Tavora, Governador, que era destas Islas, Ibi: "Al arçobispo, y obispos de esas Islas les encargo agan, que sus provisores, y demás ministros no se entremetan á conocer de las causas civiles, ni criminales de los infieles residentes, y contratantes en ellas; ni procedan contra ellos a prisión, censura, ni pena pecunaria; sino es en casos, que expresa, y notoriamente se conozca, que se endereçan contra nuestra santa fee, y religión cristiana, y a poner impedimentos a ella; y que los demás, que no fueren deste género, os los dexen a vos, y demás mis justicias reales, a quien tocaren; y asi os encargo cuydeys destos, como conviene, procediendo conforme a derecho."
85. Y Santo Tomás enseña, que los infieles en acto no son de la iglesia, sino en potencia; asi respecto de Cristo, cuya virtud infinita se estiende a salvar todos los ombres, como de parte de los infieles, que por su libertad pueden venir a la iglesia; y refiere a San Atanasio, y otros muchos santos, que lo autorizan.
86. Y a este propósito suelen traer la respuesta, que dió Atabaliba Emperador del Perú a Fray Vicente de Balverde Dominicano, que intimándole no muy prudente, ni piadoso la guerra a fuego, y sangre, sino se subjetase a los reyes de España, á quien el Summo Pontífice avía concedido la dominación, e imperio de aquellas provincias; le respondió resuelto, que no quería reconocer por superior a aquel rey, cuyo nombre jamás avía oido; ni obedecer á aquel Papa, que con tanta liberalidad dava lo que no era suyo.
87. Y el Angélico Doctor, y su escuela concluyen, que el Pontífice en lo espiritual tienen amplísima potestad comunicada de Cristo, cuyo vicario es; en los cristianos, para instituirlos, dirigirlos, y juzgarlos con santas leyes; en los infieles, para predicar, ó solicitar que se les promulgue el Evangelio; en que el obispo de Chiapa en la proposición 14. le impone obligación de derecho divino; pero no para exercer dominación, ni jurisdición temporal, como queda asentado.
88. Y así San Pedro embio á Egipto á San Marcos; y San Clemente á San Dionisio el Areopagita á las Galias, y San Gregorio a Augustino, y a sus compañeros á Inglatierra; Gregorio 2. a Bonifacio a la Germania.
89. Esta emplificación delegó Alexandro 6. a los Serenísimos Reyes de España en las Indias; y así son delegados Apostólicos.

90. Y en virtud deste indulto an tenido, y tienen poder, y autoridad sus Magestades Católicas, para azerles promulgar el Evangelio, catequizar; y disponer al baptismo; auxiliar, y amparar los convertidos; castigar los apostatas transfugas, y desertores; reprimir a los perturbantes, con tener, y escarmentar los impedientes; y a los demás actos, que conducen a este fin: y para expeler, y excluir a los Reyes, y príncipes, que pretendieren comerciar este nuevo Orbe.

91. Dedúcese finalmente destos principios constantes, que los padres doctrinantes no tienen jurisdicción temporal política, coactiva de mero, y mixto imperio, para conocer, juzgar, ni castigar corporal, ni civilmente a los indios fieles, o infieles; sino la espiritual de curas, ó parrochos en el fuero interior de la conciencia, para absolver en las confesiones penitenciales, y administrar los demás Sacramentos; en que exercen las vezes, y oficio de los obispos: y así se lo persuade el Concilio Mexicano.

92. A esto se puede responder, que estas coacciones, y castigos se enderezan a la instrucción, y disciplina de la cathechesi cristiana; y que sin estos medios no sera posible, que fructifique en los indios, gente indevota, remisa, poco inclinada a funciones de religión, sino les despierta el miedo, y les recuerda el temor: con que si se quitase esta mano, auctoridad, y poder a los padres doctrinantes, se desvanecia la obediencia, se destruía la doctrina, se arruinaría la iglesia, y se asolaría la fee en estas provincias; porque todo consiste en los azotes, palos, prisiones, grillos, zepos, bretes, y castigos de los naturales.

93. Lo 1. se satisface á este argumento, con que en nada son más admirables los indios, que en la obediencia; porque como está, es ija de la umildad, y ellos son tan umildes, y mansos de coraçon, son obedientísimos a los superiores. Quando an tenido ni primeros movimientos de contradicción á órdenes reales, ni falta de respecto al sagrado nombre de su magestad, ni deslealtad, ni imaginación de semejante exceso? Quando se a visto renitencia, ni contradicción a los alcaldes mayores, ni doctrinantes, quando les mandan no solo lo justo, y onesto, sino lo penoso, injusto, é intolerable, promptissimamente lo executan. Y sino ay quien incite, y promueva sus euexas, las fomente, persuada y solicite, ni reclaman sus agravios ni representan sus injurias en los tribunales. Quando jamás resisten las contribuciones, é imposiciones? Sino que luego se resignan, sin discurso en la obediencia, sin aliento a la repugnancia.

94. Si los indios fueran obstinados, y rebeldes a los mandatos, nunca se lloraran los daños de los repartimientos, esquipazones, fábricas, contrataciones, entierros, testamentos, fiestas, limosnas, negociaciones, tareas y demás servicios personales, y reales, que los tienen exaustos, y consumidos: su rendimiento, umildad, y obediencia ciega; es la que da lugar a estos agravios, vexaciones, y molestias: porque ni tienen resistencia a los males, ni contradicción a los peligros; sin que se atrevan a un suspiro, insensibles no al conocimiento del dolor, que bien lo conocen, y ponderan, sino a su manifestación, ira, furor, ó impaciencia. Vease lo mucho, que encomían la virtud de la obediencia en los indios aquellas illustrísimas Mitras de Osma, y Chiapa; y a los religiosos varones Joseph de Acosta, Fray Juan de Torquemada, y los demas que an istoriado las Indias con pureça, verdad, y zelo.

95. Lo 2. porque el cathequismo, predicación, e instrucción de la doctrina suelen tomar algunos, por instrumento de venganzas, por medios de vindicar sus passiones, y afectos menos ordenados; patrocinanco a la iracundia el pretexto del Santo Evangelio, como elegantemente escrivio Justino Martir, en la carta a los ermanos Zena, y Setano.

96. Lo 3. porque la religión cristiana, la fee católica, la disciplina eclesiastica no entra a palos, ni a coz, i bocado, sino con suavidad, mansedumbre, y dulzyura, como enseñó el predicador de las gentes, el precepto de Cristo a sus Apóstoles; que fuesen no como lobos a tragar ovejas, sino como ovejas en medio de los lobos; para que no matando, sino padeciendo, plantasen la fee. La violencia repugna a la religión. Y así Cristo Señor Nuestro busco la oveja errante por los montes; y después que con dificultad, y penas la halló, la echó sobre sus ombros; para enseñarnos, que los convertidos se an de firmar, y confirmar en la fee con alagos, y caricias, no con rigores, asperezas, y castigos; que en el temor, y pusilanimidad de los indios influye con más fuerza la aversión, y retiro de lo sagrado: con que quedan destituidos de los remedios penitenciales, y de las participaciones sacramentales, dice la Santa Congregación Mexicana; y S. Gregorio el grande lib. 2. Epístola 52. escrive: nueva, e inaudita es esta predicación, que a fuerza de azotes, quiere introducir la fee; y es hazerla odiosa, aborrecible, y blasfemable, como refiere S. Pablo, y otros, y el Concilio limens. 2. ibi. "Que los curatos, de cuya voluntad dependen los demás indios, sen tratados con amor, y onrosamente, enfrenando, y castigando, como es razón, la demasia, y desorden de los españoles, que los maltratan de palabras, o de mano; porque el nombre de Cristo no sea blasfemado entre los indios, y clamen con sentidas palabras: donde está el Dios de los Cristianos, que nos predican mansísimo, benignísimo, y pacientísimo Cordero, en sus afrentas, en sus injurias, en sus ignominias, en sus dolores, sacrificado infamemente en una cruz? Y que con estos motivos deseen sacudir el pesado yugo, que los oprime; quando el de Cristo Señor nuestro, su evangelio es leve y suave; y la potestad, que confirió a su promulgación no se dirige a destruir, sino a plantar, y edificar, afirma S. Pablo.

97. Desta manera se crió, procreó, creció, y augmentó la fee, derramando la sangre, y padeciendo los tormentos, los azotes, los palos, las calumnias, y las afrentas los predicadores, y no los predicados: con suavidad se introduxó, con paciencia creció, con benignidad, y sufrimiento se conserva, y las iglesias de regiones nuevamente adquiridas se an de governar por el rito primitivo de la Católica.

Las armas subjetan las cervices, la religión convence los entendimientos, reduce la voluntad de los vencidos; y así viene a ser la subjeción gustosa, y materia de amor la victoria, hállanse obligados a dar gracias a la Providencia Divina, que los condujo a los resplandores de la verdad. Si experimentan rigores, penas, y castigos, están cerca de arrepentidos, y no lexos de llamarse á engaño, y a convertir las aficiones en odios, las gracias en aborrecimientos, y los cariños en miedos, temores, y orrores.

98. Presupuesta la obligación, que tienen los párrocos o curas de almas de enseñar a los niños, jóvenes, ó muchachos la doctrina cristiana, la obediencia a Dios, y a sus padres, e instruirlos en buenas costumbres los

domingos, y días festivos, según el Santo Concilio Tridentino, controvierte el gran Augustín Barbosa, si podrán compelerlos, en caso de notable negligencia, contumacia, y rebeldía, con multas, y otras comminaciones en los pueblos, municipios, villas, aldeas, o lugares fuera de las ciudades; y resueltamente tiene, que no: porque no tienen jurisdicción coactiva; y el Tridentino, quando dize, que sean compelidos con censuras, habla de los curas, a quienes an de obligar los obispos con estas penas, a que dotrinen, y enseñen la juventud; no de los niños, y muchachos, ni de sus padres; ni los prelados ordinarios pueden según derecho imponerles ningunas: pero en España está introducido por costumbre, que puedan los obispos compeler con excomunicaciones a sus subditos, a que aprendan el catecismo, y a los párrocos, ó curas, que lo enseñen, y expliquen.

99. Y estos los medios, que deven usar, para mover a los padres, que embien a sus ijos, y a los ijos, para que acudan puntualmente, es manifestarles la necesidad, encarecerles la importancia, ponderarles la utilidad deste exercicio, persuadirles con razones, y moverles con exemplo; publicarles las indulgencias, que concedió la Santidad de Pío 5. y Paulo 5.

100. Con que a todas las luces queda comprovado el intento, y asentado el defecto de jurisdición en los padres dotrinantes: y si los juezes, que entran a juzgar dudosos della, pecan mortalmente en sentir de Santo Tomás, y todos los Teólogos, que será quien ciertamente lo deve conocer; pues se halla sin título, causa, autor, ni fundamento, que se la confiera; y la firmeza, y certidumbre della deve preceder al exercicio, y conocimiento.

101. Mas tan poco se puede dexar de conceder alguna económica; pero no jurisdicional sobre la juventud, y menor edad; en cuya virtud puedan enmendarlos, corregirlos con moderada castigación, y contemplada coerción; a la manera, que se conceda a los maestros, y preceptores, a los Padres, y parientes; valiéndose de los fiscales nombrados por los señores arçobispos, y obispos (como lo dispone el Concilio Mexicano) que son en quienes reside la verdadera, propria, y cierta jurisdición espiritual eclesiástica; así por ley diocesana, como de jurisdición: y pueden en sus diócesis todo lo que el Pontífice en el Orbe universo, ecepto lo que especialmente está reservada a su Santidad.

102. Y esto a de ser, como dize una elegante ley, con animad aversion paternal; como padre, que quando acusa, excusa; quando condena, absuelve, escrive la pluma del Aguila Africana. La potestad patria consiste en la piedad, no en la atrocidad. Mas agradable, y grato es el nombre de piedad. que de potestad dixo el mismo Florente.

103. Con que me a desembarazado del asumpto implicado deste parágrafo: meditación, que pedía mas dilación, que la que dispensan las asistencias sucesivas de mi oficio. Siempre estaré rezeloso de la multiplicidad de sus defectos: que lo apresurado imposiblemente se unió con lo perfecto, en sentir del Tácito Cicerón, y el Sidonio. Excusarame quien atentamente advirtiere, que forme estos mal limados discursos, forcejando entre el genio del inquirir, y el exercicio de lo forense, que se arrebata todo el tiempo, como preciso a la profesión; e importa poco, que los aficionados a las letras sean ladrones de las oras, si todas se deven, y pagan a la obligación.

3. De Otras Especies de Servicios Reales, y Personales

1. Padecen los naturales gravámenes pesados en la distribución del substento de los alcaldes mayores, escrivanos, alguaciles etc. Porque no observan la forma, que prescrive la ordenanza 21. del govierno; ni los juezes de residencia azen exacta averiguación, como devían en este punto: y quando visitan las provincias, pueblos, y lugares de su distrito, les obligan a que los alimenten de valde, y les asistan con leña, agua, verduras, limones, tomates, chiles, cevollas, sal, vinagre, y lo demás necesario a su persona, la del escrivano, alguacil mayor, y otras que llevan de comitiva. Y en faltando qualquier circunstancia destas, los amos, criados, y esclavos, que son crueles verdugos, los azotan, y castigan rigurosamente; y así se deve mandar se guarden exactísimamente las ordenanzas. Y que las contribuciones, que se les permiten para sus alimentos, y las demás minestras, y menudencias, que les azen dar en las visitas, las paguen luego en dinero contante, tabla, y mano propria, con fee de escrivano, testigos, y asistencia de los padres doctrinantes: que se les obligue a exibir las cartas de pago en las Sindicaciones; y que faltando, se les agan de oficio satisfazer las summas todas, con pena al juez que faltare en esta inquisición de cien pesos, aplicados a la Cámara de su Magestad, y gastos de justicia, y que se bolveran a tomar de nuevo a su costa: y que examinen también, si commutaron los alimentos, ó substento en otras especies, de las que les dispensa la ordenanza, que suelen compensar el arroz en cera, las gallinas en lompotes, los pollos en Algañia; y así en los demás fructos preciosos del País, transmutando las substancias sin milagro. Y para que sea fácil verificar el desafuero los mandamientos, que despachan a estos efectos, los executa un confidente español, que en las plazas, es uno de los infantes, que paga su magestad, para servicio de los alcaldes mayores, y les ordenan expresamente, que no dexen copia en los pueblos: demostración evidente de la iniquidad, que incluyen; porque el expediente, o es justo, o es injusto, sino justo, como lo mandan? Si justo, como lo ocultan, encubren, y sepultan? Quien obra con seguridad, ni se niega a resplandores, ni se esconde a claridades; ni ama tinieblas, ni aborrece luzes. Y así se deve proveer, que el executor de estos desórdenes, incluyéndose en la contribución, que contienen muchos pueblos, en cada uno dexe copia en forma provante al Governador del, y dirigiéndose a uno solamente el original, y otorque carta de pago de los géneros, que recibiere ante el escrivano público, o real, y en su defecto ante testigos, y a ambos casos asista, y firme el padre doctrinante, con pena de quatro años de galeras al remo irrimisiblemente. Y no cumpliéndose con esta forma, los governadores no los obedescan, ni executen, porque como provaré en el n. 17. no tienen obligación de cooperar, ni cumplir órdenes illicitos, injustos, y pecaminosos con apercibimiento, que se castigaran corporalmente, y que los exhivan en las residencias de los alcaldes mayores, y el juez necesariamente los pida, y ponga en el proceso, y haga los cargos, que resultaren dellos, y de la averiguación, que sobre este artículo formaré debaxo de las comminaciones repetidas.

2. Y que no nombren, ni tengan mas Vilangos, juezes de sementera,

tenientes de governadores, alguaciles mayores, o escrivanos, ni mayordomos, que los que tuvieren títulos del govierno, y conforme a las órdenanças; porque augmentan este número, para que cada uno de los oficiales le contribuya dos, o tres pesos a la semana, o conforme paccionan la barateria. De que se siguen gravísimos daños a los demás naturales; porque estos quedan excusados de las cargas públicas: y como quiera, que se allan otros muchos exemptos, que son los principales, caveças de barangay, y los que actualmente son governadores, alguaciles mayores, oficiales, actuales de justicias, y caxa de comunidad, y los que an sido, los que ocupan, y an ocupado oficios militares, los fiscales imaginarios mayores, y menores, los mayordomos, y otros con título, que residen en el servicio de las iglesias, y conventos; viene á cargar el peso del trabajo, en los miserables Timauas contra la proporción geométrica, que se deve observar, pide toda razón, y derecho, y manda su magestad en sus reales cédulas, y en especial la tantas vezes repetida del Señor Don Juan de Silva. ibi. "Y en la elección de todos se procederá sin aceptación de personas, y de manera que así el trabajo de las distancias: como el peso de las ocupaciones, y la compensación de las otras circunstancias, en que a de aver más, y menos graveza, se reparta, y comunique con igualdad, para que todos participen de los servicios más, y menos trabajos; sin que el beneficio, y alivio de los unos recambie en agravio de los otros."

3. Y en la ordenança 15. del govierno está prevenida esta insolencia (que no guardan, aunque juran los alcaldes mayores) dice pues así. "Por aver dado muchas reservas de polos, y servicios personales a venido a caer la carga sobre los ombres mas flacos, que son los Timauas con que se van acabando y consumiendo: para cuyo remedio ordeno, y mando, que de aquí adelante no aya en los pueblos, y partes de vuestras juridiciones persona ninguna reservada de acudir a dichos polos, y servicios personales; sino fuere tan solamente los viejos de sesenta años que para ello tuvieren reserva, y los que fueren Caveças de barangay, y su hijo primogénito eredero, y subcesor en él; y los cantores, sacristanes, cocineros, y portero, que se reservan, en conformidad del auto del Doctor Santiago de Vera, de que cada año se despachan mandamientos y el Governador, teniente, y demás ministros, y oficiales de justicia, durante el año porque son nombrados, y no más. Y todos los demás acudan a los dichos polos, y servicios personales, sin embargo de que tengan reservas mías, o de mis antecesores, por qualquiera título, o causa que sea, y aunque ayan sido governadores, capitanes, y otros oficiales de guerra, o por otro qualquier título, causa y razón; ni por ser onrados, ni principales, ni por conciertos, que hagan unos con otros por razón de sus antiguedades. Solo se les guardaran sus preeminencias en actos públicos, asientos, y oficios, y otras onras semejantes, etc."

4. Y así se a de mandar cumplir con graves penas, esta ordenança en los casos, que segun las cédulas de su magestad se permiten los servicios personales, de que tratare en el parágrafo final.

5. El señor fiscal pondera otro linage de servicios, que son los indios de bagaxe, carga, o carruage, que en la Nueva España llaman Tamemes Apires en el Peru, y en estas Islas con término general de Polong, y al

servicio Opahan, de que usan frequentemente los alcaldes mayores, padres doctrinantes regulares, y seculares, los pasajeros, y algunos de los venerables, y devotos padres provinciales en las visitas de sus provincias; aunque otros con admirable exemplo y rara edificación de los pueblos, las lustran a pie por caminos fragosos, y aún casi inaccesibles, a costa de su salud, y peligro de sus vidas; sin descaezer del ardiente fervor de sus primitivos padres primeros fundadores de las religiones en estas Islas.

6. Obligan á estas azemilas racionales quando están promovidos a sus oficios, y beneficios, a que vengan desde sus municipios a esta ciudad, y les transporten la ropa, víveres, y demás cargas, y quando asisten en los partidos en todas las jornadas, que se les ofrecen, y a que condusgan sus personas a ombros en amacas, y orimones, que son unas especies de literillas, y en estas funciones ocupan mucho número de indios sin pagarles, ó en muy corta cantidad. Y se sigue otro perjuicio no menos sensible, que se azen copiosas contribuciones de dineros, y arroz en los pueblos entre los que quedan para sustento de los que van, y en mayor cantidad de la necesaria, que interceptan los governadorcillos principales, y cavezas de Barangay que son los distribuyentes.

7. Quanto sea el trabajo pesadumbre, aflicciones, y angustias desta ocupacion lamentó penoso el señor obispo de Chiapa en la relación de la destrucción de las Indias. Nueva España.

8. Y quan proivido se alle en las cédulas de su magestad, represente a V. S. en el dictamen sobre la translación del puerto de Cavite al de Lampon disc. 3. n. 3. y lo pondera bastantemente Fray Juan de Torquemada, y Antonio de Herrera, y por mucho que se exsagere, siempre quedará corto el encarecimiento, la pluma torpe, aunque mas pretenda con alado buelo remontarse a esphera de superior eloquencia, y aunque mas se aliente a colorear con pinzeles vivos de retóricos colores la justificación de las causas, y la razón de los motivos. Cite, y exorne la de 4. de diciembre de 1528. la de 4. de junio de 1570. Otra de 24 de noviembre de 601, con más parieto, un capítulo de instrucción, que se dio al virrey de Mexico el año de 1550. y al del Perú año de 1595. y en el cap. 48. fol. 15. de 1603.

9. Porque aunque es cierto, que los romanos tenían destinados, y mancipados ombres para el transporte, y comboy de los bastimentos públicos, y de más mercadurias, y cosas semejantes; y les compelian a cargarlas, en si, ó en sus bestias, sin admitirles excusación, ni dispensarles mudar el ofiçio, al qual llamavan Angaria; y quando excedía de lo ordinario, Parangaria, y Angaros, o Tangaros a los que abían de llevar estas cargas, como testifican los autores, discurriendo variamente sobre la Etimología de la palabra, Angaria, y con gran latitud sobre la imposición deste ministerio, y que Príncipes pueden imponerla; y á que vasallos, y con qué causas.

10. Y también tenían paradas de cavallos, y carros en las vías militares, para correr la posta con todo lo preciso al sustento; avio, y servicio dellos; y obligaban a los naturales de cada comarca, que así con personas, como con cavallos, mulas, bueyes, y aciendas asistiesen a estos forrages, gastos e impensas, y a construir, y reparar los establos o cavallerizas,

mansiones, citerias, posadas, ó mesones; y les llamavan cursos, y cavallos públicos cursuales, veredos, y paraveredos.

11. Y tenían asimismo obligación, a acer las transvección de las especies fiscales a su costa, y en sus cavallos, bestias, y jumeries, en que pudiera explayarse la pluma, a no contenerla el examen, y erudición de los grandes barones, que lo an ilustrado en este siglo.

12. Pero después los emperadores Adriano, Severo, y Antonio Pío, en quienes cayó más la luz de la razón, aliviaron a las provincias de peso tan intolerable, suprimiendo, y extinguiendo esta injusticia, transfiriendo en el fisco las expensas, gastos, y costas de los cursos transvección, Angarias, y Parangarias: elegantemente lo selebra el Senador Marco Aurelio Casiodoro, pareciendo, que no era justo que ombres libres sostituyesen en el oficio a las bestias; pues aun en los esclavos lo increpan San Augustín, y Clemente Alexandrino, considerando, que no puede aver cosa, que así enerve el cuerpo, y devilite las fuerzas, como la opresión de tales cargas, que seran cargos gravísimos en el Tribunal de Dios.

13. Y porque con ocasión de las palabras equíbocas, y dudosas de la cédula del año de 1543, se abría brecha a estos servicios cargosos, se despachó otra el de 1549 que se renovó, y mandó guardar por la del Escurial en 4 de julio del de 1570. con esta formalidad. "Y así desclarando la dicha ley por la presente, proibimos, e imviolablemente defendemos, que agora, ni de aquí adelante, so color de la dicha ley, ni en otra manera alguna directe, ni indirecte ningunos españoles, mercader, ni otra persona alguna que sea, que tenga origen destos reynos, ni fuera dellos de esas partes vecinos, y moradores, o estantes en las dichas Indias de qualquier estado, y condición, que sean, puedan cargar, ni carguen, ni agan cargar indio, ni indios algunos con mercadurias, o otras qualesquier cosas, llevándolas de unas partes a otros, para vender, y contratar con ellas; porque nuestra intención, y voluntad al tiempo, que mandamos azer la dicha ley, y al presente es, que por ninguna vía, ni color que sea, ninguna persona pueda cargar, ni cargue, ni aga cargar indios, aunque sea en parte de esas dichas Indias, donde no aya caminos abiertos, y bestias de cargar: porque no tubimos, ni tenemos esto por necesidad bastante; y nuestra voluntad a sido, y es, que por ninguna vía, ni manera, ni necesidad, que sea, ninguna persona de las suso dichas, y de qualquier estado, y condición, que sean, pueda cargar, ni cargue, ni aga cargar indios algunos en poca, ni en mucha cantidad, ni para mucho camino, ni para poco; ni con mucha, ni poca carga; ni con paga ni sin ella: porque en este caso nuestra determinada voluntad es de quitar, y proivir de todo en todo, que ninguna persona cargue indios en esas dichas Indias, conforme a la dicha ley."

14. Y la del año 1609. "Principalmente proibo, que en ninguna manera, ni occasión, por mucho, que inste la necesidad, consintays, que los indios se carguen, aunque la carga sea ligera, y voluntaria: porque si se diese lugar a fuesen trabajados, por esta vía, sería muy grande su opresión; y solo dispenso, en que puedan llevar la cama del doctrinero, o del corregidor, quando se mudaren de un lugar a otro: pero esto con tres limitaciones, la primera, que la carga se divida entre diferentes indios mas,

o menos, según el peso, o calidad que fuere, y la jornada sea corta, y proporcionada con el aliento, y fuerzas de los indios. La segunda, que se les pague el jornal, que vos señalaredes, tasándole en justo valor. La tercera, que en la provincia, que esto se tolerare, no aya bestias, carneros de carga, ni otros bagages; porque aviéndolos, no an de servir los indios en este ministerio. Y porque es mi voluntad, que esto se haga, pudiendose excusar, os encargo, que en las partes donde uviere falta de bestias, y carneros, procureys introducirlos; para que de esta suerte cese el trabajo de los indios."

15. Donde precisamente se limita en la cama del padre doctrinante, y del corregidor, o alcalde mayor con las modificaciones, que expresa y quando se transfirieren de unos lugares a otros de su districto, y jurisdicción; pero no en los viajes, que hizieren fuera de sus provincias; ni dentro a negocios particularles; y que para que esta dispensación tenga lugar, no a de aver cavallos, bacas, ni otros bagajes; porque aviéndolos, no se a de usar de la permisión.

16. Y exceptas estas personas, y en el caso, que había el rescripto, se a de proivir inviolablemente en todo género de personas, regulares, eclesiásticas, seculares de qualquier estado, condición, y calidad que sean, con penas corporales a los governadorcillos, fiscales intrusos; a los inductores, ó productores de los repartimientos; y que aunque se lo ordenen, y manden los alcaldes mayores, o padres doctrinantes, no lo executen; pues no están obligados estos a obedecer lo injusto, ilícito, ni proivido por su magestad, como ni aquellos a mandar sino lo onesto, justo, raçonable, y permitido por Dios, por el derecho, leyes, cédulas, y rescriptos: que no es la dirección de las acciones preceptivas la potestad, sino el decoro; ni nadie a de pensar, que puede hazer sino lo que debe hazer; ni que a de correr sin limite el arbitrio: que perficiona la fidelidad, y regula la prudencia en el imperar, no lo que se quiere, sino lo que se puede.

17. Esta proivición se a de dispensar solamente en la persona de V. S. y de los señores ministros togados de esta real audiencia: que la satisfación, confianza, méritos, y prendas, que concurren en varones tan justificados, y piden lugares tan superiores, aseguran, que usaran deste indulto con tanta templanza, y modestia, que precisamente se valdrán en casos inexcusables, que la necesidad les impela, y que miren a la pública conservación, y bien universal de las provincias, y sus naturales.

18. Y también con los ilustrísimos y reverendísimos arçobispos, y obispos, que son del consejo de su magestad, como afirman las leyes, y auctores del reyno, y el mismo rey confiesa, y titula en sus cédulas; y a tanta dignidad se deven mayores atenciones, y privilegios, porque prepondera á todas las potestades, que venera el siglo, quanto el cielo es mas precioso que la tierra, decía el Nazianzeno; son las columnas de la iglesia, pastores de las almas, sucesores de los apóstoles, onor del clero, amparo del estado secular, defensores de los Concilios, bulas, y apostólicas constituciones, maestro de la verdadera dotrina, dotores de los pueblos, medianeros, y conductos entre Dios, y los ombres, principes de los fieles de su rebaño, Dioses en la tierra, luz y sal del mundo que lo alumbran, conservan, y sazonan, para que logre los bienes eternos; los que con su valor,

sangre, constancia, y doctrina desde los apóstoles asta oy incesantemente an formado, y reformado, trabajado, y fructificado en la Cristianidad, é iglesia católica, como especiosamente escrive San Clemente.

19. Y si el Arca del testamento antiguo siendo sombra, y figura muerta, la reportaban en ombros, que mucho que a los que son viva, y verdadera arca del nuevo, la pongan no sólo los indios, sino todos los fieles sobre sus cabezas, y ombros; y más quando los van a confirmar en gracia, á confortar en la fee; a descargar, y no a cargar, a alibiar y no a augmentar sus aflicciones, fatigas, y desconsuelos; á visitar, remediar y curar sus dolores, angustias, y enfermedades espirituales.

20. Y se hallan obligados de derecho divino, y de necèsidad precisa a la defensa, protección, y amparo de estas sus ovejas umildes y mansas, y a solicitar, e instar oportuna, e importunamente por el desagravio, y reparo de sus opresiones. Así lo siente el señor obispo de Chiapa, (que también supo cumplir con esta obligación) en el segundo Tratado de la materia de los indios, Corolario 2. y lo prueba docta, y difusamente. Los obispos (dice aquella zelosa pluma) están obligados de derecho divino, et *de necessitate salutis* á exercer los actos, que propriamente son de pastores, como pertenecientes, é inclusos en su oficio, y cuydado pastoral: en estos se contiene no solamente regir, governar, enseñar los pueblos, sino preservarlos, y defenderlos en sus daños, aunque sean corporales, y temporales, principalmente las impedientes la salud espiritual, que se corrobora con los seys actos pastorales, que se constituyen en la profecía de Ezechiel, y las lucidaciones, y explicaciones de los Santos Doctores.

21. Y con esta atención los primitivos protectores de los naturales, fueron los señores obispos; el primero de México el Santo Don Fray Juan de Zumárraga de la Seráfica Religión, lo fue en la Nueva España, por provisión del Señor Emperador Carlos 5. su fecha en Burgos en 10 de enero del año de 1528, y esta fué la primera creación, è institución deste oficio: y se lucieron los aciertos de la elección de tan sagrada, y religiosa persona en la entereza, rectitud, y perfección, con que exército la protección, que le costó muchos desasosiegos, calumnias, turbaciones, y persecuciones; pero venció la verdad, y triunfó la justicia.

22. Y el primero, que uvo en estas Islas fué también su primer obispo D. Fray Domingo de Salazar del Orden de Santo Domingo, según se prueva de una cédula real dirigida a Gómez Perez Dasmariñas governante estas provincias, su data en Madrid a 17 de enero de 1593, ibi: "Cosa es muy conveniente, y necesaria, que los indios tengan protector, y defensor, como esta ordenado en el Perú, y Nueva España; y pues, como decir, el Obispo, a quien yo lo avía encargado, no puede acudir a la solicitud, actos, y diligencias judiciales, que requieren presencia personal, vos como governador pondreys el dicho defensor, y protector; y le señalareys salario competente, proveyendo, que este se le pague de las tasas de los indios por rata entre los que estuvieren en mi corona y encomendados a personas particulares; sin que para esto se toque en azienda mía, que proceda de otros géneros: pero ase de entender, que por esto no a de ser visto quitarse al obispo la superintendencia de la protección de los dichos indios."

23. Claro está a vista de tantos títulos, y vínculos de obligación miraran el alivio de sus ijos espirituales como padres amantísimos, y entraran a la parte de sus penas, procurando esfuerzos a la relevación, y no agravando la fatiga más que en lo mas necesario, e inescusable.

24. La Panga de Marivélez se deve extinguir como iniqua, y detestable. Resulta de veynte indios, que las provincias de Balayan, y Pampanga contribuyen cada mes, para vegiar, y explorar los mares; y los corregidores reciben la ración en dinero, y los naturales redimen la vexación, compran la libertad, y les venden la exempción por cien pesos, asistiendo cada provincia con cinquenta cada mes: y supuesto que solo sirve a la codicia, y no a la necesidad, y sin ellos se azen estos oficios, como es constante, parece preciso descargar la conciencia a los corregidores, removiéndoles la causa de su pecado, y la ocasión de su delicto.

25. Y nunca an de ser menos atendidos, y más exsaminados los alcaldes mayores, y otros ministros, que quando representaren las combeniencias aparentes del servicio del rey, que siendo tan recto, tan justificado, tan regulado, tan incorporado, y unido con él de Dios, algunos dellos lo azen pretexto de maldades, y capa de pecadores, con que cubren sus excesos: así como los Ebreos, que para obrar la mayor iniquidad, se valieron de servicio del César, y persuadieron a Pilatos con este título a condenar la misma innocencia, acusando la que estorvaba; y proivía a los vasallos tributar a la magestad augusta: y pondera San Augustín, que pensaron ingerirle mayor temor, para que crucificase a Cristo, paliando la pasión, y venganza con el servicio del emperador: y quando trataba de absolverle, proclamaron, que si le libraba de la muerte, no le servía como ministro; antes le deservía como enemigo: y en Roma se valían los iniquos de la imagen de los Césares, aciendo la fomento, y protección de las injurias, y ofensas que cometían.

26. El señor obispo de Chiapa en la Relación de la Destrucción de las Indias refiere un capítulo de carta, escrita del desde Santa Marta a la magestad católica del señor emperador Carlos 5. su fecha en 20 de mayo de 1541, ibi. "V. M. tiene más servidores por acá de los que piensa; porque no ay ombre de quantos ay, que no se ose decir públicamente que si saltea, o roba, destruye, o mata, o quema a los vasallos de V. M. porque le den oro, sirve a V. M. a título, que diz que de allí le viene su parte a V. M. y por tanto sería bien cristianísimo César, que V. M. diese a entender castigando a algunos rigurosamente, que no recibe servicio en cosa, que Dios es deservido."

27. El servicio del rey consiste en observar los mandamientos, y preceptos de Dios, en obedecer las leyes, instrucciones, ordenanças, y direcciones de su magestad, y de sus governadores, y ministros superiores, que le representan; en executar sus reales órdenes, cédulas, y rescriptos; en aliviar, desaogar, y conservar a los súbditos, y vasallos, principalmente a los indios como más desvalidos, y menos amparados; en auxiliarlos, y defenderlos en la libertad de personas, y aziendas: este tengo por su mayor servicio, este es el que e aprendido, y me á enseñado el derecho divino, natural, positivo, y de las gentes. Este es el que juramos, y deste se nos

toma cuenta en las sindicaciones, y visitas; y en la que emos de dar á Dios, que es la más verdadera, cierta, y estrecha.

4. De los Exactores, o Cobradores de Encomiendas, y Otros Oficiales

1. Otra peste contagiosa de los naturales, que los destruye, abrasa, y consume son los exactores, cobradores, ó publicanos (que todo es uno en el derecho) de los tributos así del rey, como de los encomenderos particulares. Quan mal sientan los Sanctos Doctores, las leyes, constituciones, y rescriptos de este linage de ombres, por su cudicia, avaricia, crueldades, violencias, y rapiñas, no es ponderable, ni exagerable. Afirman, que nacieron para eversión del género umano, calamidad de las Provincias, asolación de los pueblos, y ruina de las gentes.

2. Y no ay más que dezir en la materia, sino que Nerón, con ser un Nerón, quiso extinguir universalmente todos los tributos del imperio romano, por extirparlos de una vez, para siempre, como refiere ermosamente el Tácito.

3. Y en términos individuantes de las Indias, el Señor Don Juan de Solórzano en los lugares ilustrados, encarga mucho el cuydado destos exactores de encomiendas, por los muchos fraudes, que en ellos cada día se experimentan; y que son mas molestos, y graves a los indios, que los mismos tributos; y que sus excesos son tanto más execrables, quanto se cometen contra personas pobres, y miserables. Y así a sido grande la atención, que los Reyes nuestros señores an aplicado en reprimir estas vexaciones, como testifican Matienzo, Fray Miguel de Agia, y Josef de Acosta.

4. Y la cédula despachada al señor don Alonso Faxardo, siendo governador destas Islas, su fecha en Madrid a 9. de agosto de 1621. ibi: "También dezis, que en los títulos de las encomiendas pondreys el número de tributos, lo que pagan, y el valor de las especies, y en que parte caen, como os está mandado; y que por estar incorporadas en mi real corona algunas, que caen muy distantes de esa ciudad, y en parte que no se goza de las especies, que es lo mas considerable, las defraudan las más vezes los cobradores, diziendo, que fue mal año, y que cobraron dinero; y si confiesan algo en especie, lo venden como quieren, y sobre ello azen vexaciones a los indios: y que para que con otros tantos tributos, tuviese mi real acienda mucha más utilidad, soys de parecer, que como vayan vacando encomiendas de particulares de la Pampanga, y otras partes cerca de esa ciudad, y de buena cosecha de especies, se fuesen trocando por las distantes: con que teniendo a un particular por encomendero, serán más bien tratados los indios; y a los que estuvieren en mi real corona ningún cobrador les ará vexaçion, estando tan cerca de vos; y que así pondreys en execución lo sobre dicho, como se fuesen ofreciendo las ocasiones. Esta traça, y manera de govierno que representays es muy bueno, y así lo executareys; y en la junta de azienda ireys siempre confiriendo lo que podía ser de mayor beneficio de mi real acienda, y lo pondreys así mismo en execución; pues todo será tan onesto, y lícito, como lo confio de vos, y me avisareys de los que icieredes. Y porque

apuntays una cosa de mal govierno, y que ex exceso, y lo deveys estrañar, y castigar, no permitireys, que ningún executor, ni cobrador por sí, ni por interpositas personas, pueda comprar en pública almoneda, ni fuera della secreta, ni públicamente ningunas especies, ni cosas que devan los tributarios arrendadores, indios, o deudores reales: porque en esto suele aver grandes fraudes, y las leyes lo castigan, y proiben. Y para mayor justificación del caso en los títulos, que despacharedes a cada uno de estos cobradores, les pondreys por cláusula lo referido, con pena del quatro tanto."

5. Y el Señor Conde de Lemos en la carta repetida al señor Don Juan de Silva ibi: "Suplico a vuestra merced que pondere la importancia desto, para velar con gran cuydado sobre todos los ministros, que uvieren de tener parte en la observancia dellas; y que pueble las orcas de corregidores, encomenderos, y cobradores, y los demás vezinos desas provincias, declinando siempre en los casos de duda al rigor, y a la justicia."

6. Y su puesto, que los encomenderos están proibidos de residir en sus encomiendas, como consta de cédula despachada a esta real audiencia en Segovia a 25 de julio de 1609. Y por otra de 6 de junio del mismo año, se impone pena de diez mil pesos de oro a los virreyes, presidentes, y governadores, que concedieren licencia, sino fuera para muy de paso, o alguna cobranza, o quenta brevísima; quanto más se deve proibir a los exactores, que los Encomenderos, que por la mayor parte son casi todos illustres cavalleros, y personas de muchas prendas, meritos, y servicios; y aquellos miran los indios como agenos, para la protección, y como proprios para el provecho, según dixo el obispo de los avernos, y el Tácito acusando a Titio Vinio.

7. A los encomenderos la utilidad propria les a de mover naturalmente a solicitar la conservación, y consistencia de sus encomendados. Los exactores libran su commodidad en el estrago, y de populación de los naturales, sin mirar ni prevenir lo futuro; porque solo tienen el goze de lo presente.

8. Y así se a de mandar con graves penas, que ningún vecino de los pueblos de las encomiendas sea indio, o español, ó de otra nacion, pueda ser exactor, cobrador, o publicano: y que los que lo fueren no puedan residir de asiento, sino solamente el término preciso para la exacción: el que conceda la ordenanza 11. del govierno son tres meses; y me parece muy dilatado, y que se deve estrechar a menos: y adonde tengo noticias, que son los mayores desafueros, es en las provincias de Oton, en que se a introducido este oficio por beneficio; se a echo pretensión, y gratificación; y allí se deve aplicar más vivo el remedio, donde instan con mayor actividad los daños.

9. Ase de expeler el desorden, que an introducido de los ministros militares, de servirse de los indios Panpangos, soldados alistados, y matriculados en sueldo de su magestad en sus particulares commodidades, y negociaciones; y en que les conduzgan agua, leña, pescado, zacate; en bogavantes de sus embarcaciones, y con la misma disolución los dan, reparten, y prestan a sus amigos, y confidentes, que si fueran sus esclavos. Y aunque el rey lo tiene mandado por cédula de V. S. proivido por

ordenanzas, prevenido por vandos públicos, y castigado con penas las transgresiones, que a llegado a entender, sin embargo dura la inobediencia rebelde, y la obstinación contumaz en algunos menos temerosos de Dios, que no estiman sus almas, ni consideran como deven el juramento que azen; la obligación de restituir a su Magestad los sueldos, los daños, vejaciones, y trabajo corporal a los indios.

5. De los Principales, y Cabezas de Barangay

1. Es mas que cierto el apostegma corriente en toda la América, que ningunos son peores para los indios, que los mismos indios; y que los mayores daños son los que se causan unos a otros; y así es necesario advertir, que los naturales Pampangos, y de otras provincias tienen quatro estados de calidad, o se allan quatro especies de estado.

2. La 1. de los Cabezas de Barangay, cuya etimología communmente se afirma, procedió desde el tiempo, que se transmigraron a estas Islas, de las de Celebe, Malayo, y otras del Archipiélago. Transfretáronse en unas embarcaciones, que llaman Barangays; y en cada una conducía cada qual su familia, o algunas personas de su linage, sequito, o comitiva. A este, que era dueño, o superior de aquel vaso, titularon con nombre de cabeza del Barangay, como capitán, o señor de la embarcación. Aviendo navegado, y aportado a estas Provincias, despojaron de su posesion a los etas, negros, y zambales, que eran los naturales dellas, y los obligó la maña, y fuerza de los Estrangeros, a retirarse a los montes más intricados, que actualmente abitan; cada uno destos cabezas con su Barangay pobló, y cultivó la porción de tierra, que le cupo en el País, reteniendo la dominación governativa del Barangay, sucediendo los ijos a los padres, y unos a otros, asta la pacificación, y conversión a la fee católica, en que también an conservado el nombre, y poco menos del poder.

3. Y según la ordenanza 11 del govierno tiene cada cabeza a su cargo treynta tributantes para arriba, y no menos a quienes llaman Cabancas, y están obligados a cobrar de ellos el tributo, y después enterado al alcalde mayor de su provincia; y para la seguridad de la exacción dan fianzas.

4. Están exemptos, y sus primogénitos por la ordenanza 15. de la contribución, que llamavan Polos, y de servicios personales, cortes, y arrastres de maderas, y demás funciones del rey, que, nominan malongay; ocupan oficios políticos, y puestos militares.

5. En los Barangayes (como se refiere en la ordenanza 11. citada) se sucede en unas provincias por elección, y en otras por derecho de sangre: a la manera, que en los cazicazgos está mandado lo mismo por muchas cédulas, que están en el 4. tomo de las impresas pág. 287.

6. No aviendo sucesor legítimo, se manda que el alcalde mayor nombre un indio principal onrrado, y acreditado, y de quenta de la promoción con los motivos, y causas, que persuadieron la elección de la persona; para que reconocido por los Señores Governadores, la aprueben, o reprueben.

7. La 2. especie es de los principales, o nobles padres, abuelos, ermanos, tios, y parientes del cabeza, que lo fueron también; pero por no

aver el número prescripto de cabancas se incorporaron en el Barangay, y gozan nombre, y privilegios nobles, y principales agregados, y unidos; acuden a los Cortes, arrastres de maderas, y Malongay de su Magestad, y pueden obtener oficios públicos, políticos, y militares.

8. La 3. los que llaman onrrados decendientes de principales, que también asisten a los cortes, arrastres, y malongay, a pescar para los padres doctrinantes, alcaldes mayores, y sus oficiales, y ocupan los oficios de alguaciles, y vilangos.

9. La 4. la plebe, y vulgo, que desde su immemorial tienen nombre de Babagsay, que sirven no sólo a los cortes, arrastres, y malongay sino de bogar, cargar, y las demás obras viles baxas, y mecánicas, en que tambien se exercitan los Timauas, que son los descendientes de esclavos.

10. Estos Principales, y cabezas de Barangay forman una junta, que llaman Ambagan: Casacasa es lo que confieren entre sí, que todo se ordena e repartir de capitaciones a los demás naturales, que generalmente llaman polillo, y Ambagan, y se consume en los efectos, que arbitran; y en acabándose repiten la imposición: y aquí entran las impensas, que algunos de los alcaldes mayores, y padres doctrinantes les obligan a azer, y con la mayor parte se quedan los distribuyentes; de manera, que si se necesita de quatro, reparten ocho, para aprobecharse de lo más, y gastar siempre lo menos.

11. Y supuesto que V. S. con tanta justificación a mandado extinguir las caxas de Polon, consequentemente se a de suprimir el polillo con graves penas corporales a los principales, y cabezas de Barangay, y pecuniarias a los alcaldes mayores, que lo permitieren, toleraren, o omitieren las diligencias.

12. Los cabezas, y principales como tienen tiraniçados a los cabancas de sus barangayes, los ocupan, y a sus ijos, y ijas en sus sementeras, en sus labranzas, en sus embarcaciones, en los edificios, y reparos de sus casas, sirviéndose dellos como si fueran sus esclavos; y sin que ellos puedan reclamar contra su poder, y violencia, oprímenles la libertad totalmente; y no solo se aprovechan del sudor, y trabajo de estos desdichados, sino que los venden, y conducen a la manera, que si fuesen dueños, y señores absolutos, aunque lo son disolutos de sus personas: *verbi gratia*, si uno tubiese necesidad de cortar, arrastrar, y labrar maderas, para edificar una casa, el contrato se celebra con el cabeza, pactase el precio, y satisfácesele. Este manda a sus cabancas cumplan, y executen lo que an contratado, sin que participen un real del contrato; porque su cabeza se quedó con todo: que sólo por ser lo que dicen, que tienen imperio, y dominación despótica sobre bienes, cuerpo, y azienda.

13. También les proiben, que fabriquen casas, ni labren tierras en frente, o detras de las suyas; y si las cultivan, luego se las demuelen, y destruyen, sin que puedan representar sus agravios, ni proponer sus quexas; porque los demás cabezas, y principales sus parientes, y deudos se confederan contre el querellante, y de temor se ausentan. Los alcaldes mayores proceden con mucha tibieza; y como éstos son pobres, y aquellos ricos allan en él todo favor, y valimiento: con que seguramente cometen las ofensas, e injurias.

14. Y llega a tanto el atrevimiento, que si el Timaua tiene algún perro cazador, baca, toro, ó otro qualquier animal, o alaja que les parece bien, se le quitan con mano tirana, sin pagárselo, sino en palos, y azotes de contado.

15. Y asimismo les impiden cortar maderas, vejucos, y cañas en los montes, para la construcción de sus casas; y les proiben el derecho de pescar en los esteros, ríos, y lagunas comunes.

16. Y estos daños, y otros mayores, que cometen, los manda castigar, y remediar su magestad en sus reales cédulas; en ésta del Señor Don Juan de Silva ibi: "Os buelvo a mandar, que procedays con el cuydado, y vigilancia, que de vos confio, castigando exemplar, y rigurosamente los malos tratamientos, que los indios recibieren de sus caziques." Y advierto al menos noticioso, que en la Nueva España se llaman caziques, y en el Perú Curacas los que en estas Islas Principales, y cabezas de Barangay.

17. Y en la de Madrid de 6 de julio de 1594. dirigida al virrey del Perú ibi: "Supuesta la relación, que se tiene de los agravios molestias, y vejaciones, que los indios reciben de sus caziques, y governadores, que como poderosos cometen muchas maldades, pecados, e incestos," y otras muchas, que se allan en el 4. Tomo de las Impresas ex pag. 289. Y lo ponderan el padre Josef de Acosta, Matienzo, y otros muchos: pero imposiblemente se an de remediar en Filipinas, sino se extinguen los Barangayes, y se reduce la exacción de tributos a la forma de la Nueva España.

6. De Algvnas Advertencias Para la Resolucion, y Execucion

1. Las materias grandes nunca se sujetan a una sola acción, necesitan de muchas, y lo que con una execución es imposible con algunas se facilita, y dispone. No pueden todas las provincias a un tiempo informarse con una misma resolución; pero la disposición, y execución en las unas dispone, y encamina a las otras. Esta materia de los servicios personales y reales es justa, y justísima, y no sólo posible, sino fácil, y lo a sido en todas las Indias, donde los primeros, que movieron con exemplo, y persuadieron con obediencia fueron los señores virreyes, y ministros superiores, privándose de los indios de mita, que les repartían para los servicios de sus casas; empecando la justicia por las proprias, antes que la executasen en las agenas: que en opinión del Tácito, fue la mayor acción de su suegro Agrícola. Ceda pues ya lo imposible, pues se a visto fácil en otras provincias; y que de asentado en éstas lo que tenemos por justo en todas; y ya no se puede dudar, que sea factible, quando se vee executado en tantas.

2. Y así lo primero, que deve V. S. declarar, conformándose con la voluntad imperativa de su magestad decifrada en tantos, y tan innumerables rescriptos, es que los indios naturales de estas islas no pueden, ni deven ser compelidos a contribuyr cosa alguna; ora sea esculerta, o poculenta, o de otro qualquier género, especie, o calidad en mucha, ni en poca cantidad, sin dinero, o con dinero: ni á servir personalmente en ninguna ocupación, ministerio, ni oficio; ni a dar avio sea terrestre, o naval de embarcaciones, esquipazones, bogas, guías, amacas, orimones, cavallos, bacas, forrage, comboy, o carruage, ni bagaje, leña, agua, pescado, guevos, gallinas, y lo demás; sin excluir cosa alguna de servicio personal, o real a los alcaldes

mayores, padres doctrinantes; a los venerables, y devotos padres provinciales, ó a los visitadores, que delegan á estas funciones; a los pasajeros, correos, o personas, que conducen despachos, aunque sean de su magestad, y de su real servicio.

3. Que voluntariamente libres, sin compulsión, fuerça, ni extorsión podrán acudir, si quisieren a estos oficios, y ministerios expresados, pagándose lo primero, y ante todas cosas en dinero contante, tabla, y mano propria, sin intervención de los Governadores, principales, y cabezas de barangay, ó otros oficiales con asistencia de los Padres Doctrinantes, y alcaldes mayores, fee de escrivano, o testigos en su defecto, o otro impediento; y que sea la satisfación conforme a los aranceles.

4. En que es preciso advertir, que éstos los forman los alcaldes mayores a su arbitrio, en que vienen a ser juezes, y partes formales; por que como son los más interesados en los trabajos, y contribuciones de los indios, azen la tasación en causa propia: con que á esta luz son nulos; y mirándolos a la de la jurisdición, lo son mucho más; por no tenerla en este caso, que privativamente confio de V. S. el rey, como eligido, aprovado, y calificado de su Soberano juizio, y alta providencia; cuyos aciertos aseguro en la generosa, y real sangre, que yerve en las venas de V. S. y en las prendas, méritos, y servicios, que concurren en su persona, y le merecieron los grandes puestos, que ocupa, y los decorosos premios, que le adornan: que todo anticipadamente junto, afianzo igual correspondencia a la gratificación.

5. Pruévase de las cédulas de 2 de diciembre de 1563 y en la de 1609. ibi: "La segunda, que se les pague el jornal, que vos señaláredes tasandole en justo valor." Y la despachada a Gomez Perez Dasmariñas, governando estas Islas de 18. de junio de 1594, ibi: "Dareys orden en que los dichos religiosos no se sirvan de los indios, sino fuere en casos, y cosas muy necesarias; y entonces pagándoles lo que vos tasaredes, que merecieren por sus jornales."

6. Y así se a de mandar, que todos los alcaldes mayores, y corregidores destas Islas dentro de un mes los cercanos, y dentro de seys los distantes embien los que corren, y se observan en sus provincias a manos del señor fiscal; para que V. S. los organice, y disponga con su autoridad, y jurisdición; y se les imponga obligación con las comminaciones, que convengan, a tenerlos fixos en las casas reales de su asistencia, y que sea capítulo en el interrogatorio de la sindicación, que se les toma; y que el juez della deva azer inquisición, y examen particular, con pena de nulidad, y que se bolverá a tomar a su costa.

Que en los testamentos se observe la forma, que propuse en el S 2. n. 59. y 60.

8. En quanto a las obvenciones de los baptismos, casamientos y entierros, se agan despachos de ruego, y encargo, según la disposición, que refiere en el mismo S n. 57. en caso, que parezca, que no se deven suprimir en todo, a los señores arçobispo, y obispos, para que agan los aranceles; y a los venerables, y devotos padres provinciales, para que conforme a su obligación, los manden guardar, cumplir, y executar a sus súbditos, e inferiores: con advertencia, que faltando por su parte, se usara, y procedera

a los medios, y remedios, que dictan los sagrados cánones, concilio tridentino, y mexicano, cédulas reales de su magestad, que les encarga este cuydado, corrección, y enmienda no menos, que a sus Governadores, y ministros; y en especial en ésta del Señor Don Juan de Silva, en que individualmente abla con estas Islas, y destos servicios personales, y reales; "y a los obispos, y provinciales de las órdenes ruego, y encargo, que anden con la misma atención sobre el castigo de las culpas desta calidad que suelen cometer los doctrineros, y otras personas eclesiásticas."

9. Y que en caso, que el padre doctrinante, excediere se remueba luego del partido, y no para otro mejor: que ésto sería reducir a su fuerza los inconvenientes; enervar, y enflaquecer para siempre los remedios; y a daños de bronce, aplicar los de terciopelo; consiguiría remuneración el delicto, y reportaría commodidades el dolo.

10. Resultaría alguna vez quedar castigada la innocencia del doctrinante, que transferían de la doctrina, para acommodar al culpado, permutándosela por la que a éste le quitavan; y la que quizás nunca pudo alcanzar por otros medios, le abrirían brecha sus desórdenes; y el que la obtenia se vendría a allar en la que menos penso, despoxado sin causa de la que le mereció su observancia: con que se viera escarmentada, por puntual, la obediencia; la obstinación premiada, y la oposición remunerada.

11. Y con este expediente quedarían los remedios escarmentados, y los daños aplaudidos; pues sólo mudava de sitio el exercicio: que claro está, que los mesmos cometería en el partido, donde le transmutaban. Variabanse los feligreses, pero no la condición, y natural: donde quiera se llevara asimismo y mejorado de fortuna en la condenación. Parece, que consequentemente vendría a ser mas insolente la transgresión, y a pesar más los daños, que los remedios.

12. Mejor govierno parecerá, que las prelados los reduzgan a los santos conventos, y casas de Manila; y que los modifique súbditos, y los tiemple subjetos, no la commodidad, si la communidad, donde asistan rendidos, sin esperanza de salir de su diciplina regular, aunque se resignen a los órdenes, y preceptos de los concilios, y del rey: que tarde viene la penitencia, quando no la ofrece el amor, y dicta la reverencia. No es voluntario, ni cierto el rendimiento, que tiene por premio la victoria; y no basta el arrepentimiento para reparar el daño, quando le ocasiona la repugnancia.

13. Convendrá, para el efecto, que se despachen mandamientos a los alcaldes mayores, que de su parte inviolablemente cumplan con lo que les tocare; atiendan, y apliquen entero cuydado en que se executen los órdenes, que miran a los padres doctrinantes; y no consientan contribuciones, exacciones, ni repartimientos, ni ellos los cometan: que lo que se proibe a otro, lo dispensarán en sí con penas gravísimas, que se apresuren, y igualen con los excesos: que es sólo el modo, que se alla, para enmendarlos.

14. Y a los indios productores, inductores, e instrumentos, por donde se disponen los repartimientos, las corporales, que fueren ajustadas; y que debaxo de las mismas, no accepten, ni tomen los nombramientos de Fiscales mayores, ni menores; de mayordomos, o zeladores, sino fueren de mano de los señores arcobispo, y obispos; y que aunque los alcaldes

mayores, y padres doctrinantes les manden, o empleen en los servicios referidos, no les obedezcan, ni cumplan sus órdenes; pues como se asentó en el S 3. n. 17. están muy lexos de la obligación de executarlos; y deven cumplirlos de Dios, y del rey, como criaturas de aquella magestad, y vasallos de ésta; y que las penas, que se establecieren, y direcciones, que se construyeren se guarden precisa, e inviolablemente, sin interpretación, excepción, ni dispensación.

15. Porque las leyes ordenanzas e instrucciones sin observancia no son, sino cadáveres arrojados en las calles, y plaças, que solo sirven de escándalo de los reynos, en que tropieçan los súbditos, y ministros con la transgresión, quando avían de frutificar vivas toda su conservación, alegría, y tranquilidad; y no an de ser leyes de palabra, sino de obras como dixo gravemente el emperador Justiniano; y el no executarse redunda no solo en inobediencia, sino en desprecio del legislador. El Papa Bonifacio 8. y el Jurisconsulto Pomponio escrivieron advertidos, que de nada servia formarlas, sino avia juezes, que las iciesen guardar. Los Atenienses criaron un Magistrado, o Prefectura, a cuyos Ministros llamaron, Nomofilaces, que con coronas blancas asistían a los prefectos; para proibirles con su autoridad la frace once de las leyes, y impelerles a su exacta observancia.

16. San Ildefonso dize especiosamente en el libro del Summo bien, que la ley, que no sirve sino de embarazar papel, y gastar tinta, se devía canzelar como superflua, e infructuosa; porque la que es justa, santa, y onesta tiene por calidad necesaria, precisa, y sustancial, que se guarde cumpla, y execute.

17. Y Cristo Señor Nuestro nos enseñó con admirable exemplo la execución de las leyes, desengañando a sus discípulos, que no pensasen, que venía a quebrantarlas, sino a cumplirlas al pie de la letra.

18. Y en todos los reynos, que se rigen, y goviernan por ellas, siempre su observancia está floreciente, eterno el uso, inmortal la prática. Justiniano César lo afirmo asi: aunque los casos, que compreenden nunca succedan, siempre retienen su vigor, fuerza, y virtud.

19. Si las cédulas, órdenes, y rescriptos del rey nuestro señor no se an de observar, para que las expidió el eroico zelo de su magestad: Para que las pensó tan despacio la superior sabiduría del consejo? Para que las consultó la eminente ciencia de sus ministros? Para que las remitio la excelente prudencia de su presidente? para que las juramos nosotros? Es razón, que se disimule, ni pase en olvidos los que con tan grandes trabajos, y ardientes fatigas se constituyó?.

20. Y como importa poco, que el médico dicte remedios para la curación, sino se executan en acto las medicinas, que aplica; así se desvanecería la edición, y promulgación de las leyes, cédulas, y rescriptos, sino se exercitasen en los casos, que previenen y reparan: y así dize cuerdamente el Señor Conde de Lemos en la carta, que se a referido tantas vezes, escrivió al Señor Don Juan de Silva en este negocio de los servicios personales. Santas y prudentes son las leyes, que su magestad a establecido, para conseguir este fin; pero poco útiles serían, si en la execución no se procediese con gran cuydado.

21. Y parece, que sería buen medio, para la consecución, elegir, como

lo a deseado V. S. en las provisiones, que a echo, personas temerosas de Dios, afectas, e inclinadas al bien, y propagación de los indios, con noticia experimental, y conocimiento práctico de que en otros, que uvieren ocupado, les ayan beneficiado, y procurado sus augmentos, comodidades, y buenos tratamientos: así lo aconsejó yetro a su yerno Moyses.

22. Lo mismo mandó la serenísima emperatriz Doña Ysabel, regente de los reynos de España, por ausencia del invictísimo emperador Carlos 5. en la cédula despachada a la real audiencia de México, su fecha en Ocaña a 10 de diziembre de 1531. ibi: "Y sobre todo quales an echo buen tratamiento a los indios etc. Lo qual azed, sin tener respecto, y afición alguna; pues veys quanto esto importa al servicio de Dios y nuestro, y a la gratificación de los pobladores de esa provincia: lo qual nos embiad en los primeros navíos, que a estos reynos vinieren etc. Y será bien, que los naturales, y pobladores de esa tierra sepan de vosotros esta intención, y cuydado, que tenemos." Fray Juan de Torquemada, que refiere esta cédula en su *Monarchia Indiana* lib. 17. c. 19. fol. 293. pondera las ultimas palabras. Y será bien que los naturales de esa tierra sepan de vos, o otros esta intención etc." Y las glosa desta manera. "Es a saber, de buscar tales ombres;" y dize: "Reparo en esto; porque me olgue, quando lo allé pronunciado por aquella Santa Emperatriz y Reyna; por que con forma con lo que yo las vezes, que se a ofrecido tengo dicho y lo escriví a España al Arçobispo de Mexico, y Presidente del Consejo de Indias Don Pedro Moya de Contreras; y después se lo dí por escrito al virrey Don Luis de Velasco: que el remedio de los muchos males, que se acen a los indios principalmente consistía en que se mandase con mucho rigor, que ningún ministro de los indios en lo temporal, ni espiritual se consintiese tener más quenta con su proprio interese, que con el bien de los indios en su conservación política, y cristiandad: de suerte, que ningun tal ministro se proveyese, ni continuase, o prorogase en el cargo, aunque tuviese cédulas de su magestad expresas, sino por ser ombre útil, y provechoso para los indios, y su cristiandad; y los que mas útiles en esto se mostrasen, fuesen siempre preferidos en los mejores cargos, y prorrogados en ellos por todo el tiempo, que así lo iziezen.

23. Y para la pregunta, que me avían de azer, que a do se allarían estos tales ombres, y santos; como eran menester tan descuydados de su proprio interese, y tan zelosos del bien de sus proximos? Yo prevenía la respuesta, diciendo: que como los ombres supiesen, que se buscavan tales; y que de estos, y de otros, se vían de servir en estos ministerios, ellos se allarían, y arían fuerza a sus siniestras condiciones, o inclinaciones naturales, por ocupar oficios.

24. Y por tanto es bien, como lo dize aquella real cédula, que sepan los ombres esta intencion, y cuydado: y por averlo tenido aquel cristianísimo emperador, allo a un Diego Ramirez, ombre de recta intención y temeroso de Dios, a quien encomendo la visita de muchos pueblos y tierras desta Nueva España, donde estava informado, que estavan muy cargados, y agraviados los naturales indios; y para ello mando a su real audiencia, se le diese todo favor, y ayuda; y se le alargase el término de su comisión, y visita, si fuese menester, como parece por una su real cédula, dada en

Madrid a 12 de mayo de 1552, que fue causa de remediarse muchos excesos, así de los encomenderos en los tributos, y otras cosas, como de los corregidores, tomándoles residencia a aquel buen ombre, que no se aorraba con nadie: porque tomándosela ellos mesmos entre sí unos a otros, como comunmente se suele azer, es el juego, que dizen: azme la barba, y arete el copete; y por esto no se castigan, y enmiendan." Asta aquí este religioso Baron.

25. Y el medio, que representa, parece proporcionable al fin, quanto mejor proveer en los oficios, y administraciones a los que no an de pecar, que castigar a los que después pecaron; y quanto es más prudente dictamen prevenir, que reparar; preservar, que curar. El Tácito, en la vida de Agrícola, lo ponderó bellísimamente; y le encomia de que, con rarísima moderación deseaba más allar, que azer buenos. Y como eloquentemente escrivió Quintiliano: ninguna erida se cura tan facilmente, como se aze.

26. Vna buena elección prudente es de quien elige, y dicha de quien es escogido, pero no puede ser seguridad, mudanse en las dignidades los ánimos; y si sale mal lo que se eligió bien, no es culpa del eligente, sino del eligido: basta desear, y procurar el acierto. No pide el derecho, que adivinen; ninguno está obligado a vaticinar.

27. Muchos ay dize el Tácito con su lacónica pluma, que parece, que no son aptos; para ocupar puestos, y elevados á ellos los exerzen con estremada rectitud, integridad, y zelos incita, y mueve sus ánimos la grandeza, y confianza de los negocios. Otros, de quienes se esperaba, y prometía, que los avían de usar con gran crédito, limpieza, y desembarazo, se entorpecen, y enrudecen de manera, que lo corrompen, y destruyen todo; y aquellos vicios, que encubría, ó detenía el desvalimiento, y miseria, afectando virtudes, mientras se introducía la pretensión, descubre, y rebienta el valimiento, y fortuna en el onor conseguido; rompiendo el natural la fingida simulación de su ipocresía: calidades, y circunstancias, que es imposible pueda compreender el principe, virrey, ni governador.

28. Con buenos exemplares lo exorna felizmente el mismo Tácito: de Otón refiere, que aviendo vivido relajado en Roma, luego que le criaron prefecto de Lusitania se mudó, y la governó con santa integridad; y de Galba, que todos le uvieran juzgado por dignísimo del imperio, sino uviera imperado. De Quinto Fabio Máximo se escrive, que fue desordenadísimo asta que ascendió a las dignidades, y títulos onoríficos, en que procedió modestísimo, y gravísimo; y lo mismo afirma Budeo, de los promovidos en Atenas al senado de Areopago.

29. Y sucede muchas vezes, dize el obispo Osorio, que se engañan, y les engañaron en la elección, juzgando por bueno, y recto al que era derregalado, y perverso; ó tal vez el que en vida particular, y doméstica se alló perfecto, y modesto, en exerciendo la pública, le estraga, ó la felicidad, ó el oficio.

30. Pero en teniendo entendido, que no a de ser la duración en ellos, ni an de repetir otros, sino en quanto cumplieren las instruciones, ordenes, y direcciones, que se dispusieren en bien de los indios, todos procuraran

aventajarse en la execución; fructificaran los remedios, y se lograra el zelo, desvelo, y cuydado de V. S.

31. Otro arbitrio pulsa el Torquemada, que si pudiere ser practicable en estas Islas, y diesen lugar a su introducción las distancias cortadas de tantos mares, la exigencia de subjetos idóneos, la miseria de los oficios, y otras circunstancias, que lo azen dificil, pero no imposible, sería de gran importancia al bien público, y alivio de los naturales: que los alcaldes mayores no se sindicasen unos á otros: por que como puede corregir, ni inquirir el juez lo mismo, que va determinado, y resuleto a cometer; y como dize la ley de Partida. "Porque no sería derecho, que el que fuese a tal juzgase a los otros." Y Cicerón, que no se a de encargar la enmienda de delictos al que vive muy olvidado de contener los suyos. Y Séneca, que no ay cosa mas torpe, que oponer un ombre á otro lo que se le puede o poner a él.

32. Por San Lucas., Dixo Cristo al ipócrita: para que miras la paja en el ojo ageno, y no consideras la viga en el tuyo proprio? San Pablo: no tienes escusa, o juez, que en lo que en otro juzgas a tí te condenas: tu que enseñas á otro, no te enseñas a tí; tu que preconizas, que no urten, urtas: tu que dizes, que no adulteren, adulteras: tu que abominas los ídolos, azes sacrilegios; y tu que te precias de guardar la ley, la prevaricas.

33. Por esto mandaba Dios en el Exodo c. 25. que las tijeras de despavilar fuesen de oro purísimo, para signifiar la perfección de los que an de sindicar á otros: y Cristo lo dixo por San Juan, a los delatores, que le presentaron la adúltera.

34. El juicio de la Residencia es Santo, Sagrado, é inviolable, como instituido por el mismo Dios: es el que mantiene en esperanza a los pueblos, que an de poder pedir al que tanto temieron al mandar. Deslucimiento es en parte de la dignidad en los cargos superiores, y eminentes; pero gran fuerza de la jurisdicción, y suma rectitud en el principe, que sepamos los ministros, que no sólo tenemos mortales las personas, sino también los oficios, y que á de llegar con el fin el principio de la quenta: refiéranos este miedo, consuela, y alienta a los vasallos: nosotros por el rezelo del castigo de las culpas, que cometieremos; aquellos por la esperanza de allar satisfacción de los agravios, que les izieren. Si el Juez no es entero, recto, y puro, se desvanecen los medios, y se frustan los fines; y descargando y absolviendo á los reos sindicados, se cargan, y condenan los juezes sindicantes.

35. Pondera en el lugar ilustrado el Señor Don Juan de Palafox con la sazón, y agudeza de su grande ingenio, que luego, que Samuel quedo absuelto de su residencia, le pareció, que podría azer milagros, y los izo. Dudo, que uviera muchos en Filipinas, que los izieran después de las suyas, aunque todas piensen, que los puedan azer, y vengan canonizados en ellas: ni tampoco se puede negar, que ay otros, que las toman con entera justificación, y zelo de cumplir con la obligación de su ministerio. No se abla de los buenos; sólo se trata de advertir los inconvenientes, que resultan de los que menos se ajustaren.

36. Vltimamente clausulo el parágrafo representado a V. S. que sirviéndose de conformarse con estas proposiciones, para el mejor cobro de

las materias, que incluyen, y excusar las fatigas, tiempo, y trabaxo, que se a de aplicar, y gastar en copiarse, mande, que se impriman a expensas del oficio de govierno por agora; y los alcaldes mayores proveidos, quando se les entrieguen, podran ir contribuyendo la costa prorateada; pues siempre es preciso, que tengan estas direcciones, que continuamente les recuerden la obligación, y les acusen las transgresiones: y como quiera, que un ombre no puede azerse presente, ni disponer en muchas partes, estando en una, sino con la pluma, y el papel; y con solo este instrumento se suplen los defectos de la ausencia, que es la que causa mayores daños en el govierno. Y así decia Julio César: si quieres governar, escrive, es preciso, que las instrucciones sostituyan la persona de V. S. en cada uno de los partidos: y siendo estos muchos, consequentemente a de ser embarazoso, y prolijo el despacho; y la imprenta lo alivia, y abrevia todo.

7. Final de los Servicios Personales, y Reales, que Tocan a su Magestad

1. Svpongo, que el rey nuestro señor precisamente dispensa los repartimientos, y compulsiones de los indios en las materias de su real servicio en los casos, que miraren a la conservación, y consistencia de estas Islas, y provincias, y quando no uviere obreros voluntarios, y no de otra manera. Consta de la cédula despachada al Señor Don Juan de Silva ibi. "Primeramente mando, que no se repartan indios en más, ni menos número para grangerias particulares, ni públicas; pues a las cortes de maderas, navegaciones de Caracoas, y otras fábricas de esta calidad, en que está interesada mi Real Acienda, y la pública comodidad de esas provincias, llevareys alquilados los chinos, y Iapones, que a la sazón se allaren en Manila, y según estoy informado, avrá entre ellos suficiente número de jornaleros, que vayan a estos ministerios, si les dan el justo jornal de su trabajo: por lo menos usareys de aquellos, que quisieren alquilarse, por excusar el concurrente número de indios; y en caso, que no se pueda quitar el repartimiento, como adelante se dirá, y puesto, que los chinos y japones no quieran; o no puedan satisfacer la urgencia, y necesidad de estas obras públicas, areys diligencia con los indios para que acudan a ellas libre, y voluntariamente, usando de los medios, que os parecieren convenientes a este efecto: pero dado, que aya falta de obreros voluntarios, permiso, que se compelan algunos indios para trabajar en estas occupaciones, con las condiciones, que se siguen, y no de otra manera. Que este repartimiento no se aga sino para cosas muy forzosas, y que no se puedan escusar pues en materias tan odiosas no a de bastar el mayor beneficio de mi Real Acienda, o más comodidad de la república; y todo lo que no fuere preciso para su conservación; pesa menos, que la libertad de los indios."

2. Y en la carta del Señor Conde de Lemos ibi. "En efecto a tomado su magestad resolución en la materia de los servicios personales de los indios, aunque el consejo se a visto tan embarazado en ajustar los puntos, que contiene, que a dos años, que se anda en ésto y siempre a parecido este negocio tan intrincado y dificultoso, que apenas se podía tener por posible la concordia de la materia de estado, y la justificación; y con todo eso no quedamos satisfechos, sino con mucho escrúpulo, tanto más, considerando la dificultad, que a de tener la execución de algunos de los

órdenes de su magestad: y por cierto señor, que yo me espanto mucho del desaogo; y seguridad, conque algunos ministros de las Indias de mas y menos porte, an pasado por estos escrúpulos, y dificultades; no advirtiendo la crueldad, y violencia con que los indios son tratados, sin embargo de que son libres, como las demás naciones; y que la grandeza, y costumbre de los repartimientos sólo se justifica en las cosas que miran precisamente a la conservación de esas provincias, y presupuestas las condiciones, que van expresadas en la cédula de su magestad; todas las quales son precisas, para que se aga, lícita la compulsión de los medios; y así lo piden el derecho, y Teología de Europa: no sé yo si en las Indias ay otras leyes, y letras. que alarguen mas la licencia, y facultad de nuestro imperio."

3. Y en el fin. "Esto se a considerado para cargarle tanto la mano a vuestra merced en que escuse todos los repartimientos, que no fueren precisos para la conservación de las Islas; y en que dentro de estos límites, aya los menos trabajos de los Indios, que fueren posibles: y así emos descargado todos los ministros de acá nuestras consciencias sobre el cuydado de vuestra merced, mire, que un solo indio, que reparta, pudiéndose escusar, a de clamar y serle cruel fiscal, y acusador en el acatamiento de Dios el día del Juicio.

"Pero en caso, que los repartimientos sean forzosos (que esto se duda mucho presupuesto, que ay tantos chinos, que si les pagan bien acudiran a servir) a lo menos áganse los repartimientos con la justificación, y condiciones, que lleva la cédula: y el daño grande, que los indios reciben en el servicio, y manejo de las Caracoas, no sé con que consciencia sea tolerado asta aquí. vuestra merced por reverencia de Dios lo remedie por el camino, que mejor le pareciere, que todo se fia de su zelo, y prudencia; y no podra dezir que no le emos dado aviso bien claro del Santo intento de su magestad. El Conde de Lemos, y Andrade."

4. Y estas calidades, que prescriven las cédulas se an de verificar, y probar antecedentemente, según derecho; y ajustadas, se á de executar la compulsion con las moderaciones, y precauciones, que disponen sus decisiones, y yo referi en el dictamen sobre la translación del Puerto de Cavite al de Lampon, Discurso 4. desde el numero 10 y repetiré aquí con mucho gusto mío, por ser en favor de los indios, añadiendo las noticias, que después an adquirido mis desvelos.

5. La 1. que no se conduzgan indios de provincias distantes, y remotas, sino de las más propinquas, y confinantes: que así lo resuelvan las cédulas de 1551, de 1563, y de 1558. ibi. "Y a los que astuvieren de venir para trabajar, no los sacareys, ni consentireys sean sacados de mas lejos, que de dos leguas, o tres, aviendo necesidad," y otra del año de 1567, que se reiteró el de 1589. Y en la del señor Don Juan de Silba ibi. "que no se lleven de partes distantes."

6. Y fuera de las razones de justicia, buen govierno, y comiseración, que inspiran en la observancia desta condición, se a experimentado otro daño grave que aze más peligroso, y menos lícito el exceso, y es, que corren luego falsos rumores de que son muertos los indios; y como esto no es sólo contingente, o posible, sino casi necesario a los trabajos, inconmodidades, y desconsuelos, que padecen ausentes de sus patrias, y pueblos, con

facilidad se prueba; y las mugeres, que se tienen por viudas se casan segunda vez, viviendo el primer marido; que a sucedido muchas vezes bolver, y allar a su muger en estado de segundas bodas, sin averse disuelto las primeras: y estos casos a practicado, averiguado, y remediado en su diócesi la vigilancia grande del Señor Don Francisco Rodrigo de Cárdenas, obispo de la Nueva Segovia, cuyos encomios, por mucho, que volase la pluma, fueran más injuria, que gloria de sus virtudes, como el Tácito dixo de su Agrícola, sólo se asegura, que conservando la dignidad episcopal no a discrepado de la vida del religioso más retirado: Panegyris, que allo en San Martin Obispo Turonense Severo Sulpicio.

7. La 2. que se les paguen proporcionados salarios a los jornales justos, que mereciere el trabajo en tabla, mano propria, y dinero contante; fe de escrivano, o dos testigos, que no sean indios, ni singleyes; asistencia del padre doctrinante, y alcalde mayor, sin retardación, ni fraude: porque esto lo pide, y manda el derecho Divino, Natural, y Umano.

8. Y aún quieren que la satisfacción se haga todos los días; porque parece que se da más por alimentos, que por salarios; de donde los latinos le llamaron, Diario, y los griegos Efemeridas, como lo dice Geopónico, lib. 2. *de Re rustica.* c. 76.

9. Y en lo individual de los indios, sus servicios, y jornales afirman lo mismo Matienzo, Agia, y Josef de Acosta, y las cédulas de 1599. de 1563. y en las Instrucción [sic], que se dan a los virreyes, que están 1. tomo Impres. pág. 319 et 329. ibi. "Las pagas se agan a los mismos indios que trabajaren, y no a sus principales, ni a otra persona alguna:" y en esta dirigida al Señor Don Juan de Silva ibi. "Que se les de enteramente el hornal, que merecieren por su trabajo, y se les pague en su mano cada día, o al fin de la semana, como ellos escogieren."

10. Con que quedan escluidos, e inibidos los governadores principales y cabezas de barangay de recivir estos jornales, y de ser conductos, por donde se ministre la satisfacción del trabajo: que son tan depravados administradores, que lo usurpan, é interceptan todo, gozando el sudor ageno, y sustentándose, como tiranos, de la sangre de los pobres, y miserables Timauas.

11. Y no sólo se les an de pagar los días, que ocuparen en el trabajo actual, sino los que gastaren en ir, y bolver a sus casas, y pueblos, de donde los extrayeren: porque el tiempo todo de la ausencia cede, y se quenta en lugar de servicio; y lo dispuesto en el término, se entiende siempre constituido también en la vía, por donde a él se camina: y así ablando en las obras, que los libertos deven ir a azer a las moradas de sus patronos; y que si para ésto salen de las suyas les ayan de pagar también el jornal, nos lo enseña el derecho, y lo asientan por regla general quantos tratan de esta materia.

12. La 3. que supuesto, que su magestad (como queda dicho) no confió de menos personas, que de los de los señores virreyes, presidentes, y governadores privativamente la situación, y tasa de estos salarios, y jornales, y el número de las oras, que an de trabajar en cada día, como lo disponen la cédula de 2. de diciembre de 1563 y en la de 1609. ibi. "La segunda, que les pague el jornal que vos señalaredes tasándole en justo

valor." Y en la del Señor Don Juan de Silva. "Y señalareys las oras que uvieren de trabajar cada día, atendiendo a las pocas fuerzas, y débil complegión de los indios." Vuestra Señoría les señale el jornal, y oras, que an de ocupar en el trabajo acomodadas, y proporcionados a la débil complexion, y flaca naturaleza de los indios, como advierte clementísima, y atentamente la cédula referida.

13. Por eso Tomas Moro in *Eutop.* lib. 2. pág. 62. et se qq. acusa de injustas las provincias, que fatigan mucho los trabajadores panegyrizando a su república de Eutopia, que tenía magistrados destinados, llamados, Siphograntos, que dividían, y diputaban las oras del día a los operarios, para las fatigas personales.

14. La 4. que se remuden frequentemente, de suerte, que no se detengan más de una semana y se buelvan pagados, y gustosos a sus casas; y en su lugar sucedan, y se sobroguen otros: que aun en el derecho común se dispone que se cambien los Palatinos, que se embiaban a las provincias a las exacciones fiscales; y por eso se llamavan mitendarios.

15. Y en terminos terminantes de las Indias, Juan Matienzo, Acosta, y lo disponen apretadamente las cédulas del año de 1601. c. 15. et 18. y en el ca. 24. ibi. "Para que así su mayor trabajo, como lo que fuere alivio, se reparta igualmente entre todos:" y en la de 1609 c. 16. "Porque de estas detenciones violentas se les siguen inumerables daños, y es de los abusos, que con mayor cuydado aveys de impedir, y cautelando su libertad, de tal manera, que no padezcan violencia, ni compulsión alguna:" y la del señor Don Juan de Silva. "De manera, que así el trabajo de las distancias, como el peso de las ocupaciones, y la compensación de las demás circunstancias, en que a de aver más, o menos graveza, se reparta, y comunique con igualdad, para que todos participen de los servicios más, o menos trabajosos; sin que el beneficio, y alivio de los unos recambie en agravio de los otros."

16. La 5. que se conduzgan en tiempo, que no se desacomoden de sus aprovechamientos, de la cultura, y cura de sus campos, y labor de sus sementeras, según se manda en la misma cédula del Señor Don Juan de Silva ibi. "Que los dichos repartimientos se agan a tiempo, que no se encuentren con la sementera, y cosecha de los frutos ni las demas sazones, en que los indios an de acudir a la grangería, y administración de sus aciendas; porque mi intención es, que no se pierdan, y puedan asistir a todo; para lo qual os mando, que a la entrada del año prevengays las fábricas, o otras cosas de mi servicio, en que los indios uvieren de ocuparse; porque tomándose con tiempo, se pueda compartir de tal manera, que no reciban vejación considerable en sus aziendas, y personas."

17. La 6. que se tenga mucho cuydado con su salud; especialmente con los que en el trabajo adolescieren, se aplique mayor desvelo de curación de regalo, y asistencia, como se dispone en la cédula del año de 1601. c. 6. et 9. ibi. "Y los que enfermaren sean visitados, y curados, y se les administren los Santos Sacramentos: y en el c. 17. que sobre todo se tenga muy particular cuydado de su salud, y buen tratamiento en lo espiritual, y temporal, y que los enfermos sean muy bien curados."

18. Y en la del Señor Don Juan de Silva se expresa el especialísimo deseo, que su magestad tiene de la salud, y vida de los indios, y quanto

previne los accidentes, que se la pueden molestar y turbar, ibi. "Que presupuesta la mala disposición, y traza de las Caracoas, y que remando en ellas suelen morirse muchos; porque van sin cubierta, expuestos a las inclemencias de los temporales, os mando, que deys orden, que estas embarcaciones se mejoren, y fabriquen de manera, que puedan los indios manejarlos sin riesgo de su salud. En todo lo qual y lo demás, que mirare a su conservación, y augmento, os buelvo a mandar, que procedays con el cuydado, y vigilancia, que de vos confio." Y el mejor remedio de la enfermedad será, dejar ir libremente a curar a sus pueblos, y casas a los que adolescieren gravemente: que suele aver algunos superintendentes, cabos, oficiales, ó ministrales de tan dura cerviz, tan impiamente crueles, y tan asoyonados, que olvidados de la fe, que profesan y del Dios, que adoran, recetan a las enfermedades de estos desdichados muchos azotes, vejaciones, injurias, y agravios, obligándole a que sin embargo trabajen; queriendo dar entender, que son fingidas, y simuladas; y que las toman por pretexto, para escusarse; y la suerte, que les sobreviene con los nuevos accidentes de rigores, les desengaña ireparablemente del error, que les impresionó su pasión, mal natural, y peor inclinación. Los males se originan de los cabezas; y en la elección se aciertan, o se yerran las acciones.

19. La 7. que no se les obligue a trabajar, ni caminar en domingo, y días festivos: que fuera de ser precepto divino tercero del decálogo indispensable se manda expresamente en las cédulas del año de 1564, donde después de referir los daños, y cargos de conciencia, que resultan del abuso contrario, se manda. "Que por ningún caso, se les permita trabajar en domingos, y fiestas de guardar." Y más apretadamente la de 1609. c. 32. "Sobre todo lo qual atendereys con mucha vigilancia, a que los jornaleros oygan misa, y no trabajen los días de fiesta en beneficio de los españoles, aunque tengan bulas apostólicas, y privilegios de su Santidad."

20. La 8. que se extirpe la depravada costumbre, que se a introducido, de las opas, que es redimirse los indios a sus mismas cabezillas, y á algunos españoles, que suelen embiarse por cabos, ó ministrales; porque les indulten el trabajo, y les disimulen bolverse a sus pueblos, ó les escusen la compulsión, y libres del repartimiento, ó no los asisten para las jornadas: y luego se reconocen a las primeras luzes, sin que se necesite de ponderación, los graves daños, que resultan de este género de baratería. Lo. 1. porque por lograr, y augmentar la injusta grangería, reparten, y complen a mayor número de los que an menester las funciones. Lo 2. porque el peso, y continuación del trabajo recae siempre sobre unos mismos, que son los, que no tienen con que comprarse; sobre los pobres, sin esperanza de alivio, y desaogo; con que se despechan, y desesperadamente mueren, porque desconsoladamente viven. Lo 3. porque se pone diametralmente al bien de la causa pública, y al fin é intento, que se lleva en estos repartimientos, y piden los reales rescriptos, que es la igualdad geométrica: y así son muchas las cédulas, que con graves palabras, y penas lo proiben, llamándolo pernicioso, detestable, y lo califican por peor, que urto, y por atroz delicto: y que los señores fiscales velen en inquirirlo, examinarlo, y acusarlo, para que los juezes los manden castigar con exemplar escarmiento, como son las de los años de 1601. c. 2. 1603. 1609. c. 23, y las de 1608,

1616, 1618 y de 1620. El Señor Don Juan de Solórzano en su *Politica* lib. 2. c. 18. fol. 165.

21. Esto es lo que menos de lo que siento, y lo más de lo que ignoro esperando de la justificación de V. S. que está desaliñada fatiga á de redundar en lúcida ostentación de la causa pública, bien universal de los naturales, y general indicación de que lo deseo, solicito, y procuro: que será el mayor premio de mis estudiosos desvelos, y la más pomposa gratificación de mis empleos literarios; quando anticipadamente sólo intentarlos, aunque no llegue a glorias de conseguido, ni goze dichas de executado, tiene calificación de fructuoso, en sentir de Salviano Cicerón, y el segundo de los Plinios.

22. Y no puede ser dudable, que se le ofrece a V. S. gran materia, en que azer inmortal su nombre en todas las naciones del archipiélago en igual mérita, y bien de las provincias extirpando de raíz abusos, que deslustran, y desafueros, que deforman; con que se deverá a la piedad y liberalidad de V. S. unicamente, la renovación, que persuaden los rescriptos, y la reformación, que mandan las cédulas: cesarán los clamores de los pueblos; se suprimirán los agravios de los partidos; se olvidarán las vejaciones de las personas; será más cordial, y reverencial el amor, obediencia, y rendimiento a su majestad, mayor su nombre: y como obligado por tantos títulos, y vínculos a su exaltacion, y propagación, y á que se consiga por mano de V. S. no podré dexar de repetir siempre con nuevas instancias lo que suspendo agora, no con desmayos de ciencia, sino por acierto de meditación y seguridad infalible, de que V. S. confirme resolución a reparar de una vez los daños ponderados, aplicando los remedios prevenidos, y que a de amanecer a los naturales el festivo día, en que se aplaudan libres, y exemptos de la servidumbre, que los debilitan, de los achaques, que los extinguen. V. S. mandara lo que fuere servido, que será lo más conveniente. Manila, y agosto veinte y dos de mil, y seiscientos, y cinquenta y siete años.

Lic. Don Salvador Gomez de Espinosa y Estrada

ADDITIONAL NOTES

P. 157: The intervention of Innocent III in the Canterbury monks' elections was the result of a clash between him and King John; it resulted in England's being placed under a papal interdict (i.e. an ecclesiastical strike) until John submitted in 1213; two years later Innocent again intervened in English affairs by annulling the Magna Carta (1215).

P. 158: Bulla de la Cena: papal bulls, like hymns, are usually known by their opening words; this one, however, takes its title from the feast day on which it was annually promulgated: Maundy Thursday or In Coena Domini. Consisting of a catalogue of anathemas against transgressors, it was published yearly in Rome from 1364 to 1774, when pressure from the Catholic Enlightened Despots caused it to be dropped.

203a

P. 174: The reference to Jacobo de Valdés's De dignitate regum regnorumque Hispaniae (Granada, 1602) shows that Espinosa, though he might be at the 'end of the earth', was up to date with the latest Latin best-sellers; the fact that his reference is slightly out does not detract from this. Cf. also in this connection his reference to Juan Antonio de Vera y Figueroa's El embajador (Seville, 1620; French trans. 1635; Italian trans. 1624).

V

TWO MISSIONARY METHODS IN CHINA: MENDICANTS AND JESUITS

1579: The Franciscans' Return to China

The Spanish Franciscans' arrival in China in 1579 led to the resumption of the work of their spiritual ancestors three centuries earlier. This «Second Coming» was important for various reasons: it was the realization of a Franciscan dream; the fulfilment of a prophecy; their answer to an insistent vocation; it was also, they came to decide, «un misterio y providencia del Señor.» With hindsight we now know that it set the scene and assembled the *dramatis personae* for the opening stages of the celebrated Chinese Rites Controversy. That debate ultimately embraced East and West and intensified the early search for a policy of accommodation in missionary techniques. And though this particular controversy is over, the basic problem remains with us still, in varying forms, as for example the process of *aggiornamento*.

Accounts of the old China mission are usually put forward in simple black and white terms. The romantic story of the Jesuits has captured the imagination, and compared with them the friars come off badly — and not only in popular literature either. The mendicants are shown as reactionaries, as «medievals» in a Renaissance world, as rough intruders into an area where delicate diplomacy was needed, of being obstinately ignorant, of advocating spiritual conquest with fire and sword. But this simple view is not historically tenable, for the friars were not rigid stereotypes, and their story is more complex than is usually believed. What has been learnt of the Hispano-American missions can, *mutatis mutandis*, also be said of China:

> «Est-ce à dire que l'Eglise d'Espagne a fondé l'entreprise évangélique sur la répression, qu'elle a choisi d'effacer purement et simplement la tradition religieuse indigène, d'imposer la foi catholique et son enveloppe

européenne, sans tenir compte des conceptions et des habitudes des Péruviens? La réalité fut plus complexe.»[1]

Antonio Sisto Rosso OFM., has said that «the Mendicants were the heirs of Catholic tradition as found in the West and East, and not a single feature of the so-called Jesuit method was alien to them.»[2] Nevertheless, one is far more likely to read that «The Franciscans... swooped down upon China aflame with hopes of converting the pagans, but failed because they refused to compromise with existing customs and beliefs... they arrogantly announced the superiority of Western culture and demanded that the Chinese conform.» After which it may be confusing to be told that the assertion that «nunca se hará nada [en China], si no va el evangelio en una mano, y la espada en la otra» was not made by a «swooping» friar, but by a prominent Jesuit.[3] And some would find it surprising to learn from a leading authority on the subject that the «*rêve chinois* so industriously fostered by the Jesuits in the next two centuries, and which influenced Leibniz and other European thinkers of the "Enlightenment" so profoundly, got off to a good start» in the work of friars whose affection and admiration for China, and zeal for studying its languages and mysteries, were no less keen than the enthusiasm of their more celebrated Jesuit colleagues.[4]

Nevertheless, there is more than one *leyenda negra.* So the idea persists that a glorious opportunity was lost in Asia solely through the intransigence of pedantic moralists, and for the sake of a few trifling scruples.[5]

In the interests of balance I intend here to present the situation as the friars saw it, because it is important to know what the friars believed they were opposing. Consequently, I shall try to examine the friars' evangelistic passports, their humanist credentials, their attitudes and their

---

1 P. Duviols, *La lutte contre les religions autochtones dans le Pérou colonial,* Lima, 1971, 339.

2 A. S. Rosso, OFM. *Apostolic Legations to China of the 18th Century,* South Pasadena, 1948, 109.

3 Or that the declaration that the two essential qualifications for the China mission were «Christ Crucified and Chinese,» was not made by a 17th-century friar, but by a 20th-century Jesuit General: Wlodimir Ledochowski, *Selected Writings,* Chicago (ad usum nostrorum privatum tantum), 1945, 717.

4 C. R. Boxer, *South China in the Sixteenth Century,* London, Hakluyt Society, 1953, xci.

5 Eg: John Davis, quoted in P. J. D'Orleans, *The History of the Two Tartar Conquerors of China,* London, Hakluyt Society, 1854, p. iii; Francis Mahoney, *The Works of Father Prout,* London, 1835, 49.

earlier experience, to see if and how all this prepared them for the China mission. For, besides their *recados*, the mendicants took to Asia a vast and varied experience of mission activity. They had, first, their own tradition of missionary work and accommodation; they had their experience as evangelists among the Moors of Granada; they had their experience gained amongst Indians and colonists in America and the Philippines; they had their experience among the Chinese and Japanese in Manila by which to profit. Finally, they had their own Japan mission where they were distinguishing themselves. Each area was different; no one was an exact model for another, but each taught the need for adaptability, and each served as a collective preparation for the next. All this experience worked on two levels: it taught them to evolve novel techniques for novel circumstances; but it also developed in them an awareness of certain dangers which, in turn, begot caution: it placed them on their guard against over-optimism. In a word, it made them realistic.

But we are entitled to ask what became of this rich experience when the mendicants crossed the South China Sea; did they arrive in China, the «Central Country,» having learnt nothing and having forgotten everything?

«The great differences that disturb the peace of mankind are not about ends, but means.» But such differences are difficult to contain for they have a dynamic quality of their own which spreads into other more personal areas. And since every theological dispute is at bottom human, the human dimension is important in any assessment of the missionary controversies about the methods and techniques suited to China. Thus many of the missionaries (Jesuits and mendicants) took with them to Asia a sense of unease *vis-à-vis* their other colleagues from whom they differed in their approach to the problems of the new mission. For instance, the still disputed theory of Probabilism was being applied there with confidence by one group and resisted with alarm by the other. In such circumstances dispute was inevitable. And the more important the end, the more bitter the dispute about the means to achieve that end.

The first Catholic missions to China took place in the 13th century. Expeditions were made to Asia by friar John of Pian del Carpine (1245-7) and William of Ruisbroeck (1253-5), and their accounts reached friar Roger Bacon who was probably «the first to relate missionary activity to scientific observation»; other friar missionaries to China included John of Montecorvino (1289-1328), the first Archbishop of Peking (1307). It was he who translated the New Testament, Psalter and Missal into the Tartar language in which he said Mass in his Cathedral. His early efforts at acculturation («*ut multos Christo lucrifaciant*») could set a model for future missionaries in China, the Central Country. There were other Franciscan missions to China in the fourteenth century but eventually these died out for various reasons: the Black Death in Europe, the fall of the Mongol (Yüan) Dynasty in China, the succession of the Ming in 1368, and the obstructions put in their way by the Muslims in the Middle East. [6]

So, though these early Franciscan efforts could not be followed up, China was not forgotten, and the papacy continued to appoint prelates to Cambaluc (Peking) until 1426. In the sixteenth century a Jesuit in Asia (St Francis Xavier) and a Franciscan in Mexico (friar Juan de Zumárraga) gazed longingly towards the Central Country, symbolically foretelling the pincer movement by Jesuit and mendicant from East and West. Throughout that century fresh exploratory expeditions were made until, finally, a friar and a Jesuit managed to enter China at almost the same time: Father Melchor Nunes Barreto (1555-6) and fray Gaspar da Cruz (1556). From then onwards, more and more religious sought to follow, including the famous Augustinian sinologist, fray Martín de Rada. The first group of modern Franciscans, fray Pedro de Alfaro and companions, entered the empire in 1579. Four years later the Jesuits established themselves, and Catholicism, on a permanent basis in the form of the mission of Matteo Ricci and Michele Ruggieri.

---

[6] Rosso, *Apostolic Legations,* 13-15; Celsus Kelly, OFM., *La Austrialia del Espíritu Santo,* Cambridge, 1966, 117-19; and the detailed account in D. F. Lach, *Asia in the Making of Europe,* I (i), 30-48: «The Revelation of Cathay.» For a full discussion of early contacts between Europe and China, and for the correspondences between the final failure of the Crusades and the great voyages of discovery see also Joseph Needham, *Science and Civilisation in China,* Cambridge University Press, 5 vols. (in progress) who quotes «one of the most famous hadiths of the Prophet: «Seek for learning though it be far away as China.» He notes that Spanish Muslims travelled as far as China in the thirteenth century: I, 216-8, 225, III, 522; IV (Pt 3), 502 ff. Needham shows that the interest was not all one-sided: the Chinese also sought the Far West, and their Admiral Cheng Ho, («the Chinese Vasco da Gama») found his way down the African coast as far as Mombasa. These efforts, however, did not continue, and in 1434, when Gil Eanes was doubling Cape Bojador, the last Chinese expedition to Africa returned home. See, for Catholic missions in mediaeval China and India: Jean Richard, *Orient et Occident au Moyen Age: contacts et relations* (*viie-xves.*), London, 1976: a stimulating series of articles which goes beyond what the title would imply.

MENDICANT AND JESUIT IN SEARCH OF CHINA

The Apostolic Age is defined by Paul's addressing himself to non-Jews. The Age of Discovery can be seen as another such era: the Christian message was now to be delivered to all races of men and to the whole world. In this work Franciscans played a major role. Associated from the start with Columbus, whose projects they favoured and furthered, they were also active in the early Portuguese voyages of reconnaissance. Jaime Cortesão makes high claims for the Franciscan contribution to humanist studies at this time, and others follow him: «As is well known, the early years of the Franciscan order coincided with a striking renewal of interest in the study of geography and in the production of travel literature, two fields of humane scholarship in which the Franciscans were to achieve notable success in the later medieval centuries. The renewal can be attributed to the development of an original philosophy of nature among the Franciscans, stemming out of their involved and intense approach to Nature and to Man.» [7] The Franciscans spread rapidly both to east and west. They had long been active in the colonization and conversion of the Azores, Madeira, the Cape Verde Islands. They were involved in Cabral's voyage to India in 1500; by 1505 they were in Ceylon and soon resumed in Cochin and southern Malabar the work of their spiritual predecessor, John Marignolli OFM, who had worked there in 1346-7. [8] As early as 1525 they started evangelizing in Celebes. In the West, they were quickly established in Cuba where they had opened a school by 1502, spreading further west and south quickly, so that by 1529 they were beginning missions in the Argentine and Paraguay areas.

But their most celebrated success was achieved in Mexico where the famous «Twelve Franciscan Apostles» began evangelizing immediately after the conquest. From there they were later to cross the Pacific to the Philippines, the «gateway to Asia.» For the first time in history the Church, if it did not cover the whole earth, had footholds nearly everywhere in preparation for future establishment.

In America particularly, the friars grasped at what they saw as the opportunity to create a utopia, a chance to return to the purity of the

---

[7] Quoted in *An Account of Sierra Leone* by André DONELHA, edited by A. TEIXEIRA DA MOTA and P. E. H. HAIR, Lisboa, 1977, 37.

[8] LACH, *Asia*, I (i), 231, 281; KELLY, *La Austrialia*, I, 117.

primitive apostolic church, a Catholicism which would not require a Reformation because it would be uncontaminated by the vices and the corruption of Europe. But by the middle of the sixteenth century the golden age of colonization of Mexico was fading fast; disappointment and frustration discouraged many friars, and the work of evangelisation had become mere routine. The last years of fray Bernardino de Sahagún show us the slow death of one of the first of the American myths. Once again the insistent call of China was heard. Not, of course, that it had ever been entirely silent, for even fray Martín de Valencia, the very leader of the Mexican «Twelve Apostles,» had longed to move on there. One of the attractions of China was the belief that the people there were highly intelligent and posed a greater challenge than the intellectually docile Amerindians. Fr. Custos Valencia never fulfilled these hopes, and the Franciscan chronicler, Jerónimo de Mendieta, believed that his disappointment was destined, that God selects an apostle for each region of the world, and that it was the vocation of Valencia to remain in Mexico. [9] There, accordingly, he died, lamenting: «Fraudatus sum a desiderio meo.» Even such apparently dedicated American evangelists as fray Bartolomé de las Casas were tempted by the bait of China. In a moment of spiritual crisis he, too, toyed with the idea of leaving New Spain for Asia, together with fray Juan de Zumárraga and fray Domingo de Betanzos.

Other individual friars were influenced by sinomania: the friar who accepted the first bishopric of the Philippines allegedly did so because it would bring him nearer to China (yet, later, heavily involved in his new responsabilities, he was to complain of those «frailes que piavan por irse a China.») The Central Country seems to have been the topic of conversation even during recreation periods if we may judge from fray Pedro de Alfaro, who recalled how «después de la sobremesa, tomamos por de postre el tratar las cosas de la China.» Some had no doubt that it was the right and privilege of the Franciscans to convert the East. Fray Paulo da Trindade's seventeenth-century *Conquista Espiritual do Oriente* devotes a chapter to the theme of «Como a Conquista Espiritual do Oriente por razão da antiga posse se devia de direito aos Frades menores e como eles foram os primeiros que vieram a India.» Others sought dramatic solutions to their problem, and one of them «en

---

[9] Jerónimo de MENDIETA, OFM., *Historia eclesiástica indiana,* IV, Mexico, 1945, 29-33; Juan de TORQUEMADA, OFM., *Monarchía indiana,* Madrid, 1723, III, 415.

el año de 1571... se quiso vender por esclavo para poder de este modo entrar en la China.» [10] Still other enthusiasts, seeking justification for their plans, enlisted Chinese prophecies that they were destined to be conquered one day by an alien people with long beards and large «cats' eyes.» [11]

There were also Jesuits just as keen to enter China. For instance, José de Acosta had first sought to go to Asia; America only came into his mind after the start of the Jesuits' Florida mission; and the martyr, Isaac Jogues, was fascinated by the idea that Lake Superior might be the legendary road to China. [12] This zeal was partly aroused by the Jesuits' publications, private and public, on the East. There were non-Jesuit works also. The *Tractado* of the Dominican Gaspar da Cruz (Evora, 1569) and the *Discurso* of Bernardino de Escalante (Seville, 1577) were the first two books on the Central Country published in Europe, but the real best-seller on the subject in sixteenth-century Europe was the *Historia* of the Augustinian Juan González de Mendoza (Rome, 1585). [13] Some of these mendicant works irritated Jesuits who found themselves in the impossible position of advertising China and Japan, while at the same time keeping those same missions to themselves. They therefore denounced those Spanish publications which drew attention to the possibilities, challenges and attractions of China. Ricci and his colleagues, still hoping to enter the empire admitted that «Se em algum tempo virmos com nossos olhos aberta esta porta, veremos huma conversão a major que ouve desda primitiva Igreja ategora,» but denounced annoying

---

10 The best study of this topic is that of J. Beckmann, SMB., *China im Blickfeld der mexikanischen Bettelorden des 16. Jahrhunderts* in: «Neue Zeitschrift für Missionswissenschaft,» 19 (1963) 81-92, 195-214; 20 (1964) 27-41, 89-108; see also A. Chavez, OFM., *The Oroz Codex*, Washington, 1972, 136, 184 ff

11 Such alleged prophecies are not uncommon and range from Africa to central America: for these, see Diogo de Couto, *Década V*, livro 8, ch. 12; *Sínica Franciscana*, II, 132; Juan Gonzalez de Mendoza, *The History of the Great and Mighty Kingdom of China*, I, London, Hakluyt Soc., 1853, xliv, 76; II, 163.

12 Some would-be missionaries were frightened off the American missions by stories of the disputes between clergy and *encomenderos* and the complicated «casos de conciencia.» One Jesuit Father wrote to the General: «Mi inclinación siempre ha sido para las Indias del rey de Portugal, y para las del Emperador, nunca.» This attitude, of course, implies ignorance of the complexities of the Rites Controversy in China. See L. Lopetegui, SJ., *José de Acosta y las misiones*, Madrid, 1942, 44.

13 See Lach, *Asia*, I, (ii), 742 ff., Boxer, *South China*, passim. Less important, but symptomatic, is *The Strange and marueilous Newes... of China* published in England in 1577, which reported how «There hath been made within this citie of Mexico general prayers and supplications, beseeching the Almightie God to lighten this strange people with the knowledge of holy fayth and woorde...» R. McLachlan, *A Sixteenth-Century Account of China...* in: «Papers of Far Eastern History,» Canberra, 12 (1915) 71-86

exaggerations in others which were stirring up alarming interest: «Habbiamo inteso che per via de' forastieri furno a Roma le nove della conversione con qualche excesso della verità [and] l'India occidentale e l'Europa ne erano tutte in commozione.» That the Jesuits were equally busy may be judged from the ninety letters from Asia published by them in Alcalá in 1575, relating their achievements, printing a gazeteer of place names in the Indian Ocean, and giving a brief description of Japan. The dedication reveals that 1,000 copies were printed and distributed free of cost. Sometimes this passion for the Far East irritated Jesuits elsewhere who felt their work was being slighted: Jeronimo Roiz, for instance, wrote lamenting that Japan and China got all the limelight. In a letter from Cochin in 1569 he described his own labours so that, «charissimos hermanos, verán que no es como allá se piensa, que sólo en Japón y China ha christiandad.» [14]

Not all the favourable publicity came from books, pamphlets, or extravagant rumour. Some Chinese and Japanese travelled to Mexico, some as far as Spain itself, and even «into other kingdomes further off.» Later still there were Chinese slaves in Mexico, well able to play the part of those Angli who seemed more like «Angeli» to Gregory the Great, and moved him to seek the conversion of the English. In much the same way, the Chinese attracted attention, aroused interest and presented a challenge. Their natural qualities and their bright intelligence made their conversion imperative. The first Franciscans to arrive in Manila confessed that their desire to go over into the Central Country had been heightened by their intercourse with those individual Chinese they had already encountered. [15]

* * *

Of the four mission centres in Asia (Goa, Malacca, Macao and Manila) only the last lay in the Spanish zone of influence. Unlike Macao and

---

[14] Pasquale D'ELIA, *Fonti Ricciane*, II, Rome, 1942, 268-9; António da SILVA REGO, *Documentação para a História das missões do padroado português do Oriente, India*, XI, Lisboa, 1955, 23; *Occasional Paper No. 17*, University of Minnesota Library, May 1977, 12; R. STREIT, OMI, *Bibliotheca Missionum*, XI, Aachen 1928, 414-5.

[15] BEDE, The Venerable, *Hist. Eccles. Anglorum*, II, ch. i; LACH, *Asia*, I (ii), 791; R. KONETZKE, *Col. de docs. para la hist. de la formación social de Hispanoamérica*, Madrid, 1958, II (i), 291, 438; C. R. BOXER, *Notes on Chinese Abroad in the Late Ming and Early Manchu Periods... 1500-1750*, «T'ien Hsia Monthly,» IX (1939) 448-49. The old Franciscan convent of Cuernavaca has a mural depicting the martyrs of 1597 which, apparently, is the work of a contemporary Japanese artist in Mexico.

Malacca (and to some extent Goa), Manila was not dominated by the Jesuits in the ecclesiastical sphere. The Orders had established themselves there as follows: Augustinians (1565), Franciscans (1578), Dominicans (1587), and in 1581, the Jesuits. In 1579 a bishopric was established (suffragan to Mexico, 6,000 miles away) and by 1620 an entire hierarchy was organised with some two million Christians in its care. From this springboard the friars made their leap into China, the Central Country, and they used it as a base for moving into Japan and even, during the 1590s, into Siam and Cambodia. All through the second half of the sixteenth century missionaries of the various Orders made a series of sallies into China, among them the Franciscan fray Pedro de Alfaro and his companions.[16] Alfaro, the newly-appointed Custos of the Philippine Islands, had arrived in Manila in June 1578 after a successful voyage which had included something akin to a triumphal progress across Mexico, «ben veduti et accarezzati dalli frati Minori dell'Osservanza, che furono i primi religiosi, li quali convertirono quella Nova Spagna.»

Jesuit-Portuguese alarm at all these moves expressed itself in a number of ways, among which was the securing from Gregory XIII of a bull *Super Specula* (1576) erecting Macao into a diocese comprising «forever» all China, Japan and the surrounding islands, a suffragan of Goa, and under Portuguese patronage.[17] The Macao missionaries, writes Lach (oc I 296), «with their heavy investments in the silk trade, were as fearful as the Portuguese about condoning or encouraging actions to which the Chinese might respond unfavourably» and the civic authorities also «were extremely anxious not to anger the Chinese and were particularly fearful that illegal entries of the mainland would endanger commerce.»

Equally, however, the friars could not be expected to give up lightly what they regarded as their vocation; so, undeterred, they continued to look towards China as their ultimate goal. Members of the groups that arrived in Manila in 1578 with Alfaro were restless and, finally, unable to resist the lure of China, five of them, including Alfaro, left for Canton without the permission of the civic authorities of Manila. They wrote

---

16 For a schematic outline of missionary attempts to enter China in the sixteenth century see *Sinica Franciscana*, II, xxxiii, and D'ELIA, *Fonti Ricciane*, I, 139 n.

17 See ROSSO, *Apostolic Legations*, 49; LACH, *Asia*, I (i), 296-8. For a brief biography of Alfaro see *Sinica Franciscana*, II, 163; and for some idea of the still primitive nature of the Philippine colony and of the urgent need to staff and equip it, see Luis MURO, *Soldados de Nueva España a Filipinas (1575)*, in: «Historia Mexicana,» 19 (1969) 466-91.

back from China to the Philippines, expressing the conviction that they had no hope of staying inside the empire and, as Alfaro put it, in curiously chivalresque language, «morir aquí todos en esta demanda.» But their journey had served its purpose, since they had borne witness, and had even left behind them one of their companions «como por señal y prenda hasta el día del juicio, donde no tendrán escusa estos infieles, pues ya por parte de los Portugueses y nuestra se les ha ofrecido la paz evangélica.» Eventually, denounced by the Portuguese, driven from Canton, they nevertheless managed to establish a Franciscan convent in Macao, with a view to a permanent mission some time in the future. [18]

The arrival of the two groups (Jesuits from Macao and friars from Manila) took place at more or less the same time, and each moved gradually nearer the common goal: an establishment in mainland China. In this the Jesuits were the more fortunate. These pioneers quickly concluded that the new harvest-field required special techniques, for the Chinese were extremely xenophobic, being both suspicious and contemptuous of all «foreign barbarians.» One friar was later to describe the situation by saying wryly that the Chinese regarded Europeans in the way that Europeans regarded the Amerindians. The different European nationals were seen by the Chinese as merely members of different tribes, and they would have been stunned and scandalised if they had known that eventually their «Central Flowery Country» was to become, for the Jesuits, merely a vice-province of the Society's international organisation.

The Jesuit tactic: The Mandarin-missionaries

The Jesuits pioneers began with a false start. They first dressed as Buddhist priests, until, realizing that these were not greatly respected, they changed to the silk robes of the literati, or scholar gentry, from whose ranks were recruited the mandarins who administered the Empire. The Fathers adopted Chinese manners; they let their beards grow, they

---

[18] In time, the Manila authorities, both civic and ecclesiastic, came to resent those Religious who arrived merely to move on to China; such expeditions were eventually forbidden. On the other hand, it came to be recognised that it was the chance of entering China from the Philippines that induced many friars to go there, and of these some stayed on, instead of leaving. Alfaro was therefore credited with, accidentally as it were, having increased the number of volunteers for the Islands. Cf. Lorenzo Perez, OFM., *Cartas y relaciones del Japón*, I, Madrid, 1916, 19-20 with A. Valignano, S.J., *Sumario de las cosas del Japón*, ed. J. L. Alvarez-Taladriz, Tokyo, 1954, 296.

kept servants, and they gave expensive presents to the influential. Since a stigma attached to any official who travelled on foot, they had themselves carried about in sedan-chairs. This way of life was costly, and eventually, in order to support themselves and keep the mission independent, they were obliged to become merchants and traders. There was nothing surprising in any of this, for it was the same realistic policy that they followed elsewhere. Jesuits, they proclaimed, were prepared to do everything possible to bring the Gospel to the unconverted; ready to become literati to the Chinese, or indeed anything to anybody. [19]

Ricci also realised the enormity of the work involved in persuading an ancient and highly developed civilisation to change its ways of life by adopting Christianity. Their task was all the harder because the Chinese seemed unlike any other people; they seemed so choked with intellectual pride (that greatest of all obstacles to the Faith) that even the possibility of capturing their respect was remote; much more so was the hope of converting them. [20] Then Ricci saw how to approach this sophisticated people: he would rely on their curiosity and love of knowledge. His campaign began. Natural charm helped him to make friends: the Chinese saw him as a «person of virtue, with a curly beard, blue eyes, a voice like a great bell; intelligent, witty, and of manifold ability; he could read off anything he had once glanced at» (he was admired for everything, even for his hearty appetite). His prodigious memory helped him master Chinese, which in time he came to write unaided, though he usually sought correction before publication. Not an astronomer, he had however studied mathematics under Christopher Clavius in Rome, and cosmography in Portugal under Pedro Nunez. Moreover, during the five years' long journey from Europe he had devoted his leisure to the study of the natural sciences. He also brought with him a number of maps and scientific instruments which he now decided to use as bait. Gradually, polite visits to educated officials developed into discussions with them; amused tolerance on their part yielded to questioning when it was discovered that, surprisingly, there was something to be learnt from the newcomer. Ricci grasped every opportunity. He observed errors in the Chinese mathematical

---

19 This, of course, was not something unknown to the Franciscans; see, for example, Pedro BORGES, OFM., *Métodos misionales de la cristianización de América: Siglo XVI,* Madrid, 1960, 101-110.

20 For a sympathetic view of Ricci's life and work in China see G. L. HARRIS, *The Mission of Matteo Ricci, SJ: A Case Study of an Effort at Guided Culture Change...* in: «Monumenta Serica,» 25 (1966) 1-168.

texts which he pointed out and corrected. Above all he captured interest with his world map, showing Europe and America to the Chinese for the first time. But Ricci himself claimed that his treatise on friendship «won more credit for me and for Europe than anything else we've done», for the Chinese seemed more interested in moral philosophy than in science. This, however, was but the beginning. All the time, from his arrival in 1583 to his reaching Peking in 1601, Ricci kept his eye firmly fixed in the direction of the imperial Dragon Throne, realizing that in such a rigid hierarchical society the best hope for Christianity lay in obtaining the Emperor's favour. In China, as elsewhere in Asia, the Jesuits gave first priority to the conversion of the ruling class rather than to the lowly. It was the policy laid down in their Constitutions and so carried out in their practice. The economists' so-called «trickle-down» theory could pay dividends as converted rulers brought their people into the Church behind them; so, «We should begin at the top... mathematics are very useful in the whole of the East. How else could we approach these very proud kings?» asked one of the Jesuits.

None but courtiers and high officials had any contact with the Emperor, the «Son of Heaven,» who dwelt in god-like splendour and isolation in Peking inside the Forbidden City which was controlled by the imperial eunuchs. For eighteen years Ricci worked conscientiously, and waited quietly, until at last after managing to establish himself near the capital, he sent to the palace a number of gifts to excite the Emperor's interest: books, paintings of Christian subjects, a clavichord, maps, and, above all, a striking clock. As he had hoped, the clock intrigued the Emperor, and when it wound down Ricci was summoned to carry out «repairs.» Thus he succeeded in his plan and, perhaps for the first time since John of Montecorvino (1289-1328), a European entered the palace. Although he never saw the Emperor himself, the Jesuit continued his efforts, striving to make himself indispensable — holding open that door which he had prised ajar so patiently. He had given his colleagues an example of the use of «human means» for divine ends, and since the wisdom of his imaginative policy was apparent, the Society now began its policy of sending to China some of its most talented members: mathematicians, architects, court painters, topographers; mechanics such as Father Magalhães, who made a clockwork puppet that could walk for fifteen minutes; and Father Verbiest, who seems to have invented a rudimentary form of steam engine. Since they were ready to turn their hands to anything in the cause, they even cast cannon for the imperial armies. In time, the Jesuits became part of the state bureaucracy and for two hundred years were the interpreters between East and West.

If Ricci had to do no more than insinuate himself into the Emperor's favour all would have been achieved, but, unfortunately for the Jesuits, there were other obstacles between them and their goal. There were, for example, two serious problems which demanded solution. The first, a semantic obstacle, the so-called «Term» question, concerned the problem of the correct Chinese word for the Deity. There were two possible words, *T'ien* and *Shang-ti,* and it was essential to decide which of them coincided more nearly with the Christian conception of God as the supreme Spirit who alone exists of himself, is infinite in all perfections and who rewards and punishes for all eternity. This matter was vital and urgent, since the translation of prayers and the liturgy into Chinese was practically impossible until a decision was reached. Furthermore, if, as some feared, the Chinese had no word for God, then it followed that they were a nation of atheists. Ricci could find no word corresponding to the Christian concept of God, but he began to use the term *T'ien chu,* meaning «Master of Heaven,» because it seemed to him that the Chinese adored Heaven as the supreme numen, and so by referring to God as the «Master of Heaven,» the Christians were showing that their God was greater than Heaven. This solution did not satisfy all his colleagues, some of whom feared that the Chinese word might have connotations unknown to them which would detract from or contaminate the Christian idea of God. (In fact, the Chinese had no concept or word for a Creation *ex nihilo* but this was not yet known to the missionaries. This semantic problem, the «Term» question, deeply troubled the Fathers for years, and was serious enough to drive one of them to suicide). [21]

The second problem had more widespread consequences, for it concerned the Rites performed by the Chinese in honour of their ancestors. These ceremonies, —which it was impious to neglect— were practised by the entire nation from Emperor to peasant, and involved the offering of meat, fruit, silk, perfumes, and the burning of joss-sticks and paper money before the corpse, the grave, or a commemorative tablet (*p'aiwei*). Dating

---

21 An old problem, it had disturbed newly-arrived Buddhists in second-century China: should they adopt existing (i.e. Taoist) technical terms, risking fatal distortions of their message? And for the term problem in modern science (e.g. chemistry) see NEEDHAM, *Science and Civilisation,* II, 409; V (3), 255.

back to the beginning of recorded history, these rites were the foundation of the social system of the Empire. Interference with them was bound to cause violent reactions. Parallel with these were still more ceremonies, part of the state cult of Confucius, performed by the literati, or scholar-gentry. The minor, twicemonthly, ceremonies consisted in prostrations (the *kotow*), and the offering of incense in honour of the Sage. But at the Spring and Autumn equinoxes the rites were far more solemn: dead animals and food were offered up; the devotees taking part usually fasted and abstained from sexual intercourse before the ceremony. The missionaries clearly had to decide whether or not these practices were religious, whether or not they were sacrifices or mere civic commemorations, and whether they could be permitted to Christian converts.

There were also, confusingly, other popular practices based on primitive animism, or derived from Taoist and Buddhist mythology: these were rejected and banned by all the missionaries, since they were clearly defined as superstitious. The rites in honour of ancestors and of Confucius were more difficult to define. For twenty years Ricci had studied the rites, which, he was encouraged to note, were not accompanied by any prayers to the dead or to Confucius. He had been assured that the rites were meant only to inculcate obedience to parents and to authority in general; as a result he concluded that they were only civil acts. Ricci was not always sure of his ground, but putting the much-disputed theory of Probabilism (see p. 100 below) to one of its most dramatic uses, he declared that the ancestor rites were «certainly not idolatrous and perhaps not even superstitious.»[22] The seeds of dissension lay in all this, and within a few years the question was being hotly debated not only by missionaries in China but by philosophers in Europe.

Back in the field of action, Ricci advanced another theory which, though at first sight apparently a masterstroke, was later turned against him, both by the Chinese and by those missionaries opposed to his methods. He appealed to texts in classical Chinese literature to prove that the religion of China had been monotheistic in former times. He concentrated on showing the Chinese the similarities between their own

---

[22] «sta tutto questo fuori di ogni idolatria, e forse che anco si possi dire non esser nessuna superstitione, sebene serà meglio commutar questo in limosine al poveri per le anime di tali defunti, quando saranno christiani»: D'ELIA, *Fonti Ricciane*, I, 118.

ancient religious beliefs and Christianity. To his sympathisers, Ricci seemed to be assuring the Chinese, as Paul had done the Athenians, that he had come to preach their «Unknown, unrecognised, God.» Like Paul, he too quoted adroitly from their own classics. He did not accuse them of being in the wrong but assured them they were merely different: that was all. There were advantages in this approach: Chinese pride was not upset by seeming arrogance on his part; the converts need not fear that their ancestors, whom they venerated, had been damned. Confucianism was a *preparatio evangelica* whose adherents were at a stage of arrested development on their unconscious journey towards Christ. [23]

Ricci's approach was seductive, but dangerous. Seductive because by stressing analogies he could show that his Faith was not something new, foreign and consequently barbaric, but was rather something common to both civilisations; identical in essentials, if not in accidents, to the creed of their ancestors. Indeed, Christianity became a «new» link with the old, lost, but still venerated past. Dangerous, because his approach could lead to syncretism, and end in a vague amorphous amalgam of Chinese and Christian beliefs. [24] This danger seemed to some to be all the greater because Ricci now produced a Chinese catechism in which he made no mention of six out of the seven Catholic sacraments and (like the early friars in Mexico) he ignored the six «Commandments of the Church» which constitute a form of psychological discipline for the Catholic. His catechism (again like the first friars' in Mexico) was a brief synopsis of Christian teaching based on natural reason, and suited to the exigencies of the situation.

The Apostle Paul, preaching to the Athenians, was given a polite hearing until he mentioned the resurrection of the dead. At this he lost his listeners' respect, for they were revolted by the idea of a «standing up of corpses.» The Chinese, for their part, were equally scandalised at the concept of the Crucifixion. Asians revealed a love of self-control by presenting the dying Buddha with a serene smile on his lips. Beside this the agony of Christ on the Cross was shocking. Must he not have been

---

[23] It is possible to see here some link with Karl Rahner's theory of the «Anonymous Christian,» which has also caused some heart-burning recently.

[24] Ricci's attitude is not unknown in some contemporary thinking. In 1975 an English Benedictine monk is recorded as declaring that Tibetan Buddhist services are «the Catholic divine office in an unfamiliar rite.»

a criminal to be so put to death and were not his worshippers sadists? Faced with this reaction, Ricci and the early Jesuits were careful not to display the Crucifix too freely, nor to discuss the Passion of the Saviour until they were sure of the seriousness of their enquirers. «Es verdad,» admitted Father Francisco Hurtado to the Jesuit General in 1636, «tenemos la imagen de Christo Señor nuestro en la cruz, recogida y no en público; pero no escondemos su misterio a los dignos en el catechismo; *si el tiempo da lugar* [my italics] se explica toda la Pasión del Señor a los que han de recibir el santo baptismo.» [25] It seems likely that the Jesuits distinguished between the *Crucifix* and the *Cross;* and that they were cautious about public displays of the former.

In short, Ricci, carrying out the policy of being all things to all men, for the greater glory of God, was taking a calculated risk But in trying to soothe Chinese susceptibilities, he was ruffling those of many of his colleagues and of all of his critics. Pascal, when he came to hear of it, was shocked by such «conduite obligeante et accommodante,»[26] by this «estrange zèle, nouvelle charité.» His version of what the China Jesuits were allegedly doing was put down baldly, without qualifications; and his account was important because many of the readers of his *Provincial Letters* believed it implicitly. In time their «conduite accommodante» was to lead the whole Society of Jesus into one of the gravest of the many controversies it had to face; and one which, in the end, contributed much to the legends about the Order and to those beliefs which led to its suppression by Clement XIV in 1773.

But this could not have been apparent in the beginning. China presented an enormous problem, but the sort of problem the vigorous young Society welcomed. The Central Country and its people were the answer to a Jesuit's prayer. First it was a vast empire governed by a refined sophisticated aristocracy who would only be converted by intellectual superiors. No Jesuit doubted that the Order most fitted to this task was his own, which, «although the merest newcomer to the Church has been chosen by Divine dispensation and made into the first, after St. Thomas

---

25 Quoted in Spanish in *Archivum Franciscanum Historicum,* VIII, 583; and in Latin in the *Informatio de praxi Missionariorum,* Paris, 1700, 16.

26 He took the phrase from a French Jesuit, Denis Petau (1583-1652), author of the *Pénitence publique.*

the Apostle, to cultivate the remote Orient.»[27] Secondly, the Jesuits were in the specially privileged position of having China and Japan as their monopoly granted to them by Gregory XIII's Bull *Ex pastorali officio* of 1585. This donation was as bitterly resented by the friars as it was jealously guarded by the Jesuits.

The Friars Glimpse Jesuit China

The Jesuits, then, in the persons of Ricci and Ruggieri, had managed to establish themselves on the mainland from their Portuguese-held toehold in Macao. But the mendicants based in Manila continued to make individual forays into China, since this seemed to them legal after Clement VIII's constitution *Onerosa pastoralis* of 1600 granting them permission to enter the Jesuit monopoly. This belief was strengthened by a further papal decree of 1633, after which the mendicants' efforts to enter China increased.

To return to China was, for them, more than a duty: it was a joy. They may have lost all collective knowledge of their previous mission to Peking, but they certainly saw themselves as heirs of a tradition, as following in the footsteps of St Francis whose mission to the Muslims they now recalled as an inspiration.[28] Friars began to arrive in China during the 1630s. In the following decade, when coastguard surveillance declined as a result of the disruptions brought about by the Manchu invasion of the empire, it became possible for the friars to go directly across from Manila to the maritime province of Fukien, thus avoiding the obstacles raised by the Jesuits and Portuguese in Macao. What they found in the mission surprised the friars: what happened astonished them.

---

[27] «... sebene il nome hè di tre, nella realità sono più di trecento le sette di questo regno, et ogni giorno vanno pullulando altre nove... Contra questo mostro della idolatria sinica, ... si mosse la nostra Compagnia di Giesù... a far guerra da parti sì lontane, ... per liberare le misere anime dalla perditione eterna...» (Ricci, in D'Elia, oc. I, 131, 135). And cf: «... muchas veces hablando entre nosotros, decimos nos parece cosa milagrosa estar como estamos los pocos Padres que en la China ay ... y llegó el negocio desta mission de la China a tal termo, que parece cosa más milagrosa que humana...» (P. Pantoja and P. Valignano in D'Elia, oc. II, 268n).

[28] «Non mi e stato discaro l'intender questi primi vostri fervori per una santa imitatione delli antiche soldati della christiana militia mandati, per quanto ho inteso, dal B. Francesco a una citta di Mori ove da un'alta torre predicavano ancora loro a Mahomettani et poi morirono nell'Africa, gloriosi martiri» [1220] (fra Giovanni B. Lucarelli, *Viaggio dell'Indie*, «Sinica Franciscana,» II, 23) and see also the «Relación del viage» of fray Francisco de Escalona who lists the countries where the OFM have worked and suffered (omitting Mexico!) and concludes that «no contentos con esto buscan otros nuevos mundos como es Japón y la gran China» (ib., 224 ff).

In 1635 two celebrated mendicants (the Franciscan, Antonio Caballero de Santa María, and the Dominican, Juan Bautista Morales) reached the mainland after having short-circuited Macao. Undaunted by the open hostility of those Jesuits they encountered, they continued the language studies which they had already begun in the Philippines, where they worked among the large Chinese trading community there. They also set about further study of the religions of China, going over the same ground as the Jesuits had done. Their suspicious were aroused by their language teacher, who defined the word *ch'i* as meaning «a sacrifice, like the Mass,» as well as being the proper way to honour one's ancestors.

Accordingly the two friars decided to investigate the matter personally and they arranged, without being seen, to attend one such ceremony performed by a Christian family, the Miu. They were greatly disturbed by what they saw: in a richly decorated hall, with tablets bearing the names of ancestors inscribed in gold letters, was an altar-table bearing food, flowers, red wax candles, incense tapers and joss sticks. «The divine office,» directed by a Master of Ceremonies, included ritual prostrations, the sharing out of the «sacrificial» foods of goat's flesh and pork, and libations of wine. The presiding official solemnly intoned the exhortations of Confucius, and gold and silver paper money was burnt to pay for the expenses of the dead in the beyond. The friars concluded that this was no mere civic ceremony, but a religious act in which, they said, nothing more was needed to make it into a sacrifice.

This experience, together with their readings of Chinese texts, led them to disagree with Ricci. The Rites which he found were «certainly not idolatrous, and perhaps not even superstitious,» were in their eyes certainly superstitious and more than likely idolatrous. And where the First Commandment was concerned they were prepared to be unpopular. Other, later, reports, seemed unbelievable. Friars who had seen the Jesuit Church in Peking alleged that it contained two altars, one dedicated to Christ and the other to the Emperor of China; and it was to this latter that Chinese visitors seemed to be paying reverence. To many friars, therefore, it seemed that they were, like Ezekiel, witnessing abominations in the Church.

It would have been prudent of the Jesuits to have come forward at this point to explain to the friars the reasons for any apparent eccentricities on their part. But this the Fathers would not do. Unfortunately, besides the two principal problems there were a host of lesser ones, which all served to cloud the issues and increase general unease. The friars found themselves differing in most respects from the Fathers' conception of the mission. They declared, for instance, that Christian missionaries should live poorly, observing their vows of poverty and begging their way through the country instead of «sallying forth in sedan-chairs, and rustling silk, whenever they stirred.» [29] Moreover, they disagreed with the Jesuit policy of conversion from the top, holding that the poor were the more naturally inclined to Christianity. But where they were most intransigent was on the question of the Rites. Where the Jesuits tended to compromise, the friars tended to the opposite view. Before long they denounced the religion taught in China by the Jesuits as contaminated with idolatry, and soon saw themselves, like Joshua, come to lead the people into the true Promised Land.

The friars' main fear was that the Jesuit strategy would ultimately imperil the whole mission, endanger the spiritual well-being of the converts, whose newly-acquired faith they regarded as merely «pegada con saliba.» There seemed also to be a danger that the Fathers were laying the foundations of a Chinese «national» church, with its own rules and concessions, which could not be altered later without the risk of creating groups of «new» and «old» Christians. This danger has been admitted by later writers. [30] One result of this situation was that the friars in their assesssment of the China Jesuits often seem genuinely baffled. The

---

29 Some Jesuits seem to have suffered scruples on this point. The celebrated Father Verbiest is reported to have said that it was «una cosa fea que saliesse en público el Varón Apostólico, vestido de seda, sino se ceñía interiormente con una cadena.» P. A. Thomas, SJ., *Carta circular acerca de la muerte de P. Fernando Verbiest,* Madrid, 1691, 10.

30 The Jesuit Vice-Provincial Furtado explained to the Pope (1640) «Ad evitanda tanta mala ne gentiles talem de nobis nostrisque neophytis concipiant opinionem, in hunc usque diem non convocamos populum, nec conventum instituimus in publicis plateis et compitis... ideoque domi suae vel in nostris, privatim intra domesticos parietes, legem Dei praedicamus...». Pastor Gutiérrez, SJ., comments on this quotation: «¿Aparecería ... laudable a los ojos de los mendicantes la táctica jesuítica de descartar toda pública predicación y no presentar el mensaje evangélico sino a puertas cerradas, como quien teme exponer a la gentilidad ... las verdades y los misterios de nuestra religión? Creemos sinceramente que, a pesar de las apologías de los jesuitas, era en ocasiones muy difícil a los mendicantes el arrojar de sí esta mala impresión.» And, again, «Los jesuitas corrían, a no dudarlo, peligro de quedar indefinidamente estancados en el estado inicial e «infantil,» pues no era cierto, ni mucho menos, que aquellos cristianos, acostumbrados a un Catolicismo muelle (que también los conducía a la Patria) se hallasen más tarde dispuestos a conmutarlo por una ascética más severa y conforme al espíritu de Jesús.» P. Gutierrez, SJ., *Dos métodos del apostolado en China,* «Missionalia Hispanica,» 3 (1946) 565, 570. But it is only fair to say that these are minority views among Jesuits past and present.

Fathers in the Central Country seemed different from Jesuits in some other places. The Franciscan Caballero de Santa María sums it up neatly: «en las historias de Inglaterra se lee, que una cosa, que parecerà a qualquiera, ansi a prima faz, de poca importancia como era, que el Catholico rezara la oracion del Pater noster en voz alta juntamente con los Hereges, nunca quisieron venir en ello unos Santos Martires de la Compañía, que estando ya al pie del patibulo, les pedian los Hereges... ...y quisieron antes morir, que tal hazer...» [31]

The Jesuits too had their accusations to make. They saw the mendicants as guilty of looking upon the China scene through entirely European eyes, and of condemning what they did not understand. More specifically, they alleged that some friars who reached Peking in 1637 had caused trouble by threatening, or at least discussing, a Spanish invasion and conquest of China. [32] This was, of course, a serious accusation and Santa María discusses it fully. He dismissed as frivolous any notion that the allegation had any firm basis. But he admitted that there might be some half truths in it. For example, at that very time the Tartars were invading China, and this might well have been the subject of conversation — indeed, it would have been unnatural if the topic had *not* been mentioned, given its importance for the future of the mission. Caballero de Santa María suggests that the friars and Jesuits would perhaps have been comparing the courage of the invaders with the alleged cowardice of the Chinese, which was a commonplace amongst Europeans at the time. If this casual conversation in an after-dinner chat (*en un papassar*) had caused trouble how did this happen?

Caballero de Santa María answers his own conundrum. Either the threats had been uttered aloud, publicly, outside the area of the Jesuit compound, and in Chinese; that was too stupid to contemplate: or, they were remarks made inside the Jesuit quarters, in Latin, Spanish, or

---

31 Santa María quoted in NAVARRETE, *Controversias* 553 (full bibliographical details of Navarrete's works at p. 88 below). Santa María is probably recalling the case of the English martyr Edmund Campion, SJ., as told by Diego de YEPES, *Historia de la persecución de Inglaterra*, Madrid, 1599, 334-5.

32 True or false, it might have been more discreet for the Jesuits to pass lightly over this matter, since the leading advocate of the fire-and-sword approach to the mission was one of their own men: Alonso Sánchez, SJ., who got as far as seeking an interview with Philip II in order to propose the plan. Ironically, though the friars in China were thought intolerant of the ceremonies and rites, in Manila they were denounced by Jesuits for their laxity towards Chinese syncretic practices (see page 76 below).

Portuguese, so that no one could understand them except the Fathers. The implication is clear: the story was either a fabrication or a deliberate misconstruing of an innocent conversation; and it must have been the Fathers who reported it secretly to convert mandarins as an excuse to have the unwelcome friars deported and discouraged from returning.[33]

In their desire to keep China as a monopoly for themselves the Jesuits were firm: «El que no entra por la puerta es ladrón y no pastor,» they declared, knowing that the gate of Portuguese Macao was closed to Spanish friars. They also showed single-mindedness in their treatment of friars who «crept in like thieves,» Sentimentality was not allowed to sway them, and one Franciscan, fray Martín Ignacio de Loyola, who managed to enter the empire, was bundled out again unceremoniously even though he was a nephew of the Jesuits' founder, St. Ignatius. The friar's story was that the Jesuits had laid false information against him. There were other such incidents. Strongarm tactics were used by Jesuits to get rid of other friars who reached Peking. Father Manuel Dias in 1634 had the Franciscan Antonio Caballero de Santa María tied up by his converts and carried off. On the other occasion [1637] the two friars were «arrested» by convert mandarins who, in secret collaboration with the Jesuits, laid on a straight-faced farce, hoping to frighten off not only them, but any other adventurous mendicants. The friars were interrogated in the Jesuit compound, were reprimanded severely and told they would be deported. It was not intended that the friars should discover that these officials «from higher quarters» were Jesuit converts, willingly playing a part in the comedy, but in fact they were recognised, having been seen on an earlier occasion in Macao.

This sort of behaviour gave the China mission a unique quality of its own. And letters which the Jesuits later wrote to each other on this subject eventually became public and did nothing to allay suspicions. Friar Caba-

---

33 Santa María, who had a nice sense of humour (e.g.: O. MAAS, OFM., *Cartas de China*, Seville, 1917, I, 123) was somewhat amused by the Jesuits' determination to have their cake and to eat it: when it was convenient they denounced the friars for ignorance of the Chinese language, but when it suited their book, as here, the friars were suddenly shown to be dangerously fluent. Santa María's discussion of the topic is in NAVARRETE, *Controversias*, 541 ff. A model case of subjective judgment occurs with friar Domenico Maria Sarpetri, OP., a mendicant who, unusually, agreed with the Jesuit view. Accordingly he is deferentially paraded by Jesuits as a skilled witness and «litterarum sinarum peritus,» etc. e.g. Philippe COUPLET, SJ., *Confucius Sinarum Philosophus*, Paris, 1687, cix; and similarly in P. P. INTORCETTA, *De cultu sinensi*, Paris, 1700, 224.

llero de Santa María, by collating the dates of these letters, concluded that the Jesuit Vice-Provincial, in his version of the affair, was describing in the past tense events which had not yet taken place at the time he was writing, thereby proffering evidence that the whole affair was a hatched-up plot. [34] A friar, relating this, deftly inserted a phrase from the Gospels with telling effect: «vinieron dos mandarines con alguaciles y verdugos, *cum fustibus et armis...*» And Santa María, lamenting this method of apparently welcoming, then deporting, friars, described it as follows: «... al principio les han recibido con cara de la entrada y recibimiento de Domingo de Ramos, pero luego, como por debaxo de la capa se les ha seguido las tinieblas de la Passion de Viernes Santo.» In later years some Jesuits, however, apologised to friars whom they had had highjacked or otherwise immobilised; Santa María related how one Jesuit, who had been instructed to get rid of him, had refused to do so and wrote to his General that he had no intention of wrangling with other Religious. [35]

The friars had objective reasons for believing they had a right to preach in China, and they were even willing to limit themselves to certain areas in the empire if that would solve the problem. They were accustomed to opposition from the Jesuits: «Es viejo en la Compañía no querer otros Regulares en las Misiones» wrote one friar. The outspoken friar Buenaventura Ibáñez complained «sic Patres quantum potuerunt fecerunt ad nos extra vineam dominicam expellendos et quamvis non nos occiderunt, saltem in judicis gentilis manus tradiderunt... quasi cum pontificibus et pharisaeis dicerent Pilato: *nobis non licet occidere quemquam*»[36] Nevertheless the situation in China appeared to puzzle some friars. From the time of Marco Polo («Il Milione») onwards, it had been a cliché for travellers to report home that they did not expect to be believed when they described the wonders of China. Now friar Ibáñez found a fresh angle: describing these and similar events in that strange mission-field, he lamented, «Hoc in curia romana erit omnibus incredible et sic tacens non amplius de hoc loquar.» For the Jesuits, who seemed able to accommodate themselves to the

34 Unless, of course, «el dicho Padre fue propheta que escrivía lo futuro» (Santa María in NAVARRETE, *Controversias*, 554 ff.). A more prosaic explanation might be that the Vice-Provincial absentmindedly put the wrong date on his letter. The truth of the incident is not however in doubt. But the Jesuits did not limit themselves to kidnapping friars; they sometimes had to connive at exiling each other, as Father Schall did with Fathers Furtado and Martini: G. H. DUNNE, SJ., *Generation of Giants*, London, 1962, 331-2: and *quibus igitur credemus, si fidem laudantibus non habemus?*

35 Fr. General Vitelleschi, SJ., had ordered his China subjects (1616) to avoid giving hospitality to friars, on account of the possible danger involved: DUNNE, oc., 239.

36 *Sinica Franciscana*, III, 142.

sophisticated Chinese, were unable to bring themselves to show the friars that same tact, diplomacy and understanding. Believing that the mission was their monopoly, they refused to enter into discussions with men who, they held, had no right to be there. [37] So that later, when accused of denouncing what they did not understand, the friars could rightly reply that they had vainly sought for advice and counsel. In frustration the friars eventually decided to appeal to the authorities in Macao and Manila. A meeting of theologians of the religious orders was called to discuss the China mission and its problems. The Jesuits, however, refused to join in; and this was a fatal decision, for peace between the two groups became impossible from then on. This, it seems to me, was a decisive turning point in the affair.

A Dominican who had been in China, Juan Bautista Morales, made the initial overtures, but without success. Father Bernard-Maitre, SJ., describes the situation as follows: «Il n'en obtient une fois de plus que des excuses polies et se résout à aller en personne plaider sa cause à Rome» and again: «l'on doit reconnaître qu'en cette délicate affaire, les deux missionnaires de Manille se comportèrent très correctement. Après avoir vainement essayé d'obtenir satisfaction, pour leurs doutes, de leurs voisins jésuites, ils portèrent la cause aux supérieurs ecclésiastiques de Macao.» [38] Earlier Jesuit writers tended to take a more severe view of this procedure: «ritus gentis Europaeo oculo considerans, miris scrupulis agitari coepere... *omnia ad Europaeam consuetudinem exigens* [my italics] ... nihil proinde mirum, si praejudiciis occupatus ... primus [Morales] bellum ritibus Sinicis indixit.» [39]

Thus the Chinese Rites Controversy began, for everything seemed to conspire to make it inevitable. The Macao and Manila Jesuits in general preserved silence; but for one of them the strain was too great. A Spanish Father, Bartolomé Roboredo, the Procurator of the Japan and China province, felt that an answer to the mendicants was overdue. Accordingly, with more energy than anything else, he threw himself into the fray

---

37 The China Jesuits' intense possessiveness over their mission aroused irritation even amongst themselves, and it can be detected in Ricci's complaint (with which an uncommitted observer can sympathise) that he must submit his writings about China to fellow-Jesuit censors outside the empire.

38 Henri BERNARD-MAITRE, SJ., *Un Dossier bibliographique de la fin du xviie siècle sur la Question des Termes Chinois*, in: «Recherches de Science Religieuse, 36 (1949) 52; idem, *Histoire universelle de Missions catholiques*, II, Paris, 35, 341. See also Rosso, *Apostolic Legations*, 110.

39 G. PRAY, SJ., *Historia Controversiarum de Ritibus Sinicis*, Budapest, 1789, 18-19, 61.

by publishing in Manila a defence of his colleagues in the China mission. He considered this an opportune moment to do so because all Manila was ringing with gossip about the novelties and mysteries of the new church. Quite why Roboredo should have felt himself equipped for the task must remain a puzzle, for he had not been in China except for a few months in Macao. His apologia appeared en 26 December, 1638 and instantly created a sensation: «L'effet en est désastreux, car il concède l'essentiel de la thèse des adversaires, c'est-à-dire que les rites chinois permis aux chrétiens sont véritablement superstitieux!... la pratique des Jésuites de Chine, telle qu'elle avait été avouée par Roboredo, ne pouvait être que condamnée ... Le scandale est immense.» [40]

Roboredo talked of Chinese «idols,» «altars» and «sacrifices» but tried to justify attendance at the Rites by saying that a cross was put upon the altar to which the convert could direct his devotions and intentions. In an interesting slip he told the friars why they should not blame the Jesuits in China for their troubles: «Estas son las causas verdaderas de los destierros, prisiones, açotes, y Iglesias derribadas, y más trabajos, que los Religiosos [mendicantes] dichos han padecido en China, no la contradición de nuestros Padres, ni la amistad de los Mandarines que los favorecen, ni sólo el odio de los Gentiles y Christianos, *por no permitirles à ellos sus idolatrías,* y honras políticas; y assí no tienen que quexarse de otro alguno, sino de sí mismos.» And other remarks by him were equally disturbing: «Bien obrarían nuestros Padres en China, si tal, o tal vez baptizassen a aquellos Cathecúmenos, que tienen propósito general de no quebrantar la Ley de Dios, sin hablarles en estas, o aquellas cosas particulares con que se quebranta, principalmente en las supradichas (idolatrías) que tienen tan arrygadas en sus coraçones... [41] The effect

---

[40] BERNARD-MAITRE, *Dossier,* 51, 53; INTORCETTA, *De cultu sinensi* [1668], 297, on Roboredo's ignorance.

[41] Quoted in NAVARRETE, *Controversias,* 80, 501; my italics. (For details on Navarrete, see p. 88 below). The mendicants would also have been confused by the celebrated Jesuit Alexandre de RHODES who in his *Voyages,* Paris, 1653, p. 54, declares of the Chinese: «Un de leurs faux Dieux est un certain Confucius... Il n'est pas croyable combien ils ont respect pour lui; nous avons peine de persuader aux chrétiens qui se convertissent de ne pas fléchir les genoux devant ses statues, qu'ils ont quasi tous dans leurs maisons; et ceux qui ont fait courir le bruit, que les jésuites permettent cette idolâtrie à leurs néophytes, me permettront de leur dire qu'il sont très mal informés...» Of this passage, Benno Biermann, the Dominican historian, declares that Rhodes's lack of knowledge is amazing seeing that he was a missionary in Indo-China, where the Rites had the same meaning, and in 1640 he was in Macao where the Rites were thoroughly discussed. B. BIERMANN, *Die Anfänge der neueren Dominikanermission in China,* Münster in Westfalen, 1927, 175.

of this disastrous intervention, coming at such a critical time, cannot be overestimated, especially since Roboredo claimed that he was basing himself upon material submitted to the Father General by the Father Visitor for Japan and China, who, he noted, with his great knowledge of the mission obviously knew more than anyone in Macao or Manila about Jesuit practice and usage in China.

The bewildered mendicants were put in agony by this turn of events. One Provincial, Clemente Gan, made a moving and ecumenical plea to the Jesuit Visitor: «No se espante V. P. que nos haga mucha dificultad esto y otras muchas cosas ... que verdaderamente nos han espantado mucho ... Házenos grandíssima dificultad que a sacrificios manifiestamente idolátricos como confiessa ... puedan concurrir y aún ser Ministros los Christianos ... y así en nombre de esta mi Provincia, suplico a V. P. se averiguen amigablemente estas cosas, que nos ofrecemos a seguir, quanto hecha esta diligencia, se declarare poder seguirse, aunque sea contra lo que sentimos. Tanto como esto deseamos la paz. El modo de averiguarse, ordene V. P. como fuere servido ... teniéndolo VV. PP. tan mirado, todo, o casi todo ha de salir en favor de la Compañía, y no avrá cisma, ni diversidad de doctrinas en China ... Quanto a no ir unos a los pueblos de los otros, también passaremos por qualquier concierto moderado, que V. P. ordenare, y con esto escusaremos no pequeño escándalo, que ha de aver en España y Roma, si allá se averiguan cosas semejantes ... Espero muy alegre respuesta no sólo para mis Religiosos, sino para los Angeles de paz y Autor de ella, y que se ha de celebrar en el Cielo, si la tuuiéremos en China.» [42]

Nothing came of this appeal; there was no joint discussion; nor did the Jesuits disown Roboredo immediately. The Visitor replied to the friars, but had no help to offer; and as for Father Roboredo, the Visitor contented himself with the grimly ambiguous remark that «el dará razón de lo que allí escrivió.» [43] At this point the mendicants, in desperation, decided to send an agent to Rome for consultations and a ruling.

---

[42] Quoted in NAVARRETE, ib., 335-6; original in *Archivo de Santo Domingo*, Manila, tom. 30, fol. 5.

[43] Poor Father Roboredo's ill-judged loyalty brought him nothing but trouble: he was dismissed the Society, «certè non propter virtutis excessum,» said INTORCETTA, o.c., 223, 303. But the disowning and dismissal came too late: irreparable harm had now been done; his word was taken as the policy of the Society, baffling though it seemed.

Fr. Roboredo signified more than the friars knew. He was a symbol of a deep malaise within the community of China Jesuits. He was a witness to their divisions and the differences amongst themselves. Roboredo's laudable Pauline injunction (*idem sapiamus, idem dicamus omnes*) was doubly unfortunate, for though it was addressed to the friars, it was as if he were talking over his shoulder to his own men of the «Ricci school.» When, later on, the friars discovered that not all the Jesuits in China were convinced of the legality of the Ricci strategy, this added to their own scruples. A contemporary friar, speaking on behalf of his baffled colleagues, expresses their dilemma: «A quién hemos de seguir, a los antiguos [Ricci's generation] o a los modernos? a los leídos y experimentados en los libros Chinicos, y los más doctos de la Compañía en China, o al P. Intorcetta? ... el mayor argumento, que tenemos en nuestro favor, es que ningún caso, ni parecer, que ayamos seguido, se hallará no averle primero enseñado los Missionarios de la Compañía... la discordia, y discrepancia que ha avido en opinar, ha estado entre los de la Compañía, y no en nosotros con ella; pues quando entramos en la Missión, ya estaban divididos, y opuestos, a los quales era del todo impossible acomodarnos: *Filii vestri ipsi sint testes contra eos.*» [44]

Of course during Ricci's lifetime there had been a superficial unity among the Fathers; and not until he was dead did an open rift occur. Quite soon after that, there was a full range of opinion within the Jesuit ranks: extremists at one side agreed entirely with Ricci; moderates in the middle were cautious and had qualifications to make; on the other side there were those who opposed all temporising, and in varying degrees shared the views of the friars. Father Jean Valat was regarded with suspicion by his fellow Jesuits, but to the mendicants he was an ally and a source of consolation, for he forbade the suspect ceremonies to his converts. Another Jesuit, Father Lobo, witnessing the Confucian Rites

---

[44] The irony of this statement should not be missed: «Era del todo impossible *acomodarnos* [a los Jesuitas]» because the Fathers were divided amongst themselves. The friar is here saying more than he realised: the friars' problem was that, before accommodating their teaching to the Chinese, they had to try to understand the wholly baffling strategy of the Jesuits, who remained silent and disunited. The friars, in short, were experiencing the dilemma described in PASCAL'S, *First Provincial Letter* where the writer is discussing «pouvoir prochain.» Asked to explain it, he replies to his questioner: "Je l'entends au sens des molinistes [ie: Jesuits]." A quoi mon homme, sans s'émouvoir: "Auxquels des molinistes," me dit-il, "me renvoyez-vou?" Je les lui offris tous ensemble, comme ne faisant qu'un même corps et n'agissant que par un même esprit. Mais il me dit: "vous êtes bien peu instruit. Ils sont si peu dans les mêmes sentiments, qu'ils en ont de tout contraires.»

for the first time, excelled the friars themselves in a demonstration of outraged orthodoxy, for he almost fainted: «me temblaron las carnes, erizaron los cabellos, el rostro descolorido y sin sangre en él, que todo se me avía recogido en el corazón.» [45] Some of these dissident Jesuits held high office and were influential in the Society. Luis da Gama, a narrow-minded Portuguese who made the friars look recklessly lax, was the official Father Visitor for China and Japan, and he caused considerable trouble to his Jesuit colleagues before they managed to have him overruled. The Jesuit João Rodríguez, nicknamed «The Interpreter,» who had been in the East since the age of sixteen, was a bitter adversary of his colleagues' accommodation technique, and his prestige as a linguist made his evidence weighty. But the most damaging defection of all was that of Father Niccolò Longobardo, who had been chosen by Ricci himself, and was considered theologically sound enough to succeed him as Superior of the mission.

The situation in China was therefore extremely disturbing for the Society, which took pride in its ability to swing the whole ecclesiastical corps into concerted action, with no undisciplined stragglers hanging back. [46] Furthermore, the split in their ranks came to weaken the Jesuits' position precisely when they felt the need to stand together in face of the friars' intervention. Not all the disunity was over theological principles either: Lach refers to the «internecine struggle going on in his [Maffei's] day within the Society over the question of a military attack upon China» (Lach, oc I (ii), 805). Henri Bernard-Maitre, SJ., makes the point that this Jesuit disunity means that one should not talk of Jesuits' and Friars' attitudes in the Rites Controversy; both groups had members who strayed over the mental frontier into the other's territory.

Conferences were summoned to discuss the Jesuits' internal disagreements (there were no fewer than 74 meetings up to 1665): everything possible was done to suppress their differences, which, meantime, were to be kept a secret amongst themselves and withheld from all

---

45 Later on Lobo was dismissed the Society; he ended his days as a secular priest in Macao, where his friends used to provoke him by joking about his having genuflected to the Emperor's portrait in the Jesuits' Peking Church during his earlier career as a missionary in the interior.

46 It must be admitted, however, that not everyone sees the Jesuits as a totally disciplined and united body: «The Society of Jesus could be described as a group of individuals working against each other for the greater glory of God»: A. L. Martin, *The Jesuit Mystique*, in: «The Sixteenth Century Journal,» 4 (1973) 33. For Rodrigues, see Michael Cooper, SJ., *Rodrigues, The Interpreter*, New York, 1974.

outsiders. Any evidence of dissension was ordered to be destroyed, and the writings of the anti-Ricci faction were burnt. More than fifty controversial Jesuit memoranda are recorded as having been written up to the time of the mendicants' arrival in the 1630s; all have disappeared, probably by order: «ad extinguendas opinionum dissensiones.» [47] The most important of these condemned treatises was the one by Longobardo, a copy of which, unfortunately for the Jesuits, escaped their family *auto da fé*, fell into the friars' hands, and was later published by them. It played a significant part in the subsequent controversy.

The treatise had been written in 1623-4, when Longobardo, having taken over command of the mission, found his scruples exacerbated by objections from the Jesuits in Japan who were troubled about the correct translation of Christian concepts. After taking advice Longobardo wrote his memorandum, refusing the pleas of those brethren who begged him to follow what they regarded as a ray of hope, but what Longobardo, to the satisfaction of the friars, dismissed as a will-o'-the-wisp.

Some ten years after Longobardo wrote his memorandum, the Vice-Provincial Francisco Furtado ordered it burnt, to the great indignation of the friars when they came to hear of it. The copy that survived had been given in secret to the Franciscan Santa María by Father Jean Valat, the French Jesuit who was always friendly to the friars.

On the death of Ricci in 1610 some of his colleagues had suspected there might be danger for them from dissidents in their ranks, and so discharged a flood of writings aimed at preempting the situation by presenting their picture of China to Europe. [48] It must be stressed, however, that on the whole the majority of the Fathers accepted the Ricci approach to the Rites, which became official policy within the Order, and those who dissented did not influence Jesuit mission programmes or methods, though they strengthened the anxieties of the mendicants.

GRANADA, MEXICO, MANILA: FRANCISCAN REHEARSALS FOR CHINA

We have seen the early friars distressed by their first glimpse of the Jesuits' China and what was apparently a foretaste of a new Christian Asia. It is fitting to pause here in order to examine the background of

---

[47] «Thus,» says Pastor, briskly, optimistically, and wrongly, «thus the disputes among the Jesuits were disposed of.» *Popes*, Eng. tr. 33:403.

[48] B. GUY, *The French Image of China before and after Voltaire*, Geneva, 1963, 61.

the friars, and their preparation for this obviously particularly delicate missionfield.

Francis of Assisi was the first religious Founder to include a special chapter on missions in his Rule, which, for instance, exempted his friars from monastic observances during missionary work. This ideal he placed at the heart of the Franciscan movement. Yet its originality and modernity, is often overlooked. [49] It was to remain a perpetual source of inspiration for generations of his friars. The spirit of the Order was to teach more by example than by word: «plus exemplo quam verbo.» Seraphic love took precedence over all: in St Bonaventure's words: «alii principaliter intendunt speculationi et postea unctioni. Alii [OFM] principaliter unctioni et postea speculationi. Et utinam iste amor vel unctio non recedat.» [50] In accordance with this theme, the Franciscan movement, based upon the teaching of «the most beloved of medieval saints,» aimed at an ideal of gentleness, humility and humanity. «Francis's vision and originality consisted in sending out men who rejoiced in poverty as a positive, exciting, romantic thing; who were happy to be poorer than the poor, humbler than the humble, more ignorant than the ignorant.» [51] Such a spirit made an appeal wherever the Franciscans went. For instance, Joseph Needham discussing «potlatch,» an element in Chinese culture which attained its greatest heights of expression in Taoist texts, finds similarities between the thought of Francis and of Lao Tzu: «This conception of *jang* (yieldingness) reaches its highest point in *Lao Tzu*:

"Therefore the Sage
Puts himself in the background, yet is always to the fore
Remains outside, but is always here.
Is it not just because he does not strive for any personal end
That all his personal ends are fulfilled?"

One cannot help being reminded of some of the great Christian poetical paradoxes, e.g. "having nothing and yet possessing all things." And St Francis:

---

49 On this, see the succint account «of the Franciscan world-wide apostolate — the missionary ideal and action of the friars, their contribution to geographical knowledge,» especially with reference to the Pacific, in Kelly, *La Australia*, 117-20.

50 H. Felder, OFM Cap., *Geschichte der Wissenschaftlichen Studien im Franziskanerorden*, Freiburg im Breisgau, 1904, 29-30; H. O. Taylor, *The Medieval Mind*, II, London, 1936, 396.

51 C. N. L. Brooke, *The Missionary at Home: 1000-1250*, in G. J. Cuming, (ed.), *The Mission of the Church and the Propagation of Faith*, Cambridge, 1970, 62.

"C'est en donnant qu'on reçoit
C'est en s'oubliant qu'on trouve;
C'est en pardonnant qu'on est pardonné;
C'est en mourant qu'on ressuscite à l'éternelle vie!» [52]

Donald Lach links Franciscan customs and practices with Eastern variants: «Their versions of mendicant asceticism were highly reminiscent of Buddhist and Hindu practices: the knotted cord, etc... The Franciscan reverence for birds and animals might also be related to Hindu antecedents as well as a generally responsive and open-minded attitude towards nature which can best be appreciated by reading the accounts of their [OFM] overland missions to Asia.» [53] In view of all this, one is not entirely surprised to learn of the existence of a Buddhist Franciscan Society in Japan.

Another characteristic of the Franciscans has exerted a powerful attraction on both rich and poor: their devotion to holy Poverty, the Franciscan «Eighth Sacrament.» It is clear from many contemporary sources that this quality made the friars particularly suitable for the missions in Mexico, the Philippines, and Japan. The celebrated Manila judge, Antonio de Morga, informed Philip II that in his opinion Japan «is kept quiet by the Franciscans whom we have there.» And the Franciscan fray Pedro Bautista in the 1590s explained their success in Japan and the lack of opposition from the government by pointing out that the Franciscans, unlike the Jesuits, were not dedicated to proselytizing rich and influential people but were content to work with the poor. [54] Similarly, disinterested Englishmen reported from Mexico in the sixteenth century that the Indians there «have the friers in great reverence: the occasion is, that by them and by their meanes they are free and out of bondage,» and the natives themselves said that this was «porque estos

---

[52] NEEDHAM, *Science and Civilisation*, II, 62. Fr. Antonio Sisto Rosso, OFM., tells me that this prayer, though fully Franciscan in Spirit, is not in fact by the Saint. There is an article in *Archivum Franciscanum Historicum*, 68 (1975) 450-453.

[53] LACH, *Asia*, II (iii), 1978, 399.

[54] LACH, OC, I, 307; Antonio de MORGA, *Sucesos de las islas Filipinas* [1609], ed. J. S. CUMMINS, Cambridge, Hakluyt Society 1971, 21, 336. For a study of the significance of holy poverty in Asia today, and the relevance of charismatic poverty to our own times, see Justinian CHERUPALLIKAT, OFM Cap., *Witness Potential of Evangelical Poverty in India*, Immensee, 1975. Though the work deals with India, much of what it says can be applied more widely.

andan pobres y descalzos como nosotros.»[55] The friar-chronicler Motolinía draws a vivid contrast between the well-to-do colonists, and the friars with their dwellings which were akin to the cells of the Desert Fathers: «que más parecen sepultura que no casas.» Another chronicler, Mendieta, declares that the Franciscans' very lifestyle was a form of preaching «y suplió la falta de milagros que en la primitiva Iglesia hubo y en esta nueva no fueron menester.» Motolinía himself impressed the Indians when they first saw him, one of the «Twelve Apostles of Mexico,» walking barefoot from Vera Cruz to Mexico. Indeed so much so that (naturally oblivious of the significance of what they were doing) they nicknamed him in Nahuatl with the same name as that given to St Francis himself: «Motolinía, il poverello.» In other words, «Franciscan» was a synonym for holy poverty. A Jesuit writing from Cochin in 1566, describing the local natives' dress, had only to say that it was «trage más pobre que el de San Francisco»[56] for his meaning to be taken.

This devotion to poverty led the friars to concentrate on the lowly, since they believed that evangelisation upwards was more likely to succeed. Antonio de Santa María puts it succintly: «no nos parece mala señal que comience el Evangelio por los pobres.» At the same time, of course, the friars in China hoped for imperial favour and for permission to preach freely, just as the Jesuits for their part did not neglect the poor, though they concentrated on the upper classes. Each group had its natural affinities; neither restricted itself to them exclusively.[57]

Rigid though the friars' vow of poverty was, and deep as was their devotion to it (it affected even the vestments and decorations of their churches), they were flexible enough to alter it when need arose. As early on as the first mission to the Mongols they gave evidence of their adaptability: «In order to make missionary work possible, [from 1300 onwards] a number of unusual privileges had to be granted... they were

55 «A Relation of the commodities of Nova Hispania, and the maners of the inhabitants, written by Henry Hawks, merchant which lived for five yeeres in the sayd countrey» [1572], in Richard HAKLUYT, *Voyages*, London, Everyman ed., VI, 1962, 288; MOTOLINIA, *Historia de los indios*, Trat. 3, chap 4.

56 SILVA REGO, oc., X, 66. Another instance of the equation, Franciscan = poverty, is to be found in a letter of Gerard Peregrine of Castello, who worked as a bishop on the Mongol mission. In 1318 he describes himself: «I, brother Peregrine, appointed a Bishop of Poverty in another world...» in A. C. MOULE, *Christians in China before 1550*, London 1930, 207; LACH, oc., I (i), 40.

57 But the friars had a good point when they claimed that they could minister to those poorer Chinese who would obviously be too frightened to approach a Jesuit-mandarin to ask for confession or some similar service.

permitted, contrary to their rule, to carry money, to wear clothes other than their habit, and to grow beards. The Mongols were nomads; if they were to be evangelized, the missionaries must also adopt the nomad way of life. About 1335 we have word of small groups of Franciscans, who wore Mongol dress, followed the Mongol «hordes,» and carried portable altars and vessels on wagons very much like those of the pastoral people to whom they ministered... these «mobile convents» were far more successful than others in winning converts.» [58]

The friars' medieval missionary experience has already been referred to, but needs recapitulating here. The early Spanish Franciscans worked in Asia, competing with the Muslims for the spiritual conquest of the Mongols; they worked also in North Africa, and in their own homeland amongst the Moors of Granada. Here, in addition to their Founder's prescriptions, they had the example of Ramon Lull, a Tertiary, and a champion of the apostolate by peaceful persuasion, who himself died a martyr in 1316. Lull spent part of his life advocating missionary colleges, to be organised in what would now be thought of as a thoroughly modern spirit. The evangelising of the Muslims in Spain has a particular significance. During the medieval period Spain was unique in Western Europe: conquered by Muslims in 711 AD, she remained occupied (in varying degrees) down to 1492. Of the Christian lands conquered by Islam, the Iberian Peninsula was the first to be successfully recovered; indeed the only one until 1699, which witnessed the freeing of Hungary. And of the lands conquered by Islam, Spain alone has reverted to its original religion. This *Reconquista* from Arab domination obviously had a profound effect upon Spanish life, character and national outlook; an effect still detected, even today, from Madrid to Manila. [59]

Nevertheless, it is an oversimplification to see the reconquest of Spain simply as an eight centuries' long crusade of Cross against Crescent, and Faith against Fable. The religious situation, even in that frontier world, was marked by tolerance and respect as well as by zeal and

---

58 Stephen NEILL, *A History of Christian Missions* (Harmondsworth, Penguin Books, 1977), 128-9. It is often claimed that the friars, through an obstinate rigidity, refused to wear other than their religious habits. In fact they were willing to adapt to local circumstances without scruples, doffing the habit, or changing it: though brown is the usual colour of the Franciscan robes, in Mexico they wore blue; and their English nickname, «Greyfriars,» speaks for itself.

59 For all this see Derek LOMAX's excellent study, *The Reconquest of Spain*, London, 1978.

militancy. Christian knights sometimes fought as mercenaries for Muslim rulers (the Cid Campeador instantly comes to mind) and changed sides without embarrassment or accusation. Art forms on both sides of that often blurred frontier were characterized by a strong tendency to acculturation, indicative of a mutual respect and admiration. Craftsmen from Granada, brought in to embellish the alcázar of Seville for Pedro el Cruel, left behind inscriptions calling down the «blessing of Allah upon the Lord Sultan,» that is, upon King Pedro. Similarly, there have been found parish churches with the Message, «There is no God but God, and Muhammad is his Prophet,» side by side with Gospel texts, in the plaster-work. This is not to say, of course, that there was any religious acculturation which might have resulted in an intermediate religion. But some fascinating neighbourliness is reported: for example, from Murcia in 1463 where Muslims travelled into Christian territory to venerate the shrine of San Ginés de la Jara, formerly a Muslim sanctuary. San Ginés was reputed to work miracles at this shared shrine for Muslim and Christian alike. Some Moors even came from North Africa with this aim: «suelen venir, de intento, de varias partes de Berbería. Explícanse, diciendo: que es San Ginés el mayor Santo, y más piadoso, que ay en el Cielo: pues no sólo atiende a las peticiones, y súplicas de los Fieles Moros, si también de los christianos: y al fin, hechando todo el resto a su expresión, y elogio, dicen que San Ginés, estar Pariente de su Gran Profeta Mahoma.» [60]

Yet one consequence of this conquest by Islam, and Spain's unique recovery from it, is sometimes said to be seen in the religious inflexibility of the Spaniard of the sixteenth and seventeenth centuries: «La psicología de los misioneros españoles no estaba en general, preparada para aquel conato de adaptación. Como veremos, el contraste con los jesuitas no ibéricos de China es patente... es quizás el problema más delicado.» Spaniards developed «una ortodoxia incapaz de compromisos,» and they were not as suitable as the Italians who were «influenciados por el Renacimiento, o los alemanes, acostumbrados a convivir con protestantes.» [61] This may or may not be true. Certainly it is easier to assert than to prove. It is not immediately clear why living with recently-defeated

---

[60] This paragraph is based on Angus MACKAY'S, *The ballad and the frontier in late mediaeval Spain*, «BULLETIN OF HISPANIC STUDIES,» 53 (1976) 15-33.

[61] P. DAMBORIENA, SJ., *La Salvación en las religiones no cristianas*, Madrid, 1973, 107, 113.

Muslims should make a man less tolerant than one living with recently-born Protestant heretics. But whatever the answer, it is tiresome to see that old slogan of «Spanien das Land ohne Renaissance» being brought forward once again, even if only by implication. Surely, that was refuted many years ago when Dámaso Alonso declared, in ringing tones: «Y cuando nos pregunten si existe el Renacimiento español, podremos contestar: Existe por estas, esas y aquellas razones ... O simplemente por esto: porque esté Fray Luis de León.» And fray Luis, of course, was a mendicant friar. [62]

A different explanation for a Spanish inability to compromise might have nothing to do with Renaissance or Reformation, or with Reconquest and Trent: it might be that there (as in Ireland, Poland and Romania traditionally; and in presentday Albania temporarily), the old religion is a major part of the collective assertion of unity and nationhood. The Reconquest did, no doubt, leave Spaniards sensitive and nervous, as is summed up in the phrase, «hay moros en la costa.» But there is also a positive side, for it imbued some Spaniards with a zeal for evangelization, and this is nowhere more clearly demonstrated than in the work of the Friars Minor in their Andalusian mission. In 1496 the Minorites of the Holy Gospel custody moved down to Granada where they preached a simple straightforward Christianity to both the spiritually neglected Christians and to the Muslim farmers and townsfolk. These friars were considered ideal for this work since they lived in small communities and subsisted on the minimum of charity. Kubler points out that they had the status of «predicadores apostólicos» and that, in the words of the bull of Alexander VI (1496), they were «to preach the word of God and the Holy Gospel throughout the world, among faithful and infidel alike.» In this way they

---

62 D. Alonso, *Ensayos sobre poesía española,* Buenos Aires, 1946, 170. See also A. Bell, *Luis de León: A Study of the Spanish Renaissance,* Oxford, 1925; and we ought to bear in mind that in the second half of the sixteenth century many of the friars were university trained, knew Latin, Greek and Hebrew, were well read in the classics and the Fathers. If Italians, being «influenced by the Renaissance,» were therefore more flexible than Iberians, we are left with the question why this same influence failed, apparently, to affect the Roman Curia which legislated in the Rites Controversy. In resisting flabby generalisations, one would not, of course, deny Italian broadmindedness, as evidenced in Ricci, Valignano and de Nobili; heterodox Italians of the period showed a similar breadth of vision and spirit: «Out of Italy ... emerged the greatest leaders of tolerant Protestantism in Europe»: Henry Kamen, *The Rise of Toleration,* London, 1967, 81; and cf: «The impassioned plea for religious toleration, ... was the most far-reaching Italian contribution to the Reformation,» writes Philip McNair in *History,* 60 (1975) 361.

were preparing themselves, all unconsciously, for their missionary work in America some twenty years afterwards, and for their labours in Asia some years after that. There is perhaps a symbolic connection between the Muslims of Granada and the Amerindians, in that fray Martín de Valencia, leader of the «Twelve Apostles» of Mexico, had earlier volunteered three times to preach among the Arabs before being posted to the New World.[63]

The number of the twelve apostles of Mexico was deliberately and symbolically chosen («quoniam hic fuit numerus discipulorum Christi») by their Minister-General, Francisco de Quiñones, later Cardinal de Santa Cruz. The Twelve were the contemporaries of St Ignatius, Santa Teresa and San Juan de la Cruz. Though they had medieval roots they were entirely «modern» men. They were distinguished by boldness of outlook, so that in dealing with them, the historians (e.g. Bataillon, Beckmann, Kubler, McAndrew, Ricard) resort constantly to the word «radicals,» and stress their acute sense of the need for reform. They included scholars, saints and martyrs (the first American martyr was a Franciscan, appropriately), even men of royal blood. They were selected to meet the demands of Cortés who wanted special men, able to stand comparison with the fanatically chaste and strict Aztec priests. The friars responded to the call and its exigencies.

For the first time those to be converted were not Muslims, Jews, nor animists; and so one finds astonishing the capacity of the friars to work without any precise blue-print or model. They had to improvise and to rely largely on intuition. Yet writes McAndrew, «Still surprising today are the speed with which they worked, the numbers converted, the extent of the territory involved and the ingenious means worked out by a handful of unarmed friars.» New concepts had to be formed, new techniques developed; a new voice had to be found for a new church in a New World. America, in short, was sheer novelty. Indeed the radical mentality and spirituality of these missionaries and their methods of conversion have struck McAndrew very forcibly: «If the simplifications and emphases of the early friars seem liberal now, they were indeed

[63] For the background to all this see G. KUBLER, *Mexican Architecture of the Sixteenth Century*, 2 vols. London, 1948, and J. MCANDREW, *The Open-Air Churches of Sixteenth-Century Mexico*: *Atrios, Posas, Open Chapels and other Studies*, Cambridge, Mass., 1965, 5-7, 30-1. Both these fascinating works range more widely than their titles suggest: both deal with the historical and intellectual background of the Apostles of Mexico.

bold then. The return to first principles could have been Erasmian, for Erasmus was much read and admired by the [Franciscan] Observants, and Bishop Zumárraga paraphrased him in his *Doctrina Breve* (1544) so extensively that Bishop Montufar later suppressed it.»[64] Marcel Bataillon has studied Erasmus in America through the Franciscans' work: Zumárraga, in particular, he finds was impressed by «Herasmo,» and: «A pesar de las apariencias, es entre los frailes de temple apostólico donde hay que buscar la huella profunda, eficaz, de Erasmo en el Nuevo Mundo. Esto supone una revisión de los tópicos corrientes acerca de la mal llamada Contrarreforma y de lo que Erasmo significa en la crisis religiosa del siglo 16.»[65] There is no doubt that the principles of Erasmus greatly affected some of the American Franciscans, leading them to contemplate the birth of a fresh, primitive Church in New Spain and elsewhere. «Así se fundará en el Nuevo Mundo una "Iglesia nueva y primitiva," mientras los cristianos de Europa se empeñan, como dice Erasmo, en "meter un mundo en el cristianismo y torcer la Escritura divina hasta conformarla con las costumbres del tiempo" en vez de "enmendar las costumbres y enderezarlas con la regla de las Escrituras."» Zumárraga wanted to protect the new church from some of the religious ceremonies and customs of Europe, «aunque en otras tierras y gentes se pudiese tolerar... en ninguna manera se debe sufrir ni consentir entre los naturales desta nueva Iglesia.»[66] With sentiments like these it is not surprising, however farfetched it seems, that an influence as radical as that of Savonarola has been detected among the early Franciscans in Mexico. Yet radical and spiritually adventurous as they were, the friars kept within the bounds of orthodoxy: «lo que la Historia deberá siempre al franciscanismo será haber contenido esa corriente de espiritualidad en la obediencia a Roma.»[67]

There is further evidence of their «modernity» in their enthusiastic use of the famous catechism of Constantino Ponce de la Fuente.[68] This *Suma de doctrina cristiana,* by a famous preacher of Seville cathedral, aimed to present the bare essentials of Catholicism: Faith and works; Creed, and Commandments. The book's very title suggests the intention

---

64 McAndrew, oc., 53-4.

65 M. Bataillon, *Érasme et l'Espagne,* Span. tr., Mexico 1966, 831.

66 Bataillon, oc., 821, 826.

67 J. A. Maravall, *La Utopía político-religiosa de los Franciscanos en Nueva España,* «*Estudios Americanos,*» 1 (1949) 199-227; Bataillon, oc., 819 ff

68 This is studied in Bataillon, oc; it was also used by Jesuits in Brazil and Asia; St Francis Xavier thought it was «muy necesario llevarlo a la China.»

to present a pared-down fundamentalist version of Catholicism shorn of all that the author judged to be mere accretions. Inevitably, Ponce fell under suspicion; and Bataillon links the case with that of Carranza.[69] But this is hardly surprising, since although the *Suma* makes no mention of Erasmus, the book is redolent of the erasmian spirit, as Bataillon points out.

The *Suma* appeared in 1543. It was an instant best-seller, being reprinted within three months of its appearance. Bishop Zumárraga, who wished to introduce printing into New Spain to help in the task of evangelisation, produced a Mexican edition (1545-6), declaring that it contained «todo lo principal y necesario que el cristiano debe saber y obrar y lo que más conviene predicar a los indios.» Like Ricci later on in China, Ponce omitted five of the six Commandments of the Church, and his *Suma* names only three of the seven sacraments: baptism, confession and communion. But the *Suma* pleased the friars for these reasons, and also because it left unmentioned everything likely to create confusion with the Indians' pagan past, «dejando,» said Zumárraga, «los sermones de otra materia para más adelante.»

The spirit that led the friars to adopt Ponce's radical catechism was no mere flash in the pan: it certainly seems to have lived on in New Spain long after it had died out, or had been suppressed, in the mother country. Bataillon sums up the situation well: «Evangelismo, paulinismo: éste es, al fin y al cabo, el espíritu de los apóstoles que de España y Portugal, desde "los Doce" de Fr. Martín de Valencia hasta las misiones primitivas de los jesuitas, salen a la conquista espiritual de las muchedumbres no cristianas de América y de Asia.»[70]

The friars also brought to New Spain an intense curiosity about the nature of Indian religion and culture. Here they were fortunate, for the Indian priests' chronicles were longer and fuller than those of any other culture except the Chinese.

---

69 As late as 1887 the *Suma* could still give scandal: Menéndez Pelayo found it «más peligroso por lo que calla que por lo que dice,» noting its failure to mention papal supremacy, purgatory, or indulgences, *inter alia*. But this was precisely what the friars wished to avoid at that stage of their work: «cuadraba más, a lo menos para esta gente y tiempo presente, y aún para algunos años adelante no ternán necesidad de otra doctrina» (Zumárraga in BATAILLON, oc., 826).

70 BATAILLON, 828; and cf: «Baste lo dicho para situar lo que se puede llamar erasmismo en las *Doctrinas cristianas* del Obispo Zumárraga, y mostrar que en ellas la utilización de Erasmo no procede de capricho o de pereza, sino que corresponde al sentido profundo de la evangelización tal como la entendían aquellos hombres» (821).

«The result [of mendicant work] was a methodically arranged mass of carefully verified information on the gods worshipped by the Indians, their fiestas, their ideas on immortality and death ceremonies, astrology, witch doctors, rhetoric and philosophy, lords, governments, merchants and mechanical arts, vices and virtues, animals, birds, fish, herbs, trees, fruit, and flowers, and on the conquest of Mexico as the Indians saw it.» [71]

This zeal is neatly symbolised for us by friar Motolinía (Mendieta's «curioso investigador de los tiempos y verdades») who, when the Spaniards reached Popocatepetl on their way across Mexico, could not be deterred from climbing and inspecting it. It was Motolinía who in 1528 made a long and dangerous journey down to Nicaragua in order to study the local Indians' religious beliefs. Lach points out that the new love of nature discovered in the thirteenth century by the Franciscans led to «curiosity about all its forms [which] is exemplified in the observations of the friars and other travellers who made the overland trek to China and back again» in the thirteenth century. [72] This curiosity was certainly still alive in the 16th century. On the other hand, much of the interest in native religions was motivated by a utilitarian principle: they had to be understood in order to be destroyed, as well as to enable the friars to ease the psychological upheaval implied by conversion. To these missionaries (Ricard singles out the Franciscans' interest in «ethnographic and linguistic studies» and their «greater concern with training a native clergy») we are indebted for their rich language works, and their chronicles of the cultural and moral life of the newly-discovered inhabitants of the New World. [73]

The outstanding scholar in sixteenth-century Mexico was the Franciscan, Bernardino de Sahagún (c. 1499-1590), the «father of ethnological investigation in the New World.» His work was not superseded until recent times. Fray Bernardino set himself to investigate the beliefs and culture of the Aztecs, and in this he had three aims: to show his fellow spiritual physicians how to recognise the disease they had come to cure; to record a Nahuatl vocabulary as an aid to the future conversion of the Indians, and, thirdly, to reveal through the study of the pre-conquest past that the natives were not barbarians. He must have been born

---

71 L. HANKE, *B. Arzáns de Orsúa's History of Potosi*, Providence, 1965, 7.

72 LACH, oc., II (iii), 483-5.

73 Robert RICARD, *The Spiritual Conquest of Mexico... 1523-72* (English edition), Berkeley and Los Angeles, 1966, 285.

with a gift for research; obviously untrained, he devised a new method of ethnographical investigation. His devotion is self-evident. His work gives one the feeling that though he became a research scientist for religious reasons, he ended by being one for scientific reasons.

Sahagún's *Historia general de las cosas de la Nueva España* was based on material gathered from ten or twelve elderly Indian informants. He was also helped not only by his own fluent knowledge of Nahuatl but also by four youths who were influenced by both cultures, and who were able to write their language in Latin letters. The situation was ideal: willing informants and an investigator who was loved and respected, and who was prudent enough to put his raw material «through a sieve three times» to be more certain of its authenticity. The final results were written in Nahuatl by Sahagún and later re-written in Spanish. Specialists have found his work is meticulous and able to stand every critical test that modern research can apply. It is an encyclopedia of the Nahua people, an attempt to recover the ancient Aztec mind and to record the pre-conquest oral tradition before it died for ever.

It is noticeable that Sahagún in Mexico was facing many of the same basic problems (terminology, ritual, etc.) confronting his Jesuit contemporary Matteo Ricci, in China. Yet the work of Sahagún has been comparatively neglected. Had he belonged to a more publicity-minded Order we should have hosts of studies and editions of his work. As it is, the Mexican scholar Miguel León-Portilla has had to call attention to the need for further study of the Opus Sahagunense, and he makes a significant appeal: «Almost four centuries after the writing of the Spanish text it seems to be time to prepare a critical edition of it.» [74]

Where faith and morals were not involved, then, the best friars sought to adjust to their converts; and they sought to inform themselves what was morally neutral and permissible in the native culture. [75] With good reason, then, a recent writer has declared that «the term *tabula rasa* is too sweeping when applied to the Franciscans' understanding and use. Their concern was not to sweep away the Indian culture in order to expose a clean slate... in terms of their own theoretical and working

74 In Munro S. EDMONSON (ed.): *Sixteenth-century Mexico: The Work of Sahagún*, Albuquerque, New Mexico, 1974, 250.

75 «Opportune autem rerum Indicarum, quibus, ipsi non modo interfuimus, sed et praefuimus, aliqua adhibuimus exempla» (Diego de VALADES, OFM., *Rhetórica Christiana*, s.l., 1579; preface, sin pag.).

perspectives they had no intention of making the Indians over into a Spanish mould... in so far as they understood their mission, it was not to Hispanicize the Indians.» [76] It is worth repeating that if their missions to the Moors of Granada did not establish a model for the Franciscans in New Spain, it is precisely because not being as rigid as is so often alleged, they were open to new ways and methods, capable of moving forward from one position to another, and they did not try to impose Andalusian solutions to American problems. [77]

All the evangelists were guilty of iconoclasm, irrespective of the religious order they belonged to. McAndrew, discussing their destruction of pagan temples and native antiquities in Mexico, laments an aesthetic tragedy which was an inevitable corollary of conquest. But Ricard makes the point that they were only consistent and logical: they could hardly be expected to leave untouched what would clearly become pilgrimage centres and rallying points for the old religion. Destroying pagan religious sites would leave the Indians in a religious vacuum which would make them turn more willingly to the consolations of Christianity. It is also important to recall that the old religion the missionaries were combatting involved ceremonies which they would find shocking: human sacrifice, cannibalism. Moreover the culture that the friars had encountered expected them to destroy the old shrines: the Aztecs, for example, always burnt the holy places of any tribe they conquered, and the Nahuatl pictogram for «conquest» was a burning temple. Finally, the missionaries were not professional, not even amateur, antiquarians. [78]

The friars acted under orders to destroy in order to rebuild; «ut falsis ritibus extirpatis, vera religio plantetur» (*Universalis Ecclesiae*, 1508) explained Rome; and a royal cédula of 1523 ran: «Ordenamos y mandamos ... que en todas aquellas provincias, hagan derribar y derriben, quitar y quiten los ídolos, aras y adoratorios de la gentilidad y sus sacrificios.» It was explained that to do otherwise would be to condone the eternal death of millions. But, at the same time, the Consejo de Indias urged

[76] E. E. SYLVEST, *Motifs of Franciscan Mission Theory in sixteenth-century New Spain*, Washington, 1975, 101, 130.

[77] Valadés's comparisons between the Amerindian converts and the converted Moors of Granada, suggest that the friar-missionaries had improved as a result of their first lessons: Valadés, oc., Part iv, chap. xi. xii.

[78] RICARD, oc., 35 ff., BORGES, oc., 88; MCANDREW, oc., 179.

the preservation of all things «que no fueren contra nuestra sagrada religión.» [79]

McAndrew (oc 179 ff) reminds us that iconoclasm and the wanton destruction of beautiful buildings was no novelty to Europeans: we have only to recall the Sack of Rome (1527), and a little later the dissolution of the English monasteries under Henry VIII and the fury of the Puritans a century later. McAndrew makes a good point: «Much of Catholic Mexico City was built of the stones of pagan Tenochtitlan in the same years and in the same way that much of Catholic Counter-Reformation Rome was being built of the stones of pagan Rome.» This theme is developed by E. R. Chamberlin who quotes Pastor to the effect that «the feeling we designate piety, reverence [for an ancient structure in its own right] seemed unknown in the Middle Ages.»

As the friars in Mexico were destroying in order to rebuild, precisely the same was happening in Rome. «Julius II decided to demolish the 1,200 year old Constantinian basilica in order to build a new one... the oldest, largest, most sacred building in Christendom was knocked down as though it was a peasant's hovel...» and the great architect Bramante, who «acted like some Goth or Vandal» in the enterprise, earned himself the nickname of *Il Ruinante*. Quite soon after Julius's decision in 1505, the «most important part of the old basilica disappeared in a fury of destruction that did not spare the very tombs of the Popes... the demolition of old St Peter's was carried out at the hands of its guardians, for the greatest destroyers of Rome were Romans.» The city was treated as a quarry to supply materials for new buildings «more in keeping with the spirit of the age.» Chamberlin dates the change in the attitude to the past, and the consciousness of aesthetic sacrilege, as taking place «some time during the year 1505,» when complaints began to be made. Later still, Sixtus V, who they said seemed «bent on the destruction of Rome,» was begged to desist. If «the spirit of the age» demanded that Rome be destroyed by her very guardians in order to be rebuilt, then the pagan glories and wonders of Mexico-Tenochtitlan could hardly hope to escape a similar fate. [80]

In other fields the friars showed great flexibility: Damboriena writes of «magníficas pruebas de adaptación al medio ambiente» in the American church; McAndrew finds astonishing divergences from European ritual

---

79 DAMBORIENA, OC., 114, 115, 121, 123.

80 E. R. CHAMBERLIN, *The Death and Resurrection of Rome*, in: «History Today,» 28 (1978) 304-12.

practice; even Dunne grudgingly admits that «adaptation was not unknown in Mexico and South America.» As much as possible was taken over from the native culture, christened, and put to use for the better evangelisation of the Indian. The missionaries were particularly successful with para-liturgical devotions: they experimented with such traditional Catholic usages as the rosary and holy water, and liturgical decorations such as candles and flowers, in order to attract the natives' interest. Songs and dances from the pagan past were christianized, with the result that «el pueblo indio pudo seguir durante mayor o menor tiempo... practicando sus antiguos cultos en la forma cristiana americanizada.» [81]

Music was used also. The discoverer of this missionary technique was fray Pedro de Gante, who first showed the way. A great deal of the early missionary success was due (on the purely human level) to this emotional conditioning through the skilful use of music. [82] The missionary theatre was also original and serviceable. The first friars used the *auto*, or allegorical play, as a species of catechism: it became a half-way house between ritual and drama. Spanish plays were adapted and fused with elements of the then incipient Indian theatre, with choral dances and pantomime-type performances. Las Casas, following Motolinía, discusses plays performed by Indians; one in particular, for the feast of Corpus Christi, 1536, seemed excellent: «si en ella se hallaran el summo Pontífice y el Emperador con sus cortes, holgarán mucho de verla... si en Roma se hiciera, fuera sonada en el mundo.» A theological sense was given to all these entertainments and they became in fact dramatised devotions. Pious Catholic legends were put over in the native languages: before long the Wolf of Gubbio appeared in Aztec guise. [83]

One particular novelty introduced by the friars into New Spain has aroused admiration and wonder, namely the atrio-church or open-air

---

81 DAMBORIENA, oc., 120, 122; MCANDREW, oc., 205, 366; DUNNE, oc., 229; E. DUSSEL, *Hipótesis para una historia de la Iglesia en América Latina*, Barcelona, 1967, 83.

82 A. E. LEMMON, SJ., *The Jesuits and Music in Mexico,* «*Archivum Historicum Societatis Jesu,*» 46 (1977) 197.

83 RICARD, oc., 104-5; E. A. ARMSTRONG, *St. Francis: Nature Mystic. Nature Stories in the Franciscan Legend,* Berkeley, 1973, 216. B. de LAS CASAS, *Apologética historia,* chaps. 63-4. There is an excellent brief summary of the missionary theatre and its subsequent development in B. W. DIFFIE, *Latin-American Civilization: Colonial Period,* New York, 1967, 534-5. Diffie comments on the survival of themes which are now incongruous: «Indians who never heard of a Moor in any other connection still engage solemnly and vigorously in mock battles in which the Moors are driven out, from where it is not exactly clear.» (534).

church. McAndrew, who has studied this phenomenon and explained the ideology behind it, describes these buildings as «what may be the most dramatic American architectural innovation before the skyscraper,» and shows how they were «called into being in the sixteenth century by the urgencies of a vast campaign of religious conversion, ... the outdoor church can be properly understood today only as a product of that conversion, and of some of the peculiar local conditions.» He goes on to claim that such a novelty («an amazing divarication»), so closely connected to the celebration of Mass, must surely «have raised suspicions of unorthodoxy bordering on heresy. It is astonishing that Spaniards were able to accept and even encourage their use.» These churches, which were needed to cope with the vast crowds of converts, were sponsored by friars; the secular clergy did not favour them, and eventually they were forbidden. They turned the Mass from a traditionally indoor rite into an outdoor one, and there was no European tradition for this use of a church forecourt as a nave. Their novelty is revealed in the way that the chroniclers who mention them always go on to describe them, realizing they would be difficult for their readers to imagine. [84]

* * *

Hernán Cortés, not satisfied with his conquest of Mexico, was determined to explore the Pacific. And the Franciscans, with their world-wide vision, encouraged this desire to look beyond the confines of New Spain.

The first stage on the westward journey to Asia led inevitably to the Philippines. In comparison with the conquest of Mexico, the impact of the Spanish upon the Islands was relatively pacific. The Spaniards who reached there had been tutored by the experience inherited from Mexico: they brought forty years' knowledge of colonial life, and had already learnt to establish old, and to create new, institutions to meet the circumstances. This shows itself in the work of missionaries too. They had refined their methods; they had lost the apocalyptic spirit which had driven them into haste in New Spain; they had now learnt for instance to abandon the practice of baptizing without prior instruction. They had also emerged as the natural protectors of natives. Just as the

---

84 McAndrew, oc., vii, 205 ff. The word «heresy» seems rather exaggerated, but the author is clearly impressed.

«Twelve Apostles» had found a symbolic name for the Franciscan custody in New Spain, so the first friars in Manila named theirs after St Gregory the Great. Here, as in America, adaptation was practised where it seemed possible; folk customs were christianized; as before, such popular Catholic devotions as would appeal to the Filipinos were introduced: rosaries, medals, processions, music, singing (children were taught the catechism in song). In all this there were few novelties. But in time Manila was to produce an unforeseen bonus, for it was to introduce the friars to large communities of Chinese and Japanese. (Later on, as many as 20,000 Chinese were there at one time.) The local Parián thus gave the missionaries an opportunity to acquaint themselves with Chinese customs, religious beliefs, and languages. Friars, both Franciscans and Dominicans, worked with these two foreign communities.[85]

Though it was a friar who declared that «Ricci, Pantoja, Aleni... y otros tales fueron los Gigantes de la Missión de la China,»[86] the mendicants themselves, even in the early days, could produce their own giants: from the Franciscans, Santa María; from the Dominicans, Cobo; from the Augustinians, Rada. These, like the «Twelve Apostles» in New Spain, «would be hard to match.»[87] Ricci had been preceded by José de Acosta, but both were preceded in their turn, by the Franciscan Sahagún. But «giants» and «titans» apart, there was probably not a great deal of difference between the average Jesuit and his friar colleague. Indeed, the former might have been at a disadvantage in not having had any serious pastoral experience before embarking on the China mission, whereas the friar would most likely have served in priory or parish in the Americas or the Philippines during his journey to Asia. Hence the friars could say, indeed one of them did say: «todos los padres Jesuitas que acá vienen por misionarios, no son Salomones en la ciencia como ellos lo blasonan,» because «el primer Bautismo que hace el P. Francés, Alemán o Italiano es en China.» As for the training of some Jesuits, it was not

---

85 And sometimes showed them a tolerance which troubled local Jesuits. At least on one occasion they were denounced to the Inquisition by Fathers Vello and Sola for allowing Chinese to celebrate the full moon in ways which seemed to the Jesuits to mix «devilish practices» with Christian piety. There is a certain irony about the idea of Chinese syncretism under mendicant auspices! (*Arch. Gen. de la Nación*, Mexico City, *Inquisition*, 442, ff. 259-63; 520, Exp. 245).

86 NAVARRETE, *Controversias*, 356-7: bibliographical details at p. 88 below.

87 MCANDREW, OC., 30; «the twelve,» in their turn, are called the «generación de titanes» in E. J. PALOMERAS, SJ., *Diego de Valadés, OFM*: *Evangelista y Humanista de la Nueva España*, Mexico, 1962, 115.

a carping friar but an irritable Father, who dismissed some of his own colleagues by complaining: «son teólogos de Goa.» [88]

Despite what has been said of the friars' methods in America, it is still frequently alleged that they were hostile to «cultural adaptation» and the use of «human means.» A recent study of the China mission describes the Franciscans' alleged «abhorrence for every measure of cultural adaptation, which they regarded as a betrayal of the faith,» and quotes Buenaventura Ibáñez OFM., as denouncing the Jesuits' methods as «purely human means, directly contrary to those used by the Apostles...» But in fact it was this very same Ibáñez who described how he had undertaken some clock repair work to help him make friends with the Chinese: «Cualquier medio que sea por el cual se consigue el fin tan alto que se pretende de poder predicar el santo Evangelio a esta gentilidad, ¿se podrá condenar por mal e inútil? No, por cierto.» In other words the friar is not opposed to human means, only to what seemed excessive reliance upon them, for divine ends.

Of course the friars who distinguished themselves by their use of human means in America were not always motivated by self-interest, but often acted in the cause of culture and humanity, as well as of religion. [89] Marcelino Menéndez y Pelayo, in his study of Ecuador, singles out the Franciscans for special praise: «a las órdenes monásticas, y especialmente a la de San Francisco, se debió la primera cultura del país y el establecimiento de las primeras escuelas, así como a un franciscano, el P. Jodoco Rickle, se había debido la introducción de la primera semilla

---

88 Antonio de SANTA MARIA in *Sinica Franciscana*, II, 374; NAVARRETE, *Controversias*, 197, 331. Indeed some of the Jesuits might not even have finished their training before being despatched to the mission: in this connection c.f the situation in the English mission: «It is not generally understood that the first Jesuits who came to England had not yet completed their training; few, if any, save J. Heywood, had been solemnly professed.» Bernard BASSET, SJ., *The Engish Jesuits*, London, 1967, 123. On the vocations of the early Jesuits see the fascinating paper by T. V. COHEN, *Why the Jesuits Joined: 1540-1600*, «Canadian Historical Papers,» Otawa, 1974, 237-58; this is a study of the Spanish, Portuguese and Polish provinces of the Society, based on questionnaires and spiritual autobiographies. Also relevant are L. LUKÁCS, SJ., *De Graduum diversitate*, «Archivum Historicum Soc. Jesu,» 37 (1968) 237-316 (in Latin); summarised in Spanish in *Diferencia entre profesos y coadjutores - Historia*, «Información SJ., Revista internacional dirigida a los Jesuitas,» I (1969) 310-14.

89 For examples, see M. R. PAZOS, OFM., *Los misioneros franciscanos de Méjico y la enseñanza técnica que dieron a los indios*, *AIA*, 32 (1973) 149-190, and the bibliography given there; and IDEM, *Los misioneros franciscanos de Méjico y sus hospitales para indios*, *AIA*, 14 (1954) 339-78. RICARD, oc., 135-160. J. A. MACKAY, *The Other Spanish Christ, A Study in the Spiritual History of Spain and South America*, London, 1932, 38.

de trigo.» Friars acted as surgeons, civil engineers, architects, developed canals and irrigation systems («it would have been astonishing if the Spaniards had not kept their veneration for water which is still today so striking in the Peninsula,» says Ricard) transforming desert areas into fruitful land, and making possible the cultivation of, for example, the prickly pear for cochineal. [90] Fray Juan de Zumárraga even requested convert Moors be sent from old to New Spain to teach the cultivation of mulberry trees and the method of producing silk. Children too were taught farming as a form of recreation, sometimes almost as a species of catechism, since such manual skills were regarded as a means of moral uplift, apart from their intrinsic value. The missionary, writes McAndrew, had to be able to cook, sew, barber, tailor, nurse, build, teach; all the better if he could also be a jeweller, blacksmith, painter, sculptor and had some notion of design and embroidery. This went on for many generations. Franciscans «did much to promote agriculture and stock raising. Great herds of horses, mules and cattle came into existence. Sugar, bananas, maize, cassava, rice and beans were extensively cultivated. Cacao and coffee plantations were developed.» The mission thus became a social welfare agency in many areas, and after the friars were displaced in Mexico, writes Kubler, «for eleven generations no equivalent agency emerged to resume the humanization of Indian society. Only in the twentieth century was the work of rural education and welfare begun again, by a government whose unacknowledged archetype is the Mendicant organization of the sixteenth century.»[91] These efforts to improve the lot of the poor and lowly, to whom the Franciscans were devoted, were not peculiar to America. Realizing that seraphic ardour alone was not sufficient, the friars carried out a programme of «human means» as an adjunct to preaching, in the Philippines, Japan and China.

In the Philippines friars provided their own ethnologists, such as fray Juan de Plasencia, OFM, and there too they introduced novel farming

---

90 A letter quoted in TORQUEMADA (*Monarchía indiana,* 1723 ed. III, 131) comes from a friar demanding that iron be sent to his mission; it was important for the manufacture of agricultural tools. There is an interesting study of the significance of metal tools and implements as «human means» in A. METAUX, *The Revolution of the Ax,* «Diogenes,» 25 (Spring, 1959) 30-32.

91 M. MENENDEZ PELAYO, *Historia de la poesía hispano-americana,* II, Madrid, 1948, 7. RICARD, oc., 145; MCANDREW, oc., 29; K. S. LATOURETTE, *A History of the Expansion of Christianity,* III, New York 1939, 138; KUBLER, oc., I, 21.

techniques, new seeds, fruits, even animals.[92] The friars also produced their «advocates of the Indians» in the Philippines, after the manner of Las Casas in Central America. Indeed it was largely the gentle persuasion of the mendicants that made the conquest relatively bloodless, as has been said above. Franciscan zeal for the natives is recalled by the President of the Philippine Historical Conservation Society who in 1977 in a reference to the modern administrators of CARE, described them as «the Franciscans of our own century, for they also go about as they did alleviating pain and hunger» ... «that Order [OFM], with all justice, can be said to have developed and organised a good fourth of our country.»[93]

In Japan, as in China, local needs were different, so the friars' methods differed to meet the situation. Once more they showed themselves able to produce linguists, teachers, writers, even envoys; and they took up medicine, establishing hospitals and nursing lepers, though this was also thought to be an excellent way of leading to the conversion of the Chinese.[94] Buenaventura Ibáñez, OFM, whom we have just seen condemned for denouncing Jesuit methods, shows that in fact he was far from hostile to them; indeed, he was anticipating modern mission practice when he wrote from China in 1650 «Yo no hallo otro mejor camino para todo, como es por medio de un religioso sirujano, al qual cada día lo avrán menester mandarines y governantes para ellos o los de su casa, por cuyo medio tendrá entrada también el ministro, y será dellos soco-

---

92 LATOURETTE, oc., III, 318-9 gives more detail. See also J. L. PHELAN, *The Hispanization of the Philippine Islands*, Madison, 1959, *passim;* MORGA, oc., (ed. Cummins), 27, 254, 255; Marcelo de RIBADENEIRA, OFM., *Historia de las Islas del archipiélago filipino y reinos de la Gran China, Tartaria, Cochinchina, Malaca, Siam, Cambodge y Japón*, 2nd ed. Madrid, 1947, 48.

93 CARE: an acronym: «Cooperative for American Relief Everywhere,» a private organisation which distributes food and funds to the needy in foreign countries. Alonso FELIX Jr., in *The Philippine Chronicles of fray San Antonio*, tr. and ed. P. Picornell, Manila, Historical Conservation Society, 1977, v, x.

94 «Es la medicina para las conversiones uno de los medios más suaves y eficaces que hay en la Iglesia para atraer las almas y *a veces aprovecha más que la teología*, como se vio por experiencia... [my italics].» *Sinica Franciscana*, II, 288. C. R. BOXER, *Friar Juan Pobre of Zamora and his Lost and Found «Ystoria» of 1598-1603*: *(Lilly Ms. BM. 617)*, «The Indiana University Bookman,» No. 10, November, 1969, 41; Idem, *The Christian Century in Japan, 1549-1650*, Berkeley and London, 1951, discusses Franciscan hospitals and their care of lepers, 204, 233, 419, 477, 479; and at p. 235: «Fray Juan Pobre says that learned bonzes, who could not be convinced by purely theological arguments, on passing by the [OFM] Kyoto hospice and seeing the friars washing the lepers' feet, exclaimed, «We do not want any more arguments. This is it! There must be salvation.»

rrido con limosnas y amparado de los malechores, y se sembrará la semilla del Evangelio con menos sudor y a poca costa. Deste mesmo parecer es... Fr. Antonio de santa María.»[95] And Antonio de Morga, writing to Philip II, praised the Franciscans in Japan for their hospital work which won them sympathy, and led to conversions.[96]

The friars who reached China in 1579, then, with these traditions behind them, felt in no way inferior to the Jesuits. Nor should it be lightly assumed that they were unlearned or untalented. If, for example, Bernardino de Sahagún is known as the father of Mexican ethnography, it is another friar, Martín de Rada, whom a generous Jesuit has dubbed «the father of modern Sinology.»[97] Henri Bernard-Maitre SJ., describes friar Rada as «l'un des fondateurs de la sinologie.» The friar's account of his voyage was published in Europe in the work of his fellow-mendicant González de Mendoza, «et nul ouvrage, pas même les Commentaires du P. Ricci... ne contribua davantage à répandre dans le gran public des notions sérieuses sur la Chine et ses institutions.»[98]

Rada's accomplishments and achievements have also drawn praise from Boxer and Lach: a tireless missionary, Rada is credited with «having evangelised almost single-handed Cebú and Panay.» His linguistic skills, revealed earlier in his career in Paris and subsequently in Mexico, stood him in good stead in the Philippines, where Visayan proved an easy language after Otomí. Later, he was to prepare a work, now lost, on Chinese. In the Philippines he also found time to make astronomical observations and calculations, and studied the problems of the longitude and of the

---

95 in *Sinica Franciscana*, III, 22: Antonio de Santa María OFM., also urged that missionaries should use medicine in the missions, in his *Respuesta* quoted in Navarrete, oc., 548 ff. (see p. 88 below) citing the example of the Nestorians of a thousand years earlier who «daban de comer al hambriento, de vestir al desnudo, que curauan a los enfermos, y que enterrauan (pero no que sacrificauan, ni que ofrecían algo) a los muertos.» The words in brackets are clearly a dig at the Jesuits' permissiveness.

96 MORGA, oc., 3, 16. In Japan both Jesuits and Franciscans seem to have shown great originality in the use of «human means.» The Jesuit Alexander Valignano asked permission for the Fathers to lend out money at interest at the rate of ten per cent which would compare favourably with the local usurers' rate of seventy per cent, and would add «great luster to our Religion.» The Franciscans were said to have opened fencing schools to attract potential converts to their Kyoto convent (BOXER, *Christian Century*, 203, 235).

97 For eulogies of Rada, «the flower and phoenix of the mathematical arts of Spain,» see BOXER, *South China in the sixteenth century*, lxxv-viii, where we read: «It is high time he was given credit for being the first European writer on China who clearly and correctly identified this country with Marco Polo's Cathay.»

98 H. BERNARD-MAITRE, SJ., *Aux portes de la Chine: 1514-1588*, Tientsin, 1933, 105, 113.

demarcation line established by the papacy between the Portuguese and Spanish zones of interest. Like the later Jesuits in China, he is to be found writing home for more scientific books to replace those lost at sea or in other vicissitudes: «of geometry I have here only Euclid and Archimedes; of astronomy, Ptolemy and Copernicus...» [99]

The Franciscans in China: Reactions and Problems

The friars, in general, were under no illusions about the difficulty of converting the Chinese. One mendicant reported that «los chinos, no son como los indios que con cualquier razón se convencen sino que arguyen y replican a la respuesta... plugiera al señor pudieran venir por acá los maestros de Salamanca, que en muchas ocasiones tuvieran muy mucho donde emplear bien sus talentos.» Again: «se debe poner mucho cuidado en elegir ministros para China, que no se han de tomar del montón; no es lo mismo ser apto para el ministerio en Manila que serlo para China.» Antonio de Santa María meant the same, though he was brief: «Los chinos aunque sean agrícolas no son tontos.» [100]

The ideal man, said the friars, should be healthy, energetic, pious, sound in his theological learning, and with linguistic talents. In character a missionary must be calm, urbane, modest, long-suffering; for the Chinese are converted through the eyes, not through the ears, that is, by good example, not argument. But above, all, the volunteers must be realists; over-scrupulous romantic dreamers, would-be mystics and saints, «are best left in their priories»; sometimes one has to «dejar a Dios por Dios» in order to deal with the task at hand. Loneliness could be one of the greatest crosses of the China mission and the priest had to be prepared to live alone for long periods. Friar Pedro de Piñuela spent eight years without a companion, sometimes going for ten months at a stretch without seeing a European, and with no other recreation but to go out on a clear night

99 Friar Rada's interest in Copernicus is another warning against cliché and stereotyping; nor was he alone: among others, San Juan de la Cruz apparently accepted the new astronomy; and it was an Augustinian friar, Diego de Zúñiga, who adopted it for the official syllabus of Salamanca University (1561). This adoption of the Copernican system must not be overstressed, however, for it met with opposition: it was attacked by a Jesuit, Father Pineda (O. H. Green, *Spain and the Western Tradition*, III, Madison, 1968, 234).

100 Francisco Varo, OP., to his Provincial, 1667: *OP Archives*, Manila, vol. 28, n. p; fray Bernardo de la Encarnación, 1689, in Maas, *Cartas de China*, II, Seville, 1917, 21; Santa María to P. Gen. Oliva, SJ., 1650; *SJ Archives Rome*, Japsin 162.

to gaze at the stars. It was particularly trying («esta es una de mis cruces») for a Mexican creole, «porque tenemos fama de parleros.» [101]

A recent writer claims that the mendicants were disturbed by such «Jesuit innovations» as learning the language of the country in which they were working; and asserts that previously this principle of cultural adaptation had been ignored. [102] This is difficult to understand, for there was no novelty here. As has been said already, the friars in thirteenth-century China had said Mass in the Tartar language and in medieval Spain had set up their own missionary schools of Arabic and Hebrew, under the influence of men of practical experience such as Ramón Lull (the Franciscan Tertiary who advocated conversion by persuasion) and William of Ruisbroeck after his return from Asia. Prospective missionaries were methodically prepared in such institutes as the language schools in Murcia and Miramar. To the friars, linguistic studies were an addition to theology. Their expression for language-learning showed they realized it was a new development, responding to new needs; for them it was «la teología que de todo punto ignoró San Agustín.» [103]

The friars, who had produced a host or grammars, dictionaries and vocabularies of Amerindian languages, were no less diligent in the Philippines, where they applied themselves to the study of such languages as Tagalog (e.g. fray Juan de Plasencia's pioneer grammar and dictionary), as well as Chinese and Japanese. For just as the Jesuits trained their men in Macao, so the friars (like the «China-watchers» of our own day), finding the mainland closed, were obliged to study Chinese language and culture in Formosa (Taiwan) or amongst the large Chinese community in Manila. And they were, it seems, no less eager than their modern counterparts. Sometimes they were denounced for this very zeal. Governor Diego Fajardo (1644-53) complained of one friar who «apenas había desembarcado, quando se puso a enseñar a algunos de dichos Religiosos

---

101 *Sinica Franciscana,* IV, 1942, 280. Piñuela seems to have been a charming character: there is a study of him by A. Sisto Rosso, OFM., in *Franciscan Studies,* 8 (1948) 250-74.

102 This scarcely needs refuting: but to match one quotation for another we might quote Motolinía's remark that «frailes hay que predican en tres lenguas todas diferentes,» *Historia de los Indios,* trat. III, chap. 3.

103 Modern Jesuits too seem to have a high opinion of outstanding linguists: «exceptional skill in any difficult foreign language can compensate for lack of that knowledge which is required for the profession of the four vows.» Ledochowski, oc, 129, 917.

la lengua Mandarina que es diferente de la de los Chinos del Parián [in Manila] que no sirve sino en China.» [104]

Another outstanding friar Sinologue was fray Juan Cobo, OP., who ministered to the Chinese in Manila from 1586-1592. His studies led to the translation into Spanish of a collection of 673 Chinese aphorisms, taken from the writings of 110 different authors. [105] The Franciscans began studying Chinese immediately on their arrival in the Philippines and by the 1580s the Audiencia was informing Philip II that there were friars among them capable of preaching to the local community. The mendicants' studies were quickly put on a formal footing and the Franciscans devised an intensive course for newcomers. The Divine Office and community Masses were said before dawn, and then the whole of their available time until dinner was devoted to private study and conversation practice. Any friar who accidentally spoke Latin or Spanish was punished. In the afternoon, following Vespers, there were formal classes until supper time. Some time before 1604 there was an official examination system with two examiners in Chinese appointed for the work. The scheme seems to have been successful, for in 1610 the Portuguese bishop of Macao (admittedly himself a friar) was writing to their superior in Rome to congratulate him on such accomplished subjetcs.

Jesuits, as has been said above, frequently alleged that friars went into China ignorant of the language. Such allegations are understandable: they were part of what the Fathers deemed essential to their strategy of keeping mendicants out of China; they were also in part natural exaggerations, and in part may have been due to misunderstandings, because the friars tended to concentrate on the Fukien and other dialects. This dialect would not be easily understood in Peking, where the court Jesuits could diagnose mendicant «ignorance.» Fortunately the written language could be read and understood from one end of the empire to

---

104 P. PASTELLS, SJ., *Historia general de Filipinas*, Barcelona, 1923, IX, civ. And for an example of this zeal see the remarks of Fray Francisco de Jesús ESCALONA in *Sinica Franciscana*, II, 217, 246; and also 40, 41, 176.

105 LACH, oc., (ii), 805-6 has warm praise for Cobo; also BOXER, *Christian Century*, 161. See also B. BIERMANN, *Chinesische Sprachstudien in Manila*, Neue Zeitschrift für Missionswissenschaft, 7 (1951) 18-23, and P. Hermann KÖSTER SVD., *Zum ersten chinesischen Katechismus auf den Philippinen*: Nachtrag, Zeitschrift für Missionswissenschaft und Religionswissenschaft, 39 (1955) 55-57.

the other, so that concentration on one particular dialect did not prevent the friars from studying the all-important classical texts. [106]

The mendicants in America had studied closely the nature of the natives, their languages, customs and religions; and their resultant controversies and discussions had produced such results as the bull *Sublimis Deus*, to mention only one significant example. In the same tradition, the friars now set themselves to study the problems they faced in China, responding enthusiastically to the challenges presented by the Central Country. One must here insist again on what was said at the beginning: the China legend so industriously fostered by later Jesuits had been launched first by friars, and their affection and admiration for China and their zeal in studying its languages and mysteries were no less than that of the Jesuits. Henri Bernard-Maitre SJ. resists the temptation to be more daring, but it is interesting that he can at any rate go so far as to say: «Nous n'oserons point dire cependant que les essais des jésuites italiens en China se soient directement inspirés de ces antécédents.» [107] The friars soon came to respect the intelligence of the Chinese, their natural interest in ethics and in moral questions; and in China, as in America, many mendicants were moved to echo St Augustine: «Ecce pagani doctores fidelium facti sunt.» Naturally their major preoccupation was with the religious beliefs and practices of the Chinese.

The Jesuits who reached China did so via Portuguese India, where by and large they kept to the coasts, since the Portuguese, their patrons, did not attempt inland conquests. Friar Diego Aduarte noted this: the Portuguese, he declared, do not serve the Faith fully since they are content to hold the ports they have, in order to secure the sea for their trading activities. [108] Everywhere the Fathers went they saw deeply entrenched religious beliefs, held by millions. They must have seen that, in human terms, they had no hope of supplanting them. But they relied on the domino theory: Asia, in general, seemed morally and culturally subservient to the Central Country, so that the conversion of the latter would induce the surrounding nations to follow suit. Father Antoine Thomas, for example, was expressing this widely held conviction (which

---

106 The difference is such that on one occasion in 1937, during the Sino-Japanese war, Cantonese-speaking pilots who landed in north China were killed by locals who took them for Japanese (*Ex relatione* C. R. Boxer).

107 Bernard-Maitre, oc., 117.

108 Letter of 26 June, 1598, quoted in *AIA*, 38 (1935) 455-58.

dates back to Xavier) when he wrote: «I myself believe that the conversion of the whole East is dependent upon that of China alone: so nothing, however insignificant, must be neglected to promote this end.»[109] China, the key to Asia, therefore became a Jesuit obsession.

The friars shared this view though it was modified by their experience. They did not underrate the difficulties lying before them, but they reached the East by the Spanish route, across America and via the Philippines, and everywhere they saw evidence of the success of the methods of their brethren. They were therefore less psychologically resigned to compromise.

To summarise, the mendicants were at least as learned as the Fathers in theology and philosophy, and certainly no less zealous nor less perspicacious, and often they were more experienced in practical evangelical and pastoral work. But both groups had different standpoints, from which they approached the common task.

* * *

In a world of confused and confusing beliefs, it seemed inevitable to the friars that Christianity must be declared in an assertive (which does not mean aggressive) manner, preaching the kerygma: announcing a call to all men to submit to the Almighty and seek salvation in the dead and risen Christ. The friars acted as heralds of the kingdom and of its king: unfolding the Good News to the heathen for the first time (Luke 24: 47). In this they showed a certain Pauline audacity. They could have had little hope of vast conversions, but their duty was to declare their message without being inhibited by human respect, or from fear of martyrdom.[110] Initially, they made tactical blunders, though often it could be argued that these were a reaction against the apparent over-delicacy and timidity of the Jesuits. The friars later admitted these early mistakes, but reminded their accusers that they had quickly learnt from them and had restrained their ardour with prudence. This was true, for the mendicants soon modified their attitude without departing from their general principles. They took fewer risks; they no longer preached openly

109 P. A. Thomas, SJ., to the Duchess of Aveiro, from Macao, 2 February, 1683, in Maggs's Catalogue No. 455: *Bibliotheca Asiatica*, ii (1924) 91.

110 Jesuits complained that the friars seemed more intent on earning themselves private palms of martyrdom than on converting the Chinese. Sometimes the choice seemed simply to lie between mathematics and martyrdom; whether to be a mandarin or a missionary.

in the streets, and confined their proselytising to churches, where they could more freely discuss and argue with their listeners. Before Sunday Mass their congregations were divided into two groups and recited a Dialogue Rosary: before the service there was a catechism lesson followed by questions on the Creed, and in this work the friars were assisted by trained catechists. The Chinese were sharp in argument and used to take quotations from the missionaries' writings and turn them against the preacher; their remarkably acute questions always went to the heart of a problem. One friar warned his successors that the missionary who had not got his feet firmly in the stirrups would quickly find himself flat on the ground. Another friar described the situation as similar to that in Japan, where the Zen priests «asked questions which even Aquinas and Scotus could not answer satisfactorily.» In these arguments the Chinese were helped by Muslims, who often took over the debate while the Chinese stood by, listening, and carefully noting reactions.

The mendicants were keenly aware of the need to adapt themselves and their message to the Chinese. The problem lay in deciding how far to adapt, and in what respects. It seemed to them that the proclamation of the Gospel was essential: without the kerygma, the didache is a mere ethical system, not a doctrine of salvation. Herein lay the danger in the «Riccista» approach, as the friars saw it. They were conscious that they had no mandate to delay or to water down the essence of the message entrusted to them, no matter how desirable it might seem from a temporary point of view. What was watered down, might end by being watered away.[111]

The friars would not compromise where they suspected there was superstition (let alone idolatry), yet they did not, contrary to much popular belief, interfere unnecessarily. They had not done so in America, they had not done so in the Philippines, they did not attempt to do so now in China. Even had they felt so inclined they would have been restrained by the denunciation of mindless «Europeanism» in the

---

111 «It was by kerygma, says Paul, not by didache, that it pleased God to save men» (C. H. DODD, *The Apostolic Preaching*, 1936, London, 8 ff.). The *locus classicus* is I Cor XV, 1 ff. Contemporary events have revealed this danger; Thomas Ohm, while stressing the need for adaptation, discusses the possible dangers inherent therein, in «Akkommodation,» *Handbuch theologischer Grundbegriffe*, I (1962) 25-30. See also the discussions in the *Concise Dictionary of the Christian World Mission*, ed. S. Neill, London, 1970: «Accommodation» by S. NEILL; «Acculturation» by Frank LYNCH, SJ., and «Syncretism» by H. W. TURNER.

now celebrated decree of Propaganda Fide, issued in 1656: «Quid enim absurdius quam Galliam, Hispaniam, aut Italiam... in Sinas invehere? Non haec sed fidem importate... admiramini et laudate ea quae laudem merentur.» Nor did they need to be reminded of such time-honoured tags as Augustine's «In unaquaque provincia servandum esse, quod neque contra fidem, neque honestos mores fieri solet»; or Aquinas's «Nunquam aufert Apostolus consuetudinem, quae non impedit salutem. Ritus non impediens salutem non debet mutari propter vocationem ad fidem.»

The friar in the seventeenth-century China mission who is regarded by his critics as the epitome of bigotry and the most narrow-minded, intransigent and severe of all the mendicants was not a Franciscan, but a Dominican: Domingo Fernández Navarrete. Accordingly, he is worth quoting on the question of allowing civic ceremony and political practice to the converts. He poses the problem: «Si es imprudencia quitar al Chino lo político,» and then proceeds to discuss the matter: «Parece que la resolución deste punto es fácil, y cierto el dezir, que es imprudencia intentar quitar al Chino lo político, y civil, que por millares de años tienen assentado, y establecido aquella Nación... No sólo hemos sido los de las dos [mendicant] Religiones notados desto, sino también Padres muy graves de la Compañía [de Jesús]... Confiesso, que siento mucho, quando veo escrito en papeles, y oygo dezir a algunos que no permitimos lo político a los Chinas, y que por esto ay pocos Christianos, se siguen alborotos, y se cierra la puerta para la conversón, &c. ... suponer y assentar en que es pure político, y luego afirmar, que no lo queremos permitir es calumnia clara, y injuria conocida, bautizada con nombre de imprudencia. Siempre fuy y fuymos de parecer, que lo político y civil, no sólo se debe permitir, sino aprobar positivamente; siempre me pareció mal el dezir, que se ha de permitir lo político, si lo político es bueno y razonable, como de hecho lo es, no se permite, sino que se aprueba, se admire [sic], y abraça; y no siendo esto impedimento para la Ley de Dios, ¿por qué se ha de quitar, o llegar a ello? *Gratia non destruit sed perficit naturam.* Tampoco destruye la policía, perficionala, sí. Viene aquí lo que en otra parte escriví de San Agustín, Epist. 18, cap. 5: Que lo que no se opone a la Fe, o buenas costumbres, no se debe variar, sino dexarlo en su ser; conviene con Santo Thomás, que dixo en otro lugar, que ay costumbres, que *Nec prosunt, nec obsunt,* a lo que toca a nuestra Religión, en lo qual no se debe meter el Missionario. ... Que no convenga mudar al Chino su policía, lo dize con brevedad Cayetano sobre el mesmo lugar de San Pablo: *Quia suavior est homini Ritus sibi consuetus.* ... en ninguna manera nos metemos, ni tratamos de lo Civil, y Político, sino sólo de lo ceremonial y Religioso de aquella Nación. Aquí está el punto de la dificultad.» [112]

It was this same friar who believed in accommodation as far as possible, but his notion of what was reasonable and possible differed somewhat from the definition of those Jesuits who followed Ricci. One formative element in his attitude, at least in part, was his respect for the Chinese; he could not see why it was necessary to adjust Christianity for a people as intellectually superior as they were, a people in every way capable of assimilating its doctrine whole and entire. He made an attempt, however, to find a middle way out of the dilemma besetting him, and he laid down a number of practical rules: the missionary should be cautious, never showing any sign of over-confidence, should be gentle and he should never rely upon scripture quotations in argument, for, admirable though they were for beating down a heretic, they were obviously useless in China. The Chinese must be dealt with on their own ground, and argued with out of their own books, which must be quoted at them; and at all times the basis of argument was to be natural reason.

In similar spirit he urged that: «se debe extender lo posible la Theulugía [sic], para favorecer, en quanto se pudiere a las plantas tiernas, que como no han llegado a echar raíces, están expuestas a que cualquier ventecillo dé con ellas en tierra.» Again, elsewhere: «andémosles aora con blanduras, y suavidades; muy bien saldrán de sus errores y pecados. *Durus predicator contra duros in malo veniebat*» [113]

This is a «narrow-minded mendicant» view; but at the same time there were limits to benevolence and benignity; a priest was a «compass, not

---

[112] «The Church, from the beginning down to our own time, has always followed this wise practice: let not the Gospel on being introduced into any new land destroy or extinguish whatever its people possess that is naturally good, just or beautiful»: PIUS XII, *Evangelii Praecones*, 1951. Despite these claims not everyone is convinced, and it is possible to find a modern writer stating that «the Church in Japan, China and other eastern nations, has allowed the converted Catholics to keep their civic customs, thus coming round to what the [seventeenth-century China] Jesuits allowed them.»

[113] D. FERNANDEZ NAVARRETE, OP., *Tratados históricos... de China*, Madrid, 1676, 438; idem., *Controversias antiguas y modernas... de la gran China*, Madrid (printed,

a weathercock turning before every oriental breeze»: «no seamos missionarios cocineros o taberneros que guisemos la doctrina al paladar de los Gentiles... no conviene seamos camaleones.» There was even a quotation from Confucius to fit the case: «... nos dexó buen exemplo el Confucio, el qual... dize: "Yo soy pregonero de doctrina, no inventor de ella, la que yo enseño al mundo, no es nueva, ni imaginación mía, es de los antiguos"...» [114] The friars were not prepared to countenance novelties where they believed the First Commandment was involved. They were also prepared to see many reject them and turn away because their message was too demanding; like the rich fool in the Gospels.

* * *

The Chinese devotion to ancestors presented many serious problems for the missionaries. Among these was the question of the eternal fate of Confucius. Had he been damned or saved? Now here great prudence and caution were required, and whatever the friars may have thought privately they learnt to be careful. For example, the Franciscan Caballero de Santa María explained how the mendicants dealt with mandarins' questions: «quando hablassen con alguno, cordura tenían para hablar con cortesía y la razón en la mano ... y quando acerca de las cosas de sus difuntos y Kumçu les han hablado, no ha sido con la aspereza, que aquí pintan los Padres [Jesuitas], sino procurando con razón conservarlos, con cortesía, y buen modo; y si no lo oyen assí, bien saben con buena sazón y palabras de benevolencia despedirse de ellos &c.» [115] Yet writers such as T. I. Dunin-Szpot, SJ., asserted that the mendicants «*sine necessitate* [my italics] dicunt et docent eum (Confucium) cum aliis inferni poenis torqueri»; but the answer to this and similar allegation had been given by a friar years before: «no nos hizo el Señor tan imprudentes e ignorantes... nuestro estilo pues es en no tratar estos puntos con los gentiles, que no muestran afición a el baptismo y si ellos lo tocan procuramos divertir la plática.» [116]

---

but not published, though there are copies in the *Biblioteca Nacional*, Madrid; *Santa Cruz Library*, Valladolid; *British Library*, London; the *Angelica Library*, Rome; *Jesuit Archives*, Rome; *Public Library*, New York),46-7, 98, 292, 400; idem, MS: «Ratificación de verdades,» *Biblioteca Nacional*, Madrid, MS. No. 7522, fol. 33.

114 NAVARRETE, *Tratados*, 153; *Controversias*, 8, 174, 230, 394, 399-400.

115 Quoted in NAVARRETE, *Controversias*, 543.

116 GUTIERREZ, oc., 567; fr. Francisco Varo, *Declaración*, «British Museum Add.» Mss. No. 16, 933, fol. 239.

The precise problem of the salvation or otherwise of non-Christians was no new problem though it had been made acute by the discovery of the New World. Missionaries there were frequently asked why God had not sent them earlier, to save the dead ancestors. To this they were wont to answer in the terms of the old scholastic dictum: «facienti quod in se est, Deus non denegat gratiam.» [117] This, or something similar, is found in Origen who, commenting on John 13:17, has this: «And to all reasonable souls it hath been said above: Whatsoever things any of you did in ignorance, not knowing God clearly, all his sins shall be forgiven him.» [118]

The sort of embarrassing situation in which a missionary often found himself is as follows: a priest, here named «Ai Ju-lüeh,» is being quizzed by the writer, Huang Chen, concerning the fate of the ancestors of the Chinese. The questioner is troubled about the Christian teaching that a man should only have one wife, since Chinese ancestor-veneration made it inevitable that there should be concubines and secondary wives. Huang Chen writes: «Their [Christian] religion has ten commandments, and they say that if concubines are taken because no son has been born, then one has broken a great commandment and must certainly enter hell. If this is so, then the sage emperors and illustrious kings who have hitherto possessed concubines will not be able to avoid the hell of the Lord of Heaven [of the Christians].

I made enquiries concerning this matter and asked: "King Wen possessed many queens and concubines, what do you say to this?" Ai Ju-lüeh thought deeply for a long time, but did not reply. The second day I again enquired about this, and again he thought deeply, but did not answer. On the third day I enquired yet again and said. "You must explain the meaning of this clearly, setting up a principle valid for ever. Only in this way can you bring people to understand and take refuge in this religion, being completely free from doubt." Ai again thought deeply for a considerable period of time, and then said with great hesitation: "At the outset I did not wish to speak, but now I will indeed speak." Again he hesitated for a long time and then said slowly: "I shall speak to you, elder brother, but in the presence of others I would certainly say nothing. I fear that King Wen too has entered hell!" Then hesitatingly, changing his line of speech, he said: "Let us talk about principles instead

---

117 See L. Capéran, *Le problème de salut des infidèles*, 2vv. Toulouse, 1935. This work has been re-written for an up-dated 1961 edition.

118 Quoted in M. R. James, *Apocryphal New Testament*, Oxford, 1953, 18.

of personalities, for it could be that King Wen later repented bitterly, and is therefore not a subject for discussion."

Now, their religion maintains that after a commandment has been broken it is possible to return to the Lord of Heaven and to repent with sincerity. Thus the punishment of hell can be avoided. But if right up the drawing of the last breath one refuses to repent, then, alas, nothing will avail.

These are poverty-stricken and evasive phrases with which they defame and slander sage men.» [119]

Contrary to what many would assume, the embarrassed missionary «Ai Ju-lüeh», here cornerned into making a harsh statement rather than a compromise, was not a narrow-minded mendicant, but the celebrated Jesuit Giulio Aleni (1582-1649). Aleni was praised by friar and Father alike: the Jesuit Gabriel de Magalhães called him «outro Xavier,» and Father Ignácio Lobo described him as «learned, and one of the most intelligent men we have in China today. In both word and deed he is circumspect. Everything he does is preceded by mature reflection»; and Friar Antonio de Santa María concurs: «courteous, learned and able... a master of the Chinese language, he was really the oracle of the province in which he lived.» A modern Jesuit declares that «Aleni was well acquainted with Chinese psychology... one of the greatest of the early Jesuits... [with] an extraordinary mastery of Chinese culture. It is related that he never failed to observe in minute detail the ritual of cultivated society [which] endeared him to the hearts of most of those who met him ... he was widely known as the "Western Confucius."» [120]

Nothing could show more clearly the manifold and complex problems of the China mission, and how Jesuit Fathers, for all their renowned skills, suffered as much as friars when faced with persistent questioners. It also shows that the Fathers, like the friars, sometimes put a limit to their concessions. In other words, it suggests that the general picture of the all-accommodating and permissive Jesuit is as overdrawn as is the picture of the harsh, non-compromising friar.

* * *

---

119 Quoted in D. LANCASHIRE, *Anti-Christian Polemics in 17th-century China,* Church History, 38 (1969) 231-2.

120 Magalhães: Biblioteca da Ajuda, Lisboa, Jesuitas na Asia, 49-V-12, f. 511; DUNNE, oc., 147, 188, 191, 260-62.

Another problem confronting the missionaries has already been touched upon, namely the nature of the Rites practised by the Chinese in honour of Confucius and of the dead. Ricci (as has been said above) had already decided that these Rites were *perhaps* innocent of superstition; with this diagnosis the friars differed. One of the reasons for this divergence of interpretation lay in that those Jesuits who agreed with Ricci (the «Riccistas») sought their explanation of the Rites in the ancient classical texts; but the friars, and those dissident Jesuits who agreed with them, based their understanding of contemporary Chinese religious thought not upon the classics themselves, but upon the later commentators on those same texts. An analogy might be drawn between those Christians who go directly to the Bible for their conception of their Faith, and those who, instead, prefer tradition and the Fathers of the Church for their interpretation. The friars emphasized this analogy by pointing out that Christians would resent foreigners who, within a few years of their arrival in Europe, began explicating the Scriptures in a sense contrary to that of the Fathers and contemporary theologians.

The question of the permissibility of the Rites involved yet another problem. The Chinese, who were largely indifferent to doctrinal niceties, could not easily understand the Christian concept of exclusiveness; for them, one religion did not necessarily preclude belief in yet another, and a Chinese could practise different cults without any embarrassment. «The three doctrines of Confucianism, Taoism, Buddhism,» said the proverb, «like seeds, leaves, and flowers, all spring from the same root.» Or, as the Wan-li Emperor expressed it: «Buddhism and Taoism are the wings of Confucianism.» To do as the Jesuits did, and permit converts to keep some of their former Rites, on the grounds that they were «*probably*» not superstitious, seemed to many friars to be underrating the risks; to be dangerously like condoning the traditional Chinese attitude to syncretism; to be cooperating with an innate tendency to assimilate and harmonize incompatibles.

In this the friars were obviously influenced by their past experience. In Manila they had made converts of Chinese who seemed zealous Catholics, but who had sometimes turned out to be mere «rice Christians», or else had been suddenly detected observing their old rites in cheerful conjunction with their newly-adopted creed. This led to a fear that the Chinese were inconstant and must be tried and proved in their faith before being trusted. The friars' earlier experiences in America had made them cautious. Long before, friar Motolinía had noted how the Aztecs, who seemed to have one hundred gods, had no objection to adding yet another, namely that of their conquerors. In this they too seemed like the Chinese who were ready to see their three cults of Buddhism, Taoism, Confucianism (the *San Chiao*) move over to make way for a fourth. Christ would be merely an addition to the national pantheon.

For the friars there was a terrible irony in all this. In America their contemporaries had constantly to fight native underground resistance movements. There, idols and pagan statuettes were hidden on the Catholic altar, behind the Cross or Christ's image, so that they could still be adored in disguise by natives who were practising their own form of «directing the intention.» And this persisted despite unceasing and strict vigilance. Yet in China, or so it seemed to the friars, some converts were being permitted to do just the opposite: they placed their Crosses upon the pagan altars, so that Christ could be adored discreetly, humiliatingly, in shared devotions in which He took second place. In Mexico the old gods skulked in the background; in China perhaps it was Christ who would never leave the shadows. This permissiveness moreover was being practised in a land where tolerance of all beliefs («an amiable politeness towards possibilities») made it especially necessary for Catholicism to retain its distinctive features as firmly as possible if it was to survive and retain its identity. [121]

* * *

There remained yet another problem: the so-called Term Question (see p. 45 above). This was no novelty for the friars when they arrived in China, with their collective American experience behind them. This delicate problem arose early on in their work in New Spain: «There were partisan views which tended to end in compromise. How were Christian names and concepts unknown to the natives to be rendered? Should a Nahuatl equivalent be given for *Espíritu Santo*, for *ángel*, *alma?* Was God to be rendered as *teotl?*» The use of Spanish terms, it was argued,

---

121 There can be no doubt that any Church established by the Jesuits on a two-tiered system, in which initiates adored Christ Crucified behind closed doors, first-stage neophytes being held back from such mysteries, would inevitably have aroused the suspicions of the Chinese authorities. This is not to say that such a proposal was mooted; but any system even remotely resembling it would suffice to bring down trouble upon the Christians.

would «make Christian teachings superficial and unassimilated in the native mentality»; those who opposed Nahuatl usage feared it would contaminate Christian doctrine with pagan concepts.[122] Sometimes the friars were even obliged to alter Latin liturgical texts: in Mexico a Latin word was deleted from the Mass because of possible misunderstanding by the Indians: «Papa» was the Nahuatl word for a priest, so that in the Collect of the Mass «Papam» was replaced by «Pontificem nostrum» lest the converts should think their old priests were being commemorated. Sometimes the friars' tolerance of native expressions had unhappy results, as when the Blessed Virgin was confounded in the popular mind with the old goddess Tonantzin.[123]

But far more dramatic in its consequences was the problem of the public display of the crucifix in China. Here again, the friars had previous experience of the problem, though in a slightly different form. The Mexican Indians had an intense devotion to the cross, some form of which had been revered by them before the conquest, unrelated therefore to Christianity. To the Tlascalans, for example, the cross was a representation of the four cardinal points of the compass and was known as «the tree that sustains life.» Of this devotion fray Motolinía writes: «Está tan ensalzada en esta tierra la señal de la cruz por todos los pueblos y caminos, que se dice que ninguna parte de la cristiandad está más ensalzada, ni adonde tantas ni tales ni tan altas cruces haya.»[124]

The conquistadores in their initial progress across Mexico had erected a cross in each town they passed through. To avoid desecration, the figure of Christ had been omitted from many of these monuments: the symbols of the Passion replaced the representation of the Saviour. Some crosses, for instance, were enriched with the Crown of Thorns at the intersection of the arms, and there were dripping patches of blood where the nails had been; others showed the Franciscan escutcheon of the Five Wounds; sometimes episodes of the Passion were carved on the shaft and arms. McAndrew finds nothing similar to these monumental crosses

---

[122] Charles E. Dibble, *The Nahuatlization of Christianity* in Edmonson, oc., 226-7; for a neat summary of the problem see F. Esteve Barba, *Cultura virreinal*, Barcelona, 1965, 78, 142; and Ricard, oc., 287; Phelan, *Hispanization*, 57.

[123] Term problems remain with us: a recent letter in the *London Times* objects to the use of the expression «the Lord's Table»: «to Catholics the use of the word «table» is inadequate and even ... mildly offensive. Tables are for meals: God's sacrifice is offered upon an altar.» *Times*, 2 February 1978.

[124] Motolinía, *Historia de los indios de la Nueva España*, Trat. II, ch. 9.

anywhere in Europe. And at least one of them he described as being «as ferocious as any pre-conquest sculpture.» [125]

This intense Indian devotion to the Cross was sometimes spoilt for the friars when on occasions they discovered it was contaminated. Motolinía lamented that the friars had been informed that sometimes «los indios escondían los ídolos y ponían en los pies de las cruces o en aquellas gradas debajo de las piedras.» Sometimes, too, emblems from the pre-Christian past were incorporated into the crosses by native artists. In one church in Michoacán the Franciscan escutcheon is depicted with a small obsidian disc on the intersection of the arms of Christ and St Francis, and there are other instances of this. The purpose of the disc was to endow the monument with life, as in the pagan past. [126].

The friars therefore were no strangers to problems associated with the display of the Crucifix, and were capable of adaptation and modifications to suit particular circumstances. But on arrival in China they concluded that the Jesuits were over-cautious in their keeping the cross withdrawn (See pp. 47-48 above). They were also distressed when the Jesuits, not content with this, tried to influence the friars to do the same. What one modern Jesuit considers to have been excessive timidity was regarded by the friars as baffling cowardice. [127] By reaction, and anxious to show that they at least were ready to «preach Christ and Him Crucified» without shame, they tended (in the beginning, it must be stressed) to make the Cross the centre of their preaching. The friars believed that they had been sent «ut dicant in nationibus quia Dominus regnavit a ligno.» Or in the words of Antonio de Santa María, «[Christ] a todo el mundo se quiso mostrar crucificado, aviéndose mostrado a solos tres transfigurado.» [128]

It has been said above that, partly as a result of Pascal's Fifth Letter, it was widely believed in Europe that the Jesuits were systematically keeping the Cross from the Chinese so as not to scandalise them. Now, of course, it is unthinkable that this should have been true; but it is equally unthinkable that the friars could have invented the accusation in the unqualified form which spread abroad. There must then have been

---

125 His discussion of this remarkable example of adaptation is at oc. 247 ff.

126 R. Garcia Granados, *Reminiscencias idolátricas en monumentos coloniales,* «Anales del Instituto de Investigaciones estéticas,» II (1942) 55: and Motolinia, oc., Trat. I, chs. 3 and 4. Cf. the mingling of Islamic and Christian art motifs in Spanish late medieval churches as described above.

127 Gutierrez, oc., 555: «No se mostraron en esto dignos imitadores de Javier...»

128 Navarrete, *Controversias*, 485, 510.

some fire behind this particular smoke. In fact the friars did not make this accusation baldly; what they did complain of was that the Jesuits delayed the teaching of the Passion, lest, in Father Roboredo's words «demus sancta canibus.» The friars clarified their position: «ni decimos que no predican a Cristo Crucificado, sino que le muestran muy tarde.» Jesuit prudence, and the wish to make Christ's burden light and his yoke sweet, seemed to the friars to go too far. They claimed that the Chinese were not scandalised by the Passion; and this was incidentally confirmed by a Jesuit, Furtado, writing to his General in 1636: «Atque generaliter loquendo, habent omnes christiani summam devotionem erga hoc sanctum mysterium.» [129]

Against this must be set the account in a contemporary friar's history published in Manila in 1640. He describes how a friar colleague in China in the 1630s writes to Manila begging for «ymágenes de la Virgen del Rosario y de Cristo Crucificado. Del cual dice, que halló muy poca noticia entre los pocos fieles que halló en el Reyno, porque los ministros del Evangelio esperaban, para dár se la mayor, a que fuesen más adultos en la fe, por parecerles Dios Crucificado y muerto bocado duro para principiantes: no porque no les den noticia de El cuando los cathequiçan, sino porque después no les tratan más de este misterio, ni les muestran al Señor Crucificado, si no es el Viernes Santo, por mayor respeto y devoción: pero el padre fray Angel pensaba dár se lo a conocer con la primera de su doctrina y muy de ordinario, que es más acertado.» [130]

As a result of the friars' arrival in China, and the consequent publicity given to their allegations of tardiness on the part of the Jesuits, the latter changed their policy; but the mendicants remained suspicious and uneasy for some years towards these colleagues who had moved «con pies de plomo» in this matter. And certainly suspicions lingered on in Rome for some time. The Jesuits produced illustrated accounts of the Passion between 1635 and 1637; including, wrote Antonio de Santa María, «[uno] impresso y compuesto por el Padre Iulio Aleni de la Compañía, y se vende públicamente desde el año de treinta y siete y treinta y ocho... [131]

---

129 NAVARRETE, oc., 557; GUTIERREZ, oc., 557; BIERMANN, oc., 200.

130 Diego ADUARTE, OP., *Historia de la provincia del S. Rosario*... II, Manila, 1640, 270-1. The Jesuits sought to prevent the publication of this work.

131 Santa María, in NAVARRETE, *Controversias*, 464, 510-11. The most balanced account of all this is in BIERMANN, oc., 200 ff. Earlier (1623) Aleni had produced a geography for Chinese readers; in his description of Judaea he «presents the birth, life and ascension (but not the crucifixion) of Jesus.» This omission suggests that

THE FRIARS' HANDS ARE TIED

We end with the question asked at the beginning. The friars had plenty of collective experience as evangelists, and a history of adaptation in America. When they reached China, a few years after the Jesuits, they might have been expected to follow the policy described by Motolinía: «Proveyó sabiamente la Iglesia, que en la conversión de algunos infieles y tierras nuevas, "los ministros que a la postre vinieren se conformen con los primeros hasta tener entera noticia de la tierra y gente adonde allegaren."» [132]

In China, however, the friars seemed to forget their earlier expansiveness in America and elsewhere, and to ignore Motolinía's words. They seemed to forget that in Mexico they had encouraged that same conflation of Christian and native art forms which had, centuries earlier, grown up in Spain between Christian and Muslim. They seemed to forget that in Mexico they had accommodated the text of the very Mass itself, and permitted a special form of the Crucifix to suit local conditions; that they had looked with amiable complacency («era cosa de reir,» said Motolinía) upon a juxtaposition of the old and new religions, as when the Tlascalans brought into church cooked food, lambs and pigs, and offered wax and doves; and on All Souls' Day they permitted the Indians to come to church to make offerings (maize, bread, chickens, chocolate) for their ancestors («el día de los finados... dan muchas ofrendas por sus difuntos,» says Motolinía). [133] They seemed to have forgotten how in former times in Mexico they had adopted Classical Nahuatl usages and style in a Christian context. In one Franciscan *Doctrina Christiana*, for instance, there is a passage that can be duplicated, apart from the use of the word «God,» in a prayer to Tezcatlipoca. [134]

«the book was written as an inducement to the unconverted literati»; it also shows that «not everything published by the Jesuits mentioned the Crucifixion in the pertinent places,» in spite of DUNNE oc., 275: B. HUNG-KAY LUK, *A Study of Giulio Aleni's «Chih-fang wai chi,»* in: «Bulletin: School of Oriental and African Studies,» London, XL (1977) 67, 83.

132 MOTOLINIA, oc., Trat. II, cap. 4.

133 The Indians' offerings were later given to the poor. It is noteworthy that this christianised form of an old pagan custom, encouraged by the friars in Mexico according to MOTOLINIA (oc., Tr. I, chaps. 4, 13), is precisely what Ricci, a few years later, was hoping to see come about in China: Ricci wrote: «... this ceremony... is devoid of idolatry and perhaps it can be said that there is no superstition, although it would be better to commute this into alms for the poor...» (ROSSO, oc., 72). On the face of it, then, there should have been nothing to alarm the friars in China. But in fact there was.

134 DIBBLE, oc., 232.

Why, it may be asked, in view of all this, did the mendicants in China behave so as to lay themselves open to accusations of inflexibility and of lack of imagination. There may be a number of answers: but there is one in particular. «*Los ministros que a la postre vinieren se conformen con los primeros hasta tener entera noticia de la tierra y gente adonde allegaren...*» That is all very well; but what if the first group refuse to help the innocent newcomers, despite «a moving plea»? And what if they refuse to help them gain «una entera noticia de la tierra»; indeed connive at (if not arrange) their deportation out of it? And, worse still, what if the first group appear to have gone astray and are yet unwilling to explain themselves or their peculiar situation?

One answer is suggested by friar Antonio de Santa María who, for all that he was the most charming, gentle, and charitable of the Franciscans in the Central Country, could yet speak plainly. In 1637 he declared that their entry into the empire was a «manifiesta providencia de Dios... para que así como San Francisco y Santo Domingo fueron llamados por Dios, para el reparo de la ruina que amenazaba en el siglo xiii a la sociedad, así sus hijos han sido elegidos por Dios, para reparar los falsos cimientos sobre que se edificaba la Religión cristiana en China.»[135] In other words, there were elements in the new mission that had a marked effect on their attitude. First of all, the friars felt their hands were tied; the situation had been pre-empted by the Jesuits and the mendicants found themselves with no room for manoeuvre. They were faced, they decided, with a *tabula mixta* by the Fathers, whose possessiveness, hostility, and refusal to explain, did nothing to help the situation. In addition, the friars' discovery of the great disunity among the Jesuits themselves as to the propriety of their conduct understandably increased their own doubts.

The mendicants, as we have seen, had already encountered many of the China mission problems earlier and elsewhere. But here there was another which was totally novel: Jesuit permissiveness on such a scale, and within an alleged monopoly mission. Accordingly, it can be argued that the friars never had the chance of looking upon the China scene with untroubled eyes: Jesuit strategy inevitably turned them towards hesitation, doubt, and caution, as they were faced from the start with

---

[135] Quoted by Lorenzo PEREZ, OFM., *Los Franciscanos en el extremo Oriente*, Archivum Franciscanum Historicum, 4 (1911) 52.

what seemed inexplicable conduct in their fellow missionaries. To put it emphatically (though no friar ever went so far) it must sometimes have seemed that they would have to correct the Jesuits at the same time as they were to convert the heathen. Perhaps one novelty on the Jesuit side would have been tolerable; but there were too many unexplained procedures in that one mission field. There were missionaries who were mandarins, others who were traders, and some who were cannon-founders; missionaries who *seemed* ashamed of the Cross but ready to condone superstition, and who were so determined to keep the field to themselves as to connive at the deportation of unwanted help-mates. In part, this explains why those of the mendicant tradition who had felt no qualms about using the fundamentalist catechism of Ponce de la Fuente in Mexico now shrank suspiciously from Ricci's catechism, though it was based on roughly similar principles.

«*Para reparar los falsos cimientos sobre que se edificaba la Religión cristiana en China*...» Caballero de Santa María obviously felt obliged to take a severe view of what seemed Jesuit laxity; so the friars were forced to jettison many of their own inclinations to experiment and to adopt a broadminded approach. The Jesuits, it may be thought, were praiseworthy, but the friars were realistic. For China had a long history of absorbing would-be conquerors, spiritual or any other kind. Mencius had said: «I have heard of barbarians being converted by China, but I have never heard of China being converted by barbarians.» To the friars it seemed that the Jesuits were marching, hypnotised, into those open, all-enveloping arms. In that world of amorphous, hazy, beliefs and agnosticisms, with disturbing rituals (described by some Chinese as civic, by others again, including the still respectable Father Roboredo, as superstitious, even religious), the friars clearly felt the need to stand up straight and eschew equivocation. [136] That is to say, the friars feared the Jesuits' concessions

---

136 «... aquella babilonia de libros y doctrinas exquisitíssimas, y con letras y vocablos llenos de equivocaciones, símbolos y enigmas...» (NAVARRETE, *Controversias* 153). And again: «... la sencillez y ... pureza de la santa Fe, la qual no admite mezcla de tantas invenciones Gentilicas, solo pastadas y dissimuladas con sola capa de humana policia, con solas unas precisiones, que haze la imaginacion...» (Santa María in ibid, 513, 553). Even Jesuits were sometimes confused: «Quam perplexos habuerit et sollicitos primos divinae Legis praecones (Riccium maximè) tanta varietas et confusio dogmatum, Sectarum, Librorum, Interpretum»: P. COUPLET, SJ., *Confucius Sinarum philosophus*, Paris, 1687, lx. The contemporary English Protestant, Samuel Purchas, praising the Jesuits' work in Asia, thought that if the Chinese were converted it did not matter which Christian Church they joined; any would be better than none. «Better a mixed

for the very reason that the Freethinkers were later to welcome them: they seemed to forward the cause of Deism because their converts would soon lose any sense of precise religious identity.

There was a further problem. The Jesuits justified their decisions by appealing to the theory of Probabilism, which was itself then being hotly debated by the theologians. [137] The friars were not impressed by what they regarded as a dubious theory, and they preferred safety to mere probability. One is reminded of Pascal, again, «Je ne me contente pas du probable, je cherche le sûr.» The Jesuits' methodology was expressed in the formula: «ritus Sinenses possunt tolerari quia solide probabile est illos esse licitos.» Yet the Fathers sometimes admitted they were skating on theologically thin ice. The celebrated Fr. Schall wrote in 1650 to fray Timoteo de San Antonio to concede that «Quamquam illud quod hactenus Paternitates vestrae secutae sunt, et magis probabile est et tutum, nostrum tamen *probabilitate non caret* [my italics], atque omnino illud sequi convenit.» This admission that the mendicants' method was safer was also repeated by another prominent Jesuit, Francesco Brancati, who declared «Nemo ex nostra Societate unquam condemnavit practicam opinionem Patrum aliorum; nam bene novimus nostram opinionem non esse demonstrationem, sed se continere intra limites opinionis probabilis.» [138]

The differences were not only abstract and theological. Though delicate, this aspect cannot be ignored, for there can be no doubt that the Jesuit

---

truth, then total errour: better a maymed Christ, than none at all.» The friars could not be expected to appreciate this view. Perhaps they saw where this would lead in time: e.g. in the nineteenth century a Bishop in China «thought that Roman Catholics had been wrong in introducing the doctrine of Transubstantiation in China» since it caused the Chinese to think foreigners were cannibals. (Victor PURCELL, in *The Historical Journal*, 6 (1963) 146).

137 Probabilism is neatly defined by the *Oxford English Dictionary*: «The doctrine that in matters of conscience on which authorities differ, it is lawful to follow any course in support of which the authority of a recognised doctor of the Church can be cited.» A modern Jesuit refines this further: «Les probabilistes ont toujours cherché des raisons intrinsèques à la probabilité d'une opinion morale; l'autorité des auteurs renommés (critère extrinsèque) en tant suffise en quant qu'ils ont posé des motifs réels et fondés pour la probabilité d'une opinion en cause» (M. BATLLORI, SJ., *De historia SJ in Gallia*, «Archivum Historicum SJ,» 35 (1966) 258. Anxiety over the permissiveness implied in Probabilism provoked Probabiliorism, «according to which it is claimed in opposition to probabilism that that side on which the evidence preponderates is more probably right and therefore ought to be followed.» One may feel that this encapsulates the friars' attitude in the China mission.

138 GUTIERREZ, OC., 522; NAVARRETE, *Controversias*, 318; INTORCETTA, *De cultu sinensi*, quotes Schall's remarks; but suggests that his statement that the friars' method was «magis probabile et tutum» was meant ironically (303-4). This may be so: Schall was notoriously sarcastic.

attitude of superiority, their irritating tendency to address other colleagues *de haut en bas*, caused natural resentment. This had been a mark of the Jesuit from the beginning, and it was a result of their party spirit. For example, «When in Rome a father mentioned Texeda [a Franciscan distinguished for his holiness] as an example of humility to a novice, Ignatius told him with that severe expression he had, when he gave a scolding: are there no examples of humility in the Society to give a novice and he forbade him to have any further conversation with the novices.» [139] Where Ignatius led other Jesuits followed, and «Polanco's official history has this to say about the Jesuits' special standing: "It must be confessed that experience teaches that a very close friendship with priests who are not of the Society, even though in other respects they are good and spiritual men and actively help others, is not to be cultivated.» [140]

CONVERSION BY SCIENCE OR MEDICINE

It may be of interest to assess here the Jesuits' and the friars' proposals to win over the Chinese by the use of human means. The friars were anticipating modern practice in deciding on medicine, and they also enjoyed considerable success. But they failed in their chief aim: to convert through medicine. One leper is reported to have returned to thank Christ, but few Chinese are recorded as having accepted the Faith as a result of being cured of some physical illness. Moreover, medical practice could be dangerous sometimes, especially if the missionary failed to cure some important dignitary who might well harbour resentment or suspect an attempt to harm him. [141] (We have a contemporary example of this from the opposite pole: Transcendental Meditation, recently introduced into the West as a species of mental hygiene and psychological welfare,

---

139 Quoted by P. Penning de VRIES, SJ., *Protestants and other Spirituals*, «Archivum Historicum Soc. Jesu,» 40 (1971) 478-9. Possibly Ignatius here feared «alumbrado» influence.

140 Quoted in M. FOSS, *The Founding of the Jesuits, 1540*, London, 1969, 136. The intense pride that the contemporary Jesuit felt in the Society is nowhere more clearly depicted than in the extraordinary jubilee volume published by them in 1640, the *Imago Primi Saeculi*, a strange work which deserves a study all to itself. It contains a number of references to the China missions, including one apparent tilt at the friars: «Ingenti hic opus fuit & patientia & prudentia, ne inconsultus fervor simul cum Societate spem omnem istius tam nobilis tamque immensi Regni exterminaret» (397).

141 For examples of mistaken diagnoses and the result see F. PRANDI (ed.), *Memoirs of Father Ripa*, London, 1844, 42.

has also been denounced as a veiled form of Hinduism and its propagators of being disguised missionaries).

The Jesuits, with their advocacy of science as a mission aid, also had problems. At first however this was not apparent, for Ricci and his colleagues had arrived in China at a lucky moment for their strategy. Chinese science was then in decline, as it had been since the fifteenth century. There was no one to tell the Jesuits of the Central Country's former mathematical glories, that Chinese science had often been in advance of the West during the Middle Ages, or that the three inventions reckoned by Bacon to be the keys to the transformation of Europe all came from China: printing, gunpowder and the compass. [142] It is noteworthy that Columbus's voyages in search of a westward route to China were made possible by two Chinese inventions: The magnetic compass and the sternpost rudder.

But in other ways the scientist-missionaries were less fortunate. In Europe, science was making such strides that the Church was not always ready to assimilate the newest theories, and the Jesuits had to conform. Thus, they soon found that their role as purveyors of scientific knowledge was becoming ambiguous, that they were no longer able to play fully their adopted part. The condemnation of Galileo created a major crisis for them. News of Galileo's work had reached China in 1615, relatively quickly for those days, and the Jesuits propagated his theories as long as they could. But after his denunciation by Rome the «new» science they were preaching became essentially medieval. The Fathers transmitted knowledge of Galileo's telescopes, but they could not transmit the Copernican heliocentric theory, thus retarding rather than advancing Chinese astronomy: «Urania's feet were bound,» as Joseph Needham puts it. [143] As a result Copernican ideas were not known in China until the

---

[142] Many Chinese suspected this was so. The K'ang-hsi emperor himself declared that since all mathematics derive from the Book of Changes, western methods were obviously Chinese in origin. See also the remark of Joseph Needham: «There was a Jesuit transmission in all these sciences (chemistry, botany, zoology) but it was westwards, not eastwards.» (NEEDHAM, oc., V (3), 221). For this section I have relied on Needham, especially his vols. III and V.

[143] «Jesuit astronomy... was basically characteristic of Europe *before* the Copernican Revolution. In 1650 it may have resembled that taught by conservative astronomers in Europe, but by 1700 it was ludicrously absolete...» Kiyosi YABUUTI, *Chinese Astronomy: Development and Limiting Factors* in: S. NAKAYAMA, *Chinese Science. In honour of the 70th birthday of J. Needham,* Cambridge, Mass., 1973, 100-102. Cf. also: «On the whole one concludes that the Jesuit contribution [to Chinese science] was not an unmixed blessing» (NEEDHAM, oc., III, 447); and: «on balance I would have to

beginning of the nineteenth century. In the long run, then, the strategy of calling Western science to commend Western religion was dangerous, for in time, when the Chinese discovered the Jesuits' suppressions of the discoveries of Galileo and others, they would come to doubt the validity of their religious teaching, since both had been deliberately linked.

Also to be considered is the effect of this strategy upon the character of the Fathers themselves. Not being disinterested scientists they were sometimes tempted to resort to parlour-tricks, rather than pure experiments, in order to gain an end. [144] In the early years they were often thought by the Chinese to be alchemists. Joseph Needham discusses this: «If the Jesuits were assumed now and then to be alchemists and magicians there is some reason for believing that they had only themselves to thank.

This is illustrated in a fascinating letter addressed from Peking in the autumn of 1735 by Dominique Parrenin... to one of the Academicians in Paris,... Parrenin recalls... that being in attendance on the Khang-Hsi emperor during a winter hunting expedition, he had found himself drawn on to convince a group of scholars, including two Ministers of State and ten Han-Lin Academicians, that one could make water freeze near a hot brazier... when the experiment was tried with a bowl of snow standing in a dish of water, he managed to slip some saltpetre surreptitiously into the cup, ... and induced the water in the saucer to freeze solid although quite close to the fire... The success of his demonstration was complete, but he neither told nor explained what he had done. The next day he worked another «miracle» when he produced a powder which «could blow a hole through an iron spoon,» awakening still further the admiration of the company, one of whom remarked that thenceforward he would feel compelled to believe anything Parrenin said, and feared that he might therefore be deceived. "I am incapable of deceiving anyone," said Parrenin "and on the contrary would be only too happy to be able to undeceive you from the religious errors which you are in, and which

---

conclude that their work was favorable... It is nevertheless the case that in certain respects (as for example their adherence to the Ptolemaic world-view, the crystalline spheres of medieval cosmology...) they did have a retarding effect» (*ex relatione* J. Needham).

144 Maritain bitingly dismisses the figure of the Jesuit-scientist whom he defines as an apologist in disguise: «A-t-on jamais vu un savant s'agenouiller devant le monde (à moins que par chance il ne soit jésuite, mais alors ce n'est pas un pur savant, c'est un apologiste déguisé)?»: Jacques MARITAIN, *Le Paysan de la Garonne*, Paris, 1966, 85.

are of far greater consequence for your happiness than the ignorance of a few natural phenomena."

On yet another occasion, when he had impressed his audience by a scientific demonstration of this kind, he addressed them as follows: "you must remember that you are giving me your word that you will hereafter listen to me with greater docility when I speak to you of a subject far more elevated and of infinite advantage to you since it will gain for you eternal felicity." And he concluded his account [to Paris] by saying that in dealing with Chinese scholars "one must gain their esteem by a knowledge of natural things, which mostly they lack, but about which they are curious to learn — nothing better disposes them to attend to our preaching of the sacred truths of Christianity."

Dominique Parrenin was an outstanding linguist, an estimable man and a devoted priest, yet his action in using physico-chemical knowledge to perform tricks with the object of inducing belief in the body of religious dogma which he represented, and without explaining the meaning of his demonstrations to his listeners, was something we may find it hard to forgive today... seen in the light of the ethic of the scientific world community of today there was something almost sacrilegious in Parrenin's attitude. Thaumaturgy was in bad taste, to say the least, when what was called for at that particular time and place, in eighteenth-century China, was the transmission of true chemical knowledge and understanding.» [145]

Scientific skill brought other dangers: it could arouse jealousy in the powerful, and bring still more problems. The persecution of 1664 was believed by the friars to stem from the resentment of Chinese astronomers who had been proved wrong in an experiment carried out by the Jesuit

---

[145] NEEDHAM oc., V (3) 255-7; quotations slightly abbreviated. For an earlier instance of misguided, if well-intentioned, use of «superior knowledge» for divine ends, see the account of Schall's drafting of a fictitious oracle, allegedly based on astronomical observations, used as a means of reprimanding the Shun-chi emperor in 1654: Rosso oc., 116-118. These scientific aberrations might be paralleled in the theological field by the Jesuits' development of the theory of «Figurism» in China. This thesis (defended only by a handful of French Fathers) maintained that both the Old and New Testaments, the Fall and Redemption, even the Immaculate Conception, were foreshadowed in the ancient Chinese classics. Such ideas alarmed the majority of Jesuits, and most outsiders, and showed how Ricci's cautious Probabilism had moved into fantastic areas. Flexibility is admirable, but it is in the very nature of elastic to grow looser. For Figurism, see the essential and sober study of Virgile PINOT, *La Chine et la formation de l'Esprit philosophique en France (1640-1740)*, Paris, 1932, 281-366.

Father Adam Schall.[146] From this belief there came the joking pun, «One Adam got us driven out of Paradise, and another out of China»; and the parody of St Paul's words, «We have all sinned in Adam.»

* * *

Ultimately then the Fathers' stratagems were bound to fail. They hoped to win the Chinese for the Faith with the bait of their science, but just as the seventeenth-century Englishmen of the Royal Society received with gratitude their contributions to geographical and mathematical knowledge but repudiated their religion, so too the literati of China learnt to distinguish between «new» science and the «western» religion.

The conversion of China to Catholicism remains, for many, one of the «might-have-beens» of history; and those who hold this view of the matter are quick to blame the friars for its failure to come about. The truth is that both groups were destined to fail, for there would have to be limits to even the most complaisant Jesuit's flexibility. The matter was summed up succintly by an 18th-century Chinese Emperor: «In China, the teaching of the sages and worthies has always enlightened us. Who among us will destroy the tablets of their deceased parents and discontinue sacrifice to their ancestors, and pay the same homage to the [Christian] Lord of Heaven as they did to their own parents and ancestors? This is the first Commandment of their dogma, yet it would be the first obstacle to our adopting it.»[147]

Douglas Lancashire (oc 240-1) ponders whether Ricci's policy of «completing Confucianism» and grafting Christianity on to the Chinese tradition could have succeeded if there had been no Rites Controversy.

---

146 It was an incident later recalled by the K'ang-hsi emperor: «I realized, too, that Western mathematics has its uses. I first grew interested in this subject shortly after I came to the throne, during the confrontations between the Jesuit Adam Schall and his Chinese critic, Yang Kuang-hsien, when the two men argued the merits of their respective techniques by the Wu-men Gate and none of the great officials there knew what was going on.»: Jonathan D. SPENCE, *Emperor of China: Self-portrait of K'ang-hsi*, New York, 1974, 72.

147 LO-SHU FU, *A Documentary Chronicle of Sino-Western Relations (1644-1820)*, Tucson, II, 1966, 339. Some realistic Jesuits saw the impossibility of making K'ang-hsi into a new Constantine: «... exceptuando milagre, ... he moralmente impossivel que o Emperador da China se possa fazer Christão...» G. MAGALHAES, SJ., *The Annual Letter for 1673-74*, Ajuda Library, Lisboa, Jesuitas na Asia, 49-V-16, fol. 183 r/v. This has been put more bluntly by Professor C. R. Boxer: «They [the Jesuits] had little more chance of converting the Emperor of China, than they had of baptizing the Man in the Moon,» in *Indonesië*, 9 (1956), 345-8.

He concludes that there were two major obstacles to Ricci's dream: Christianity would have had to replace both Buddhism and Taoism, while simultaneously emulating Buddhism by exerting an influence upon Confucianism, which (it was suspected) the Christians would want ultimately to eliminate. Such an achievement sounds impossible in human terms; and all the more so when the very heralds of the Faith seemed to be yielding to the notorious syncretistic «pull» of Chinese culture. The specialist historian Latourette (oc III, 355) finds «it is by no means certain that had Rome taken the opposite position and sanctioned the Jesuit accommodation to Chinese culture Christianity would have made more headway.» Even Gutiérrez (oc 530) admits that, praiseworthy though it might be, the Jesuits' policy brought dangers with it: it might «declinar en ocasiones a un laxismo comprometedor para el mensaje evangélico del que eran portadores.» In a recent book [148] René Laurentin comments on how Nestorian Christianity, if we may judge from the Nestorian Monument (discovered in the 17th century), had been impregnated with Buddhist, Taoist and Confucian elements, just as China had earlier sinicized Buddhism before accepting it. [149] Owen Lattimore finds a third example of this ability to absorb and transform a foreign teaching in the Chinese take-over of communism: Marxism-Leninism-Stalinism in China has been reworked and suffered a sea-change, to emerge as the Thought of Chairman Mao. Lattimore goes on to ask this question: «If Rome had accepted the Jesuit contention that the veneration of ancestors was not a pagan worship but an admissible respect for genealogy in a family-grouped civilisation of high quality, would the outcome have been the Christianisation of China in a desirable form, or the sinisation of Christianity to an unacceptable degree?» [150] The unanswered question remains; but there seems little doubt of the reply.

* * *

---

148 R. LAURENTIN, *Chine et Christianisme. Après les Occasions Manquées,* Paris, 1977.

149 «Buddhism became more and more Chinese and more acceptable to the Chinese. I call this process the Sinicization of Buddhism in China»: Kenneth K. K. CH'EN, *The Chinese Transformation of Buddhism,* Princeton, 1973, 5-13; also see his *Buddhism in China,* Princeton, 1964, 484-5. And even the 17th-century Manchu conquerors of China had felt the need to compromise as much as possible by assimilating themselves to the customs of the Empire.

150 O. LATTIMORE, in *The Month,* XI, 2nd NS (1978), 170.

The Church took the problem of defining the nature of the Chinese Rites very seriously.[151] As early as 1644 fray Antonio de Santa María had warned Urban VIII, in his desire to do the right thing, that a condemnation of the Rites might lead to the extinction of Christianity in China. The Pope, however, firmly answered that there could be no compromise with truth. Later, Clement XI declared that the missions must be free not only of formal superstition, but from the very suspicion of such a thing; the freer the field of weeds, the more fruitful the harvest.[152] But the Jesuits continued to be convinced that their position was justifiable; and Rome continued uneasy and increasingly suspicious.

Finally the Rites were prohibited to converts as being intolerably syncretistic: they were forbidden «quia mali, non mali quia prohibiti.» Decrees to this effect were issued and all the resources of the *stylus curiae* were brought into play to prevent evasions and delaying tactics. Clement XI's *Ex illa die* (1715) was followed by the definitive *Ex quo singulari* (which repeated the text of *Ex illa die* within its own text) issued in 1742 by Benedict XIV, «The Pope of the Dialogue.» The care with which the matter was studied in Rome is described by an English Jesuit, Joseph Rickaby: «the question was examined and re-examined at Rome during more than forty years, under six Popes, Innocent XII, Clement XI, Innocent XIII, Benedict XIII, Clement XII and Benedict XIV. Chinese witnesses and Chinese documents were consulted in abundance. Every facility of representation was allowed and taken advantage of. The last Pope who examined the matter was a man of prodigious learning, the best canonist of his age, and had, in various subordinate official capacities, followed the question from the first. Yet Benedict XIV took exactly the same view as Clement XI... Certainly the argument from testimony is very strong.»[153]

* * *

Blame for any failure in China cannot be neatly apportioned. In any case, it seems as though the Central Country was always beyond conversion, except through revolution, and the Chinese Rites Controversy

---

151 Pastor thinks that it was probably as a result of the Holy See's experience with its diplomatists in China that Clement XI founded his special school for diplomats: *Popes*, Eng. tr., 33: 490. Fr. Antonio Sisto Rosso, OFM, however, informs me that the school was founded in 1701, only months after Clement XI's election. The Pope approved the foundation; the project was started just when the Maillard de Tournon legation was in the making.

152 Quoted in PASTOR, oc., 33: 428.

153 Joseph RICKABY, SJ., *Clement XI and the Chinese Rites, The Month*, 73 (1891), 79.

was only a seventeenth-century version of an old phenomenon. The adaptation of Buddhism to Chinese taste has already been noticed, and some see the failure of the Nestorians as linked to the same question of accommodation: «Apparently the mistake made by the Nestorian preachers was that of being ashamed of their faith, and trying to recommend it merely as a branch of Buddhism. There is always a temptation and always a danger in Mission work, to soften down the edges of our faith, to represent it as something not so very new, not so very different from what is already known; such a policy may avoid immediate difficulties, but afterwards it tends towards defeat; the Christianity which has conquered has been that which is urged with distinctness amounting to harshness. It seems as if the compromising nature of Nestorianism was the reason why, when Buddhism fell, it was entangled in that fall and then forgotten.» [154]

Without fully accepting this verdict, one can agree that the Nestorians erred in failing to raise up native workers and in relying too much upon Imperial favour. The State protection of religion leads to a risk of state corruption of religion, for the Church has more to fear from Constantine than from Nero, as Cardinal Suhard has said. [155]

In the Rites Controversy it is misleading to divide the parties into «Europeanisers» and «Sinicisants» *tout court*, for that makes a general problem merely provincial, and limits a situation which is both ancient and modern, and knows no boundaries. It is not so much the search for compromise, but the degree of that compromise which is at issue: the difficulty is to determine how far to go, to decide where accommodation slides into syncretism and at what point it leads to deformation of the Message. All this was known to the missionaries in Ming and Ch'ing China, but the friars in particular were acutely conscious that one can only relax one's grip after having taken hold, not before.

The problems of that mission were not peculiar to the time or place, then, for it was simply a variant of an everrecurring discussion in the Church: *aggiornamento*. To that extent the Rites Controversy still continues.*

---

[154] The Reverend Lord William GASCOYNE-CECIL, in P. Y. SAEKI, *The Nestorian Monument in China*, London, 1928, iii.

[155] P. Y. SAEKI, oc., 159; Emmanuel Cardinal SUHARD, *Essor ou déclin de l'Eglise. Lettre pastorale: Carême 1947*, Paris, 1947, which deals perceptively with the need for accommodation, the dangers inherent in it, and the consequent dilemma.

* I am most grateful to Fr. A. Sisto Rosso, OFM., and to Professor C. R. Boxer, for reading this article in draft form, and for their very helpful comments and suggestions.

ADDITIONAL NOTES

P. 68: For some analysis of Zumárraga's Doctrina christiana, see W.B. Jones, 'Evangelical Catholicism in Early Colonial Mexico', The Americas, XXIII (1967), pp. 423-432; and see also Robert Ricard, Nouvelles études religieuses (Paris, 1973), pp. 98ff. On Ponce de la Fuente, see P.M. Piñero in Archivo Hispalense, LXIII (1980), pp. 301-312.

P. 74: Pedro de Gante did not invent the technique, but he did introduce European music into America as a missionary aid. This was not of course the first time that music had been so used: according to the Venerable Bede it was the beauty of Plainsong that first attracted British converts to the Church in England. In Spain, after the fall of Granada (1492), the Franciscan Hernando de Talavera, hoping to attract Muslims to the Faith, used the spectacular Corpus festivities in much the same way. Spaniards, accustomed to the phenomenon of religious dance (e.g. in the cathedrals of Seville and Granada), used native Indian dance to evangelical purpose in both Mexico and Peru; see, for instance, B.Ares Q., 'Las danzas de los indios: un camino para la evangelización', Revista de Indias, XLIV (1984), pp. 445-463. The great Jesuit António Vieira approved of all this "in order to show the Indians that the new religion is not a sad one".

P. 80 note 97: Nevertheless, some writers still wrongly believe that it was not friar Rada but the Jesuit brother Bento de Goes who made this identification: e.g. Jonathan D. Spence, The Memory Palace of Matteo Ricci (London, 1985), pp. 125-126.

P. 82 paragraph 1: The book referred to is Generation of Giants by Father G.H. Dunne, SJ., who must have known nothing of the friars' centuries-old interest in languages as an obviously essential medium of conversion: e.g. the proposals of Ramón Lull (fl. 1300) for the study of Arabic; mendicant use of the Tartar vernacular in thirteenth-century China and their later studies of the Amerindian languages by such as friar Domingo de Santo Tomás, OP. ('the Father of American Philology'); or their Chinese studies in Manila which led the French Jesuit scholar Henri Bernard-Maitre to call friar Martín de Rada the 'Father of modern Sinology'. And, long before the friars came into being, the Benedictine monks of Cluny produced Europe's first translation of the Koran for missiological purposes. What happened in China, therefore, cannot by any stretch of the imagination be presented as a Jesuit 'innovation' which unnerved the friars.

VI

FRAY DOMINGO NAVARRETE: A SOURCE FOR QUESNAY

Of all the thinkers associated with the French Encyclopaedia who helped to change the face of France in the eighteenth century the most conservative group was that of the economists known as the Physiocrats. These, less idealistic than the philosophers, chose as their starting point that which was, not that which ought to be. They advocated a form of feudal utopia where a wise prince was to rule according to the dictates of the Natural Law, ensuring the happiness of his people by every means, but principally by favouring agriculture which was considered by the Physiocrats to be the basis of the sound state. And they believed that they had found the realisation of their ideal in the absolute monarchy of China where, they declared, a benevolent despotism had preserved the peace and happiness of the inhabitants of the Empire for centuries. In Europe such a wise and benevolent ruler could speed forward the slow process of the Enlightenment by issuing decrees to cut any Gordian knots.

The master of this school of economists was François Quesnay (1694-1774), a physician at the court of Louis XV. His interest in economics led to his contributing two articles to the Encyclopaedia, *Grains* and *Fermiers*, in which he urged a more intensive agricultural programme for the nation. His *Table Economique* (1758), generally considered to be the manifesto of the Physiocrats, proclaims that the well-being of the state rests on the prosperity of the national agricultural economy. " Poor peasants make a poor kingdom ; and a poor kingdom means a poor king," was the tenor of the exhortation. Quesnay's disciples received his declaration with acclaim, and Mirabeau went so far as to say that the three greatest inventions of mankind had been writing, coinage, and the *Table Economique*. In fact, Quesnay's work is important as an attempt to analyse wealth in national terms ; he may be considered the founder of the science of Political Economy, since he was the first economist to bring scientific method and status to what had previously been treated unmethodically. It is in his *Despotisme de la Chine* (1767) that Quesnay turns to the study of China and presents it as the exemplar of his theories. Not all the *philosophes* were agreed that China was Utopia, but the economists were unanimous on this point and Mirabeau could summarily dismiss their critics as blind men. On the eve of the Revolution there were many thinkers in France prepared to examine any suggested remedy for social evils and Quesnay's description of China was such as to impress most people : " le plus beau pays de l'univers, le plus peuplé et le plus florissant royaume que l'on connaisse" ; and its social doctrine, he declared, " mérite de servir de modèle à tous les États."[1]

China had long been the subject of incredible accounts. It had earned Marco Polo the nickname of " *Il milione* " and had given to Spanish a catch-phrase : " cuento chino ". But Quesnay had faith in his informants, for he was relying on " le témoignage unanime de plusieurs personnes dont l'état et l'intelligence garantissaient la fidélité de leurs rapports." In face of their evidence, " L'incertitude fit place à la conviction ; celle-ci entraîna à la surprise et l'admiration." Quesnay, therefore, felt that he could be quite dogmatic : " je me suis aperçu, au contraire, par les relations de la Chine, que sa constitution est fondée sur des lois sages et irrévocables, que l'empereur fait observer, et qu'il observe lui-même exactement." (564, 565.)

Quesnay had been attracted by the utopian descriptions of the ancient civilisation of the Incas, but he turned to China for his model not only because it seemed to him to furnish the finest example of what he himself was advocating, but also because China was almost universally admired in the century of the *rêve chinois*, and Quesnay realised that he could best help his cause by appealing to a vogue already popular, and to writers on China who were already known, respected and admired. Writers in the eighteenth century, and perhaps those dealing with agricultural topics more than others, were wont to copy freely from each other,[2] and Quesnay, true to this tendency, did so himself. At the same time he was anxious to appear entirely original and therefore he consistently avoided acknowledging any indebtedness to earlier writers. His *Despotisme de la Chine*, however, is strikingly different in that here he not only acknowledged his sources but even went to the other extreme and cited authors whose works he may only have known at second-hand, although he obviously wanted to give the impression that he had studied them himself (566). Clearly, this change of policy was dictated by the desire to support his theories by an appeal to the popular Chinese vogue, and to recognised authorities on the subject.[3]

[1] P. C. Newman (editor), *Source Readings in Economic Thought* (New York 1954), 93 ; V. Pinot, " Les physiocrates et la Chine au xviiie siècle ", *Revue d'Histoire Moderne et Contemporaine*, VIII (1906/7), 200-14 ; J. B. Bury, *The Idea of Progress* (London 1920), 172 ff ; G. F. Hudson, *Europe and China* (London 1931), 322 ; A. Reichwein, *China and Europe* (London 1925), 101 ff ; Max Beer, *An Inquiry into Physiocracy* (London 1939), 110 ; G. Weulersse, *Le Mouvement Physiocratique en France* (Paris 1910), II, 136-37 ; F. Quesnay (edited A. Oncken), *Oeuvres Economiques et Philosophiques* (Paris 1888), 577, 636.

[2] S. Pargellis and D. J. Medley (eds.), *A Bibliography of British History, The Eighteenth Century*, 1714-1789 (Oxford 1951), 153. Not that this tendency to copy was peculiar to the eighteenth century ; Caxa de Leruela, for example, begins his *Restauración de la antigua abundancia de España* (Naples 1631) with a warning : " Ojo a la fecha paraque se conozca, que los que han tocado este punto despues della lo tomaron de aqui " (pp. 1-2).

[3] L. A. Maverick, *China a Model for Europe* (San Antonio 1946), 126-28. A. Reichwein, *op. cit.*, 103, 164.

It is usually claimed, not only by Europeans but also by Chinese writers, that the Physiocrats owed their knowledge of China to their reading of the works of the Jesuit missionaries.[1] This of course is partly true, but they also drew upon other writers and Quesnay acknowledges as sources not only the works of the French Jesuit Father Du Halde, but also claims to have consulted the works of the Italian Gemelli Carreri, George Anson, Mendes Pinto, the Dutch travellers and also " Navarette, Espagnol et missionnaire dominicain . . . et plusieurs autres." However, since the whole passage containing this acknowledgement is lifted verbatim from what was his real source of information on China, the *Mélanges interéssans et curieux* of Rousselot de Surgy, there is no evidence that Quesnay knew at first-hand the authorities he cites. He wished, however, to give the impression that he was acquainted with these works, and his reference to Fray Domingo Navarrete (Castrogeriz, 1618—Santo Domingo, 1686), recalls the fact that this friar was once sufficiently known as an authority on China to serve as an ally for the Physiocrats and as a support for their economic doctrines. Nowadays, Navarrete is remembered only occasionally, and then chiefly to be rebuked for his activities as the leading opponent of the evangelising techniques of the famous Jesuit-mandarins of the seventeenth-century mission to China. To those familiar with Navarrete only in this role it is difficult to understand how he could have been the " sage archeveque " of Voltaire,[2] for he appears rather to be a typical example of the narrow-minded " fraile idiota " who destroyed the work of the more cultured Jesuits and thus led eventually to the failure of the first sustained contact between East and West in modern times. In reality, Navarrete was very different from his popular portrait. His deep concern for religious orthodoxy and his fear of doctrinal novelties did not limit his interest in material problems, nor did it curb in any way his enthusiasm for the way of life and the system of government he found in China. His *Tratados históricos de la monarchía de China* (Madrid 1676) has an important place in the history of ideas for in its day it was widely read, and translated, either in whole or in part, into French, German, and Italian. In English a selection appeared in Astley's *Voyages*, but the complete translation was included in seven editions of Churchill's monumental *Collection of Voyages*, where it appeared as the first item after Locke's enthusiastic General Preface. Navarrete's *Tratados* is an extremely interesting work and is almost the only important Spanish contribution to the varied and voluminous literature which gave rise to the *rêve chinois* in eighteenth-century Europe. Had Quesnay

[1] E.g., T. K. Chuan in *T'ien Hsia* I (1935), 594.

[2] Voltaire, *Oeuvres complètes* (Paris 1878), XI, 178 and 180.

taken the trouble to consult it personally he would have found a great deal of material to support his theories.[1]

Fray Domingo Navarrete left Spain in 1646, and after having served as a missionary in the Philippines, he went to China in 1658 and remained there until 1670 when he left for Rome to report on the state of the mission. The years during his absence abroad had been mortal for Spain. In that time the disintegration of the national economy had become more pronounced. Inept rulers, selfish favourites, idle nobles and heavy taxation all help to account for the decline of the country. There were other contributory reasons : the expulsion of the Moors and Jews ; the neglect of the land ; the rapid swelling of the urban population ; the constant stream of people to the colonies which led to the gradual depopulation of the country, so that the Venetian Ambassador in 1680 could describe Spain as being like the Libyan desert. Moreover, the notorious *afán de nobleza* had adverse effects which reinforced the decline. The proverbial phrase was that " el no vivir de rentas no es trato de nobles " and the spirit it represented was shown in the unwillingness to undertake menial tasks. The Moroccan ambassador in 1680 had commented that the lower classes refused to perform the duties of their state because in Spain apparently even " the dregs of the populace " considered themselves superior to the rest of Christendom.[2] Pepys, too, had seen the same : even a bare-footed beggar had his slashed sleeves and bands sewn on to his shirt. And for the business of farming, grooming horses, or serving the towns with water, foreigners were employed, even Frenchmen, who were allowed to remain in times when there was trouble between the two countries, " as not knowing how to want them." Such an attitude had a serious effect on industry and Spain had to buy more and more goods from abroad, with the result that the commerce of the country rapidly passed into the hands of foreigners ; already by mid-century people were complaining that everything, from " el abanico hasta el rosario," had to be imported. Not all the gold and silver from the Indies could suffice to make up for such shortcomings ; indeed these very riches were themselves a weakness. Caxa de Leruela realised that " no bastan las riquezas, y tesoros, que las Monarquias acomulan de otras Prouincias, a suplir el defecto de los frutos natiuos de la patria, antes son causa de distraerse los naturales y dexar sus propias tierras incultas, y adulterar sus loables costumbres antiguas, . . . quanto oro, y plata le entra de las Indias parece tesoro de duendes, y que el mismo viento que lo trahe lo lleba (31.)" Earlier, another of the keen-eyed Venetians witnessing this national agony, had

[1] A. and J. Churchill, *A Collection of Voyages and Travels* (London 1704-52), 6 vols. ; Thomas Astley, *A New General Collection of Voyages and Travels* (London 1745), 4 vols.

[2] J. Juderías, *España en tiempo de Carlos II el hechizado* (Madrid 1912), 117.

said the same: Spain's silver flowed from her "as rain from a roof."[1]

This was the Spain that Navarrete knew. The Spain he left in 1646 had been limping; the Spain to which he returned in 1673 was an almost crippled giant. The journey across the peninsula from Lisbon, on his way to report to Rome, had shocked him. He was astonished and depressed, at the waste land, at the lack of everything, even, at times, of bread. And it all appeared worse to him because he had not himself witnessed the slow decline but had had his eyes sharpened by the contrast with other countries. Like so many others in his time he never ceased to deplore the contemporary state of affairs, and to urge remedies. But where the treatise-writers relied on theory, where Quevedo preached in poetry and fantasy fiction, where Góngora showed an innocent community guided by nature, where Saavedra Fajardo and Caxa de Leruela interpreted the meaning of emblems, Navarrete and the travellers brought word of a utopia already existing, and indeed flourishing, at the other side of the world. Navarrete presented for study and imitation not so much a Noble Savage as a Wise Sage, and a Wise Sage who lived in a paradise which could with profit be copied, for "a la verdad todo él es un jardín hermoso, y una apacible y amena floresta,"[2] a paradise ruled by a benevolent despot aided by philosophers as wise and good as any in Plato's dream. The *Tratados*, with its enthusiastic account of China, ceaselessly comments on how much better things are ordered there, and the work helped to prepare the ground for much of what Quesnay was later to say, for both these writers, though separated in time by almost a century, found themselves in a somewhat similar situation, and both had the same lesson to teach. It is not, therefore, surprising that the *Despotisme de la Chine* and the *Tratados históricos* frequently coincide.

One of the characteristics of the Chinese Empire that appealed to both Quesnay and Navarrete was the paternal monarchy which seemed to rule there. For Navarrete this was the rare fulfilment of Aquinas's demand that a good king strive always "paterno regimine subditos regere." Navarrete explained that among the Chinese it was a maxim that the people must obey the Emperor with filial obedience, and that he in turn had to love his subjects like a father and always study to find ways of showing his care for them. Quesnay had Navarrete's word for it that the Emperor never abused this obedience on the part of his people:

[1] Eli F. Heckscher, *Mercantilism* (London 1935), II, 180.

[2] Domingo Fernández Navarrete, *Tratados históricos de la monarchia de China* (Madrid 1676), 2.

" ces princes gouvernent-ils avec beaucoup de douceur et se font une étude de faire éclater leur affection paternelle." (614.)

Navarrete, in whose *Tratados* the teaching of the Chinese sage Mencius appears for the first time in a European vernacular, quotes him with approval on this ideal relationship between Emperor and subject : " si el rey gobierna solo con las leyes, y usa solo de castigos, y penas, conseguirá, que le obedezca por temor el pueblo ; pero no es de suyo durable este gobierno. Si gobernare con virtud y amor, conseguirá, que los vasallos le obedezcan de voluntad, y que se averguencen de obrar mal." (143.) He touches on a more topical point when he goes on to discuss the custom of buying from abroad. The Chinese were far too wise to do so : " Dice el Chino que no necesita de cosa alguna de Reynos extraños, en que tiene mucha razon. Esta es buena razon de estado. En otros reynos se podia hacer lo mesmo, no se hace, porque no quieren." (60.) Navarrete, and later Quesnay, comment on the tax system of China which seemed to them admirable. In particular, Navarrete noted that it placed burdens only on broad shoulders and did not strangle the peasantry who were the source of the national strength and upon whom everything depended : " Que se cargue a quien tiene fuerzas, bien se ajusta a la razon ; pero que se eche el peso al que por su flaqueza no se puede tener en pie, no lleva camino." (104.) Nor could the demands of the monarchy justify any such proceeding for " el Rey es para el Reyno, no el Reyno para el Rey." (104.)[1] Navarrete, much more specific than Quesnay, quotes precise examples. He compared the indifference of the Spaniards towards their Indian subjects in the Philippines with the zeal of the Tartar conquerors of China for their Chinese vassals. The Philippine natives, whose lot he had studied at close hand, exercised the consciences and charity of the friar-missionaries in the colony : " el mayor trabajo que los Religiosos tenemos en los Pueblos de Indios, es, ver lo que padecen, y el buscar medios, y caminos para consolarles." (305.) It was a state of affairs that could not exist in China. And there were other contrasts to be drawn. For instance, he noted that the care of the Chinese for their slaves was exemplary ; very different from the attitude that he was to encounter and condemn when, some years later, as Archbishop of Santo Domingo, he tried to ease the lot of the negroes on the island. " Tengo para mi que cumplen los Chinas mejor, que muchos Europeos, en mirar assi en salud, como en enfermedad por esta pobre gente." (237.)[2]

[1] Selections from the works of Mencius appeared in the Jesuit Martini's Latin history of China, the *Sinicae Historiae Decas Prima* (1658) ; Navarrete's selection from Mencius appeared in Spanish in his *Tratados*.

[2] For further evidence of the friars' care for the Filipinos see J. L. Phelan, " Ideological Aspects of the Conquest of the Philippines ", in *The Americas*, XIII (1957), 231.

The China so admired by the "sinomaniacs" of the eighteenth century often bore little resemblance to the reality. And Quesnay himself is guilty of altering his sources the better to present a utopian version of the government and institutions of the "Middle Kingdom".[1] Navarrete had paved the way, for he also deliberately edited his material to the same end. This is nowhere more clearly shown than in the account of his imprisonment during the persecution of Christians in 1664. The evidence of other friars, his colleagues, shows that they suffered the inconveniences that might be expected from confinement in an Asiatic prison in the seventeenth century. None of this, however, is mentioned by Navarrete. He described his confinement for forty days in Hang-chau prison and this establishment, like everything else in his China, was near perfection. "El todo me parece vna Republica bien concertada . . . ni vozes, ni alboroto, ni menos riñas se veían, ni oían más que si fuera una casa de novicios bien governada, de que no poco nos admirabamos." (16.) Everything was extremely clean; there were laundries, shops, and special married-quarters. There was also a fine, well-appointed temple much frequented by the prisoners. Furthermore, although the men's and women's prisons adjoined and had a communicating door, the men were observed to keep strictly to themselves and there was no impropriety. The poorer prisoners were given a daily ration of rice which was more than adequate since there was always enough left over for them to use part of it for bartering. But the most striking feature of all was the behaviour of the prisoners themselves. "Notamos con atencion, la cortesia, grauedad, y buena vrbanidad con que se tratauan entre si aquellos hombres, y la que vsaban con nosotros; es cosa increible esto para los de aca. Si en nuestras carceles entraran dos Chinos, Iapones, o Tunquines, que hizieran con ellos los demas presos?" (17.)[2] It must have been a startling description for those who were more accustomed to the prisons described in the *Buscón*; even in the France of a century later it could be held up as worthy of contemplation: "les prisons de la Chine ne paraissent ni horribles, ni aussi malpropres que celles d'Europe; elles sont fort spacieuses, bien disposées et commodes . . . 'Mais ce qui es surtout admirable dans les prisons chinoises, dit Navaret, qui y avait été renfermé avec d'autres missionnaires, c'est que nous y fûmes tous traités avec douceur et avec autant de respect que si nous eussions été d'un rang distingué.'" (619.)

All these points were of common interest to Quesnay and Navarrete, but there were more important coincidences in the passages of their works

[1] V. Pinot, *op. cit.*, 204; and see also Ting Tchao-Ts'ing, *Les Descriptions de la Chine par les Français* (1650-1750), (Paris 1928), 99-104.

[2] But cf., for example, the more realistic account of Navarrete's colleague Fray Antonio de Santa María OFM, in *Sinica Franciscana* (Quaracchi presso Firenze), II (1933), 502-606.

which deal with agriculture. Quesnay found much support and much to please him in the works of such writers as Navarrete, especially in the excerpts from Mencius. And in a period when rural economics had become a new fashionable interest (" un fanatisme, une maladie, l'agromanie, la folie de l'agriculture," its enemies called it) and the *rêve chinois* was at its height, the writings of the missionaries became extremely popular.[1]

Navarrete's laudatory account of conditions in China must, of course, be put into perspective by reading it against the contemporary background. Agriculture in late seventeenth-century Spain was in a deplorable state. Foreign wars, risings within the Peninsula, and increasing emigration, had helped to drain away men and money. Farmers were discouraged by the fixed prices at which they had to sell their goods irrespective of how much it cost them to raise the product they were selling, and irrespective of the richness or poverty of the harvest. The privileges granted to the cattle-farmers, and the estates of the Church, either untilled or often uneconomically maintained, consumed much useful land. The nobles were for the most part uninterested in the cultivation of their estates and set aside extensive domains for the creation of hunting-grounds or pleasure-parks; at the same time, absenteeism, which had been growing under Philip IV, increased under Charles II who attempted to take measures to prevent it. The landowners treated their tenants as sponges to be mercilessly squeezed so that the proverb warned " en lugar de señorío no hagas tu nido, y si lo hizo el padre no lo haga el hijo."[2] The widespread poverty seemed all the worse because it existed in a land which was widely, and perhaps with some exaggeration, held to be rich and productive if tended. Pedro Fernández Navarrete, in his *Conservación de Monarquías*, had commented on this: " ninguna Provincia del mundo puede hacer ventaja, y pocas hacen competencia, a España asi en la fertilidad como en la riqueza . . . como todos los autores que hablan de España lo afirman." In the Cortes of 1662, the last of the century, much the same had been said: " Es cierto, que del Reino más opulento por riqueza y por estar compuesto de todos los frutos y cosas necesarias para la vida humana, sin que por ningún uso necesite de las Provincias estranjeras, y con el comercio de las Indias dueño de los minerales del oro y la plata, se ha reducido a un estado tan miserable, sin gente, despoblado lo más y mejor del Reino." During the latter part of the seventeenth century there was a widespread recognition in Europe of the need to increase population as a means towards economic security: economists were declaring that the riches of

[1] Weulersse, *op. cit.* II, 151 ff.

[2] Juderias, *op. cit.*, 121-24; C. Viñas y Mey, *El problema de la tierra en la España de los siglos XVI-XVII* (Madrid 1941), 65-68; 139.

a nation depended on the numbers of its people, and they pointed to Spain as an example and warning. " People are the real Strength and Riches of a Country," declared Davenant, going on to add " we see how Impotent Spain is for want of Inhabitants, with their Mines of Gold, and Silver and the best Ports and Soil in the World."[1]

It was in contrast to this that Navarrete presented his picture of China. He was no economist in the technical sense ; his approach to the problem was mainly that of a moralist, but at the same time he was a keen observer, inquisitive about all he saw around him, a man who had taken careful note of farming methods in Asia and had no doubt discussed the subject with others. Moreover, the missionaries were in a position to be well-informed on this matter since one of their most important converts had been the scholar-statesman, Hsü Kuang-Ch'i, an authority on agriculture whose chief work, " *The Complete Treatise on Agriculture* ", was published in Peking in 1640.[2] Navarrete explained how he had noted with particular pleasure that farmers as a class were highly respected among the Chinese ; the Emperor guarded them with special care and was always ready to come to their help in time of need. In the social scale they were allotted the first place in the hierarchy of non-literary classes, thus preceding the merchants and artisans. This was because the farmer was considered to be working for the welfare of the nation as a whole, whereas the merchant worked only for his own personal profit. Aquinas, following Aristotle, had considered that agricultural workers ought to have preference over others and this was not by any means the only time that Navarrete had seen how much the pagan Chinese showed themselves in conformity with Christian ideals—often, indeed, more than the Christians themselves. On a more practical level he noted how the farmers profited by the sensible taxation system which worked in their favour and encouraged industry and effort. And since the peasants were so highly thought of, and—more to the point—so well cared for, it is not surprising that Navarrete found them tirelessly energetic : " son continuos en el trabajo ; y si tuvieran los sustentos y vino que tienen los Manchegos no hubiera en el mundo quien les hiziera ventaja alguna en su oficio y exercicio ; toda la vida están en las sementeras, si les sobre algo de tiempo, luego al punto van al monte a cortar leña, a la huerta a componer su hortaliça, o a cortar canas &c de suerte que jamás están

[1] J. L. Sureda Carrión, *La hacienda castellana y los economistas del siglo XVII* (Madrid 1949), 89-91 ; Heckscher, *op. cit.* II, 158-59.

[2] This important and influential study, which touches upon all aspects of its subject, was in fact a work of Jesuit-Chinese co-operation and incorporated Jesuit writings on hydraulics. See L. A. Maverick, " Hsü Kuang-Ch'i, A Chinese Authority on Agriculture " in *Agricultural History*, XIV (1940), 143 ff ; also *Check-list of the Exhibition in the Princeton University Library*, April 1957, 23.

ociosos." (55.) For the same reason the peasants had an incentive to cultivate every inch of the land; according to Navarrete there was not so much as a hand's breadth of ground in all China that lay idle. The farmers strove constantly to improve the quality of the soil and in this respect ingenuity knew no bounds: " no se halla cuerno, huesso, ni plumas, que no lo quemen, y hagan ceniças para fecundar la tierra." (57.) All this was as Quesnay would have it be, and he notes, with some surprise but complete approval: " On fait même trafic d'ordures encore plus sales, pour fertiliser la terre; dans toutes les provinces de la Chine, on voit une infinité de gens qui portent des seaux à cet usage; . . . Dans toutes les villes il y a des lieux publics dont les maîtres tirent de grands avantages." (581.)[1]

It is little wonder that the Physiocrats were enraptured by such visions from an agrarian wonderland, and they linked the peace and order which was said to prevail in the Chinese empire with the agricultural prosperity of the country: " Il n'y a donc que les nations agricoles qui puissent constituer des empires fixes et durables, susceptibles d'un gouvernement général, invariable, assujetti exactement à l'ordre immuable des lois naturelles." (647.)

On the subject of agriculture Navarrete frequently, and pointedly, comments on the attitude of the paternal Chinese Emperors towards their peasantry. Indeed, agriculture was first taught in China by an Emperor. From him, and from Confucius and Mencius, succeeding rulers learnt the importance of caring for their farmers. (94.) This, said the two sages, was the first duty of a king: " Gobernar un Reyno tiene sus leyes, pero amparar a los labradores, y mirar por ellos es lo mas principal." (235.) Navarrete quotes anecdotes to show how various Emperors obeyed this injunction in periods of national crisis: there was, for example, the inspiring generosity of Shun-chih, father of the reigning Emperor, when the harvest was poor and his people in distress. (138.) "Buen Ti," an Emperor who " preciauase mucho de ser padre y pastor de sus vasallos," always exempted from taxation those of his subjects who were opening up new land. It was a custom that Navarrete approved: " buena diligencia y linda regla de gouierno, para que abunde el sustento." (115.) Another Emperor took his sons to see the peasants working the fields and said to each in turn: " reparad hijo en el trabajo, que estos pobres tienen todo el año para que vos, y yo tengamos que comer. Por esto cuydé siempre de favorecer a esta gente, porque sin su sudor y callos no hay Imperio ni

[1] On the value of good manuring Caxa de Leruela had already expatiated. To those who complained that the land was " tired " he retorted that it would be fruitful if it were frequently manured and quoted a saying from Cuenca: " Que si los ladrones supieran, que cosa era estiercol, no hurtaran otra cosa," to which he himself added that " vulgarmẽte dicẽ los rusticos q agua y estiercol hacẽ milagros." *Op. cit.*, 21-22. See C. R. Boxer, *South China in the Sixteenth Century* (London 1953), 8-9; 120-21.

Reyno para mi ni para vos. En cualquiera señor de Europa," comments Navarrete, " merecía ser celebrado este dicho." (114.) Another story he tells concerns an Emperor who went into the fields during a locust plague and harangued the insects, calling on them to kill him and to leave the peasants with what little they had. When they ignored him the Emperor attempted a sacrificial suicide, swallowing locusts to force them to feed on his entrails instead of on the crops. Immediately, reported Navarrete, the swarm rose from the harvest and departed without returning again : " premió Dios las entrañas piadosas del Emperador, y el celo del bien de su Pueblo." (106.) All these stories had their point, for whatever else he was, Navarrete could not be accused of being naïve. There was a purpose, for instance, in his further comment on this same Emperor, who said : " Governar un Imperio es como curar una enfermedad ; si el que sana della se descuida o desmanda, vuelve a recaer, y corre mayor riesgo su vida. Y assi os pido, Consejeros mios, que en todo tiempo, y a todas horas me deis aviso, me reprehendeis de cuanto os pareciere voy descaminado. Diría mas Filipo Segundo ? " (106.)

From hints to kings Navarrete passes to comment on the behaviour of the nobles who, though they " think themselves fine Catholics," nevertheless sin against the Natural Law by possessing large idle estates which are forbidden the poor, who are prohibited from fishing, hunting, or even cutting wood there. Mencius had reminded rulers that the Empire was founded on the work and sweat of the peasants, and to ignore this injunction was more than unjust, it was also foolish. This advice Navarrete saw fit to pass on to viceroys, and remembering what he had seen in the Philippines, he glossed Mencius by saying : " si con los de Manila se hiciera asi, la tierra abundara más en frutos con no pocas creces de la Casa Real. Muchos de aquellas Islas no quieren trabajar, porque quanto cogen se les va en repartimientos ; no sembrando, no cogen y quedan exemptos dellos. Assi lo dice el Indio, y asi se lo he oido yo." (55.) The Indians and their hard lot were in his mind when he related another story, which he thought the Governor of the Philippines would do well to bear in mind the next time the rice crop failed. An Emperor of China, when told of a drought in one of the provinces, was so upset that he spent the night crying for his people ; the next morning he ordered the suspension of all taxes for the area and the result of this kindly action was that " acudió Dios a la piedad del Emperador," for almost immediately " cayó tanta agua, que la tierra quedó harta, y satisfecha conque cesó la carestía del sustento." (113.) There were lessons not only for colonial governors, but also for minor officials. It might, for instance, be prudent to imitate the mandarin of "Xan Jung" province who, when obliged to imprison some malefactors at harvest-time, had pity on them and allowed them to leave prison daily in order to tend to their crops. They were, of course, on their word bound to return to prison in the evenings ; since, like all Navarrete's Chinese, they were above reproach, none failed in this respect and the experiment became a tradition. (128.)

Navarrete, in his account of the Chinese utopia, singled out for special praise the Emperor's picturesque custom of performing the ceremony of guiding the plough at the start of the spring tilling : " El Emperador mismo araba la tierra, sembraba trigo, y sazonado, lo segaba, y recogía ; mandaba a sus hijos, y grandes, hiciesen lo mismo (para) que experimentasen el sudor, y trabajo, que cuesta a los Labradores el cultivar la tierra, hasta coger los frutos y mantenimientos, de que se sustentan todos. De donde se seguirá moderación en el gasto, y conceder privilegios a los que toda la vida andan en el campo, expuestos a las inclemencias de el Cielo. Fuera muy bueno, introducir esta ceremonia, para que algunos no sustentasen tantos animales, y para que los señores se compadecieran de sus vasallos." (108.) Of all the beneficient activities of the Chinese emperors this ploughing ceremony seemed the most romantic and attracted comment from, among others, Diderot, Montesquieu and Voltaire. Raynal regretted that it was not performed in France instead of the " many religious feasts which seem to be invented by idleness to make the country a barren waste." So enthusiastic was Raynal's account that he felt constrained to add a warning : " it is not to be imagined that the court of Peking are actually engaged in the labours of rural life." In 1756, Quesnay, through La Pompadour, persuaded Louis XV to perform the ploughing ceremony in imitation of the Chinese emperors. Had Navarrete been still alive he would have hailed this event, for he would have been unaware that the performance was not unique outside China ; one of the oldest *chansons de geste* related that Charlemagne on arrival in Constantinople found king Hugh ploughing with a golden plough, and in Spain Lope had a play which dealt with a similar incident.[1]

Other Iberian writers before Navarrete had praised the Chinese and found there were lessons to be learnt in the Middle Kingdom. Caxa de Leruela and Martínez de la Mata, for instance, and Mexía de la Higuera who, writing in 1647, had commended the paternal care of the Emperor for his people. Fray Gaspar da Cruz, a Portuguese Dominican, and Fray Martín de Rada, a Spanish Augustinian friar, had commented on the agricultural skill of the Chinese and on how they cultivated even the tops of crags and rocks where it seemed they could not possibly gain anything. Later Spanish writers also quoted China as a model worth following. But

[1] A. Haggerty Krappe, " The Ploughman King ", in *Revue Hispanique*, XLVI (1919), pp. 516-46 on Lope's play *El Rey Bamba*. G. Raynal, *A Philosophical and Political History of the . . . Indies* (Edinburgh 1782), I, 86-7.

Domingo Navarrete differs from all these in that where they merely make isolated comments he maintains a consistent exaltation of the Empire and his praise for the new utopia is all-embracing : " En esto, y otras cosas he escrito, y escriuiré mil vezes, que excede aquella nacion a quantas ay en el mundo." (337.)[1] His account went far towards creating the climate of opinion in which Leibnitz could in his *Novissima Sinica* (1697) declare that the Chinese were superior to the ancient Greeks : " credo si quis sapiens, non formae Dearum, sed excellentiae populorum judex lectus esset, pomum aureum Sinensibus daturum esset." In this Quesnay agreed (591) with Leibnitz and Navarrete for he believed that the teaching of the Chinese moralists surpassed that of the Seven Sages themselves.

Quesnay and Navarrete shared many theories. They were similar in that they lived through an age of crisis, were disturbed by the state of their respective countries, and both turned to China, where agriculture was so well protected, and apparently flourished, in order to find an answer alike to the economic problem of seventeenth-century Spain and eighteenth-century France. Quesnay went further than Navarrete in that he regarded agrarian reform as the panacea for national ills ; Navarrete, more of a moralist, saw it as only one means to recovery. Both men were destined to failure. The Spanish Jesuits denounced Navarrete's work to the Inquisition on purely canonistic grounds but the fact tended to bring him into discredit and his work made little impression in his own country, apart from the narrow field of religious controversy. And Quesnay came too late with his answers to current problems for in France the rumbles of the coming Revolution were near and nothing could prevent the cataclysm that was to leave not only all Europe but the new world shuddering.

In Spain efforts were made to effect national recovery, but a century after Navarrete's death Jovellanos was still impelled to make much the same lamentations in his *Informe de la Ley Agraria*. There were, he said, few countries with so much uncultivated land as Spain ; nor, he thought, could there be " un contraste más vergonzoso que ver las capitales llenas de magníficas puertas, plazas, teatros, paseos y otros monumentos de ostentación, mientras por falta de puertos, canales y caminos, está despoblado y sin cultivo su territorio, yermos y llenos de inmundicia sus pequenos lugares, y pobres y desnudos sus moradores. ¿ Quién mirará sin horror y sin lágrimas tan vergonzoso abandono en medio de la pobreza y despoblación de tan pingües territorios ? . . . ¿ no existirán entre nosotros los mismos deseos que manifestaron los Marquez,

[1] C. Viñas y Mey, *op. cit.*, 232. Boxer, *op. cit.*, 118 ; 120-1 ; 131 ; 248. Caxa de Leruela, *op. cit.*, 268 ff. B. A. Ramírez, *Bibliografía agronómica* (Madrid 1863), 86 ; 200 ; and J. Sempere y Guarinos, *Biblioteca española económico-política* (Madrid 1804), III, cxcvii-viii, and ccviii.

los Manriques, los Navarretes, los Riberas, y tantos otros venerables eclesiásticos ? "[1]

The *Informe* brought to Spain something of the ideas of Physiocracy and was widely read, but not everyone welcomed its advice or warnings. There is no evidence that Jovellanos knew the work of Domingo Navarrete at first hand, and his reference here is more likely to be to Pedro Fernández Navarrete's *Conservación de monarquías.* Nevertheless, Fray Domingo Navarrete should not be overlooked as a precursor of Jovellanos and the agrarian reformers, and historically it is unfortunate that his work in this field, at once original and stimulating, should have been ignored precisely where and when it was most needed.

[1] Jovellanos, *Obras*, in *BAE*, L, 103 ; 132 ; 138. For Jovellanos and Physiocracy see Angel del Río, Introduction to the *Obras* in the *Clásicos Castellanos* collection (Madrid 1935), I, 127 ff. For Physiocracy in Spain see also M. Colmeiro, *Historia de la economía política en España* (Madrid 1863), II, 87-88. For Jovellanos and agriculture see Colmeiro, *op. cit.*, II, 109-10 ; and also Julius Klein, *The Mesta, A Study in Spanish Economic History* (London 1920), 347. There were, apparently, few physiocrats in Spain and not all those so labelled were in fact orthodox members of the school. In this connexion see the article by Sebastián Mantilla, S.J., in *Boletín de estudios económicos*, VII (1952), 177-207, especially his comments at p. 180 on F. Quadra Salcedo's *Economistas Vascongadas* (Bilbao 1943).

ADDITIONAL NOTES

P. 37: Navarrete's recommendations of agriculture as a partial remedy for the ills of late seventeenth-century Spain were only incidental to his main purpose in writing. For this reason they have gone unnoticed in recent studies of the Chinese origins of Physiocracy. Eighteenth-century Spanish writers on the subject were likewise ignorant (cf. Sarmiento, Feijoo, Forner, Capmany; see for example the Seminario erudito, X, XX); the rêve chinois, feeble enough in Spain, was feebler still in Spanish America, but see J.M. Mariluz Urquijo, 'La China, utopia rioplatense del siglo 18', Revista de Historia de América, 98 (Jul-Dec 1984), pp. 7-31, and also A. Braojos Garrido, 'El Semanario de Agricultura y Artes (1832-1833), un periódico fisiócrata en la Sevilla de fines del Antiguo Régimen', Archivo Hispalense, LXIII (1980), pp. 67-106.

VII

PRESENT LOCATION OF THE Pei-t'ang Library

THE former Jesuit library in Peking is a celebrated collection of books which has merited the attention of historians, sinologists, bibliographers.[1] Professor L. Carrington Goodrich (Far Eastern Quarterly) has commented of it that "it seems hardly necessary to dwell on the importance of this library" which so many scholars have drawn upon for their studies of the European contribution to Chinese intellectual and cultural life in the seventeenth and eighteenth centuries.

The first Catholic missionaries to China in the sixteenth century, like their counterparts in Japan, were deeply impressed by the civilization and sophistication of the people they met. The Jesuits in China, under the guidance of the brilliant and versatile Father Matteo Ricci, decided upon a programme of preaching their faith and at the same time spreading abroad knowledge of European scientific method.[2] For their work in the fields of mathematics, engineering, astronomy, hydraulics, the reform of the Chinese calendar, etc., they required the best and latest books from Europe.[3] By the end of the century a number of appeals for scientific books had been sent back home to Europe by the China missionaries; and these appeals continued unceasingly through the years. Perhaps the person who may be said to have done most to build up the mission library in Peking was the Belgian Jesuit priest, Father Nicholas Trigault, who was sent to Europe in 1613 on a mission which included the task of collecting suitable books.[4] By the time he returned to China in 1620 Trigault had collected a total of 629 volumes, including gifts from Cosimo II de Medici of Florence and the Duke of Parma. The prize of this collection was a gift of about 500 volumes presented to the mission by Pope Paul V. These books were richly bound in red leather with the Jesuit monogram on one cover and the pope's coat of arms on the other. In time, other collections were added, including the libraries of Bishops Souza and Gouvea and that of the papal legate, Mezzabarba. Naturally, not all these books were purely scientific for they embraced many branches of learning. There were books produced by the master-printers of Asia and Europe and they included works in the following languages: French, English, Latin, Italian, Greek, German, Spanish, Portuguese, Dutch, Hebrew, Polish, Slavonic. Father Verhaeren's *Catalogue* (1949) lists 4101 titles in 5133 volumes which constituted a mine of information and learning from which two centuries of Chinese Christian literature was derived. The library, therefore, served both as a form of intermediary between East and West, and as part of the Jesuits' *bibliothekenstrategie*, or "apostolate of the press."

By the eighteenth century there were four Catholic churches in Peking, built at the cardinal points of the city, and each of them had its own library. These were as follows: the greater Portuguese Church, the South Church or Nan-t'ang, which contained the richest library since it was the oldest, had been established by Father Matteo Ricci, and included the books donated by Pope Paul V; the lesser Portuguese Church, the East Church or Tung-t'ang; the North Church, or Pei-t'ang, established by the French Jesuit mission in 1696; and the West Church, or Hsi-t'ang, founded by a Lazarist Father, working under Propaganda Fide, in 1725[5]. The collection of books known in later times as the "Pei-t'ang Library," came from different sources and the core of the collection did not, in fact, belong to the Pei-t'ang or North Church itself, but rather, as has been said above, to the South Church, or Nan-t'ang, which in its heyday was the center of the Jesuit Vice-Province of China and the residence of the Jesuit astronomers working in the Court in the imperial service. It was only after many vicissitudes that the collection came to settle in the Pei-t'ang and to take its final name from that particular church. The reader who requires full details of this transition is referred to the Introduction to the Verhaeren *Catalogue*.

The fate of the libraries depended upon the fate of the Fathers themselves. Often they were in danger. For example, when the Ming dynasty fell in the 1640s, Peking was in a state of confusion as the supporters of each side fought one another in a month-long struggle. On that occasion the Nan-t'ang, with its precious library, was almost destroyed. But the celebrated German Jesuit, Father Adam Schall von Bell, refused to leave the capital and remained at his post, successfully defending the mission center almost single-handed.

In 1688 the first French Jesuit group arrived. These were supported and financed by Louis XIV and they entered into friendly rivalry with their Portuguese brethren in the matter of building up a library of religious and scientific work. After the suppression of the Society in 1773 the Jesuits' possessions passed into the hands of the Vincentians, who cared for them during the troubled years of the early nineteenth century. In 1838, when Mgr. Pires, the last Catholic European Priest still in China, lay dying, he entrusted what remained of the precious collections of books into the care of the Archimandrite of the Russian Orthodox Mission in Peking, who was not interfered with during those difficult days since he had diplomatic status. The books remained in Russian charge until 1860 when Catholic missionaries returned to Peking and received back the old library thus charitably guarded for them. These books were then housed in the old Pei-t'ang, which was reopened by the newcomers. So it comes about that the former Jesuit library from the Nan-t'ang, together with other acquisitions, passed to the Pei-t'ang, and henceforth became known popularly as the "Pei-t'ang Library."

However, all danger was not over by any means. For in 1864 the Pei-t'ang was almost burnt down and some of the books actually caught fire, although in the end they were saved from destruction. Again, in 1900 the famous library was menaced by the Boxers' siege of Peking, when the Pei-t'ang in particular was the focus of attack. Later still it came through the perils of the Sino-Japanese War. At that time the library was being catalogued by Father Verhaeren who, although an enemy alien, was permitted by the Japanese authorities to continue his work because they recognised that it was of international importance. The preparation of the catalogue, therefore, continued throughout the war and during the subsequent civil war in China.

The last words in Fr. Verhaeren's Introduction, dated January 21, 1949, make poignant reading: "This was written in the midst of all the agony of a siege of the capital which began last December 13. Up to the present time the library has not suffered the slightest damage.... Let us hope that yet once again the scourge of war will spare this venerable heritage received from our Fathers."

During the civil war and the reconstitution of China that followed after 1949, the fate of the library remained unknown and some concern was felt for its survival and safety. The present writer is able to report that the library, or at least a good part of it, still exists, is in good condition, is being well cared for, and is available for consultation in Peking. However, it no longer exists as a separate entity, for it has been absorbed, in alphabetical order, into the Rare Books Section, the so-called "Valuable Collection," of the Peking Municipal Library, the Peiching T'ushukuan[6].

Since the former Jesuit collection has apparently lost its previous identity it is, naturally, pointless to enquire in Peking for the Pei-t'ang Library for this name now conveys nothing to the librarians in charge of it. The present writer stumbled on the Pei-t'ang books only by accident after noticing that the card-index catalogue of the Rare Books Section cited amongst its holdings a copy of the *Tratados históricos de la China* by the Spanish Dominican missionary, Father Domingo Fernández Navarrete.[7] It seemed highly unlikely that any library in Peking other than that of the old Jesuit mission would have held a copy of so specialised a book. This volume was requested and on arrival turned out to have *two* catalogue numbers inscribed on it, one of which, obviously the older number, was recognised by chance as being that of the copy of the *Tratados* belonging to the former Pei-t'ang Library, namely, No. 3396, quoted in the Verhaeren *Catalogue* the writer had seen once before. This suggested, obviously, that other Pei-t'ang books might also be there. And, in fact, a random check through the card-index catalogue of the Rare Books Section in search of other books known to have formed part of the Pei-t'ang Library revealed, in every instance, that the work in question was there. For instance, among the books remembered, found in the card-index catalogue, requested, and produced, was the copy of Clavius's *Astrolabium*, Romae, 1593 (Verhaeren Catalogue, item 1291), with its autograph dedication by the author to his former pupil, Father Matteo Ricci: *P. Mathaeo Riccio donum auctoris alla China*. This book also bore a library stamp reading: *Bibliotheca Domus SS Salvatoris + Peking*. The dedication proves beyond doubt that this is the copy once owned by Ricci himself. Another well-known Pei-t'ang book is the *Opus geometricum*, Gandavi, 1668, by Gregory de St Vincent, S.J.,[8] which bears a title-page dedication as follows: *R. P. Ferdinando Verbiest S.J., mittit R. P. Manderscheidt ex Poenitentiaria Romana S. Petri*, as described by Verhaeren, *Catalogue*, item 2651. Other books called for in this random fashion proved also to be from the old Pei-t'ang Library, for there were volumes of the papal collection presented to the mission by Paul v which were easily identifiable from their red leather binding and the double coat of arms described above. Some other books had burnt page-endings and were undoubtedly survivors of the fire in 1864. No copy of the Verhaeren *Catalogue* is listed as available in the Rare Books Section for consultation. A reader must therefore rely on his own knowledge of specific books, which can then be sought in the card-index catalogue of the Rare Books Section. (It might, however, be worthwhile to ask one of the librarians if there is any possibility of seeing a copy of Verhaeren.) On the other hand, experiment suggested that the books from the former Pei-t'ang Library might be traced in the card-index because the Pei-t'ang books all seemed to be catalogued with a plain number, whereas all other holdings in the Rare Books Section seemed to have their numbers prefaced with a letter *V*, presumably meaning *Valuable Collection*. It also appeared that the works formerly belonging to the Pei-t'ang Library are all on *printed* cards, whereas the other European rare books in the Peking library (but not belonging to the Pei-t'ang), are on *typed* cards. No exception to this was found, and if the surmise is correct it would, therefore, be possible even without the use of, or knowledge of, the Verhaeren *Catalogue*, to single out the old Pei-t'ang holdings from the general collection of European rare books by calling for every volume which appears in the Peking Library catalogue of rare books on a *printed* card with a *plain number* for its call-mark. The present writer must emphasize that this is only a rough rule of thumb and may not be infallible by any means—but in a random survey it held good.

Included in the Peking "Valuable Collection"

but not recorded in Verhaeren as having belonged to the Pei-t'ang collection, were such works as Noël Alexandre, *Lettere d'un dottore di Teologia*, Colonia, 1700; A. A. Georgii (or Giorgi), O.E.S.A., *Alphabetum Tibetanum*, Romae, 1762; and another *Alphabetum tangutanum, sive tibetanum* (edd. Amaduzzi and Beligatti(?)), Romae, 1773; Scipione Amati, *Historia del regno di Voxù del Giapone*, Romae, 1615; and a manuscript of fragments of a Catholic catechism in Chinese, with Latin notes, by Matteo Ricci, and dated 1588: Peking Municipal Library press-mark: V/BX. 1960. R49.[9]

There are also a number of modern works of varied interest and worth, and some oddities, such as a typewritten "despatch from the Tsungli Yamen to the Foreign Minister on the occasion of the moving of the coffin of Te Tsung Ching Huang-ti, 1909"; a manuscript on the dredging of the Woosung Bar in 1880; an anonymous, undated manuscript of 50 pages entitled "Elementa linguae sinicae"; and some labour contracts, in Chinese and Spanish, relating to *Emigración china para el Perú y la isla de Cuba, 1869*. There is also a four-page manuscript translation into Latin of a Chinese ode by "Prince Fu" in praise of Father Francesco Sambiasi, S.J., translated by Sambiasi himself.[10] This latter is apparently from the old Metropolitan Library. Also there is a manuscript copy of part of a long letter by Father Ferdinand Verbiest, S.J., dated August 15, 1678, making an appeal for more Jesuits for the mission. The letter is printed in the *Correspondance de Ferdinand Verbiest, S.J.*, edited by H. Josson and L. Willaert, S.J., Bruxelles, 1938, pp. 231-53; this manuscript copy begins at the words "Annis superioribus quando PP Procuratores . . . " and it, too, comes from the Metropolitan Library.

Peking Library, where the Pei-t'ang collection is now housed, lies on the north side of Wen Chin Street just west of the Peihai Park[11] in the central part of the city. It is the successor of the former Metropolitan Library which dated from the later part of the Ch'ing dynasty and in 1958 it contained 5.66 million books. Foreign visitors are likely to find themselves registered at the Hsin Chiao Hotel in the old Legation Quarter of the city, and from there to the Library it is an easy journey by the No. 3 trolley-bus which runs along the route from Chien Kuo Men to Peking Zoo[12]. On the way there the bus goes through Wang Fu Jing Street which contains some interesting second-hand bookshops, especially the Chung Kuo Bookshop in the Tung An Bazaar[13] where in 1965 it was still possible to pick up an occasional remainder from one of the old mission libraries, such as an odd volume bearing the library stamp of the Jesuit school of languages at Chabanel (*Bibliotheca Domus Chabanel, IHS*), or of the Vicar Apostolic of Su Chow.

Dismounting from the trolley-bus at the entrance to the Peihai Park, the visitor should walk westwards past the park, cross the wide bridge over the lake, and then turn in at the second gate in the red wall on the right-hand side of the street. This is the entrance to the library compound. The building itself, in the classical style, lies straight ahead, surrounded by a large garden. On the right-hand side of the entrance hall, just inside the main door of the building, is a window at which a reader's ticket may be obtained. The regulations are simple, and the staff very willing to help. (Visitors who do not speak Chinese might usefully carry a letter asking for an English-speaking librarian to be brought. Such a letter can easily be got from a member of the staff of the tourist office in the hotel.)

To obtain a reader's ticket, a passport, or similar document, should be produced, and a letter of introduction from a consulate or academic institute is always an advantage.

Before entering the library proper, cases etc. should be deposited in the cloakroom on the left-hand side of the entrance, immediately opposite the window where the reader's ticket is obtained. There are ten reading rooms in all, but to reach the Rare Books Section one makes a sharp right turn after entering the library, and the reading room is at the end of the corridor. The catalogue of rare European books is on the left of the entrance to the Rare Books reading room in a row of card-index cabinets, the last eight drawers of which contain the cards referring to the books of the "Valuable Collection" and, therefore, of the Pei-t'ang Library also. The call-mark or catalogue number, is printed or typed on the top left-hand side of the card. These drawers may be removed from their cabinets and may be taken over to the reader's table. Pens and *biros* are prohibited, and only pencils may be used when making notes in this section of the library. Books must be read from the individual lecterns provided at each reader's place. A maximum of five works may be called for at any one time. When requesting a book, a form, which is available at the attendant's desk, must be completed in duplicate. The layout of this application form is as follows:

Reader's Name	Library ticket No.	Seat No.	Reader's Name	Library ticket No.	Seat No.
Catalogue No.	Author		Catalogue No.	Author	
No. of Vols.	Title of Work		No. of Vols.	Title of Work	

The library is open from 8.30 a.m. to 12 noon and from 2.00 p.m. until 6 p.m. It is closed on Saturdays, and on January 1, May 1, October 1, and on certain other national holidays.

The writer had only a limited amount of time at his disposal in Peking, much of which was spent in locating the Pei-t'ang collection so that in the end there remained all too little opportunity to consult the books themselves in a leisurely way. These notes are, therefore, offered in the hope that they may be of some assistance to any student visiting Peking in the future for the purpose of consulting this unique collection of books which are rare in themselves and rich in their associations.

[1] See for example, Johannes Laures, S.J., "Die alte Missionsbibliothek im Pei-t'ang zu Peking," *Monumenta Nipponica*, 1939, II, 124-139; Henri Bernard, S.J., "Une Bibliothèque Medicale de la Renaissance conservée à Peking," *Bulletin de l'Université l'Aurore*, Shanghai, 1947, VIII, 99-118; Edmond Lamalle, S. I., "La Propagande du P. N. Trigault en faveur des Missions de China (1616)," *Archivum Historicum Societatis Jesu*, Rome, 1940, IX, 49-120; J.B. Thierry, C.M., "Catalogus Bibliothecae Domûs Pe-Tang Congregationis Missionis Pekini Sinarum, 1862," *Monumenta Serica*, Peiping, 1939–40, IV, 605-15; J. Van den Brandt, C.M., "La Bibliothèque du Pé-t'ang: Notes Historiques," *Ibid.*, pp. 616-621; Hubert Verhaeren, C.M., "La Bibliothèque Chinoise du Pet'ang," *Ibid.*, pp. 622-626; Louis Wei Tsing-sing, "Le Saint-Siège, la France et la Chine sous la pontificat de León XIII," *Neue Zeitschrift für Missionswissenschaft*, Beckenreid, 1965, XXI, 252-271; but, in particular, see Hubert Verhaeren *C.M., Catalogue de la Bibliothèque du Pé-t'ang*, Peking, 1949, a scholarly work and a labour of love, reviewed by Professor L. Carrington Goodrich, *Far Eastern Quarterly*, Menasha, 1951, X, 208-210. It is pleasant to be able to record that Fr. Verhaeren, now in his 90th year and living in Paris, is still an insatiable student of Chinese. The Introduction to his *Catalogue* is the best and most complete history of the Pei-t'ang Library.

[2] The definitive exposition of the Jesuits' scientific work in China is to be found in the third volume of the massive study by Joseph Needham, *Science and Civilisation in China*, Cambridge, 1954 (*in progress*). For a special aspect of the question see also P. M. D'Elia S. J., *Galileo in China*, Cambridge, Mass., 1960.

[3] "Western learning in such sciences as mathematics, astronomy, calendar-making, water conservancy, mechanics, geography and physiology was brought to China by Catholic missionaries during the Ming period .... Verbiest and other Catholic missionaries spread Western scientific

knowledge..." Chien Po-tsan, Shao Hsun-cheng, Hu Hua, *Concise History of China*, Peking, 1964, pp. 77, 85. It would, however, be incorrect to present the missionaries as bringing the first scientific light to the benighted Chinese, and Needham, *Science and Civilization* shows that much that appeared to be "new" western scientific learning was, in fact, already old in China, but had been forgotten during the decline of the Ming dynasty. The Jesuits, however, helped to promote a revival of scientific interest for which they deserve every credit.

[4] For Trigault, see Louis Pfister, S.J., *Notices biographiques et bibliographiques*, Shanghai, 1932, pp. 111-120.

[5] Nan-t'ang 南堂, Tung-t'ang 東堂, Pei-t'ang 北堂, Hsi-t'ang 西堂.

[6] 北京図書館

[7] See J. S. Cummins, ed., *The Travels and Controversies of Friar Domingo Navarrete* (1618–86), 2 vols, Hakluyt Society, London, 1962.

[8] For this see, C. Naux, "L'*Opus Geometricum* de Grégoire de Saint-Vincent," *Revue d'histoire des sciences*, Paris, 1962, XV, 93-104.

[9] See P.M. D'Elia, S.J., *Fonti Ricciane*, Rome, 1949, II, 32.

[10] For the Prince of Fu (Chu Yu-sung, + 1646) see A.W. Hummel, *Eminent Chinese of the Ch'ing Period*, 1644–1912, Washington, 1943, pp. 195-196; and for Sambiasi see Pfister, pp. 126-143.

[11] Wen Chin Street 文津街, Peihai Park 北海公園

[12] Hsin Chiao Hotel 新僑飯店, Chien Kuo Men 建国門, Peking Zoo 北京動物園

[13] Fu Jing Street 王府井, Chung Kuo Book- shop 中国書店, Tung An Bazaar 東安市場.

INDEX